Pathways to Fiscal Reform in the United States

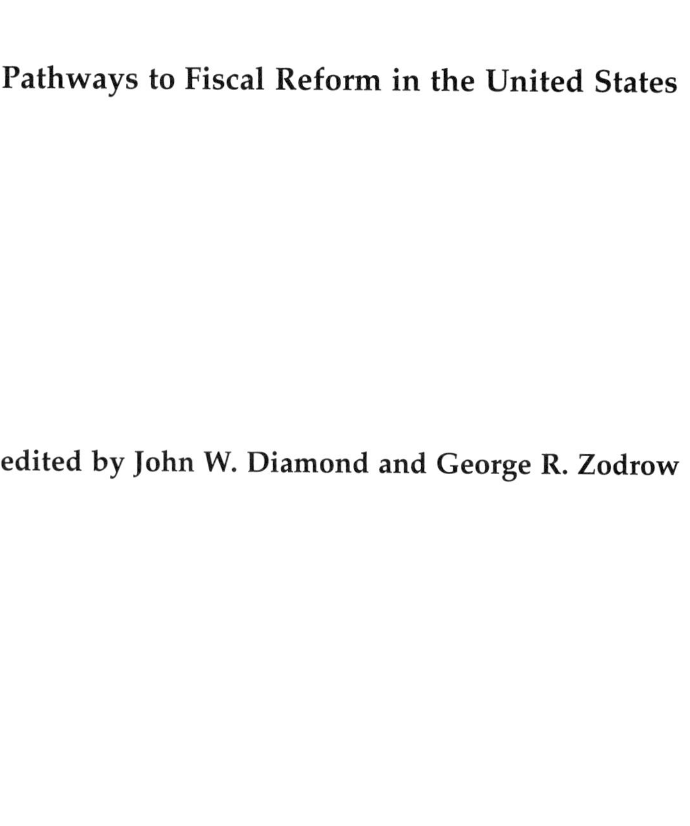

Pathways to Fiscal Reform in the United States

edited by John W. Diamond and George R. Zodrow

The MIT Press
Cambridge, Massachusetts
London, England

MIT Press books may be purchased at special quantity discounts for business or sales promotional use. For information, please email special_sales@mitpress.mit.edu.

This book was set in Palatino LT Std by Toppan Best-set Premedia Limited, Hong Kong. Printed and bound in the United States of America.

Library of Congress Cataloging-in-Publication Data

Pathways to fiscal reform in the United States / edited by John W. Diamond and George R. Zodrow.
pages cm
Includes bibliographical references and index.
ISBN 978-0-262-02830-1 (hardcover : alk. paper) 1. Fiscal policy—United States. 2. Taxation—United States. 3. Debts, Public—United States. 4. United States—Economic policy—2009- I. Diamond, John W. II. Zodrow, George R.
HJ257.3.P37 2014
339.5′20973—dc23
2014017748

10 9 8 7 6 5 4 3 2 1

To those depending on us to find a pathway to fiscal reform, especially
Jack, Evan, and Cade Diamond
Katherine and Laura Zodrow

Contents

Contributors

Henry J. Aaron

The Brookings Institution

James Alm

Tulane University

Rosanne Altshuler

Rutgers University

Daniel Baneman

Urban-Brookings Tax Policy Center

Joe Barnes

Rice University

Robert J. Carroll

Ernst & Young LLP

Ruud A. de Mooij

International Monetary Fund

John W. Diamond

Rice University

Jagadeesh Gokhale

Cato Institute

Jane G. Gravelle

Congressional Research Service

Peter R. Hartley

Rice University

Vivian Ho
Rice University

John Kitchen
U.S. Department of the Treasury

Edward D. Kleinbard
University of Southern California

John Mutti
Grinnell College

Thomas S. Neubig
Ernst & Young LLP

Mark V. Pauly
University of Pennsylvania

Rudolph G. Penner
Urban Institute

Andrew J. Rettenmaier
Texas A&M University

Shanna Rose
Claremont McKenna College

Joseph Rosenberg
Urban-Brookings Tax Policy Center

Daniel L. Smith
New York University

Eric Toder
Urban-Brookings Tax Policy Center

Alan D. Viard
American Enterprise Institute

Roberton Williams
Urban-Brookings Tax Policy Center

George R. Zodrow
Rice University

List of Figures

List of Tables

Preface

The severe fiscal problems that the United States faces have been the focus of much attention in recent years, and several groups have proposed ambitious plans for fiscal reforms that would address the deficit and debt problems facing the nation through various combinations of expenditure reductions and revenue-increasing tax reforms.

The chapters that follow, which were presented initially at an October 2011 conference sponsored by the James A. Baker III Institute for Public Policy at Rice University, examine the pathways that tax and expenditure reform might take if the fiscal problems in the United States are to be successfully addressed. They focus on (1) reforms of entitlement programs, especially the fiscal problems caused by increasing health care costs and an aging population; (2) federal budgetary issues and processes, including an examination of the lessons that can be learned from the fiscal constraints imposed on the U.S. states, as well as an investigation of the problems that would arise in financing an ever-increasing U.S. national debt; and (3) reforms of the individual tax system, including limitations on various popular tax expenditures, and a wide range of corporate income tax reforms, including base-broadening, rate-reducing reforms modeled after the highly successful Tax Reform Act of 1986.

This book and the conference that preceded it would not have been possible without generous contributions from Ernst & Young LLP, and the Peter G. Peterson Foundation. We also thank Baker Institute founding director Edward Djerejian for his enthusiastic support of the conference and this book, and the Baker Institute staff, especially Sonja D. Fulbright, Ryan Kirksey, Melissa Leuellen, David Martin, Shawn O'Neill, Whitney Smith, and Kevin Young, for their assistance throughout the project. Finally, we thank Victor del Carpio Neyra, Ann Hancock, and Sophia Sciabica, whose cheerful and painstaking editorial assistance was essential to the preparation of this book.

Overview

1 Directions for Fiscal Reform in the United States

John W. Diamond and George R. Zodrow

The severe fiscal problems faced by the United States—as well as many advanced economies in the Eurozone and elsewhere—have attracted much attention in recent years. It is clear that the United States is on an unsustainable dynamic path, as current fiscal policies imply federal government deficits and debt relative to gross domestic product (GDP) that will soon become the largest ever experienced and are projected to continue to increase in the absence of corrective policies (Congressional Budget Office 2013; Auerbach and Gale 2010). For example, in one long-run scenario constructed by Auerbach and Gale, current tax and expenditure policies result in primary deficits (neglecting interest payments) that increase from 1.5 percent of GDP in 2020, to nearly 6 percent of GDP in 2040, nearly 7.5 percent of GDP in 2060, and roughly 9.5 percent of GDP in 2080. These deficits are associated with increases in the ratio of debt to GDP from 70 percent in 2011 to over 200 percent in 2040, roughly 400 percent in 2060, and nearly 700 percent by 2080. In the eurozone, the recent financial crisis and the associated severe economic contraction have aggravated the growing national debt problems that many nations face, resulting in an ongoing crisis that threatens the long-term viability of the euro and has raised the specter of a national default by one or more members of the European Union. Finding economically and politically viable solutions to the pervasive problem of burgeoning national debts may be the most pressing concern facing the industrialized world today.

Although these problems have been building without much fanfare for a considerable length of time, they have become sufficiently severe that they are now drawing a great deal of attention. In the United States, several groups have published ambitious plans for fiscal reforms designed to address the debt issue through various combinations of expenditure reductions and revenue-increasing tax reforms. The most prominent of these are the plans developed by the National Commission on Fiscal Responsibility and Reform (2010), headed by Alan Simpson and Erskine Bowles, and the Debt Reduction Task Force of the Bipartisan Policy Center (2010), headed by Pete Domenici and Alice Rivlin. Similarly, many countries in Europe have developed their own plans to reduce expenditures, increase revenues, and reduce their national debts. However, it remains to be seen whether these countries will be successful in fully implementing such plans and thereby avoiding a catastrophic financial meltdown of the type vividly described by Burman, Rohaly, Rosenberg, and Lim (2010).

The chapters that follow address the difficult issues raised by fiscal reform in the current environment in the United States and examine the directions fiscal reform might take if the debt problem in the United States is to be successfully addressed. They focus on (1) reforms of entitlement programs, especially the fiscal problems caused by increasing health care costs and an aging population; (2) federal budgetary issues and processes, including an examination of the lessons that can be learned from the fiscal constraints imposed on the U.S. states, as well as an investigation of the problems that would arise in financing an ever-increasing U.S. national debt; and (3) reforms of the individual tax system, including curtailing various popular tax expenditures, and a wide range of corporate income tax reforms, including base-broadening, rate-reducing reforms modeled after the highly successful Tax Reform Act of 1986.

The next two chapters focus on federal expenditure programs. In chapter 2, Mark Pauly examines the interaction between rising health care costs—in both the public and private sectors—and the level of federal expenditures. He then evaluates options for curtailing the growth in public sector medical expenditures, especially in the Medicare program, while limiting the harm done to the health care system. In chapter 3, Jagadeesh Gokhale critiques the current method used to evaluate the financial health and sustainability of Social Security and argues for an alternative microsimulation approach that more fully accounts for individual behavior and demographic projections. Gokhale discusses estimates of Social Security's liabilities using this approach and then evaluates six alternative Social Security reform options.

Chapters 4 and 5 examine budgetary issues and processes. In chapter 4, Shanna Rose and Daniel Smith review the literature on the effectiveness of the budgetary constraints imposed on the U.S. states, including state balanced budget amendments, debt ceilings, and tax and expenditure limits—all provisions that are currently being discussed at the federal level. They conclude that relatively strict balanced budget amendments are the most successful approach to limiting the size of state governments; other approaches, including stringent debt limitations and supermajority requirements for revenue increases, also have some potential to promote fiscal restraint.

In chapter 5, John Kitchen examines the issues raised by the need to finance the U.S. government debt and the implications of alternative methods of financing the debt, including both domestic and foreign borrowing as well as monetization of the debt. Kitchen then simulates the effects of each of these approaches, focusing on their relative implications for the U.S. deficit and debt-to-GNP (gross national product) ratio.

The final three chapters examine issues related to individual and corporate tax reform. Daniel Baneman, Joseph Rosenberg, Eric Toder, and Roberton Williams examine several options to raise revenue at the individual level by limiting and in some cases combining tax expenditures. In chapter 6, they consider three alternative approaches to curtailing individual tax expenditures and then analyze variations of the three proposals that would increase the progressivity of the tax system. The discussion then turns to corporate income tax reform. Jane Gravelle begins chapter 7 by describing the most popular corporate tax expenditures that might be eliminated and then addressing the concerns of those opposed to raising the U.S. corporate rate to increase revenues. She identifies increasing taxes on foreign source income, reducing interest deductions, and curtailing the tax preference for advertising expenses as among the least distortionary reforms that would raise significant revenue. In the final chapter of this book, John Diamond, George Zodrow, Thomas Neubig, and Robert Carroll evaluate traditional base-broadening, rate-reducing reforms of the corporate income tax using a computer simulation model. They conclude that the effects of such reforms are relatively modest due to various effects that tend to offset and depend significantly on how corporate rate reductions are financed.

Health Care Reform and the U.S. Budget

In chapter 2, Mark Pauly of the University of Pennsylvania discusses the increasing cost of health care, its negative implications for the U.S. budget, and possible solutions to this fiscal problem, focusing primarily on Medicare. The growth of medical spending in both the public and private sectors in the United States and other developed countries is typically higher than GDP growth, especially over the long term, which suggests that medical care is a luxury good. Pauly notes that the new treatments available each year and the increasing success of existing treatments drive increased consumer demand for medical services. In addition, high-priced technological advances have been a major driver of medical spending growth, followed by higher prices for the services provided by health care professionals. Furthermore, these prices have increased at a faster pace in the United States than in other developed countries because the U.S. government is not the main consumer of these services. In many other developed countries, the government is the main purchaser of medical services and plays a major role in limiting price increases. However, in the United States, comparatively freer markets set these prices, which has resulted in faster price growth that is largely reflected in relatively high wages in the health care sector.

Private consumers can of course support increased spending on medical care by reallocating resources and consuming less of other goods. By comparison, the government must either raise additional tax revenue or spend less on other programs to support an increase in medical spending in the public sector. Pauly argues that raising revenue in the United States to support public funding of medical care is problematic because the excess burden of increased taxation would aggravate existing tax distortions, which are already significant. Therefore, he focuses on solutions to slowing the growth rate of U.S. public spending on medical care.

Public spending on medical care in the United States is primarily attributable to the Medicare and Medicaid programs. The growth of Medicare spending has tracked that of private spending growth, but at a slightly slower rate, while Medicaid spending patterns have differed considerably from private spending patterns. Pauly argues that public medical spending is the principal factor influencing the growth of the U.S. federal government relative to the economy; in his words, in the United States, "Leviathan wears a white lab coat."

Pauly argues that the rate of increase on public medical expenditures relative to income should be less than that of private medical spending as a fraction of income. Solutions he considers include voucher programs, means testing, removing the income tax exclusion of employer contributions toward health insurance premiums, health savings accounts, alterations to supply-side behavior, raising the age of eligibility for Medicare, and improving overall efficiency. Pauly's ideal solution to restricting the growth in public medical spending includes a politically determined level of spending growth that corresponds to the preferred rate of taxpayers who receive fully subsidized insurance. This growth rate would reflect both the taxpayers' preferred rate of spending growth and growth in the availability of new technology. For the population above the poverty level, the growth of public medical spending would be means tested. Pauly argues that under such an approach, medical spending in the public sector could be controlled while still reflecting individual preferences for health care.

Social Security Reform and the U.S. Budget

In the chapter 3, Jagadeesh Gokhale of the Cato Institute examines the financial health of the Social Security program and considers options for reform. The Social Security trustees estimate that under current law, the program's trust fund will be exhausted by 2035. In addition, because net benefits have exceeded net tax receipts since 2010, the program is now increasing the U.S. deficit rather than reducing it, as was the case in recent years. Gokhale contends that these official predictions are based on outdated methods and assumptions and that the situation is in fact even more dire than these projections would suggest.

Specifically, Gokhale argues that the model currently used by the Social Security trustees to project the system's financial condition is flawed because its projections, which are based almost exclusively on historical data, fail to adequately integrate demographic and economic factors, and in general do not incorporate enough detail. Gokhale proposes an alternative, the demographic and economic micro simulation (DEMSIM) model, which he argues addresses these issues and thus provides more accurate projections of the financial condition of the Social Security program.

Using DEMSIM, Gokhale projects a seventy-five-year liability for the Social Security program of almost $7 trillion; by comparison, the trustees' estimate is $4.1 trillion. He observes that the DEMSIM projection implies that either a 31 percent increase in tax receipts or a 22 percent decrease in benefits would be required for the Social Security trust fund to maintain solvency. In contrast, if no modifications are made to the current tax and benefit structure, Gokhale estimates the Social Security trust fund will be exhausted in 2029.

Gokhale concludes by evaluating six reforms of the Social Security system using the DEMSIM model. He describes two of these proposals as conservative, two as liberal, and two as in the center of the political spectrum and notes that they range from dedicating new tax revenues to the Social Security system to diverting existing payroll taxes to personal accounts. The reforms reduce the infinite horizon liability of the program by at least 80 percent compared to the baseline of DEMSIM's projections, with the exception of one of the liberal proposals and one of the conservative proposals. Gokhale also considers the microeconomic effects of each reform, comparing projected retirement incomes and lifetime tax rates under the reforms. He concludes by restating the need for the Social Security trustees to consider the microeconomic effects of Social Security and possible reforms, as well as the use of more appropriate modeling procedures to measure both the macroeconomic effects and the fiscal health of the program.

Budget Reform in the United States

The next three chapters examine various issues related to budgetary processes and their role in reducing government debt and deficits in the United States. In Chapter 4, Shanna Rose and Daniel Smith of New York University investigate the extent to which various state budgetary rules have been successful in imposing fiscal discipline on U.S. state governments and whether the federal government should consider such provisions as a means of promoting fiscal sustainability. They note that since World War II, the federal government has ended most fiscal years in a deficit—with an average deficit of 2.74 percent of GDP. By comparison, state governments, which are subject to a variety of budgetary constraints, typically end the fiscal year with a balanced budget or a slight surplus. Accordingly, Rose and Smith review the effectiveness of various state budgetary rules—including balanced budget amendments, debt limits, and tax and expenditure limits—to determine which instruments might be successfully adapted to the federal level to control the rising level of the national debt.

Rose and Smith begin by reviewing the limited experience with budgetary rules at the federal level, noting that attempts to pass a federal balanced budget amendment have failed repeatedly. The Gramm-Rudman-Hollings Act of 1985 instituted strict deficit limits with automatic budget cuts that were to be imposed if the limits were exceeded. However, its provisions were often evaded, and the law was repealed in 1990. Shortly after, the Budget Enforcement Act of 1990 established spending caps and pay-as-you-go rules designed to promote the fiscal sustainability of entitlement programs and tax cuts. However, the act was also subject to evasion and manipulation. It expired in the early 2000s, only to be implemented again recently with more exemptions, further restricting its potential for success.

Rose and Smith then analyze the effectiveness of various institutional budgetary constraints at the subnational level. For example, nearly every state government is subject to a balanced budget amendment. The literature indicates that these amendments have been fairly successful in limiting debts and deficits, especially in states that have rules that preclude carryover of deficits across budget years rather than simply more easily manipulated ex ante rules.

Rose and Smith note that studies on state debt limits have been inconclusive regarding their success in limiting government spending. They observe that although state debt limits are inevitably more binding constraints than federal debt limits since states are unable to print their own money, state debt limits are still relatively easy to evade. For example, since state debt limits are applicable to only guaranteed debt, state governments can establish entities that issue debt that is not subjected to the debt limits.

Finally, the authors note that states have recently increased their use of tax and expenditure limits to encourage fiscal discipline. However, studies that have examined the success of these limits indicate that they have had little, if any, impact in constraining public sector growth among states. Similarly, Rose and Smith find that the line item veto has had minimal success in restricting public spending.

Rose and Smith conclude that the state experience suggests that strict balanced budget amendments and debt limits have been the most effective instruments in constraining state deficits and debt, although they note that such provisions may also have had some deleterious consequences. They also note that institutional and political barriers will make it difficult to impose such constraints on the federal government, but that such barriers may be surmountable given the urgency of the current fiscal situation.

Can the World Finance the United States's Debt?

In chapter 5, John Kitchen of the U.S. Department of the Treasury examines another aspect of the debt problem facing the United States:

the need to finance the debt and the economic effects of alternative methods of financing it. He considers three primary sources of funding—domestic and foreign private funding, foreign official funding, and domestic monetary funding—as well as one scenario that assumes a successful generic policy reform that would reduce the deficit and debt. Kitchen focuses his analysis on the medium-term effects and implications of each scenario for the next ten years, using as a benchmark the projections of the CBO.

Kitchen begins by describing the composition of the ownership of U.S. debt in recent years. He observes that foreign holdings of Treasury outstanding debt, especially by foreign governments, have increased from 17 percent in 1999 to 35 percent in 2010. In addition, U.S. Federal Reserve debt holdings have increased in recent years, as well as its holdings of government-sponsored enterprise debt. For purposes of his model, Kitchen assumes that the Federal Reserve's expanded balance sheet size will be unchanged through 2013 before contracting to its usual size by 2018, at which point, according to the CBO projections, the economy will have returned to its original growth rate. Nevertheless, the U.S. debt will continue to grow at an unsustainable rate under this scenario.

Kitchen summarizes the main effects of each alternative source of funding as follows. Generalized private funding results in higher interest rates, which in turn cause lower investment rates and reduced growth. Generalized foreign official funding implies that both the U.S. government deficit and its net export deficit increase, which implies growing international debt imbalances and larger interest payments to foreigners. By comparison, if the U.S. Federal Reserve finances (monetizes) the debt, the result is higher inflation, higher nominal interest rates, and capital losses to bondholders. Kitchen's numerical simulations indicate that reductions in the federal deficit as a percent of GNP are smallest under private funding and foreign official funding, as the debt-to-GNP ratio declines from 8.4 percent in 2011 to 6.4 percent and 6.3 percent, respectively, in 2021; by comparison, the deficit declines to 5.3 percent of GNP under the scenario with domestic official funding. Federal debt as a percent of GNP increases from 66.5 percent in 2011 to 92.0 percent under the private funding scenario, 92.3 percent under the foreign official funding scenario, and 72.3 percent under the Federal Reserve funding scenario in 2021, relative to the base case scenario in 2021 of a federal debt of 60.8 percent. Under the generic policy reform scenario, which includes a successful fundamental tax reform and a reduction in government expenditures of $5 trillion through 2021, the federal deficit declines to 0.6 percent of GNP and the federal debt declines to 57.7 percent of GNP by 2021. The results of the last simulation highlight the unsustainable nature of current fiscal policy and the necessity for reform.

Individual and Corporate Tax Reform

The final three chapters examine issues related to reform of the individual and corporate income taxes as a means of addressing the debt problem in the United States. In chapter 6, Daniel Baneman, Joseph Rosenberg, Eric Toder, and Roberton Williams of the Urban-Brookings Tax Policy Center examine how revenues might be raised by reforming individual tax expenditures. The authors note that the Tax Reform Act of 1986 was successful in reducing tax expenditures from 9 percent to 6 percent of GDP, but that tax expenditures have since increased to roughly 7 percent of GDP. The 2012 budget for the United States lists 173 tax expenditures, most of which affect businesses rather than individuals; total individual tax expenditures in 2011 were in excess of $1.1 trillion, approximately 6 percent of GDP. Of these individual tax expenditures, 24 percent benefit the top 1 percent of the income distribution, approximately 67 percent accrue to the top quintile of the income distribution, and only 3 percent go to the lowest quintile of the income distribution. At the same time, however, tax expenditures reduce effective federal tax rates by the most for the two lowest quintiles and by roughly a third for the rest of the income distribution. Hence, attempts to eliminate tax expenditures are politically difficult since they are popular among many taxpayers and potential voters.

Baneman, Rosenberg, Toder, and Williams consider three alternative ways of reducing the revenue costs (and thus the value) of individual tax expenditures: (1) the replacement of six major tax expenditures with a combined 15 percent credit; (2) a cap on the total of seven major tax expenditures to 4 percent of adjusted gross income (AGI); and (3) a 35 percent "haircut" that reduces the value of a set of tax expenditures by 35 percent. The three alternatives are designed so that they would initially result in roughly similar tax increases on average. However, the authors also account for behavioral responses to each of the modifications of tax expenditures, which explains the differences in revenue raised under the various scenarios. Although not all taxpayers are affected by these changes in individual tax expenditures, those who are experience a reduction in after-tax income on average of just below 2 percent. The AGI limit would affect only one-third of households, while the 15 percent credit (35 percent haircut) would affect 40 (54) percent of households. The AGI limit would also raise more revenue than the other two proposals in its first year: $30 billion versus $14 billion (for the 35 percent haircut) and $10 billion (for the 15 percent credit). The authors also consider several modifications of these three proposals. Not treating the 15 percent tax rate on dividends and capital gains as a tax expenditure under the various alternative scenarios would limit the progressivity of the reforms and reduce tax revenues. By comparison, excluding the child credit from the list of affected tax expenditures would increase the progressivity of the AGI limit and haircut scenarios. Baneman, Rosenberg, Toder, and Williams conclude that over the course of the decade, the 15 percent tax credit would raise the most revenue: $2.8 trillion.

Corporate Tax Reform

The final two chapters consider issues in corporate income tax reform. In chapter 7, Jane Gravelle of the Congressional Research Service considers a wide variety of ways of increasing corporate income tax revenues, focusing on base-broadening modifications and reforms. The thirty largest corporate tax expenditures total $137 billion, which equals roughly 31 percent of corporate revenue. Gravelle identifies accelerated depreciation, deferred taxation of foreign source income, tax-favored bonds, the research and experimentation credit, and the production activities deduction as the largest corporate tax expenditures, and notes that the top ten provisions account for 85 percent of total tax expenditures. For example, replacing the deferral of foreign source income with a deduction for foreign taxes paid would produce approximately $123 billion in increased revenue in 2014, while using formula apportionment to determine taxable income would result in a revenue increase of $105 billion.

One of the major considerations in thinking about corporate income tax reform is the effects of globalization. In particular, many observers have argued that international tax competition and increasingly mobile international capital imply that the U.S. corporate tax rate should be reduced. Gravelle is skeptical, however; she estimates that although a 10 percentage point cut in the corporate rate would generate some short-term output gains as well as a 3 percent increase in revenues from less profit shifting, those gains would be eroded within ten years of the rate cut by the negative investment effects of the resulting increase in the deficit and interest rates.

Another revenue-raising alternative that Gravelle explores is increasing the foreign source income base by moving to a territorial tax system that exempts foreign source income, the approach that most other countries use. Many proponents find the territorial tax system appealing because it increases the ability of U.S. corporations to compete with firms from the countries that have a territorial system, and some argue that the increase in foreign investment that results from such a tax would simultaneously result in more investment in the United States. However, Gravelle stresses that these arguments ignore the results from some theoretical models, and she also questions the importance of tax effects in the decision making of investors.

Gravelle concludes with numerous suggestions and remarks on the best corporate-revenue-raising options. She argues that the reform proposals that would raise the most revenue with the least distortion are increasing taxes on foreign source income, abolishing the title passage rule, reducing the deductions for interest expense and the deductions for advertising, and modifying the system so that pass-through entities would be taxed as corporations. While the alternatives of eliminating accelerated depreciation and the productions activities deduction would increase short-term revenues with little short-term distortion, Gravelle cautions that there may be unintended consequences from these reforms. In particular, the revenues from limiting accelerated depreciation would not persist in the long run and the production activities deduction may be reasonably well targeted toward highly mobile international capital.

The Dynamic Effects of a U.S. Corporate Income Tax Rate Reduction

In the concluding chapter of this book, John Diamond and George Zodrow of Rice University, along with Thomas Neubig and Robert Carroll of Ernst & Young LLP, examine the economic effects of a rate-reducing, base-broadening corporate tax reform. They argue that using the revenues obtained from the base-broadening elimination of business tax expenditures that is the focus of Gravelle's chapter is desirable, given that the United States currently has a high statutory tax rate relative to its competitors; a rate reduction should thus both encourage investment and reduce incentives for income shifting to lower tax jurisdictions. They note, however, that a disadvantage of corporate rate reduction is that it reduces the taxation of existing capital, including capital that earns economic rents.

The authors use a dynamic, overlapping generations, computable general equilibrium model developed by Diamond and Zodrow to simulate the macroeconomic effects of various base-broadening, rate-reducing corporate tax reforms. They begin by analyzing the effects of a revenue-neutral tax reform in which corporate rate reduction is financed by eliminating all business expenditures. The reform is simulated within the context of their base model, which is extended to include an imperfectly competitive sector that earns above-normal returns, international capital flows, and income shifting. These reforms all result in declines in investment and GDP, as the benefits of rate reduction are offset by the costs of increasing the cost of capital with base-broadening measures and reducing the taxation of existing capital, including in some cases capital that earns above-normal returns.

Diamond, Zodrow, Neubig, and Carroll also consider several alternative reforms. For example, they simulate a more modest corporate rate reduction to 25 percent, financed with the elimination of business tax expenditures that have relatively small effects on the costs of capital (e.g., accelerated depreciation and most other investment incentives are maintained). Under this scenario, corporate tax reform results in increases in investment and GDP in the long run on the order of 0.5 percent. They also show that somewhat more positive effects are possible if the corporate rate reduction is financed with either increases in wage taxes (GDP increases by nearly 1 percent in the long run) or reductions in government transfers (GDP increases by about 1.3 percent in the long run), although these reforms would have different distributional implications from those that focus solely on the corporate sector.

The authors conclude that the macroeconomic effects of base-broadening, rate-reducing reforms vary significantly depending on the details of the proposals implemented. Their model simulation results suggest that reforms that finance rate reduction with the elimination of all business tax expenditures may reduce investment and GDP, while alternative reforms that retain many investment incentives or finance rate reduction with wage tax increases or cuts in government transfers are more likely to result in long run increases in investment and GDP.

Conclusion

The fiscal problems facing the United States, as well as many other countries in the industrialized world, have been well documented. Less clear are the solutions to these problems. The chapters in this book discuss a wide range of potential solutions, including reforms of the major entitlement programs and the personal and corporate income tax systems in the United States. They also examine the experience of the states and other industrialized countries to determine what lessons might be learned from coping with these issues, as well as the implications of alternative means of financing the extraordinarily large current and projected future levels of debt in the United States. Together the authors provide a wealth of information on the magnitude of the fiscal problems facing the United States, as well as the advantages and disadvantages of alternative solutions to a problem that must be solved if future generations are to inherit a vibrant economy that can generate the opportunities for growth to which we have been accustomed.

References

Auerbach, Alan J., and William G. Gale. 2010. Déjà Vu All Over Again: On the Dismal Prospects for the Federal Budget. *National Tax Journal* 63 (3): 543–60.

Burman, Leonard E., Jeffrey Rohaly, Joseph Rosenberg, and Katherine C. Lim. 2010. Catastrophic Budget Failure. *National Tax Journal* 63 (3): 561–84.

Congressional Budget Office. 2008. Revenues, Outlays, Deficits, Surpluses, and Debt held by the Public, 1968 to 2002, in Billions of Dollars. Washington, DC: Congressional Budget Office.

Congressional Budget Office. 2013. *The Budget and Economic Outlook: An Update*. Washington, DC: Congressional Budget Office.

Debt Reduction Task Force of the Bipartisan Policy Center. 2010. *Restoring America's Future: Reviving the Economy, Cutting Spending and Debt, and Creating a Simple, Pro-Growth Tax System*. Washington, DC: Bipartisan Policy Center.

National Commission on Fiscal Responsibility and Reform. 2010. *The Moment of Truth: Report of the National Commission on Fiscal Responsibility and Reform*. Washington, DC: U.S. Government Printing Office.

I Expenditure Programs

2 Medical Spending Reform and the Fiscal Future of the United States

Mark V. Pauly

The rate of growth in medical spending in the United States and most other developed countries is high most of the time and is commonly higher (over the long term) than the rate of growth in gross domestic product (GDP). Because much of medical spending affects and is affected by government spending and taxation, the growth in this share of consumption expenditures is both more important for fiscal policy and raises more potential problems than consumer spending growth in other sectors of the economy. Given the growing importance of Medicare and Medicaid, the two most important federal health care programs in the U.S. budget, and the impending expansion in Medicaid eligibility (potentially limited, though by no means stopped, by the Supreme Court decision, *National Federation of Independent Businesses, et al v. Kathleen Sebelius, Secretary of Health and Human Services, et al.*, June 28, 2012.), and subsidies for health insurance exchanges under the recent health care reform, growth in federally financed spending on health care poses a major challenge to fiscal stability today and in the future. The addition of obligations under health reform to finance subsidies for millions of lower-income nonelderly adds to the challenge. In addition, the large role played in private insurance markets by federal tax, spending, and regulatory policy means that even private spending growth is a matter of fiscal policy concern. We know that there is a problem and that current policies are not sustainable. But designing solutions that will do more good than harm requires both a clear idea of the causes of the problem and a precise and politically feasible articulation of our social goals with respect to medical care use, health insurance protection, and health outcomes of Americans. In this chapter, I describe the problem and discuss solutions.

Why Is There a Financing Problem? An Arithmetic Explanation

Before examining the content and effects of medical spending, first view it as a macroeconomic accounting issue. In economies with growing real income, consumers usually want to spend more on almost all items of consumption from one year to the next; in economic terminology, goods and services are usually "normal." It is not abnormal that some categories of spending may be more responsive to growth in income than others. I may want to spend a disproportionate share (relative to my current spending patterns) of any increase in my income on certain categories of spending.[1] That is, consumers may choose some goods to be "luxuries" in the sense that their percentage spending growth exceeds the percentage growth in income.

For goods demanded and paid for privately, this behavior raises no problems. Spending shares rise for some things as people pay for what they want and are offset by slower growth in spending for other things. But if luxury goods are financed by government, there is a mathematical proposition that may signal a problem. Since the tax base grows at approximately the same rate as income, an increasing share for a given component of spending necessarily implies higher future tax rates to finance that spending unless spending shares on other types of public activities are to shrink or deficits are to become even larger. Ever-growing marginal tax rates are a public finance economist's worst nightmare.

Historically medical spending in the United States seems to fit into the luxury category, for reasons I will discuss. Indeed, although U.S. spending is at a higher level than that of any other developed country, largely because of higher unit prices and wages in the United States (Anderson et al. 2003), the long-term rates of growth of spending in these countries are similar to that in the United States and similarly tend to grow faster than GDP (Conover 2011).

There is nothing illogical, or wrong, or problematic about a category of private consumer spending that grows more rapidly than income over a long period of time (although this cannot persist forever). Were medical spending fully privately financed, such spending growth need not be a cause for concern; as a growth industry in an otherwise bleak economic landscape, it might even be an object of cheer. But because so much medical care is publicly financed, the nearly inevitable and inexorable rise of the tax burden associated with health care spending as a percentage of both income and the tax base upsets fiscal stability and political equilibrium. I will argue both that this characteristic of medical care demand, one that is wholly natural and not anyone's fault, is the main source of the fiscal problem when medical services are publicly financed and the main reason that that problem is close to intractable without major and wrenching political choices.

Although it is not necessarily easy for people to adjust their private budgets to accommodate spending items they want to increase, they do it all the time. The problem with increased public sector spending is that income tax rates (or any other tax rates on a base correlated with income) come under strong pressure to increase to pay for what people want—even if the number of eligible persons, their age distribution, their illness levels, and all other things remained the same. The political system is, however, challenged to increase tax rates (or make other accommodations), and from an economic point of view, at some point it should stop doing so.

In what follows I first outline what we know about the reasons for this challenge for the medical care system as a whole, discuss why it is much more serious for the public sector (but also why it is hard for public and private sectors to adjust differently), and then examine potential "best of a bad lot" remedies to the fiscal problem.

What Is Special about Medical Care Spending?

It may come as a surprise to hear that at the heart of the problem of medical spending growth, is good news: at least on average, American real incomes per capita have been rising and continue to rise. American medical care (up to a point) is good for you, and it gets better every year. Not surprisingly, when people experience a rise in real income, one of the things they want to be able to do with that income is to increase their health—in the jargon terms of health policy, to increase the quantity and quality of their expected life years. We want to spend some of the happy increase in real income on living longer and better.

There are two things our health care system, flawed as it is, can do to improve our health. First, at any point in time there are additional treatments, compared to what most people are getting, that can improve their health yet further. Effective care for most people includes routine pediatric care, monitoring, screening, checking, and counseling for chronic conditions and, on rare but important occasions, serious if expensive treatments that really work. Whether the additional treatments would produce enough of an improvement to be worth their cost is an open question, but there are always useful things at the margin.

Second, each year new treatments, new procedures, and new approaches that generally work better, at least for some people some of the time, are added to the armamentarium. This "technical change" especially characterizes the research-driven medical care industry. Quality improves there, but higher-quality is sold at a higher price. Putting these two benefits from more medical care together, most people decide that it is worthwhile to have more spent on them when growing income allows it—and the percentage increase in desired spending is usually larger than the percentage increase in income.

This is not the only way to look at spending growth related to new technology. While growing income probably stimulates and surely facilitates the spread of costly new technology, some analysts believe that technology itself has an exogenous influence of its own—what is usually called the "technological imperative" (Fuchs 2011). The idea is that if they invent it, physicians will offer it and consumers necessarily will get it, whether they really want to or not. There is plenty of evidence that increased demand stimulates the progress of given technologies, but it is surely true that innovative discoveries do matter when they happen (Finkelstein 2003) and they usually slow spending growth when they happen less frequently than usual—as evidenced by the recent slowdown in the introduction of new drugs and drug spending as fewer blockbusters have been discovered. While sorting out cause and effect here is potentially important, the key fact is that the growth of spending outpaces income, regardless of its cause, and that is what I will take as given here.

As already noted, people want to spend a larger-than-previous share of spending on their health, while still spending more, just not disproportionately more, on other items of consumer spending. When my income grows, I add a big-screen TV, a more luxurious vacation destination, and an extra night out—but compared to these things, I want to bump up my medical care use even more. Of course, medical care is different: I have some choices to make about buying care at the point of service by paying more out of pocket, but mostly this increase comes about as I choose a more generous health plan and accommodate my health plan's willingness to reimburse for better care by paying higher premiums.

Less transparent in this story is what happens to public spending, especially the major public insurance plans, Medicare and Medicaid.

Empirically the evidence is pretty clear on Medicare: its spending growth per covered person closely tracks privately insured spending growth, and the total spending (including out-of-pocket payments) of Medicare beneficiaries also tracks well the path of private spending per privately insured person, though of course the level of average Medicare spending is much higher because those who are insured are older or disabled (Boccuti and Moon 2003). If there is any regularity, it is that Medicare spending is a little less "inflated" than private spending, but there is no major gap that has emerged over time (despite occasional overages and underages in terms of reimbursement, coverage, and spending).

With Medicaid, things are less clear. Medicaid can and does follow different paths from the average in different states, partly in response to changes in the number and composition of the poor and near-poor people Medicaid covers, and partly because its generally lower reimbursement policies means that it does not pay as much for the same procedures as the rest of the population does (Grannemann and Pauly 2010); there is lower cost (than if payments were greater) but less access. The divergence between Medicaid and other health care spending historically has been uneven though not dramatic, but there is little doubt that Medicaid—and especially the fifty-one different Medicaid programs in the states and the District of Columbia—can and sometimes does march to a different tune from that played by health care as a whole. That is, faced with budgetary crises, individual states cut or dramatically slow Medicaid spending per beneficiary; on those rare occasions when the budget permits (e.g., money from the tobacco settlement), they sometimes make their programs a little more generous.

In the case of both public programs, there is more going on than demanders experiencing increased demand. The primary motivation for public subsidies for health care for the old and the poor is that without them, care would be used at levels lower than what taxpayers think is appropriate—so taxpayers are willing to pay to help others. These populations (at least initially) were not insured primarily because insurance had high premiums (because of high benefits for sicker people) relative to their income; although there are always some problems in private insurance markets, even those in the Medicare population were very low demanders when Medicare was passed because being old then was virtually synonymous with being poor and high risk. That has changed a little over time as seniors' incomes have risen modestly above the poverty line, but it is still lack of affordability of efficient insurance, not lack of efficient private insurance offerings, that largely explains public support. That means, however, that the "demanders" of insurance for these populations are not entirely (or even largely) the people who will be covered, but rather the taxpayers who are financing them. This taxpayer demand for insurance for deserving others also seems to be positively related to taxpayer income, but how it is related is less well known. But even if the income elasticity of demand for others was the same as for demand for self, the rising cost of tax financing would challenge the former more than the latter.

The critical point thus far is that the largest single share of medical spending growth per capita is fueled by this demand-driven, health-improving but expensive technical change—both new products and new (and greater) use of existing products. The second major contributor to medical spending growth has been prices. Because medical care is a labor-intensive industry, most of these price increases are translations of wage increases, and wage growth in the health services sector has outpaced wage and price growth in the rest of the economy. There are some exceptions to this wage-based explanation: rising drug prices mostly benefit drug firm stockholders and scientists (and dramatic price declines when patents expire harm them), and some (small) fraction of rising insurance premiums goes to insurance firm executives, for profit and nonprofit. But still, health care spending increases are mostly health care wage increases—almost all of which are paid to American workers. Health care is not like oil or even computers. We are paying a lot more, but much of it goes to better care and better-paid American workers.

Noticeably absent from this catalogue of what we know about health care spending growth is evidence that inefficiency is a cause. An important first point is this: while there surely are inefficiency, waste, fraud, and corruption in health care, as there is in any other industry, and while (more seriously) inefficiency is probably higher in this industry than in some others, to predict higher spending growth due to inefficiency, we need to have reasons to believe that inefficiency is getting disproportionately worse every year—and that we do not know. And there surely is some inefficiency in growing spending. But the data on variations in spending across countries or states in the United States do not help us to know what is happening to changes in spending over time, and (as noted above) there is little more definitive on this subject that singles out the United States (Skinner 2011).

Thus the discussion in the Rivlin-Domenici report (Debt Reduction Task Force of the Bipartisan Policy Center 2010) that first asserts that "slowing the growth in health spending is realistic" and then points to lower spending and better outcomes in other countries is not really logical; there may be some things about other countries we should copy to lower our level of costs, but the data on growth of spending or GDP share (depending on the time period chosen) put us below many of our peers. Another example of this confusion from Rivlin-Domenici (Debt Reduction Task Force of the Bipartisan Policy Center 2010, 44) is the assertion that fee-for-service payment (mostly now limited to traditional Medicare) is a major reason for rising spending because it offers "incentives to amplify the volume of tests." If the payment rate for tests is set too high, there will be incentives to do more of them, but once the volume is boosted, there is no reason that fee-for-service payment means that it should continue to increase as time goes on.

There are some other less important causes of spending growth. Total spending obviously grows with the population, but the fact that births and net immigration exceed deaths in the United States is not something that most people would want to change. Spending per capita grows as threats to health grow; the primary threat is older age, along with the whole (and intertwined) list of obesity, HIV, asthma, and depression. It is not clear that we would want to change the fact that more Americans are living longer, and I would not want to change the fact that productive immigrants are trickling into the United States. We would like people to stay more fit, have better lifestyles, take fewer health risks, and breathe better, but cost-effective ways to effect those changes have so far proven elusive—and it is important to remember that in total, despite the worsening of health in some dimensions, we are still living longer and better than we ever have.

Working Out the Math

The story thus far about health and well-being is pretty positive. Despite some flaws in our health care system, it does deliver better care to more people every year. Not only that, but in aggregate and on average, the value of this better care is probably greater than its real resource cost (Cutler 2004). Problems arise, however, when we start to break this virtuous spending growth down into its component parts and then try to extrapolate it into the future. I will subdivide first by dividing the population by age and income (to parallel our major social programs for medical care and medical insurance) and then by examining the relationships between those component parts. I will discuss total spending and then how that aggregate does or does not hide differences in how these different parts of the population experience and are affected by spending growth.

Medical Spending's Share of GDP and Other Useless and Useful Statistics

It is commonplace to begin any discussion of the relationship of medical spending to fiscal policy with the larger issue of the relationship of total medical spending, tax financed and not, relative to GDP, and to cite the observation that for decades, medical spending relative to GDP has been higher in the United States than in any other country in the world. The usual inference or implication is that we must be doing something wrong, especially since our health outcomes are not superior to many of those in other developed countries. Of course, "doing something wrong" is meaningful only if someone has some idea of something we really could do differently.

Some of the difference does reflect something other than bad behavior about resource use. A large fraction of the difference between the U.S. share of GDP going to health care and that of other developed countries (probably more than half, although precise measurement is difficult) results from that fact that, at exchange rates based on overall purchasing power, medical care prices for many things are much higher in the United States than anywhere else. But it is even more important to note that the bulk of higher prices (with drugs as a probable exception) is caused by wages for medical workers—physicians, nurses, and even unskilled hospital workers—being higher in the United States than anywhere else (Pauly 1993; Anderson et al. 2003, 2007; Laugeson and Glied 2011). The mirror image is that the share of our workforce in health care is not out of line with the share in most other developed countries. We spend more not because we hire more people into health care and away from other industries but because we pay them more than other countries do. There may be more health care capital and equipment in the United States, but that difference is not enough to close the cost gap due to wage differentials.

Medical care prices and wages in the United States are higher for two reasons, both of which would be hard to change. In other countries, the government usually is by far the major buyer of health care and uses its large-buyer market power to hold down the prices and wages it pays; in the United States, these prices are determined in relatively free labor and product markets. The other reason is that we pay more for people to work in health care because we pay more to workers generally—and health care wages have to keep up. In short, we could have a much lower spending share if we were like the United Kingdom used to be: a nationalized health care system in a low-productivity economy. No one would want that. There might be a case for reducing payments to drug companies and doctors, but their profits or net incomes are only about 15 percent of our total spending—not enough to make a big dent and, more important, not enough to slow the growth rate for very long.

My main point here is that medical spending data, no matter how accurate, provide a very poor indicator of resource use for medical care, and it is real resource use relative to real benefit that is relevant to determining what might be better for the economy. Payments in excess of real resource use may be unfair, but they are only transfers from consumers of medical care to producers of medical care and, in contrast to other markets where we pay prices that exceed resource costs, like oil or rare earth metals, almost all the excess payments go to Americans.

There are other reasons that the health spending GDP share is one of our most misleading statistics. The level of GDP obviously affects the ratio, but it is under the control of Dr. Yellen (if it is under anyone's control), not of any medical doctor. Moreover, since shares must add up to 100 percent, if the U.S. medical spending share is regarded as excessive, some other developed country with a below-average share (like Japan) must by definition have excessive spending on some other item of consumption. (In Japan, it is housing.) Why doesn't that over-spending on housing harm the Japanese economy? At this level of generality we can only ask these debaters' rhetorical questions, but they bring us back to the main point: accurate evaluation is not helped by the misleading share data; instead it should be based on asking about the comparative value of resources used in medical care versus what those resources could have provided if they were used elsewhere (assuming it is possible to use them elsewhere).

A more meaningful statistic begins with a first difference: it is better to compare the rate of growth in medical spending with the rate of growth in GDP. Such a comparison ignores unknowable and irrelevant differences across nations in how well medical people are paid and other special characteristics like consumers' lifestyles. Of course, it would be better to convert both GDP growth and medical spending growth to real terms, either resources or consumption. As long as price changes can be assumed to be the same in medical care as in the economy as a whole, however, even comparing nominal growth rates is helpful.

In addition, growth rates are the indicators used by Medicare's trustees and most policymakers (including President Obama) to describe different scenarios. Roughly speaking, medical care spending in the United States has a long-term trend of growing at a rate about 2 to 3 percentage points above the rate of growth of GDP; policy proposals often target the health care spending growth rate to GDP + 1 percent (because that postpones the date at which medical spending will eat up all annual GDP growth by about fifty years), or in the most ambitious cost containment programs, to GDP growth only. This framing also allows us to incorporate the notion of medical spending as a historical luxury good (since that implies a growth rate above GDP).

In both the actuarial calculations in the Medicare Trustees' Report and various policy proposals, the "over-GDP" growth rate is simply treated as a policy parameter for the entire medical economy that "we" can choose as we wish. My earlier discussion implies, in contrast, that as individual consumers, we have already chosen the high rate of growth, so any collective choice of a lower rate is bound to require some give (and probably some stress) somewhere. One partial resolution of this dilemma is to note that, at least as of this writing, governmental policymakers in the United States are not responsible for or permitted to choose everyone's medical spending growth rate. If you are in the private sector, you are allowed to spend your own money on your own health care to whatever extent you wish, foolish though that may be. This choice is not entirely an individualistic one; almost all of us with private insurance obtained through a job actually get a substantial tax break that encourages us to spend more than we otherwise would. But what upset Harry and Louise at their Clinton-health-reform kitchen table was the prospect that the Clinton plan did have, as a last resort, a provision for the government to cap total spending, and even so left-of-center a commentator as Paul Krugman reminds us that is not as if the government is ever going to stop us from spending our own money (Krugman 2011). (One notable exception is for Medicare beneficiaries who take the government Part B plan; they are not allowed to pay a doctor more than Medicare permits, no matter how grateful they are or how much they want to get to see that doctor.)

There has been a recent proposal for insurers to set payment rates for all plans and all providers of care in each state to limit per capita spending growth to the growth in wages in that state (Emanuel et al. 2012). Such a system would have to reduce the growth in payments below that of wages if costly new technology is to be financed. If hospitals have to keep their wages up with wages in general, they will be required to do more with less. That will be a tall order, and there will be consumer dissatisfaction if they cannot deliver.

The focus on overall medical spending growth was adopted by the actuaries because of the long-term high correlation with Medicare spending already noted, and because decades in the future it is more plausible that one can forecast overall trends rather than individual components. But there is a key question about this linkage: Is it inevitable? If not, is changing it either feasible or desirable? Here is where the argument is going: it is plausible that if Americans' real incomes continue to grow (and return to their long-term trend), they will want their private insurance and medical care spending to continue for some time to grow as a luxury good, just as it always has. But Medicare can no longer sustain the taxes that would allow it to keep up. So either the link between Medicare and private spending must be broken, or the government has to limit private medical spending. The key question is whether it is either thinkable or desirable to use different and more differentiated models to predict or describe future medical spending trends. That is a political question, not a statistical one, and it is what I turn to next.

The Dire Fiscal Future for Medicare, and the Effect of Tax-Financed Medical Spending on the Federal Budget

Federal actuaries are required to forecast future spending on Medicare with as much accuracy and realism as they can muster. For this reason and because Medicare is the largest single category of medical spending in the federal budget, its fate is usually used to proxy what medical spending means for the government budget as a whole. I first give more detail on those projections, then turn to items that will become increasingly important if health reform is implemented as planned—Medicaid (financed jointly by the federal government and the states) and federally financed subsidies to insurance purchases in federally regulated exchanges (after 2014).

Part A (hospital) spending under Medicare is financed by payroll taxes going into a trust fund. At present that spending is a little more than half of total Medicare spending with a shrinking share (a development that requires the Medicare trustees to report on what they will do to get the general revenue funded share of Medicare back under 46 percent of total spending). The level of Part A spending is growing more rapidly than forecasted earmarked tax revenues (and has done so since 2008). The Medicare trustees conclude that Part A is not even adequately financed for the next ten years despite increases in Medicare taxes in the Affordable Care Act (ACA), and things become even worse in the longer-term projection. The balance in the trust fund is shrinking, as of the 2013 report is forecast to hit zero in 2026, and will be in serious deficit thereafter unless spending is curtailed (Board of Trustees 2013). (The timing of the day of doom for the Part A trust fund varies in different trustees' reports in different years, but they always conclude that what is uncertain is only when this will happen, not whether it will happen.)

Part B (physician care) and Part D (prescription drugs) of Medicare are financed by general revenues; spending growth on these services probably will be even more rapid. The forecast is for GDP to grow at 5.4 percent over the shorter term (next five years) projection period, while Part D will grow at 9.3 percent and Part B at 6.3 percent (ignoring the unlikely event that Congress actually implements the drastic physician pay cuts that are already in law but have always been postponed).

Putting these forecasts together, total federal spending for Medicare as a percentage of GDP is projected to double over the next twenty years and may come close to tripling after seventy-five years: from its level of 3.6 percent in2013 to 6.5 to 10 percent over 2050 to 2085. After a short-run period where forecasts depend on perfect implementation of current law, these projections of Medicare spending are driven by projections of the growth of total medical spending in the United States. Until recent years, such long-term spending was based on a simple prediction that it would grow at the rate of GDP plus 1 percent until 2085 (and at the rate of growth of GDP thereafter). Currently the excess growth is forecasted to start out higher and to trend down to zero by 2085, but with the same average excess of 1 percent over GDP over the period.

Provisions in the ACA contemplate further reductions in Medicare reimbursements and spending growth from the Independent Payment Advisory Board (IPAB), down to as low as 0.5 percent over GDP, but these have not been built into the forecasts. That is because the trustees are not certain that there are ways to reduce spending. They speculated in 2011: "It is possible that health care providers could improve their productivity [and] reduce wasteful expenditures. … For such efforts to be successful in the long range, however, providers would have to generate and sustain unprecedented levels of productivity gains. … The ability of delivery and payment methods to significantly lower cost [*sic*] growth rates is very uncertain" (Boards of Trustees 2011, 41). (In 2013 they simply say that such productivity gains would be "at a faster rate than experienced historically" [Boards of Trustees 2013, 3].)

Medical Spending and the Budget: Data for Looking Backward and Forward

As already implied by the Medicare trustees' report, the rapidly increasing growth of federal health care spending is posing problems for that important program. A good way of getting an idea of what past spending growth has meant to the overall public budget is to examine figure 2.1.

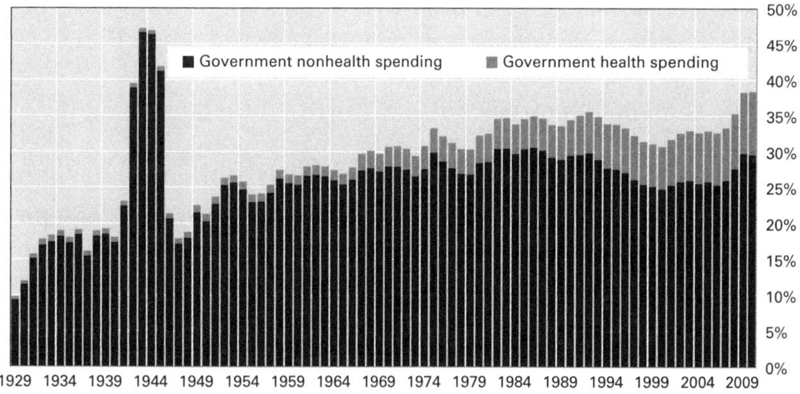

Figure 2.1
Government Health and Nonhealth Spending as a Percent of GDP. (*Note:* Data include debt service, but the entire amount appears under nonhealth spending. If allocated by shares of spending, this would increase government health spending and reduce non-health spending.) Reprinted by permission from Conover 2011.

Not only does the chart show the increasing fraction of GDP going to tax financing for medical care at all levels of government since the passage of Medicare and Medicaid in 1965, it shows that this increase is entirely responsible for the rising share of public spending in the economy as a whole. Some analysts have been disturbed about the increasing importance of government in the U.S. economy, fearing a transition to a European-style welfare state; others are less concerned about or even favor higher social spending and note that the increasing spending share has not yet been matched by as large an increase in the taxation share because of the budget deficit. Figure 2.1 makes the important point that whatever your political philosophy, in reality government spending growth has been all health care all the time. Leviathan wears a white lab coat.

The effect of this growing spending has been that Medicare, Medicaid, and the Medicaid-related Children's Health Insurance Program made up 21 percent of the fiscal year 2010 federal budget. Add to that the 20 percent for Social Security and 6 percent for interest on the debt, and half of the budget is already gone before discretionary and defense spending can be even considered. Looking forward, as the two fiscal reform commissions have noted, this pattern will continue: projected growth in federal funding for medical care, Social Security, and interest on the debt will eat up virtually all of any forecasted increased tax collections at current tax rates, especially later in the decade when the politically controversial patches in Medicare doctor payments and payments to health maintenance organizations cease to have effects.

Can We Cut Long-Term Spending Growth While Improving the Quality of Care?

The Medicare trustees' report gives us the simple answer to this question: nobody knows for sure, but it has never happened. I will now argue that although hope springs eternal, the answer for the future is also more likely to be negative than positive. The reason for a negative answer goes back to the earlier discussion of causes of spending growth: the most direct way to lower spending growth would be to lower the rate of growth of beneficial but costly technology or of wages. Doing the first will probably harm quality—for someone, in some dimension. Slowing spending growth by cutting raises for doctors and nurses and reducing increases in insurer and drug company profit need not harm quality, but here again one may wonder whether health workers or investors will really be willing to do more for less. Just wishing, or even demanding, that the system provide higher-quality, lower-cost care is not going to get you there, and yet much of the policy discussion consists of observations that because this kind of change is so needed, it will be made to happen.

One important benchmark: When we talk about "improving quality," do we mean "compared to last year" or "compared to the improvements that would otherwise have happened"? Expecting our health care system to continue to improve life expectancy is not asking too much, because (with just a few blips) it has been doing that all along. And logically, if we held real resources at about or just a little above where they are today (setting aside higher-than-average changes in medical prices) we could maintain or get a slight increase in life expectancy with lower spending growth and roughly constant tax rates to support federal programs (Pauly 2004). But I am going to assume that bringing improvements in health technology nearly to a standstill in order to save money is not what people want. Rather, they want to get even more and pay even less —a hard order to fill.

We do have evidence that it can sometimes be done. I am most familiar with work looking at the impact of specially trained nurses helping hospitalized Medicare patients make the transition back to the community (Naylor et al. 1999). Using rigorous designs, that research shows that this intervention can substantially reduce the rate of readmission to the hospital and the adverse health outcomes that either trigger or follow from it; we can save money and improve the quality of life. Some (though only a few) immunization programs using low-cost vaccines can also save more than they cost because they prevent illness and save lives; progress on this score stopped with the chicken pox vaccine. More speculatively, there is some reason to believe that greater use of some prescription drugs for asymptomatic chronic conditions like high blood pressure—if only we can get people to use them—can produce "cost offsets" by cutting the cost of physician and hospital care and keeping people healthier. The problem is that these things known to work and save money are not enough to offset the upward push of other things known to work that cost money—and these hard-won changes also do not produce continuous reductions in the rate of spending growth, only in its level as they are phased in.

There are many other discussions of prospects for saving money and lives, but little work that has the two key characteristics of proof of efficacy (not just an observation that somebody has lower costs and better outcomes, with no causal connection) and proof that they can actually be implemented in large-scale practice. The absence of evidence is not evidence of absence, so we have to temper pessimism here, but it is still worthwhile to be skeptical. Let me give two examples where doubt is warranted (though hope should never disappear).

One example may be broadly defined as "reorganized, integrated delivery systems." These are systems that typically started as large, multispecialty physician group practices that affiliated with or built hospitals and other capabilities to cover the full range of a defined voluntarily enrolled population's health care needs. Typical examples are the Mayo Clinic, the Geisinger health system, and the Kaiser health system. Although not all similar entities are equally admirable, these are the examples frequently presented to show that cost and quality need not trade off. But what do these stories prove? Investigations of how good performance is achieved have failed to identify a parsimonious list of design features consistently associated with better outcomes. Instead, qualitative factors like "physician culture" or "leadership" are usually what one ends up with after discarding the objective measures that do not work (Gawande et al. 2009). When these factors are not tautological, they suffer most from our lack of knowledge of how to produce them, or how to change them where they do exist. There may be only a small fraction of the physician workforce psychologically predisposed to be able or willing to work as well together as in these good examples—at least, no one has shown how to manufacture a culture of cooperation and allegiance to evidence—and leaders are famously born, not made. One might try (and the Obama administration is trying) to put the rewards and the information in place to identify those who work well together or lead in the right direction, but there is no evidence that would lead one to expect success.

The other example comes from the other end of the political spectrum: the argument that "competition among firms will improve the quality of care and increase efficiency" (Debt Reduction Task Force of the Bipartisan Policy Center 2010). Economic theory does say that competition is a good thing for consumer and producer welfare (if it can be fostered), but the most it says about quality and cost is that competition should lead to the lowest cost for a given quality, or the highest quality for a given cost, but not that (compared to the absence of competition, one assumes) it will necessarily produce better outcomes for both. All we can say in theory is that compared to unregulated monopoly, unregulated competition cannot lead to the combination of higher costs and worse quality. We cannot say anything in theory about how unregulated completion will compare with regulated markets (monopolistic or competitive). There are surely many examples where regulated monopolies produced too high a level of quality at high prices (air travel in the prederegulation era and "Cadillac-quality" physician care from the American Medical Association), and some where it produced very low cost but low quality or availability (the Veterans Affairs or federal vaccine programs).

This absence of theoretical certainty is, I hasten to add, not a reason to be unenthusiastic about competition, and there are a few minor examples in health care credibly cited as evidence that unregulated competition can function rather well (plastic surgery, radial keratotomy). The magic might work for more of health care, but it might not. Certainly there is no evidence that the informal data on variations in cost for given outcomes used to document inefficiency (e.g., the variations across countries or across geographic areas in the United States) find the most competitive markets at the high-quality, low-cost end of the spectrum. We should have competitive markets to be sure we have maximized our chances for a good deal, but we should not expect magic from their introduction, at least not along all dimensions of desirability. Somebody should give it a shot, but the rest of us should hold back and see how it goes. More about this later.

Cutting a Little to Save a Lot

If the jury is still out on the possibility of magic, is there something less exciting but more certain that we can contemplate? Here the answer is "market change is probable if politics will allow it." What I have in mind is what has happened in many other industries: a process of destructive innovation (or creative destruction) that, shorn of rhetoric and spin, means sacrificing some dimensions of quality to a modest extent in order to save a lot of money. In the classic business school studies, this has happened in the copier industry, the airline industry, and many other areas (Pauly 2011).

I have to admit that examples of even these arguments apply more convincingly to things that change the level of spending (and therefore affect growth only temporarily) rather than the long-run rate of growth. So I will first provide the "levels" examples and then see how they can be extended to growth rates. Minute clinics are an example of what I have in mind. The nurse practitioners who staff them are usually very capable and probably better at some tasks than the typical primary care doctor, but they cannot provide as wide a range of services. There is no harm in that: a skilled chef cannot advise you on your wine. As long as buyers and sellers know where the limits are, things can be much less costly, and even better in many dimensions—but one-stop shopping for all possible primary care needs will be a casualty.

For some unique political and economic reasons, this particular and egregious example of slightly lower quality and much lower cost did successfully enter the medical market—though its growth is now stalled. But it is the exception rather than the rule. However, I believe that regulation, law, and custom prevent a much larger and more desirable shift to this way of thinking and style of care. It is not yet acceptable for middle-class people to talk about anything but the best health care, and legal liability may prevent emergence even of what they would accept.

How can this concept be applied to technical change? To be specific, could a health plan announce that henceforth its premiums would increase only at the rate of GDP growth plus 1 percent and get there by paying current prices but buying less than the best new technology? Perhaps, but such an innovation would surely face serious challenges. So far, private insurers and hospital systems have been unwilling to go first. (Drugstores are the pioneers.) And the timing may not be right for now.

The Real Reason to Limit Public Spending and the Results for Two-Class Medicine

I have already shown some of the fearful numbers about the impact on the federal budget or GDP shares if medical care spending trends continue. But what if that kind of growth is what people want because it is worth it to them? That high medical spending growth is natural is what both history and sophisticated econometric studies tell us. So why not just plan on doing whatever needs to be done in the federal budget—spending cuts elsewhere or tax increases—to accommodate what citizens desire? That they would prefer to have this outcome at less cost makes for good politics but bad economics; taxpayers should just face the reality of ever higher taxes and like it.

The flaw in this Panglossian argument is that there is something special about publicly financed spending, even when it goes for the same things that people buy privately. That something, as I noted some time ago (Pauly 2003), is the fact that all practical tax systems impose an additional cost of moving resources from the private to the public sector—what is called the "excess burden" of taxation. It is this additional cost, one that increases exponentially as more resources are shifted, that limits both what government could and should do.

The argument is classic. If (at age seventy) I were to choose to buy a private health insurance policy, I would pay a hefty premium by diverting part of my income or assets to the purchase. I would incur a cost in terms of what other consumption I would sacrifice. Presumably I would have saved more when I was younger to be able to do this. But that would be the end of it. I save, I accumulate, and I spend—all voluntarily.

Suppose in contrast that I am taxed to pay for Medicare, and suppose it just happens that my tax share to finance my Medicare insurance equals what my private premium would have been. (I must be a somewhat-better-off-than-average and still-working senior citizen for this to happen, given the approximately 90 percent subsidy to Medicare.) I envision the same cut to my other spending, but now I look to see if there are ways I can reconfigure my income and assets to avoid having to pay so much. I might shift to tax-exempt bonds, invest in real estate, or just spend less effort consulting and writing (offset by more leisure, so it should not be a total loss). This distortion of behavior to avoid taxes applies as well to the younger generation; even though they know that Medicare needs their taxes to pay off existing seniors and to be around for them when they retire, they are individually better off trying to figure out how to pay as small a share of the bill as possible. Because we all behave this way, not only does the tax base shrink, but people do inefficient things—investors invest in inefficient opportunities, women and teenagers stay out of the labor market, and everyone hires tax advisors—so the total economic pie shrinks.

Not only that, but this excess burden cost increases as a proportion of additional tax revenues with the square of the marginal tax rate—it increases at an increasing rate. When tax rates are low, the wedge between what things really cost or yield and what people experience is small, so decisions are little distorted. But as the tax rate rises, this distortion gets worse and worse.

Current estimates of the average excess burden of the federal tax system are in the range of twenty-five to fifty cents per dollar of revenue collected. Excess burden maps the age-old trade-off between equity and efficiency; a tax instrument in which people at different income levels pay their "fair shares," like the progressive income tax, generates more excess burden than a proportional or capped tax like the payroll tax. The growth in this cost can be striking. A recent (though conjectural) estimate of the long-run marginal excess burden cost of the subsidies in health reform indicates that excess burden will increase to more than 200 percent of taxes collected if it is financed wholly by surcharges on the income tax (Baicker and Skinner 2011).

The implication is that there is a serious extra cost from expanding public financing; it is not a matter of neutrality whether the same benefits for the same people are financed publicly or privately. It is worse if you pay for health care through taxes than if you voluntarily withdraw the money from your wallet or purse. Logically this additional cost should imply a greater need to bring tax-financed spending growth to an end—which leads to the key conjecture that once this cost gets high enough, voter-taxpayers may choose to spend less in this form. While the theory about and the evidence for excess burden is strong, measurement of its magnitude is much more speculative. Moreover, evidence that its existence and size affect collective choices is also speculative. But it still seems worthwhile to spell out the concepts of what taxpayers ought to choose to do when faced with an ever-increasing inefficiency cost to ever-increasing public spending, and what they might be forced by reality to do.

The Impact of Excess Burden on Ideal Publicly Financed Medical Spending in the Federal Budget: Issues and Options

The argument thus far is that excess burden should constrain the extent to which tax-financed medical care grows over time, moving it to a lower level and different rate of growth than private spending. We usually assume that the federal tax base broadly defined grows at roughly the rate of growth of GDP. (The payroll tax base grows more slowly.) This means that a spending category that is growing faster will impose ever-increasing excess burden costs even if the rest of federal spending grows at the rate of GDP. A higher rate of growth for the remainder raises excess burden even more across the board.

Without any additional constraints, the conclusions are clear: not only should less be spent by government in any year than if financing were private, the amount should rise less rapidly with income than it would if it were privately financed. The simple manifestation of a policy that takes this concept into account is the voucher model, especially for Medicare. This idea has been around for a long time with several variants (Pauly 2008). The voucher may take the form of a uniform predetermined dollar amount, or the dollar amount may vary (usually inversely) with income or wealth. Sometimes the voucher-like arrangement takes the form of a matching subsidy (up to a limit). The definitions of qualified plans, how they will be priced and sold, whether there should be a publicly produced option, and a host of other details also need to be considered.

I want to emphasize two options and then examine their political desirability and feasibility. One option, probably the more common, imagines that the voucher is a predetermined amount that can be legally and easily supplemented by a client's private spending should the client choose to do so. The other option limits this supplementation to a greater or lesser extent: by forbidding "balance payment" entirely, capping the options for supplementation, making supplementation a regulated and constrained market. Neither option is nearly as attractive as today's Medicare, but today's Medicare is unsustainable.

Either way, there is one common characteristic: the dollar amount of public spending for vouchers or subsidies should grow no more rapidly than a limit that is politically chosen, even if this is a slower rate of growth than would otherwise have occurred for the nominal benefit package or packages available to recipients of subsidies, and a slower rate than in the private sector. For example, if private insurance premiums for the unsubsidized population (actually a tiny fraction of Americans, as we shall see) are the benchmark, the public subsidy would potentially grow at a slower rate than these private premiums.

Analysis and opinions of the two options are strongly affected by views on diversity in medical spending and insurance coverage, a bland term for "two-class medicine" (or "multiclass medicine"). Some think that even (and perhaps especially) in a society where both resources to pay for health care and preferences for what kind of health care to get with those resources vary substantially over the population, allowing some to get more than others by spending their own money is unacceptable. Others take the view that public concern should be limited primarily to setting a floor of access or health outcomes below which no one should fall, but not to setting a ceiling above which none can rise.

This preference is based on ethical, not economic, principles. Simple economics would have regarded allowing demand variations, whatever their cause, to be manifested in what people get as an efficient outcome, given the distribution of initial resources; the inequity of allowing the rich to get more medical spending would be traced to the income distribution policies that allow the rich to have more resources in the first place. There are economic approaches that allow citizens to have preferences over the consumption of their fellow citizens, but they are complex and speculative.

The Tax Exclusion and Private Spending

The fiscal consequences of growing medical spending discussed thus far relate to the government's role as a buyer of health care or health insurance for various client subpopulations. There is, however, another feature of public policy that affects both the budget and medical spending. A set of provisions in federal tax policy allows a person's tax liability to be affected by what he or she does with regard to private health insurance and health care. The largest component of this set is the tax exclusion for employment-based health insurance. This exclusion takes two forms. One is the exclusion from taxable income of the part of worker compensation used to pay the employer share of worker-only and family health insurance premiums. The other form is the exclusion from taxation of the worker's explicit premium for either kind of insurance if paid as part of a cafeteria plan that allows parts of wages to be set aside for payment for certain kinds of benefits. The total "tax cost" of these exclusions at all levels of government currently amounts to roughly $200 billion, which is about 25 percent of total premiums for employment-based health insurance. (These calculations are all based on the assumption that the total payment for insurance comes from what would have been worker wages; under this theory, the worker always pays 100 percent of the cost of insurance so there is no possibility, and no concern, about employers shifting the burden of paying for insurance to workers.) Some additional tax deductions and exclusions are allowed by law, although their revenue consequences are much smaller: the exclusion of up to $2,500 per year in a tax-shielded flexible spending account, the deduction from personal income tax of high levels of out-of-pocket medical spending, and some tax advantages for health savings accounts.

The potential impact of removing or capping these tax preferences on health insurance coverage is not negligible. Although estimates are far from certain, a reasonable estimate is that removal of the tax exclusion, by causing people to choose insurance plans with higher levels of cost sharing, might reduce spending covered by group insurance from 10 to 20 percent (Phelps 2003). This would translate into a reduction in overall spending of 6 to 12 percent. In addition, removal of the tax exclusion would raise substantial additional tax revenues in a way that does not generate excess burden, and it would do so whether workers cut back on their coverage, since more taxes would be collected on payments for insurance if they did not cut back or on higher taxable money income if they did.

What is both more hopeful but more challenging is whether these cuts in tax subsidies would slow the rate of growth in addition to cutting its level. In theory, higher cost sharing does not necessarily slow the rate of growth. There is some evidence that spending growth is inversely related to the level of out-of-pocket payment, but the results are not definitive. This point is also related to the policy sensitivity to two-class medicine, discussed earlier. The Rivlin-Domenici report holds out the hope that this step would lower private sector spending growth enough to keep it close to the necessary cuts in public sector spending growth, so that a gap between the two sectors would not emerge. Anything is possible, but there is no definitive evidence that changing the tax treatment will lower private spending growth over the long term to anything near the rates that would match the needed cuts in public spending growth.

Policy Options for Containing Government Spending Growth

I have already commented on the primary decision regarding public spending: either limit it and permit supplementation, or limit and cap overall spending by not permitting (or discouraging) supplementation. It is this latter (spending cap) model that leads to questions of how Medicaid and the public Medicare option might change how it reimburses providers and charges premiums and out-of-pocket payments to those who are insured. Assume that there is to be only one plan that recipients of subsidized coverage can choose. It has to limit spending growth to a predetermined level. How might it best do so?

The most obvious point is that it should use a mix of strategies since moving on many margins is likely to do less harm than focusing all the changes on any one item. On the provider side, the most important thing to know is the answer to the provider problem posed earlier: When providers are told that they will only get a given (lower-than-otherwise) amount and they are to do the best they can, what will they do? We need to know provider supply behavior. If Medicare, Medicaid, and the subsidized plans in exchanges got together and proposed to pay doctors and hospitals less, would providers avoid these patients (we already know that happens with Medicaid), and to what extent? There will only be a shrunken private sector left, so not all physicians can shift to concierge medicine. And as we saw, private insurers with no tax subsidy may choose to copy these cuts.

In theory, the answer depends on both the level of payment and the form it takes. Begin with the simplest case: accountable care organizations (fostered by the ACA), which have swept the field, signed up everyone and taken responsibility for their care, and are receiving de facto risk-adjusted capitation payments. Compared to what otherwise would have happened, what would they cut? The simplest story is that they should cut whatever is the least cost effective. They might be assisted in doing so or in defending what they are doing by comparative effectiveness research evidence provided by the government's new program if there had previously been uncertainty or controversy about effectiveness. However, the relevant changes would not be movement to more effective but less costly alternatives (which provides the policy case for this information) but rather movement toward slightly less effective but much less costly alternatives. They might also be assisted by the IPAB if it ordered, sanctioned, or justified the lower-quality care—for example, by stipulating that using lower-cost but better-outcome hospitals at considerable distance represented higher-quality care, even if the travel and inconvenience cost was greater than the value of improved health outcomes.

Things might predictably be different if the payment system is different—even if the final bill for the government remained the same. For example, suppose Medicare (and Medicaid) continued to pay hospitals per diagnosis-related group (DRG) and doctors per designated service, but limited the annual update enough to achieve lower spending growth (offsetting any target income behavior by physicians by reducing fees still further). Doctors might just take fewer Medicare patients, increasing delays, travel time, and the like. Hospitals presumably would not decline patients but would reduce some dimensions of the quality of care that they render per discharge. But the outcome would not necessarily be worse than under capitation, since the low prices cap the alleged fee-for-service incentive to do more.

On the demand side, there are two broad strategies. The simpler, already discussed in the context of rising spending, is for the government simply to make less available as the implicit voucher for public coverage, so beneficiaries must either themselves pay for more coverage and more use or go without. The second is a more paternalistic and more targeted approach to "patient engagement," where things are designed not just to save money but channel, nudge, or require consumers/patients to do what policymakers think is best for them. (The political divide between these two approaches is obvious.) The choice between the two cannot be settled by appeal to "market failure" under the voucher strategy, challenging though it may be to consumers and insurance markets, without also providing evidence of how well government can make rationing choices under the government control strategy.

Means-Testing Government Health Insurance

A frequently discussed method of shifting both costs and the power to choose to consumers is to contemplate means testing of both premiums and benefits in public programs. Lower-income people are usually left out, because it is assumed that they cannot afford to pay on their own (even though there is no definition and no test for "affordability"). What these lower-income people get for free could be what is available in the market, or the government could directly control the services to this population—or some combination of control and market supply. When there are potentially strict limits on what the "non-means-tested" population gets, means testing is then not necessarily a totally bad thing for those who must pay. They do have to hand over their own money, but in return they get greater freedom to choose what they want.

There is a simple and compelling logic that says that tax-financed funding should not be used to subsidize health insurance or care for people with income or wealth high enough to pay entirely on their own. By extension, people who can pay some of the cost because their income is moderately high should do so. This "means testing" or "income conditioning" of subsidies obviously characterizes Medicaid: a person is eligible only when poor. It also characterizes the planned insurance programs for individuals and small businesses offered through exchanges, where subsidies are on a sliding scale—but are available up to 400 percent of the poverty line. In the exchanges, only poor people get very generous coverage at no cost, while those partially subsidized would have to pay extra for such coverage.

Means testing does not now generally characterize Medicare: a low-income senior can get subsidized coverage, but so can a billionaire. There are some modest adjustments for very high-income people in terms of higher Part B premiums and for very low-income people in terms of more generous Part D benefits—and the poorest seniors are also eligible for Medicaid. which picks up much of what Medicare does not cover. But generally Medicare's subsidies flow to people because they are elderly, are disabled, or have failed kidneys, not because they are poor.

This characteristic has made many policymakers, including President Obama, discuss the possibility of greater means testing in Medicare. Whether presented by Republican or Democrat, this change is suggested regretfully. If we could continue with today's Medicare "as we know it," we would, and few argue that means testing in itself is a good thing. Rather, it is viewed as a way of preserving much of Medicare, otherwise at serious risk, that is superior to other alternatives.

There are some soft and unresolved policy issues here. For one thing, although everyone talks about "affordability," no one knows what it means or exactly how much someone at some income level can "afford." Ultimately affordability is a subjective (and therefore inevitably controversial) political judgment (Bundorf and Pauly 2006). More seriously, when subsidies in a program fall as income rises, that constitutes an effective tax on income, which can generate excess burden. So although the purpose of means testing is to reduce public spending and thus reduce the excess burden of taxation, an offsetting excess burden is created elsewhere in the income distribution. The "net" tax on income (as income rises taxes go up and subsidies go down) is what matters.

We can say something about extremes: a small program that cuts spending by subsidizing only the very poor and then steeply phases out probably has low net excess burden since it distorts incentives (even though strongly) for only a small part of the population. And higher taxes paid out of current income arguably distort work effort decisions more than the prospect of lower Medicare benefits if the higher current income means higher pensions after retirement. Finally, the strongest argument against means testing for Medicare (or Social Security) is that it would weaken middle-class support for such programs if they are less beneficial to the middle class; if one takes as given that the program is a good thing, this is bad political economy. A less biased view of democracy would imagine that the middle class should not be manipulated into supporting social insurance but should be permitted to choose it—and the net lifetime subsidy it appears to transfer to lower-income people—in a transparent way. Moreover, if Medicare will have to make cuts in program quality across the board without means testing—if it will come to look more like Medicaid as a payer—those cuts may well erode middle-class support much more effectively than under income conditioning. which preserves a substantial core level of tax-financed support for insurance for seniors.

But the real question about means testing Medicare is whether it would be worth the political trouble—whether it is a way to seriously lower the level or the growth rate of government spending on the program. The prospect of having seniors pay more for Medicare is a complicated question—first because of conflicting data, but fundamentally because it raises deep issues about consumer behavior and social values.

The more seniors there are who can "afford" to pay additionally for Medicare, the better. We do not know where the boundaries are on affordability, but we are pretty sure it is higher the higher one's income, other things equal. Here we get mixed results. The fraction of seniors in households with incomes below the poverty line is smaller than for the rest of the population in the United States. But so is the fraction of people with incomes above 400 percent of the poverty line. Many elderly households make it into the lower middle class because Social Security benefits are enough to put them there—but they have little room to spare.

One of the "other things" that affect affordability is wealth. Here again we get conflicting evidence. Seniors at any income level have more wealth than other Americans. In part that is housing wealth; they have a fully paid-up mortgage on their house. In part the wealth is their retirement fund that (especially at today's low interest rates) generates the moderate incomes they report. The conflict arises because neither of these items represents idle wealth—seniors want to live in their homes, and they want to live on their retirement funds. Of course, the presence of these two sources of wealth also means they are better off and can enjoy higher consumption than younger people with the same income: with no mortgage to pay and the ability to draw on my retirement fund, I can consume considerably more than the income I report to the IRS, or at least a much larger fraction compared to when I was young.

Table 2.1
Alternative Medicare Tax Rate Scenarios

Percent of Population Means-Tested as "Non-Low-Income"	Real Growth in Medicare Spending per Non-Means-Tested Beneficiary	2035 Tax Rate as Percent of GDP
0	GDP + 1 percent (approx. 2.8 percent)	6.0[a]
40	GDP + 1 percent	4.6
60	GDP + 1 percent	3.9

Source: Pauly (2004).
a. This figure assumes that the GDP growth rate equals the "excess" Medicare population growth rate.

So what might be possible? The calculations in table 2.1 provide a rough idea. The first line shows that with no means testing and spending growth limits, the Medicare spending burden will be about 6 percent of GDP. (Without growth limits, it would be 10 percent.) Taking that as a benchmark, the next two lines show the effect of limiting real spending growth by means-testing higher-income elderly populations. As can be seen, these steps reduce the spending burden relative to GDP to a range of roughly 4 to 5 percent. The last line shows the effect of very aggressive means testing, boosting the proportion of the population subject to means testing to 60 percent of all seniors, actually provides little incremental benefit.

These illustrative calculations show that means testing will help, but for it to make a serious dent in spending growth it will have to be dramatic and it will have to be associated with something to slow the growth in spending. I discuss a way to do this below.

Means Testing, Public Spending Growth, and the Transition from Work to Retirement

The implication of the previous discussion is that there is serious potential in means testing for Medicare, but it will be difficult to implement. One reason is the same point discussed earlier: the real problem with Medicare is not the level of public funding but its rate of growth. Tapping wealthier seniors will help with the level, but not obviously with the rate of growth. However, I dealt with this problem in my earlier work by suggesting, in effect, that means testing be limited to payment for growth in excess of some baseline rate the public sector can afford. That would, by definition, have an impact on the long-run rate of growth in public spending. If the growth in wealthy seniors paralleled the growth in GDP overall, that would be a positive (and offsetting) factor.

There is a deeper problem. For reasons we do not well understand, household consumption levels tend to drop dramatically when people retire—even though economic models say that people should save, buy annuities, and establish pensions so that they can keep up their consumption after retirement. Basically a very large chunk of the upper middle class seems to disappear after retirement. Less precisely measured but probably true is that the rate of growth of income (broadly defined to include growth in the value of wealth like unrealized capital gains) also seems to slow dramatically after retirement. The original premise was that desired growth in medical spending is driven by or facilitated by growth in income. But if seniors' incomes do not grow much, maybe they would not be willing to pay much more for new technology. Medicare's financing means that we do not now ask them to pay, but one might use what they would have valued as a benchmark for what society should buy—and what they value may be relatively modest growth.

This may be good logical news, because it means that slower growth even in total spending for seniors—the kind of pattern that raises the specter of two-class medicine—may actually be efficient even without considering the excess burden of tax finance.

Some Odds and Ends: Other Solutions to the Fiscal Problem

Here I briefly comment on two other smaller policy changes intended to help Medicare's fiscal future: raising the age of eligibility and doing something about the cost-increasing effects of voluntary Medigap insurance.

The arguments for raising the age of Medicare eligibility for seniors are similar to those already made (and implemented into law) for Social Security: people are living much longer than when these programs were passed, so the promise (if there was one) to help people as they get older should be adjusted to reflect a commitment for a given number of expected years at the end of life, not a commitment at a given fixed age.

Raising the age of eligibility does help with Social Security, because benefit payments (given the age at which the person retires) are fixed.

If I am going to get $2,000 per month from Social Security when I retire, postponing the age at which I can collect that amount by two years saves the taxpayers $48,000 plus interest. Medicare is a little different. Average medical benefit costs are on the order of $10,000 per Medicare beneficiary, but they start out lower at age sixty-five, rise until the person is in his or her mid-eighties, and then decline as people eschew heroic measures as the probability of death rises. This means that raising the age of eligibility will save something, but not as much (as a proportion of total costs) as a similar step in Social Security. The other difference is that the need to pay for medical spending does not go away even if Medicare does; the alternative to insurance coverage is not zero spending. If people have to arrange insurance in other ways, they will find it to be expensive. And if their incomes are low to moderate and they are no longer working for a firm that offers benefits, they will qualify for subsidies under the exchanges in the ACA. For both of these reasons, the fiscal benefits from raising the age of eligibility, while still positive, are not as large as they might seem.

The other change—for which there is a stronger argument in theory—has to do with Medigap. The government-run Medicare program has some fairly serious cost-sharing provisions intended to constrain use and spending: a hefty deductible for inpatient care and 20 percent coinsurance without limit for Part B (physician) services, cost sharing for prescription drugs, coupled with declining coverage for long hospital stays. Most seniors have reacted to these gaps in coverage by voluntarily purchasing private but federally regulated Medigap insurance. They pay the full cost of the premium that covers what the Medigap plans pay out (and fairly substantial administrative costs and profits too), but they get financial protection. The problem is that they also get a mitigation of the cost-sharing incentives to be frugal in the use of care paid for by the government plan. The evidence is strong (though not definitive) that people with Medigap impose higher costs on the government plans than those without. Proposed solutions involve banning Medigap coverage of some of the cost sharing, or the better idea of taxing Medigap to collect the costs it imposes on Medicare. President Obama has recently proposed the latter.

Both of these steps might help constrain the costs of Medicare, but their contribution is likely to be modest. The stronger argument for them is that they improve the design of the current system, targeting help better and reducing inefficiency. This may help permit some parts of the current system to better play a role in a reformed arrangement.

Putting the Pieces Together

What does this discussion imply for how we will or how we should deal with the serious effect of medical spending growth on the federal budget? We begin by noting that this is not a false alarm. Still, it is not as if the sky will fall tomorrow, and the political problem is that it is always easier to postpone dealing with a falling sky until it starts to happen—but then it is probably too late to deal with it sensibly, if at all. Economics, even political economy, has little to add to the oft-told tale of defective telescopic faculties in politics; it only tells us that we need Cassandras to keep making the point that something has to be done, and better sooner than later.

My ideal solution to the problem of rising health care spending would be one that focused on the problem of rising health care spending. Specifically, there would be two politically chosen levels of spending growth. One would represent the taxpayers' choice about the benchmark rate of spending growth (and therefore the rate of addition of beneficial but costly new technology) that would be made available to the poor and near poor, who receive 100 percent subsidized insurance. For the rest of the population, current real levels of public spending per beneficiary would be sustained, but support for growth would be means-tested. For the well-off, the only existing publicly funded program is Medicare, so they would be promised continuing support for Medicare with a voucher that is constant in real dollar terms. However, people at this income level would be required to pay in full for any growth in spending. They could either supplement the voucher or choose to use it for a plan whose cost is constrained to be equal to the voucher amount. For Medicare and subsidized plans in the exchanges, the rate of growth in the value of the voucher or subsidy amount would be means-tested. Probably the maximum addition would be enough to cover the increase in spending growth in the low-income benchmark plan, although there might be some reason to match private spending for especially desirable new technologies.

In all cases, people could use their voucher for either a private plan or a public plan if one exists that meets the criteria—but public plans would then have to make management decisions about how much and what kind of new technology to add. While the choice of plan is bound to be complex, I think it could be simplified if different plans adopted and specified the cost-effectiveness rule they would be using to cover new technology.

How would this work? Current views are that the social value of an additional year of high-quality health is about $50,000. Suppose that rule was chosen by the benchmark plan for the poor and those with low income; it would pay for new technologies that added "quality-adjusted" life-years for this cost or less, but it would not pay more than $50,000 per quality-adjusted life-year for other programs. (I hasten to add that I am using a $50,000 threshold here only as an example; if taxpayers were willing to pay more, they could increase the value.) Other plans, available to the nonpoor with additional private payment, could set different cost-effectiveness criteria—$100,000, $200,000, and so forth. Of course, the plans willing to pay for more costly technology that adds to health would have premiums that beneficiaries would have to pay that would be rising more rapidly than plans that chose a lower cutoff.

Of course, right now neither political discourse nor cost-effectiveness methodology is sufficient to allow this kind of differentiated and free market in medical care spending growth, and nothing will ever be perfect. But I believe that it would be possible to work toward this kind of system, especially in Medicare. I do not look forward to the need to implement this kind of system; I wish our national income growth could somehow be high enough to permit Medicare as we know it to be sustained, but that seems unlikely based on both the history of income growth and the logic that requires ever higher income growth or ever higher marginal tax rates to keep up with ever higher health spending growth.

Income Growth and the ACA Exchanges

The ACA sets up subsidies for health insurance for lower- and middle-income people, to be claimed for insurance arranged through state or federal health insurance exchanges. The annual price tag for these subsidies will be fairly high once the insurance is marketed (about $167 billion per year in 2020). Most of those costs are to be offset by cuts in Medicare (which may or may not be effective) and other taxes. The key issue, however, is the growth of this subsidy.

It would seem that subsidies would grow fairly rapidly, since the subsidy a household gets depends on the ratio of the premium for the second cheapest "silver" plan to its income. That means that subsidies would grow if premium growth outpaces income growth, as it usually has. However, the law contains an indexing provision that provides that after 2018, aggregate subsidies cannot exceed 0.5 percent of GDP, thus capping their GDP share at that level and henceforth limiting their growth to the growth rate of GDP. This will mean either that the burden on families will rise faster than their incomes or that the exchanges will have to find plans with premiums increasing more slowly than others in the private sector (employment-based group insurance). If the provision is enforced, the ACA subsidies do not help the government's fiscal problem, but except for the one-time hit as people move into exchanges, it will not add to the long-term trend. But if it proves politically difficult to have a government plan with increasing unsubsidized premiums or worsening coverage, the problem of medical spending growth will become worse.

Conclusion

Federally funded medical insurance programs cannot continue at current rates of funding and spending growth. Neither Medicare nor Medicaid as we currently know them can feasibly be retained in their current forms. Necessary reforms in grim circumstances will always look inferior to current practice, but current practice cannot persist; the policy question is how to return to sustainable financing while doing as little harm as possible. Some cuts are inevitable in the future, but they need to be rational and graceful.

Rising medical care spending is not the work of an enemy, the consequence of sloth and inattention, or even fundamentally due to distorted incentives (though there are some distortions). It arises because we seek and have the means to improve the quantity and quality of our years of life. But the public sector has special problems in keeping up with this desire, and those problems inevitably mean it will have to rein in spending sooner and with more force than in the voluntary private sector.

There are some modest steps that we know can produce modest temporary improvements across the board, and there are some promising, if unproven and unprecedented, ideas worth trying. My own preference is to increase the options for citizens to use voluntary private spending to cushion (and rationalize) the inevitable limiting of public financing, with larger transfers to bring about some fairness in the process. We do need to face and discuss the structure of systems that will allow some to get more than others in the future, but with a decent, reasonable, and sustainable foundation for all.

References

Anderson, Gerard F., Bianca K. Frogner, and Uwe E. Reinhardt. 2007. Health Spending in OECD Countries in 2004: An Update. *Health Affairs* 26 (5): 1481–89.

Anderson, Gerard F., Uwe E. Reinhardt, Peter S. Hussey, and Varduhi Petrosyan. 2003. It's the Prices, Stupid: Why the United States Is So Different from Other Countries. *Health Affairs* 22 (3): 89–105.

Baicker, Katherine, and Jonathan S. Skinner. 2011. Health Care Spending Growth and the Future of U.S. Tax Rates. *Tax Policy and the Economy* 25(1): 39–67.

Boards of Trustees, Federal Hospital Insurance and Federal Supplementary Medical Insurance Trust Funds. 2011. *The 2011 Annual Report of the Boards of Trustees of the Federal Hospital Insurance and Federal Supplementary Medical Insurance Trust Funds.* Washington, DC: Federal Hospital Insurance and Federal Supplemental Medical Insurance Trust Funds.

Boards of Trustees, Federal Hospital Insurance and Federal Supplemental Medical Insurance Trust Funds. 2013. *The 2013 Annual Report of the Board of Trustees of the Federal Hospital Insurance and Federal Supplementary Medical Insurance Trust Funds.* Washington, DC: Federal Hospital Insurance and Federal Supplemental Medical Insurance Trust Funds.

Boccuti, Cristina, and Marilyn Moon. 2003. Comparing Medicare and Private Insurance Growth Rates in Spending across Three Decades. *Health Affairs* 22 (2): 230–37.

Bundorf, M. Kate, and Mark V. Pauly. 2006. Is Health Insurance Affordable for the Uninsured? *Journal of Health Economics* 25 (4): 650–73.

Conover, Christopher J. 2011. Health Is the Health of the State. *American*, July 19. http://www.american.com/archive/2011/july/health-is-the-health-of-the-state.

Cutler, David M. 2004. *Your Money or Your Life: Strong Medicine for America's Health Care System.* New York: Oxford University Press.

Debt Reduction Task Force of the Bipartisan Policy Center. 2010. *Restoring America's Future: Reviving the Economy, Cutting Spending and Debt, and Creating a Simple, Pro-Growth Tax System.* Washington, DC: Bipartisan Policy Center.

Emanuel, Ezekiel, Neera Tanden, Stuart Altman, Scott Armstrong, Donald Berwick, François de Brantes, Maura Calsyn, et al. 2012. A Systemic Approach to Containing Health Care Spending. *New England Journal of Medicine* 367 (10): 949–54.

Finkelstein, Amy. 2003. Health Policy and Technological Change: Evidence from the Vaccine Industry. NBER Working Paper 9460, National Bureau of Economic Research, Cambridge, MA.

Fuchs, Victor R. 2011. *Who Shall Live? Health, Economics, and Social Choice.* Hackensack, NJ: World Scientific.

Gawande, Atul, Donald Berwick, Elliott Fisher, and Mark B. McClellan. 2009. Ten Steps to Better Health Care. *New York Times*, August 13, http://www.nytimes.com/2009/08/13/opinion/13gawande.html.

Grannemann, Thomas W., and Mark V. Pauly. 2010. *Medicaid Everyone Can Count On: Public Choices for Equity and Efficiency.* Washington, DC: AEI Press.

Krugman, Paul. 2011. The Conscience of a Liberal: Health Care Zombies. *New York Times*, June 5. http://krugman.blogs.nytimes.com/2011/06/05/health-care-zombies.

Laugesen, Miriam J., and Sherry A. Glied. 2011. Higher Fees Paid to U.S. Physicians Drive Higher Spending for Physician Services Compared to Other Countries. *Health Affairs* 30 (9): 1647–56.

Naylor, Mary D., Dorothy Brooten, Roberta Campbell, Barbara S. Jacobsen, Matty D. Mezey, Mark V. Pauly, and J. Sandford Schwartz. 1999. Comprehensive Discharge Planning and Home Follow-Up of Hospitalized Elders. *Journal of the American Medical Association* 218 (7): 613–20.

Pauly, Mark V. 1993. U.S. Health Care Costs: The Untold True Story. *Health Affairs* 12 (3): 152–59.

Pauly, Mark V. 2003. Should We Be Worried about High Real Medical Spending Growth in the United States? *Health Affairs* 8 (January): W3-15–27. http://content.healthaffairs.org/content/early/2003/01/08/hlthaff.w3.15.

Pauly, Mark V. 2004. Means-testing in Medicare. *Health Affairs* 8 (December): W4-546–557. http://content.healthaffairs.org/cgi/reprint/hlthaff.w4.546.

Pauly, Mark V. 2008. *Markets without Magic: How Competition Might Save Medicare*. Washington, DC: AEI Press.

Pauly, Mark V. 2011. The Trade-off between Quality, Quantity, and Cost: How to Make It —If We Must. *Health Affairs* 30 (4): 574–80.

Phelps, Charles E. 2003. *Health Economics*. Boston: Addison-Wesley.

Skinner, Jonathan S. 2011. Causes and Consequences of Regional Variations in Health Care. In *Handbook of Health Economics*, edited by Mark V. Pauly, Thomas G. Mcguire, and Pedro P. Barros, 2:45–93. Amsterdam: Elsevier.

Discussion

Vivian Ho

As Mark Pauly notes, the rising share of government spending as a percent of U.S. gross domestic product since the 1960s is almost completely accounted for by increases in federal health care spending. Medicare, Medicaid, and CHIP expenditures made up 21 percent of the FY 2010 federal budget. The federal government's spending on health care is projected to rise even further. Medicare spending will grow as more baby boomers retire and qualify for federal coverage. The Affordable Care Act (ACA) of 2010 will also expand the federal government's spending on health care. Expanded Medicaid coverage through the ACA and premium and cost-sharing subsidies for exchange plans are projected to increase the federal share of health spending from 27 percent in 2009 to 31 percent by 2010 (Keehan et al 2011).

Pauly identifies the two major underlying causes for health care spending growth as technological change (both new products and increased use of existing products) and rising prices, primarily through wage growth for physicians and other health care workers in a relatively labor-intensive industry. The significant role that technological change has played in increasing health care costs was first identified by Joseph Newhouse (1992). More recent research clarifies the role of technological change in explaining rising U.S. health care costs. Costs have risen in the United States because a set of costly treatments and procedures whose benefits are substantial for at least some patients is applied to a much larger patient population, for whom the marginal benefit of treatment converges to zero (Chandra and Skinner 2011). In addition, the United States is devoting substantial resources toward treatments for which randomized trials indicate no benefit, as well as costly procedures whose effectiveness has not been evaluated (e.g., intensity-modulated radiation therapy for prostate cancer).

Pauly notes that wage growth in the health services sector has outpaced wage and price growth in the rest of the economy. This fact has received less attention in public policy arenas and the press, even though the disparity between physicians' salaries in the United States and other member countries of the Organization for Economic Cooperation and Development (OECD) is dramatic (Berenson 2007). A recent study determined that primary care physicians in the United States had the highest earnings net of taxes among six OECD countries in 2008 ($186,582), and doctors in Australia had the lowest ($92,844). Earnings net of expenses for orthopedic surgeons were $442,450 in the U.S. and $154,380 in France (Laugesen and Glied 2011).

Yet Pauly correctly observes that medical spending data alone provide a poor indicator of the efficiency of resource use in the health care sector. Rather, one must compare real resource use relative to real benefit to determine what is best for the economy. Economists Kevin Murphy and Robert Topel (2006) have constructed a lifetime utility maximization model calibrated with empirical data from multiple U.S. sources to compare the value of health improvements that have occurred over the past decades relative to increases in medical expenditures. Their study concludes that increased longevity after 1970 yielded a "gross" social value of $95 trillion and the capitalized value of medical expenditures grew by $34 trillion, for a net gain of $61 trillion. Thus, the rising portion of the economy devoted to health care spending is in some sense worthwhile.

Yet Pauly also correctly notes that public financing of health insurance is inherently inefficient compared to private financing due to the distortionary effects of taxation on economic behavior. To support this argument, Pauly cites a recent study by Katherine Baicker and Jonathan Skinner (2011) predicting that if the increased subsidies for health insurance included in the ACA are financed wholly by increases in the income tax, the excess burden of taxation will reach more than 200 percent of taxes collected by 2060.

Medicare and Medicaid were established not on efficiency grounds but due to a collective desire to provide adequate access to health care services to the elderly and low-income persons. Yet the policymakers who founded Medicare and Medicaid in the 1960s could not have foreseen how rapidly the field of medicine would advance in future decades or predicted how expensive the resulting medical technologies would be. Even if improved medical technologies provide value to patients, the government's share of health spending is most likely politically unsustainable. If federal spending on health care continues to rise at its current rate, at some point the majority of American voters will oppose the higher taxes required to finance this spending.

In fact, evidence from other countries suggests that exceedingly higher tax rates may serve as a brake on health care spending growth. In their study, Baicker and Skinner (2011) find that OECD countries with a higher tax-to-GDP ratio in 1979 experienced significantly slower growth in health care spending between 1980 and 2008. The question still remains as to what strategy the United States will choose to restrict growth in Medicare spending.

Pauly points first to the strategy supported by all health economists I have met, which is removal of the tax exclusion for employer-provided health insurance. Current law exempts the value of employer-paid health insurance from income, Social Security, and Medicare payroll taxes. This exemption causes workers to choose greater compensation in the form of health insurance rather than wages, which increases demand for relatively generous plans. Subjecting employer-provided insurance policies to taxation would encourage employees to be price conscious when purchasing plans. Insurers would then have greater incentive to offer less generous, and less expensive, policies that could ultimately lower spending in the long run.

The ACA introduces a tax on employer-provided health insurance, but only for "Cadillac" health insurance plans: plans with premiums that will exceed $10,200 for individual coverage or $27,500 for family coverage beginning in 2018. The average annual premiums for employer-sponsored health insurance in 2011 were $5,429 for single coverage and $15,073 for family coverage (Kaiser Family Foundation 2011). Although premium costs will continue to rise prior to 2018, the majority of employer-sponsored health insurance plans are unlikely to be subject to this Cadillac tax. Pauly suggests that removing the tax exclusion for employer-provided health insurance for all plans could lower overall health spending between 6 and 12 percent. However, he cautions that this reduction may be a one-time saving, and may not control the growth rate of health spending in the long run.

So how might Medicare be redesigned if the public and the federal government choose to restrict growth in the program's expenditures? Pauly offers a solution in which taxpayers would choose a benchmark rate of spending growth that would be made available to the poor and near poor, who receive 100 percent subsidized insurance. This benchmark rate would implicitly limit these recipients' access to beneficial but costly new technology. All seniors would be issued a voucher that they may use to purchase Medicare coverage. The voucher would equal the benchmark rate of spending. Seniors could then be offered vouchers with even higher dollar amounts, but these supplements would be means-tested. This approach would allow the federal government to directly control the aggregate growth rate in expenditures for the Medicare program. Consumers would have the ability to choose between less and more generous health insurance plans, and one would rely on market competition between health insurers to deliver health care efficiently in terms of both costs and quality.

Pauly's suggestion to set aggregate spending limits for Medicare that are then used to determine the value of vouchers to purchase health insurance premiums may be preferable to Medicare's current strategy for cost control, which relies primarily on setting fixed reimbursement rates for services. While the Medicare program can attempt to restrain cost growth by restricting increases in reimbursement rates to health care providers over time, policymakers have little control over the quantity of services that providers choose to deliver. For any services for which the fixed prices exceed marginal costs, providers have an incentive to offer additional care in order to earn greater profits.

Under Pauly's model, the task of ensuring that hospitals and physicians deliver efficient care would be transferred to private insurers. Private insurers may be no better than the public sector in controlling waste in the health care system. For example, previous research concludes that a move from government-administered fee-for-service reimbursement to contracting with private health maintenance organizations for Medicaid enrollees led to higher costs and no improvement in infant mortality (Duggan 2004). However, a more recent study finds less regional variation in health care spending per capita among privately insured patients than in the Medicare population. The authors speculate that the "culture of money" among entrepreneurial physicians may be constrained by private insurance plans with their more stringent reviews of the use of medical services (Franzini et al. 2010).

An important concern regarding a voucher system for Medicare is the ability to achieve a competitive market among health insurers. One study concludes that a combination of switching costs for employers and bargaining power of insurers yields uncompetitive outcomes for consumers in an increasing number of local markets (Dafny 2010). Another study suggests that consolidation among insurers during the period 1998 to 2006 led to a 2 percentage point increase in health insurance premiums (Dafny 2012). One must achieve competitive markets for health insurance for Medicare beneficiaries if a voucher system is introduced. Otherwise federal subsidies will contribute to higher insurers' profits rather than the delivery of health care for consumers.

While a voucher system may be a good start at limiting government's spending on health care, I do not believe it is sufficient for controlling cost growth. Vouchers influence spending on health insurance. The financial incentives that health care providers face under the Medicare system must also be reformed. Medicare's current fixed-price reimbursement system rewards providers for delivering higher-quantity, as opposed to higher-quality, services. Medicare adopted the DRG payment system in the 1980s, with the hope that prespecifying fixed payments for particular admission types (e.g., acute myocardial infarction, concussion) would encourage hospitals to deliver cost-effective care. If hospitals knew that payments would remain fixed regardless of the amount of services delivered, there would be no incentive to overuse costly resources. But more than a decade ago, it was reported that over 40 percent of hospital DRGs are not related to diagnoses but to specific intensive procedures (e.g., open heart surgery or cholecystectomy) (McClellan 1997). Medicare also reimburses physicians fixed payments determined by the number and specific types of services performed. This piece-rate reward system likely explains a large portion of the higher salaries observed for U.S. physicians relative to physicians in other OECD countries.

Medicare's quantity-based reimbursement leads to waste in the health care system that has been documented in several clinical studies. A study of back pain patients determined that the real costs of treating patients with spine problems rose from $4,695 in 1997 to $6,096 in 2005. Simultaneously, self-reported mental health, physical functioning, work or school limitations, and social limitations were all worse in 2005 compared to 1997. Despite the substantial increase in health care spending, there were no documented improvements in patient well-being identified over the course of the study period (Martin et al. 2008).

Another example of waste involves patients with heart disease. Thousands of patients each year develop stable coronary artery disease. They occasionally experience ischemia, a cramping of the heart muscle due to narrowing of the coronary arteries, which can be relieved in less than ten minutes with rest or medications. One potential therapy for these patients is angioplasty, in which a thin tube is threaded into a blocked artery and a balloon on the tube's tip is inflated to restore blood flow. The American College of Cardiology and the American Heart Association recommend that all patients undergo a cardiac stress test prior to angioplasty in order to confirm sufficient ischemia, such that the procedure would be beneficial to the patient. However, a comprehensive examination of billing data indicates that only 44.5 percent of Medicare patients underwent a cardiac stress test within ninety days prior to receiving an angioplasty (Lin et al. 2008). Medicare reimburses providers for more than 800,000 angioplasty procedures per year, at a rate of $10,000 to $15,000 each. Substantial taxpayer dollars may be going toward aggressive treatment of heart disease patients for whom there is no demonstrable benefit and an increased likelihood of postintervention complications.

There are many more documented examples of waste in the health care system. I have commented on the increased use of computerized tomography scans, magnetic resonance imaging, and positron emission tomography scans for advanced diagnostic imaging (Ho 2008). The increase can be traced to generous financial incentives for physicians to self-refer patients for these tests rather than any clinical evidence of improved treatment effectiveness associated with use of these costly diagnostic techniques. The *Wall Street Journal* (Carreyrou and Tamman 2010) has described the unjustified growth in use of intensity-modulated radiation therapy for prostate cancer patients.

Pauly claims that fee-for-service payment cannot explain increased growth in Medicare spending: "If the payment rate for tests is set too high, there will be incentives to more of them, but once the volume is boosted, there is no reason that fee-for-service payment means that it should continue to increase as time goes on." However, inefficiencies from quantity-based reimbursement can grow proportionately as the number of complex technologies increases. Increasingly complex medical technologies lead to more asymmetric information between the patient/insurer and the provider regarding the marginal benefit of treatment. Higher reimbursements associated with these technologies can lead to an even greater incentive to overuse. These higher reimbursements can result from a tendency to set reimbursements based on the cost of technologies and procedures when they are relatively new. The unit costs of applying these advanced techniques may decline as they disseminate throughout the medical community and benefit from learning by doing. But it is often expensive to track the costs of these technologies regularly, so that reimbursement rates may not be adjusted downward appropriately in later years.

Medicare spending growth can be slowed by realigning health care provider incentives away from quantity-based rewards and toward remuneration based on high-quality care. Multiple strategies to reward high-quality, lower-cost health care are included in the 2010 Affordable Care Act. One strategy is pay for performance. Section 3007 of the ACA creates a new value-based payment modifier that, starting in 2015, will be used to provide differential payments to physicians based on quality and cost of care. The payment adjustments are to be budget neutral, so that some physicians would receive bonuses and others penalties under this provision (Berenson 2010). Beginning in 2012, the ACA enables Medicare to lower payments to acute care hospitals that experience higher-than-average readmission rates for certain applicable conditions. The program will begin with three applicable conditions—acute myocardial infarction, heart failure, and pneumonia—and the number of conditions will expand in 2015. Readmissions are both costly and are often a sign of poor-quality care during the initial admission. This measure thus provides an example of payment penalties for underperformance.

The ACA also introduces new initiatives in bundled payments to replace fee-for-service reimbursement. The Centers for Medicare and Medicaid Services (CMS) will bundle care for a package of services patients receive to treat a specific medical condition (e.g., heart bypass surgery or hip replacement) during a single hospital stay and/or recovery from that stay—that is known as an episode of care. By bundling payment across providers for multiple services, providers will have a greater incentive to coordinate and ensure continuity of care across settings, resulting in better care for patients. Better coordinated care can reduce unnecessary duplication of services, reduce preventable medical errors, help patients heal without harm, and lower costs.

The ACA also seeks to realign provider incentives by encouraging health care providers to organize as accountable care organizations (ACOs), groups of doctors, hospitals, and other health care providers who come together and declare themselves to Medicare as an organization that will deliver coordinated high-quality care to the Medicare patients they serve. When an ACO succeeds in both delivering high-quality care and spending health care dollars more wisely, it will share in the savings it achieves for the Medicare program.

Operationally Medicare will continue to pay individual health care providers and suppliers for specific items and services as it currently does under the existing Medicare program. CMS will also develop a benchmark for each ACO against which its performance in terms of patient care is measured. If the ACO is able to limit expenditure growth below that which is occurring in Medicare's overall fee-for-service population, and it is able to meet the quality benchmarks specified by Medicare, then it will share in the savings they achieved by providing lower-cost, higher-quality health care.[2]

The various measures in the ACA that are aimed at controlling cost growth by realigning provider incentives are ambitious, and it will take years to refine these programs before we are likely to see significant cost savings. Most health care providers have fee-for-service medicine so ingrained in their operations that it will be difficult to shift toward systems with more global payments and greater scrutiny of quality of care. Hospitals, physician clinics, and ancillary providers will also require time to develop coordinated care plans. In addition, the government is likely to take missteps in setting the initial regulations and reimbursement methods required to implement these new payment systems.

As Mark McClellan (2011, 87), a health economist and former administrator of CMS, states in an article on payment reform in health care:

> Stronger incentives for consumers to choose less-costly insurance plans, coupled with reliable evidence on their quality and cost, may lead to greater uptake of benefit designs that … provide much larger financial rewards to consumers who choose more efficient care. In turn, this could create much stronger pressure and a more favorable environment for more meaningful provider payment reforms to take hold.

We can control rising federal spending on health care in the United States. However, we cannot rely solely on limits to beneficiaries' spending on health insurance. We must alter the financial rewards the government provides to health care providers so that greater emphasis is placed on quality of care provided and less energy is wasted delivering high-cost medicine that yields no benefit to patients. Limiting beneficiaries' access to generous health insurance plans will lead to some decline in health benefits along the way. But the possibility remains that realigning provider incentives will yield improvements in outcomes and slow health care spending sufficiently, so that relatively generous health insurance plans become affordable to the majority of Medicare beneficiaries.

References

Baicker, Katherine, and Jonathan S. Skinner. 2011. Health Care Spending Growth and the Future of U.S. Tax Rates. NBER Working Paper 16772, National Bureau of Economic Research, Cambridge, MA.

Berenson, Alex. 2007. Sending Back the Doctor's Bill. *New York Times*, July 29.

Berenson, Robert A. 2010. *Moving Payment from Volume to Value: What Role for Performance Measurement?* Washington, DC: Robert Wood Johnson Foundation and the Urban Institute.

Carreyrou, John, and Maurice Tamman. 2010. A Device to Kill Cancer, Lift Revenue. *Wall Street Journal*, December 7.

Chandra, Amitabh, and Jonathan S. Skinner. 2011. Technology Growth and Expenditure Growth in Health Care. NBER Working Paper 169835, National Bureau of Economic Research, Cambridge, MA.

Dafny, Leemore. 2010. Are Health Insurance Markets Competitive? *American Economic Review* 100 (4): 1399–1431.

Dafny, Leemore, Mark Duggan, and Subramaniam Ramanarayanan. 2012. Paying a Premium on Your Premium? Consolidation in the Health Insurance Industry. *American Economic Review* 102 (2): 1161–85.

Duggan, Mark. 2004. Does Contracting Out Increase the Efficiency of Government Programs? Evidence from Medicaid HMOs. *Journal of Public Economics* 88 (12): 2549–72.

Franzini, Luisa, Osama I. Mikhail, and Jonathan S. Skinner. 2010. McAllen and El Paso Revisited: Medicare Variations Not Always Reflected in the Under-Sixty-Five Population. *Health Affairs (Project Hope)* 29 (12): 2302–9.

Ho, Vivian. 2008. Advanced Diagnostic Imaging: Benefit or Burden? *Medical Care* 46 (5): 455–57.

Kaiser Family Foundation. Health Research and Educational Trust, and NORC at the University of Chicago. 2011. *Employer Health Benefits 2011 Annual Survey.* Menlo Park, CA: Henry J. Kaiser Foundation.

Keehan, Sean P., Andrea M. Sisko, Christopher J. Truffer, John A. Poisal, Gigi A. Cuckler, Andrew J. Madison, Joseph M. Lizonitz, and Sheila D. Smith. 2011. National Health Spending Projections through 2020: Economic Recovery and Reform Drive Faster Spending Growth. *Health Affairs (Project Hope)* 30 (8): 1594–1605.

Laugesen, Miriam J., and Sherry A. Glied. 2011. Higher Fees Paid to US Physicians Drive Higher Spending for Physician Services Compared to Other Countries. *Health Affairs (Project Hope)* 30 (9): 1647–56.

Lin, Grace A., R. Adams Dudley, F. L. Lucas, David J. Malenka, Eric Vittinghoff, and Rita F. Redberg. 2008. Frequency of Stress Testing to Document Ischemia prior to Elective Percutaneous Coronary Intervention. *Journal of the American Medical Association* 300 (15): 1765–73.

Martin, Brook I., Richard A. Deyo, Sohali K. Mirza, Judith A. Turner, Bryan A. Comstock, William Hollingsworth, and Sean D. Sullivan. 2008. Expenditures and Health Status among Adults with Back and Neck Problems. *Journal of the American Medical Association* 299 (6): 656–64.

McClellan, Mark. 1997. Hospital Reimbursement Incentives: An Empirical Analysis. *Journal of Economics and Management Strategy* 6 (1): 91–128.

McClellan, Mark. 2011. Reforming Payments to Healthcare Providers: The Key to Slowing Healthcare Cost Growth While Improving Quality? *Journal of Economic Perspectives* 25 (2): 69–92.

Murphy, Kevin M., and Robert H. Topel. 2006. The Value of Health and Longevity. *Journal of Political Economy* 114 (5): 871–904.

Newhouse, Joseph P. 1992. Medical Care Costs: How Much Welfare Loss? *Journal of Economic Perspectives* 6 (3): 3–21.

Discussion

Andrew J. Rettenmaier

Overview

Mark Pauly's essay opening this chapter, like all of Pauly's other work I have read, is exceptionally well written, thorough, comprehensive, and explains the economic reasoning behind each key point in ways that economists and noneconomists can appreciate. The chapter progresses through an explanation for the rise in health care spending, how this growth affects government budgets, why tax financing burdens the economy, and the justification for reforming tax-financed health care spending.

These are the main ideas. Medical care is a luxury good, and consequently, spending rises more rapidly than income. This would not be a problem if medical care was paid for privately, but it is not. Government payments are 45 percent of national health expenditures. Tax spending, through the employer tax exclusion, amounts to another $200 billion. Given rising real incomes, health care spending will grow as a share of GDP. As a result, even if the government share remains constant, taxes must rise.

However, Pauly points out that tax financing of medical care creates an excess burden that increases exponentially as more resources are shifted from taxpayers to governments. Thus, he writes, "it is not a matter of neutrality whether the same benefits for the same people are financed publicly or privately." The presence of the excess burden should act as a brake on tax financing of medical care in both levels and relative growth rates. The policy prescriptions Pauly suggests include means-tested vouchers for Medicare beneficiaries that grow less rapidly than per capita health care growth in the private sector.

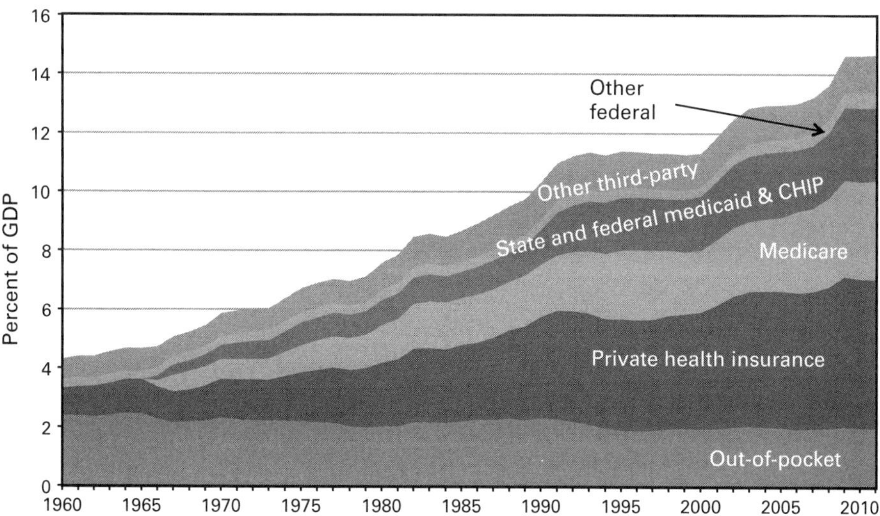

Figure 2.2
Personal Health Care Spending by Payer as a Percent of GDP.
Source: Centers for Medicare and Medicaid Services, National Health Expenditures by Type of Service and Source of Funds, 1960–2011.

The Public-Private Nature of Health Care Spending

The rise in health care spending in excess of income growth is illustrated in figure 2.2. The higher relative growth is indicated by the increasing percentage of gross domestic product (GDP) spent on health care. This sort of figure, in Pauly's assessment, has been frequently used to infer the wrong thing: that because the share of health care spending is higher in the United States than in other countries and without commensurately better health outcomes, something must be wrong. He writes, "Accurate evaluation is not helped by the misleading share data, and instead should be based on asking about comparative value of resources used in medical care versus what those resources could have provided if they were used elsewhere (assuming it is possible to use them elsewhere)."

These are valid points. Pauly also notes that the cost of labor, the majority of health care spending, is higher in the United States than elsewhere. Furthermore, in the United States, payments to health care workers are determined in a competitive market rather than by a single payer with the ability to restrict quantity and pay lower wages.

Even with these qualifications, the composition of health care spending by the payer helps establish several other observations, the most striking of which is the relatively constant share of GDP associated with out-of-pocket health care spending. From 1960 to 2011 it averaged 2.1 percent of GDP, while total personal health care spending grew from 4.3 to 14.7 percent.[3] The figure indicates that the growth in spending as a share of GDP was paid through public and private third-party payers.

Consider the changes in the composition of health care payments from 1970, or five years after the passage of Medicare and Medicaid, to 2011. In 1970, Medicare and Medicaid accounted for about 20 percent of health care spending. Private health insurance and out-of-pocket spending accounted for 22 and 40 percent, respectively. By 2011, Medicare and Medicaid's share of health care spending had doubled to 40 percent, the share paid by private health insurance grew to 34 percent, and out-of-pocket spending accounted for only 14 percent. Pauly warns that as Medicare and Medicaid grow relative to GDP, the tax burden will increase, with the concomitant escalation in the deadweight loss to the economy.

Because it is a luxury good, health care spending is expected to grow more rapidly than income on a per capita basis. However, the fact that the composition of payments changed dramatically between 1960 and 2011 indicates that other things were not held constant over this period of rising real incomes. Several studies have attributed the growth rate in real per capita health care spending to several causes, including rising real income, demographic factors, differential inflation, declining out-of-pocket spending, and technological change.

Smith, Newhouse, and Freeland (2009) find that rising incomes explain between 28 and 43 percent of health spending growth depending on their assumptions.[4] They estimate that demographic factors explain about 7 percent of real health spending growth, higher price inflation accounts for between 5 and 19 percent, declining out-of-pocket spending (or increasing insurance coverage) explains about 11 percent, and the remaining 27 to 48 percent is attributable to technological change.

Earlier studies attributed more of the growth to technological change and less to rising incomes. Thus, attributing 43 percent of real health care spending growth to rising incomes is at the upper end of the estimates. The relatively small amount of the growth that has been attributed to increasing insurance coverage is puzzling. There is well-accepted evidence that lower out-of-pocket spending increases the level of health care spending, but the evidence that it increases the growth rate is less direct. However, the contribution of increasing insurance coverage to spending growth is typically identified only by effects on the demand side of the market. Finkelstein (2007) identified supply-side responses following the introduction of Medicare and Medicaid suggesting that increasing health insurance may account for up to half of the increase in real per capita spending.

The main observations are twofold. First, real per capita health care spending has historically grown more rapidly than real per capita income growth. From 1960 to 2011 the respective real annual growth rates were 4.6 and 2.1. However, less than half of the real growth in health care spending has been attributed to rising incomes. Second, the fact that out-of-pocket spending accounts for only 14 percent of all spending today means that if it were to decline further, its effect on growth is constrained to only an additional 14 percent of the health spending pie. If it is plausible that expanding insurance coverage accounted for up to half of the increase in real per capita spending through the interaction between demand-side and supply-side effects, then the constraint on further insurance expansion may limit future demand and supply-side effects.

These observations suggest that future excess growth in health care spending may be lower than was experienced over the past fifty years. Also, reforms that increase cost sharing at the point of purchase may provoke more than just demand-side reductions; they may also reduce the growth rate in spending. Regardless of the exact cause, Pauly suggests that "the key fact is the growth of spending that outpaces income, regardless of its cause, and that is what I will take as given here."

As we have seen, the way health care is paid for in the United States has evolved. How the payment mechanism and continuing income growth will interact in the future makes predicting spending uncertain, but all forecasts point to higher relative growth in the health care sector. Figure 2.3 illustrates the impact of health care spending on primary, noninterest, federal spending. This figure is based on data from the most recent versions of the Congressional Budget Office's (CBO) *Long-Term Budget Outlook* (2011, 2012). The projections are based on the extended-baseline scenario that follows current law, including the CBO's expectations of the effects of the Affordable Care Act (ACA) on future federal spending.

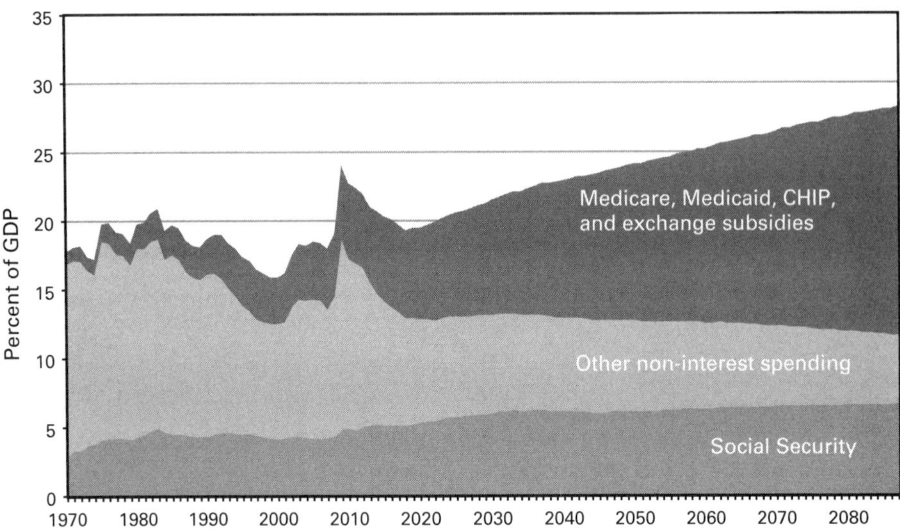

Figure 2.3
Total Primary Federal Spending as a Percent of GDP, 1970–2087.
Source: Congressional Budget Office, 2011 and 2012 Long-Term Budget Outlook. Extended Baseline Scenarios. June 2011 (1970–1999) and June 2012 (2000–2087).

This figure complements Pauly's figure 2.1, illustrating the point that growth in government spending after 1965 can largely be attributed to health care. Looking forward, all future growth in noninterest federal spending can be attributed to health care spending as well. Spending on Social Security shows a relatively modest rise due to the retirement of the baby boom generation. Both Medicare and Social Security share the same demographics, but Social Security benefits for new retirees rise with past real wage growth and then with real price growth after retirement. Consequently Social Security's growth is predictable, and its growth relative to GDP is primarily due to the demographic changes rather than the combination of demographics and health care expenditure growth in excess of GDP that drives Medicare spending. From 1970 to 2010, total primary federal spending averaged 18.6 percent of GDP. However, that average is projected to be exceeded in each year beyond 2010. By 2044, total primary spending (spending less interest payments) is expected to be 25 percent above the 1970 to 2010 average, and by the end of the projection, it will be 50 percent higher. With the CBO's alternative forecast, which assumes higher health care spending growth, primary federal spending is 50 percent higher than the long-run average by midcentury.

In 2013, total noninterest federal spending is expected to total 21 percent of GDP, with Social Security accounting for 4.8 percent, federal health care spending adding 5.5 percent, and other noninterest spending adding another 12.1 percent of GDP. Health care thus accounts for about a quarter of primary spending today, but by 2035 it will account for 42 percent, and by 2060 it will account for half.

Unless Americans want a substantially larger federal government, stemming the growth in federally financed health care spending is necessary, but Pauly makes the persuasive case that there is more to the problem than simply higher tax payments. Collecting additional taxes distorts taxpayers' behavior: they choose to work less, invest differently, and look for ways to avoid payment. It is this excess burden of taxes, writes Pauly, "one that increases exponentially as more resources are shifted, that limits both what government could and should do."

Two Ways Forward

There are multiple ways to reduce the growth rate in federal spending required to support Medicare and Medicaid. In Medicare's case, the price ceilings in the ACA's provisions and the means-tested vouchers Pauly favors provide a stark contrast in approaches. The voucher would constrain future Medicare spending from the demand side of the market rather than through the ACA-type reforms that are essentially price ceilings on the supply side of the health care market.

With the passage of the ACA in 2010, the long-run Medicare forecasts by the Medicare trustees indicated dramatic improvement in the program's funding. For example, the trustees' reports' estimates of the hospital insurance (Part A) unfunded obligation declined significantly between 2009 (pre-ACA forecast) and 2010 (post-ACA forecast). The Part A unfunded obligation is the difference between the present value of future benefit payments and the present value of future payroll taxes. When calculated over seventy-five years and based on the pre-ACA estimates from the 2009 trustees' report, the unfunded obligation was $13.4 trillion. But based on the post-ACA estimates from the 2010 report, it dropped to only $2.4 trillion. Over the infinite horizon, the 2010 trustees' report indicates that the Part A unfunded obligation is eliminated, whereas the unfunded obligation from the 2009 report was $36.4 trillion.[5] As a point of reference, the path of combined total Medicare spending based on the 2010 report estimates is about the same as would result from assuming the future per capita Medicare spending grows at the rate of per capita GDP in each year. Thus, per capita Medicare cost growth in excess of GDP growth is eliminated through the ACA provisions. One may ask then, "If the ACA achieves such substantial savings, why are policymakers still concerned about the future growth in Medicare spending?"

The answer is found in the 2010 trustees' report and in the alternative estimates accompanying the report. Each year the trustees assume that the current law, at the time the estimates are made, persists over the horizon of the forecast. However, recent history indicates that current law is often overridden. The provisions in the ACA responsible for the future savings will likely be undone by future legislative initiatives. The ACA keeps the sustainable growth rate (SGR) system in place for Part B reimbursements to physicians. At the time the 2010 report was released, these payment rates were scheduled to be reduced by over 30 percent for the next three years. The 2009 report also assumed a continuation of the SGR system for Part B, so the major difference in the forecasts comes from the reduction in payment rate updates stipulated by the ACA.[6] These reductions in payment rate updates primarily affect Part A spending, but they also affect some payment categories covered by Part B, like outpatient hospitals. The Office of the Actuary memo accompanying the 2010 report stated, "In our view (and that of the independent outside experts we consulted), neither of these update reductions is sustainable in the long range, and Congress is very likely to legislatively override or otherwise modify the reductions in the future to ensure that Medicare beneficiaries continue to have access to health care."

In the introduction of the 2010 report, the trustees direct readers to the alternative estimates:

> In view of the factors described above, it is important to note that the actual future costs for Medicare are likely to exceed those shown by the current-law projections in this report. We recommend that the projections be interpreted as an illustration of the very favorable financial outcomes that would be experienced if the productivity adjustments can be sustained in the long range—and we caution readers to recognize the great uncertainty associated with achieving this outcome. Where possible, we illustrate the potential understatement of Medicare costs and projection results by reference to an alternative projection that assumes—for purposes of illustration only—that the physician fee reductions are overridden and that the productivity adjustments are gradually phased out over the 15 years starting in 2020.[7]

The most recent set of forecasts from the 2013 Medicare trustees' report are depicted in figure 2.4.[8] The lower line reflects current law while the upper line the alternative projection. Beginning with the 2012 report,

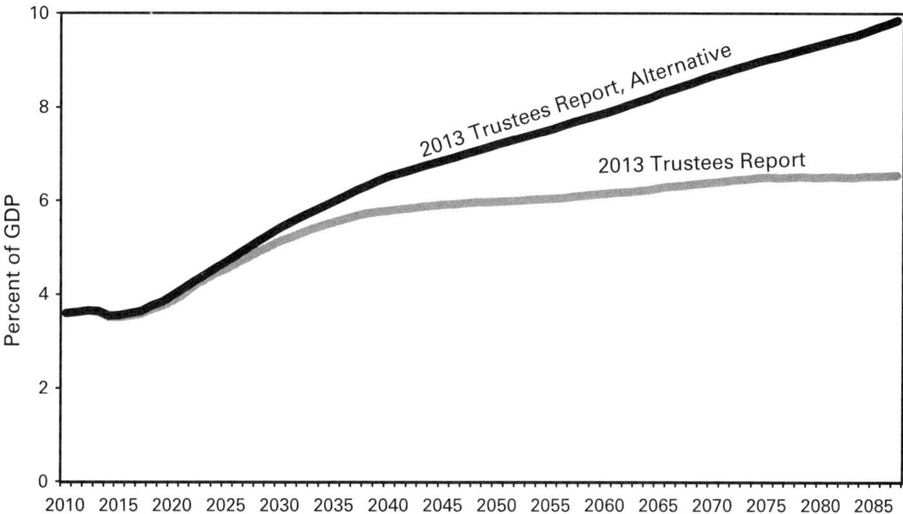

Figure 2.4
Medicare Spending from 2013 Trustees' Report.
Sources: Boards of Trustees, Federal Hospital Insurance and Federal Supplementary Medical Insurance Trust Funds (2013, table V.B3); Projected Medicare Expenditures under Illustrative Scenarios with Alternative Payment Updates to Medicare Providers, May 31, 2013.

the alternative projections were presented along with the current law projections in the first figure that appears in the report, rather than in a supplementary memorandum from the Office of the Actuary. The alternative estimates assume that the past legislative overrides of the sustainable growth rate (SGR) mechanism continue. The SGR, a provision from the Balanced Budget Act of 1997, was intended to constrain the growth in payments to physicians. However, legislation has superseded the SGR's targets. The alternative estimates also assume that the legislative history of overriding the SGR serves as an example for new stipulations in the ACA: the productivity adjustment and the Independent Payment Advisory Board's (IPAB). Both are intended to constrain spending, but both are similar the SGR. The alternative projection assumes that the productivity adjustments that primarily constrain spending growth in hospital payments are phased out over time and that the IPAB recommendations are overridden.

By 2050 total Medicare spending as a percentage of GDP based on the current law estimates is 6 percent of GDP, but with the alternative, it is 7.2 percent, or 20 percent higher. By 2080 the alternative projection is almost 45 percent higher than the current law projections. The CBO's baseline and alternative forecasts have historically exceeded the trustees' forecasts due to higher per capita spending growth assumptions. For example, under the CBO's baseline forecast, Medicare spending rises to 7.3 percent of GDP by 2050; under its alternative forecast, spending rises to 8.1 percent.

All of the varied forecasts suggest that the path of future Medicare spending is highly uncertain and dependent on legislative behavior and the forecast assumptions. Does this mean that there are no reforms that could bring about more certainty in what taxpayers will be called on to finance in the future? Are there reforms that would constrain Medicare's per beneficiary spending growth to the growth in per capita GDP (approximately the current law spending path illustrated in figure 2.4), and is such a target desirable?

Pauly argues that taking the excess burden of taxation into account leads to the conclusion that the level and the growth rate in tax-financed health care spending should be lower than in private spending. He notes that the voucher concept applied to Medicare is a natural policy application based on these conclusions and then contrasts two alternative ways to implement a voucher proposal for Medicare. In general, the voucher Pauly envisions could be means-tested, and other considerations about the insurance market would be necessary, but the two alternatives would be distinguished by whether the voucher amount could or could not be supplemented by the Medicare beneficiary.

This is the real nub of the issue. Pauly points out that the ability to supplement one's voucher will lead to more varied medical spending among seniors than would a prohibition on supplementation. The ability to supplement raises the concern of two-class medicine. But let's reconsider the ACA-type reforms. In the 2013 report, the trustees suggest that if health care providers cannot become more efficient in response to the ACA's cost-containment provisions and if other health care reimbursements continue to advance at historical rates, then "the availability and quality of health care received by Medicare beneficiaries would, under current law, fall over time relative to that received by those with private insurance."[9] In that case, higher-income retirees may exit the program, and the care provided to those who remain would gradually be characterized by reduced access, longer waits to see providers, and diminished quality. This too would produce two-class medicine.

The relatively uniform Medicare benefits that have existed up to this point have resulted in similar health care spending across seniors who had differing lifetime incomes. However, as we have seen, continuation of uniform comprehensive health insurance for seniors will become prohibitively costly in the near future. The ACA reforms that place the burden of lowering cost growth almost exclusively on providers do not appear to have engendered confidence among policymakers that they are politically durable.

If the ACA reforms are perceived as ineffective at reining in government spending growth on medical care, will the alternative reforms that Pauly outlines perform better? Altogether the reforms he suggests should have greater political durability because they are straightforward and the income-related voucher amounts and the annual growth rates can be more definitively defined. His approach also produces the benefit of increased market-based competition.

The reforms begin with reducing the tax exclusion afforded employment-related health insurance. This would lower the level of health care spending and would lessen the tax distortion in favor of health care spending. This reform changes the standard to which Medicare and Medicaid coverage is compared, and it has the potential to lower the growth rate in privately purchased health care. As Pauly adds, reducing tax expenditures raises additional revenues without increasing the excess burden.

In terms of the vouchers provided to those who rely exclusively on public assistance, the growth rate would be chosen by taxpayers. For the Medicare population, Pauly suggests a means-tested voucher that grows with general prices for high-income retirees and one that grows more rapidly for lower-income retirees, but not as rapidly as in the private, albeit reformed, health care market. With this reform, supplementation of the voucher amounts would be allowed. The parameters used to determine the Medicare voucher can include health status, income, and the growth rate target.

Looking forward, critics of a voucher proposal for Medicare patients like the one Pauly outlines will raise the following concerns: means testing will erode the support for Medicare; some patients may choose less, but presumably beneficial, health care consumption; and the variation in realized health care consumption during retirement by individuals with differing lifetime income will increase among future retirees. However, these concerns must be compared to a viable alternative future Medicare program rather than the program as it has existed up to now. As we have seen, the alternative path forward based on the payment constraints in the ACA have provoked similar concerns, but their ability to endure over time is questionable.

Federal health care spending is front and center in the debate over how the United States should deal with its current debt and forecast future deficits. Closing the funding gap, apart from ever expanding taxes, requires lower federal spending on Medicare and Medicaid. Pauly provides a compelling argument that the excess burden of taxation leads to the conclusion that tax-financed health spending should grow less rapidly than privately purchased health care, and he offers a reasonable approach to lowering federal health care spending relative to the projections. His solutions remove distortions in the health care market and require consumers to make tougher choices in the future than they have in the recent past. While health care spending may become more varied by income if means-tested vouchers are adopted for Medicare patients, the distribution of federal transfers by income will become much more progressive than they are already, and protection for lower income retirees will be preserved. Pauly reminds us that past policies cannot persist, and the path forward can indeed reduce distortions in the health care market rather than adding to them.

References

Acemoglu, Daron, Amy Finkelstein, and Matthew J. Notowidigdo. 2009. Income and Health Spending: Evidence from Oil Price Shocks. NBER Working Paper 14744, National Bureau of Economic Research, Cambridge, MA.

Boards of Trustees, Federal Hospital Insurance and Supplementary Medical Insurance Trust Funds. 2009. *Annual Report of the Boards of Trustees of the Federal Hospital Insurance and Federal Supplementary Medical Insurance Trust Funds*. Washington, DC: U.S. Government Printing Office.

Boards of Trustees, Federal Hospital Insurance and Supplementary Medical Insurance Trust Funds. 2010. *Annual Report of the Boards of Trustees of the Federal Hospital Insurance and Federal Supplementary Medical Insurance Trust Funds*. Washington, DC: U.S. Government Printing Office.

Boards of Trustees, Federal Hospital Insurance and Supplementary Medical Insurance Trust Funds. 2013. *Annual Report of the Boards of Trustees of the Federal Hospital Insurance and Federal Supplementary Medical Insurance Trust Funds*. Washington, DC: U.S. Government Printing Office.

Caldis, Todd G. 2009. *The Long-Term Projection Assumptions for Medicare and Aggregate National Health Expenditures*. Baltimore, MD: Office of the Actuary Memorandum.

Congressional Budget Office. 2011. *CBO's 2011 Long-Term Budget Outlook*. Washington, DC: Congressional Budget Office.

Congressional Budget Office. 2012. *CBO's 2012 Long-Term Budget Outlook*. Washington, DC: Congressional Budget Office.

Finkelstein, Amy. 2007. The Aggregate Effects of Health Insurance: Evidence from the Introduction of Medicare. *Quarterly Journal of Economics* 122 (1): 1–38.

Shatto, John D., and M. Kent Clemens. 2010. *Projected Medicare Expenditures under an Illustrative Scenario with Alternative Payment Updates to Medicare Providers*. Baltimore, MD: Office of the Actuary Memorandum.

Shatto, John D., and M. Kent Clemens. 2013. *Projected Medicare Expenditures under Illustrative Scenarios with Alternative Payment Updates to Medicare Providers*. Baltimore, MD: Office of the Actuary Memorandum.

Smith, Sheila, Joseph P. Newhouse, and Mark S. Freeland. 2009. Income, Insurance, and Technology: Why Does Health Spending Outpace Economic Growth? *Health Affairs* 28 (5): 1276–84.

Notes

1. Across households at a given time, medical spending appears to be higher in higher-income households (controlling for health status and insurance coverage), but not disproportionately higher. It is the way spending grows with increases in income for a given set of households that is the focus of this discussion.

2. See "Accountable Care Organizations: Improving Care Coordination for People with Medicare." http://www.healthcare.gov/news/factsheets/2011/03/accountablecare03312011a html.

3. Personal health care spending is limited to spending to treat individuals; it does not include government public health spending, administration costs, and investments in facilities and equipment. The broadest category of spending, national health expenditures was equal to 17.3 percent of GDP in 2011.

4. Their estimates assume income elasticities between 0.6 and 0.9. Using evidence from oil price shocks Acemoglu, Finkelstein, and Notowidigdo (2009) estimate an income elasticity of 0.7.

5. See table IIIB10 in the Boards of Trustees, Federal Hospital Insurance and Federal Supplementary Medical Insurance Trust Funds, 2009 and 2010.

6. The ACA provision as implemented in the 2010 trustees' report forecasts "calls for a reduction in payment updates equal to the increase in economy-wide multifactor productivity." John Shatto and M. Kent Clemens, Office of the Actuary memorandum, August 5, 2010.

7. See the Boards of Trustees, Federal Hospital Insurance and Supplementary Medical Insurance Trust Funds (2010, 3).

8. Data from Boards of Trustees, Federal Hospital Insurance and Supplementary Medical Insurance Trust Funds (2013, table V.B3) and table 5, from Shatto and Clemens, Office of the Actuary memorandum, May 31, 2013. These series are depicted in Board of Trustees of the Social Security Administration (2013, figure I.1).

9. See Boards of Trustees, Federal Hospital Insurance and Supplementary Medical Insurance Trust Funds (2013).

3 Social Security's Financial Outlook and Reforms: An Independent Evaluation

Jagadeesh Gokhale

Social Security is often described as a foundational element of the nation's social safety net. Almost all Americans are directly affected by the program, and many millions primarily depend on its benefits for supporting themselves during retirement.[1] But the program's financial condition has worsened considerably since the 2008–9 recession. In their 2007 annual report, the Social Security trustees estimated that the Old-Age and Survivors Insurance (OASI) program's trust fund would be exhausted by 2042. The trustees' annual report for 2014 brings the OASI trust funds exhaustion date forward to 2034.[2] Indeed, OASI tax revenues began to fall short of benefit expenditures in 2010, and it appears unlikely that surpluses will reemerge under the program's current rules. If the program's finances continue to worsen at this rate, it will not be long before the debate on reforming the program assumes an urgency and intensity similar to that during 1982–83, when imminent insolvency forced lawmakers to schedule a payroll tax increase, introduce a gradual increase in the retirement age, and subject Social Security benefits to income taxes.

Social Security reforms should be debated and implemented under accurate and full information about the program's financial condition under current policies and about the effects of alternative reforms on the program's overall financial condition and on different participant groups—the young and old, rich and poor, male and female, and so on.[3] But official evaluations of the program's fiscal condition and its projected finances are conducted using methods and metrics that are long outdated. Moreover, analyses of distributional effects, especially over participants' lifetimes under current policies, are not included in the trustees' annual reports on Social Security's finances. Although the topic of Social Security almost always generates a robust debate, it is likely to be misguided under the projections and analysis provided by the program's trustees and actuaries. The purpose of this opening essay in this chapter is to highlight the availability of better methods and metrics for evaluating Social Security's future finances and assessing the reforms that lawmakers, academics, budget analysts, and others have proposed.

Not only are official projections of Social Security's financial condition inaccurate, there appears to be a general reluctance to remedy the situation—even on the part of experts specifically appointed to do so. For example, the 2011 report of Social Security's independent Technical Panel on Assumptions and Methods (TPAM) fails to review and assess, and even comment on, key methodological issues posed in projecting Social Security's future finances. Without a public airing of the problems that such methodological shortcomings may introduce into official projections, we are likely to make erroneous judgments and implement suboptimal Social Security policies.

In the interest of full public disclosure, the TPAM is appointed by the Social Security Advisory Board (SSAB) but operates independently of it. As a board member, I am partly responsible for the composition of the 2011 TPAM. The board took great pains in selecting TPAM members to ensure a proper balance of expertise by including top-level economists, actuaries, demographers, and microsimulation modelers, including those with a strong background in research on the Social Security program.

Although the 2011 TPAM report contains methodological recommendations for deriving particular demographic and economic "assumptions"—those used by the program's trustees for making Social Security's financial projections—it does not evaluate the trustees' methodology for integrating them to produce those projections. An independent assessment has clarified to me that the trustees' methods contain some rather significant shortcomings. They involve issues such as the degree of detail that should be incorporated in the trustees' assumptions used to construct demographic and economic projections; their joint integration to generate financial projections, including adequately capturing important interactions among them; the reasonableness of intermediate demographic, economic, and financial outcomes; maintaining internal consistency and robustness in integrating economic and demographic assumptions over various projection horizons (the short term, seventy-five years, and in perpetuity); and, most important, the appropriateness of basing some of the assumptions exclusively on historical data—as opposed to conditioning them on projected U.S. demographic and economic features. A particular choice among alternative methods for determining and combining economic and demographic assumptions could alter the results substantially because it conditions the interplay among those forces over time differently from other choices. How should we choose among the alternatives? Unfortunately, such issues remain unaddressed by the trustees and the 2011 TPAM report drawn up to advise them.

Many lawmakers, scholars, and others have proposed Social Security reforms following their particular preferences about the program's future scope and operation. Some reform proposals have been financially evaluated ("scored") by Social Security actuaries to estimate their effects on popular measures, such as the date of trust fund exhaustion and annual balances of tax receipts and benefit payments. Official reform-scoring exercises are based on the same outdated actuarial methods used by the program's trustees to prepare Social Security's financial projections under current policies and laws.

Because Social Security directly covers 94 percent of the working population (e.g., some state and local government workers are not covered) and because the program's taxes and benefits constitute a sizable portion of most participants' budgets, it exerts a significant impact on almost all individuals and on the economy as a whole.[4] The potential for inappropriate or inadequate Social Security policy adjustments is already quite large, given that it is subject to a massive political tug-of-war between its supporters and detractors. Inaccurate financial projections and inadequate metrics that bias future policy decisions only compound the potential to adversely affect millions of participants through inappropriate or suboptimal reforms.

Assumptions and Methods in Projecting Social Security's Finances

The shortcomings in current official assessments of Social Security's financial condition are fundamental: the actuarial methods and models that the trustees use are inadequate and ill suited for making accurate financial projections. I do not say this lightly; I am well aware of the serious and severe consequences of making an unfounded charge on this issue. The reason for existing shortcomings is the absence in the trustees' projection methods of several essential ingredients, primarily the recognition that for key variables—such as fertility, mortality, productivity growth, and interest rates—assumptions based exclusively on historical data are not adequate. Important interactions among projected demographic and economic attributes of the U.S. population must be explicitly taken into account when deriving the program's financial projections under a given set of Social Security policies. Instead, under the official methodology, many of these items are based exclusively on historical data and fixed ahead of time as the trustees' "ultimate long-range assumptions."

Another shortcoming is that the trustees' actuarial methods lack a coherent framework for integrating and aggregating demographic and economic factors from the microeconomic (individual) level. And third, the trustees' projection methods are based on a seemingly arbitrary decision about the degree of detail to incorporate in estimating the "assumptions" (levels or rates of change) to be applied to the population in future years for deriving Social Security's financial outcomes.

The trustees' methods involve making parametric assumptions, including future rates of change (called the trustees' "ultimate long-range assumptions") about particular demographic and economic attributes of the population based on observed historical trends and applying them mechanically to population subgroups (or cells) distinguished by broad age categories and gender to the existing population to derive its evolution through time.[5] As the population evolves, however, the fixed parametric assumptions continue to be applied, regardless of whether they are appropriate for the projected profile and condition of the population.[6] Take assumed future fertility rates as an example. The trustees do not distinguish female fertility rates by race and education level, even though fertility rates have historically differed considerably along those dimensions. Assuming a given overall fertility rate for future years and applying it mechanically to future female populations will produce a particular population projection over the long term. But if fertility rates differ systematically by female race and education, the projected population's composition will change, with more fertile groups gaining greater representation.[7] And this change will make the future overall fertility rate that is consistent with the future composition of the female population by race and education different than the one applied to derive future fertility outcomes because the latter is based exclusively on historical data.

Such changes in the population's projected composition also have implications for other technical assumptions—for example, mortality rates, labor force participation, and labor productivity—that the trustees also base exclusively on historical data and hold fixed during all but the initial few years of the seventy-five-year projection horizon. For example, labor productivity would tend to decline if faster-growing population groups exhibit more tenuous labor force attachments, work part time rather than full time, have smaller propensities to acquire education, have larger likelihoods of remaining single rather than marrying, and so on—all of which are attributes associated with lower worker productivity. The trustees' methods ignore the effects of future changes in the composition of the population on future labor productivity and earnings growth. Instead, they assume that long-term productivity growth will remain constant at the assumed historical average except for a short-term transition through the abnormal phase of any ongoing business cycle. Under a proper methodology, however, future labor productivity should be conditioned on the composition and attributes of the projected population.[8]

In making future projections, the trustees use a cell-based method, which depends on relatively crude distributions of various population attributes by age and gender categories.[9] This method is easy to execute, but it severely constrains the type of demographic and economic processes that could be estimated and projected, including interactions between them over time. A detailed microsimulation modeling approach, where intermediate outcomes such as labor force participation rates, productivity growth, payrolls, and so on are conditioned on the demographic features of the projected population, would enable better development, integration, and internal consistency of key economic assumptions through the projection horizon. This does not mean that the microsimulation would be divorced from actual historical information and trends. Rather, the microsimulation's key drivers must be calibrated using historical information on key variables, and its operation must be validated to reproduce historical trends for intermediate outcome variables. However, it must also be designed to progressively adjust those variables so that they respond appropriately to changes in the demographic attributes of the underlying population as it evolves. Under the official methodology now used, several crucial economic variables remain frozen at historically observed rates or averages, gradually becoming unhinged from the demographic profile of the population as the forward projection is implemented. A microsimulation modeling approach is more difficult to implement than the trustees' methodology, but it is feasible in the United States because a wide range of microsurvey data sources is regularly compiled and easily accessible.

Indeed, when embedded within a growth model framework, a carefully constructed microsimulation delivers more than just a "black box." It generates insights into the likely evolution of demographic and economic components that will determine Social Security's future tax base, revenues, and benefit obligations: the evolution of the number of workers, the quality (earning capacity) of the workforce, the capital stock associated with differential propensities to save and hold financial and physical assets by demographic attributes, and so on. A well-crafted microsimulation also provides insights into different types of interactions among population groups for many variables of interest, such as the evolution of family structures, labor force participation rates, and education acquisition—attributes that will affect future earnings, payroll taxes, and Social Security benefits. Assuming fixed long-term growth rates or trends based only on historical data and ignoring the potentially large effects that projected demographic changes may exert on those key variables makes Social Security's financial projections potentially prone to sizable errors.

An important aspect of using integrated stochastic microsimulation models for making Social Security's financial projections is model validation. Given the inherent outcome uncertainty built into microsimulation models, how could one be confident about the future outcomes that it generates? Such confidence would be higher if the model were historically validated—that is, if the model implemented with historical initial conditions captures historical outcomes sufficiently accurately, on average, with acceptably small variations across multiple runs. Only after successful historical validation could one claim that the model captures and reflects the momentum of existing demographic and economic factors, including their interaction with each other over time. Microsimulation models that include a clear method for integrating economic and demographic assumptions ensure that key variables remain consistent with each other during forward runs and can be historically validated to demonstrate this consistency. Such models provide better tools for capturing future outcome uncertainty through multiple runs. They are also better suited for examining the effect of changing underlying assumptions (e.g., interest rates, fertility, net immigration) on future outcomes and on associated changes in outcome variances. Only microsimulation models with these attributes can be deemed to correctly modulate the system's response to changes in underlying assumptions (selectively or collectively) because they would maintain forward internal consistency across all relevant variables.[10]

Metrics for Evaluating the Effects of Social Security Reforms

The 1983 Social Security reforms attempted to fix the program's finances for the next seventy-five years—through 2058. But the program's total benefit expenditures already exceed its tax receipts, and the OASI trust fund is projected to run out by 2034, according to the program's trustees. Even current estimates of the program's financial solvency may prove optimistic if future economic growth remains slower than its long-term historical average. This result could emerge from unanticipated changes in demographic and economic outcomes—unanticipated because the trustees' projection techniques do not incorporate growing potentially-productivity-reducing attributes of the U.S. population into key economic assumptions about the future.

The next set of Social Security reforms should be based on better estimations of the future course of our demographics and economy. They should also be based on a proper set of financial metrics. Measurement of Social Security's solvency and sustainability requires a long time horizon, including through perpetuity, because only under such metrics can we capture the full implications of particular policy changes on the program's finances.[11] That means the trustees should retain the infinite-horizon actuarial deficit that they began reporting in 2003, together with the traditional seventy-five-year actuarial deficit and the path of annual shortfalls of the program's taxes and income compared to benefit expenditures.

Evaluating particular Social Security reform proposals also demands a thorough analysis of their effects on different population groups. Because Social Security affects almost all participants throughout their lifetimes, the program's redistributive effects should be measured and compared over the lifetimes of different population groups. However, the Social Security trustees and actuaries do not report any analysis of program (or reform) effects using micrometrics evaluated over the lifetimes of various population subgroups.

The 2007 TPAM recommends that the Social Security trustees move to a microsimulation-based estimation method. And the 2011 TPAM recommends adopting micrometrics for evaluating the program's effect on particular population groups. But progress by the Social Security Administration on adopting microsimulation projection methods, and therefore on adopting micrometrics, has been very slow. Agencies such as the Congressional Budget Office, Urban Institute, the Government

Accountability Office, and others have developed microsimulations of U.S. demographics and economy. But most such efforts have either focused on narrower policy issues or are not fully independent of the trustees' data and inputs in their development. The promise that an independent microsimulation of U.S. demographic and economy forces would yield substantial new insights motivated my development of the Demographic and Economic Micro Simulation (DEMSIM) in 2010. The results from using DEMSIM to project and estimate Social Security's financial condition and to evaluate six Social Security reform proposals are summarized in the balance of this essay.

DEMSIM

DEMSIM is a microsimulation calibrated to U.S. microdata beginning in 1970. It creates a population of about 45,000 families in 1970 (which implies a simulated U.S. population ratio of 1:5,100) in the computer. The demographic characteristics of these individuals are calibrated to match those of the overall U.S. population in 1970. Thus, the microsimulation begins with a population sample that is calibrated to be representative of the U.S. population as of 1970. The calibration to U.S. microdata is accomplished by using conditional distributions of the U.S. population according to various attributes—age, gender, race, family size and composition, education, labor force status, disability status—as reflected in the Current Population Survey (CPS) samples from the late 1960s and early 1970s.[12] Once conditional distributions of the different individual attributes listed earlier are estimated, the distributions are used to make random draws of 15,000 "families" involving about 39,000 individuals—either single individuals, single-headed families with one head and at least one child, or married couples with or without children—to closely replicate overall family sizes, family structures, and person attributes as contained in CPS's microdata sample.[13] Earnings of individuals in the simulated sample are matched to data from the Panel Survey of Income Dynamics (PSID). The simulated population is then "transitioned" forward in time by applying historical mortality, fertility, and immigration rates, to generate a new population for 1971—and so on through 2006, the last year of the historical simulation. In each year, the several demographic and economic attributes of the simulated population are matched with historical data to confirm that the simulation closely follows the pattern of historical developments observed in the United States since 1970. Thus, the simulation is closely calibrated to actual data and none of its features are independent or unrepresentative of the historically observed economic and demographic outcomes in the United States.

This historical simulation is a validated baseline—one that represents the condition of the U.S. population and economy during the mid-2000s. Because this simulation is validated historically through time, it also captures the momentum of demographic and economic forces present in the United States during the mid-2000s. The next step is to use the Social Security Administration's assumptions on demographic driver parameters—mortality, fertility, and immigration rates—to carry the demographic and economic simulation forward in time. To do so, however, DEMSIM further disaggregates those parameters along dimensions whose interactions with other population attributes are important to calibrate the future evolution of key demographic and economic variables to maintain mutual internal consistency when making Social Security's financial projections. For example, the trustees' overall fertility rates by age for years prior to 2006 are further disaggregated by female race and education levels using data from the National Center for Health Statistics (NCHS). In the case of mortality rates, the trustees' overall rates by age and gender for years prior to 2006 are further disaggregated by race, also by using NCHS data.

The Social Security trustees decompose labor force participation rates by age and gender, but not by race and education as implemented under DEMSIM. A similar remark applies to education levels and propensities to acquire education by age, gender, and race—included in DEMSIM but not considered by the Social Security trustees. Such variables, which characterize systematic differences in economic choices (or opportunities), could exert important influences on the future course of "effective labor inputs." Such a detailed projection method captures key determinants of items such as future family formation and dissolution, labor productivity, wage earnings, the payroll tax base, the degree of wage inequality, total Social Security benefits, and so on—factors that significantly influence Social Security's revenue and expenditure projections.

Projected Worker-to-Beneficiary Ratios

Because DEMSIM's demographic parameters—especially mortality and fertility rates—incorporate similar overall rates of change as the Social Security trustees' assumptions, it should produce estimates of key population ratios quite close to those of the Social Security

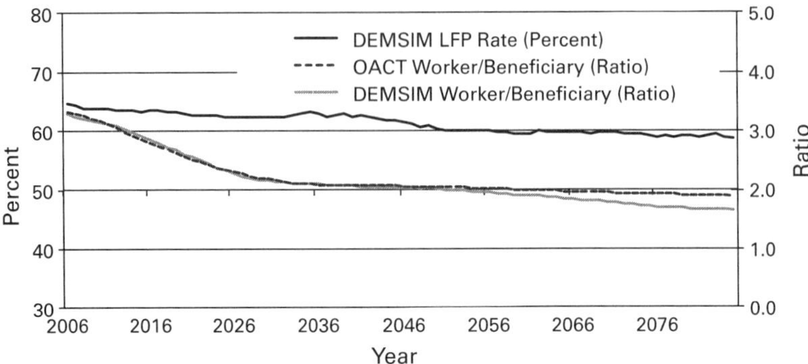

Figure 3.1
DEMSIM's Labor Force Participation Rate and the Worker/Beneficiary Ratio Projections, 2006–2080: Comparison with Social Security Trustees' Worker/Beneficiary Ratio Projections.
Source: Gokhale (2010).

trustees—at least during the first few decades of the trustees' seventy-five-year projection window. One demographic metric of special interest for this pay-as-you-go-financed transfer program is the ratio of contributors (covered workers) to beneficiaries (retirees and survivors). Figure 3.1 shows that the trustees' and DEMSIM's projected worker-to-beneficiary ratios match quite closely through the mid-2050s. The match deteriorates toward the end of the seventy-five-year period shown because of a faster decline in labor force participation (LFP) among DEMSIM's working-age individuals stemming from growth in the proportion of minority groups that exhibit less frequent labor force attachments during their working life spans.[14]

Growth in Labor and Capital Inputs

DEMSIM incorporates a growth model framework that lends internal coherence to the projection of labor earnings and the underlying demographic attributes of the projected population. Under this framework, labor earnings are assumed to be equal to each worker's marginal product from working in an economy with capital and technology inherited from the past. Capital and labor services are combined in firms to produce output—a process that also produces technical improvements over time. Total output grows over time based on growth in inputs (capital and "effective labor") and technical change, the latter calibrated to historical data based on an independent and authoritative academic study.[15] Each period's capital stock is calibrated to asset holdings by age

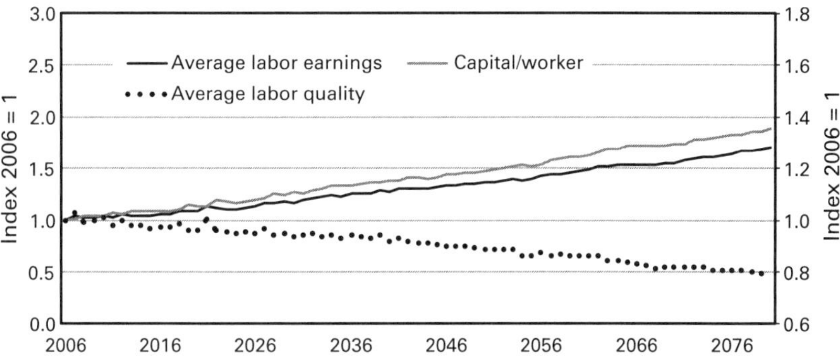

Figure 3.2
DEMSIM's Projections of Capital per Worker, Average Labor Earnings, and Average Labor Quality, 2006–2080.
Source: Gokhale (2010).

and gender estimated from microdata.[16] Asset holdings vary over the life cycle, increasing through retirement and then declining through the end of the life span. The ongoing retirement of the baby boomers means that asset drawdowns by this cohort are likely to accelerate in future years. However, positive population and productivity growth means that, consistent with projected demographic changes, those drawdowns will be dominated by asset accumulations by younger cohorts. As a result, capital per worker is projected under DEMSIM to grow during the next several decades at an average rate of 1.19 percent per year, and contribute to future output and labor productivity growth. Figure 3.2 shows DEMSIM's seventy-five-year projections of capital per worker and average labor earnings.

Labor Quantity, Quality, and Productivity

Under DEMSIM's framework, each individual's labor services depend on the person's labor force participation and his or her "labor quality." Labor quality is associated with the individual's projected demographic and economic attributes under DEMSIM—age, race, gender, marital status, family size and structure, labor force status, education level, and so on. The dependence of labor quality on those attributes is calibrated by implementing a regression of productivity-, capital-stock-, and inflation-adjusted wage earnings on those attributes using PSID panel data on earnings and person attributes.[17]

DEMSIM estimates labor quantity by simulating the assignment of full-time, part-time, and nonworking labor force status to each worker in each year—again calibrated using microdata sources. Combining labor force status with PSID earnings regression coefficients (applicable only to those working part or full time) determines the amount of effective labor input contributed by each worker. Aggregating over all workers yields simulated wage and payroll tax bases in each year. This also generates projections of the economy-wide average wage to be used in calculating Social Security's benefit basis (primary insurance amount) for each retiree. Under this method, projected wages and growth of the wage base are made contingent on the projected amounts of capital, technological change, labor quantity, and labor quality.

Although it is quite important for determining the future wage base, the future evolution of the quality of the workforce has not received any attention in official projections of Social Security's finances. DEMSIM shows that the evolution of the future workforce's labor quality is likely to exert a nontrivial impact on the evolution of the payroll base. As it turns out, although projected increases in the capital stock and continual technical change will yield positive U.S. labor productivity growth, a secular projected decline in labor quality is likely to exert a significant drag on future labor productivity growth. Ignoring labor quality, DEMSIM's calibrations produce an average labor productivity growth per worker through 2080 of 1.01 percent per year—somewhat less than the trustees' 2006 intermediate assumption of 1.10 percent per year.[18] But adding the drag generated by declining labor quality reduces annual average labor productivity growth per worker to just 0.71 percent per year. Figure 3.2 shows DEMSIM's index of projected labor quality through the year 2080.

Several demographic and economic features and trends will contribute to the projected decline in U.S. labor quality under DEMSIM. First, the retirement of the baby boomers implies exit from the workforce of the most experienced workers who are currently at peak life cycle working and earning activity. They will be replaced over time by equally experienced high-earning workers, but those cohorts will be smaller in size relative to the boomers and relative to the total workforce. Second, higher fertility among nonwhites implies that a larger fraction of the workforce will be made up of individuals with more tenuous workforce attachments—through either more years of nonemployment or higher frequencies of part-time rather than full-time work. In addition, the ongoing dissolution of family structures through fewer marriages and more divorces implies a change in social structures away from those associated with higher earnings, especially by male household heads. Under DEMSIM's projections, these labor-quality-reducing tendencies more than offset the quality-increasing effects from a better-educated future workforce. These broad trends appear to have important implications for future growth of output and tax bases, but they remain unrecognized and underappreciated among analysts concerned with Social Security's (and the nation's) future economic prospects.

One possible critique of DEMSIM's projected decline in labor quality is that a future shortage of "effective labor inputs" may induce an increase in human capital returns, spurring an offsetting behavioral response by participants who may choose to acquire more education and skills. However, estimating such a behavioral response and calibrating DEMSIM's drivers to incorporate it is fraught with significant uncertainty.[19] The absence of such "dynamic scoring" should not be taken as a denial of the possibility of a nonnegligible behavioral response. Indeed, estimating the decline in labor quality under a non-dynamic projection methodology reveals the size of the required behavioral response to fully offset the decline in labor productivity projected by assuming no response. Another relevant distinction is that this exercise is one of *projecting* Social Security's financial condition based on capturing the momentum of forces built into the U.S. population and economy. It is not, and should not be, an exercise of *forecasting* the program's finances based on conjectures about how large future behavioral responses might turn out to be. Although projecting Social Security's finances requires consistency between future demographic and economic outcomes—one that appears to be absent from official projections—it should be free of speculative content.

Social Security's Financial Condition over the Next Seventy-Five Years

DEMSIM's calculations of Social Security benefits are based on a careful individual-level calculation of benefits given each individual's wage history.[20] As such, it takes into account the impact of future changes in the distributions of wage earnings.

Social Security's benefit formula is based on each covered worker's earnings history. It indexes past earnings up to the taxable limit by a wage index of (projected) average economy-wide wage earnings, calculates average earnings over the thirty-five highest years of indexed earnings, and applies the program's progressive bend-point formula to derive the primary insurance amount (PIA), the retirement benefit for those who elect to begin benefit collection at full retirement age. It is modified for early and late benefit collection (as distinct from retirement) and constitutes the basis for calculating auxiliary benefits flowing from each worker's earnings—spousal, divorcee, child, survivor, and so on. Thus, the progressivity of the bend-point formula influences all types of OASI benefits. It implies, in particular, that under a given time series of average economy-wide wages, changes in wage inequality will alter benefits per dollar of total wage earnings.

How would this work? Under the current bend point formula, each additional dollar of average monthly indexed earnings (AIME) generates additional PIA (benefits) of ninety cents for those with low earnings (and therefore low AIME) during their lifetimes. The marginal AIME-to-PIA conversion rates are 32 percent for those with moderately high AIME and 15 percent for those with highest AIMEs. Thus, a person's total benefits increase with AIME, but the rate of increase declines as AIME increases. This means that a mean preserving decline in inequality in AIME or wages would increase benefits per dollar of wages; conversely, a more unequal wage distribution would decrease benefits per dollar of wages.

DEMSIM projects that the United States is likely to experience a reduction (possibly a slower rate of increase) of wage inequality during the next two decades as the baby boomers, currently in their highest earning phase of their life cycle, retire. Later, once the boomers are fully retired and positive labor productivity growth increases total earnings but more workers exhibit lower labor force attachments and other attributes associated with lower productivity, cross-section wage inequality is likely to reverse course (or accelerate).

Compositional changes in the attributes of the U.S. workforce that are projected under DEMSIM suggest therefore that benefits per dollar of payrolls and payroll taxes would increase initially—until baby boomers' retirement transition is completed. During the 2030s, however, the pace of this increase will slow. Under DEMSIM's projections, wage inequality continues to increase gradually after 2030. Nevertheless, benefit expenditures continue to outpace total OASI revenues because of projected increases in longevity and retirement life spans in the long term. DEMSIM's pattern of faster increases in benefits relative to payroll taxes during the next two decades, followed by a slow but steady long-term increase in the gap between benefits and payroll taxes, is shown in figure 3.3. DEMSIM's projected OASI tax-receipts trajectory is consistently lower than the trustees' trajectory through

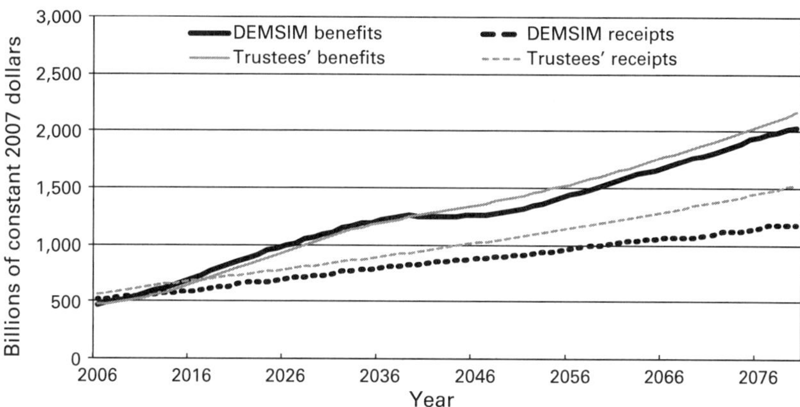

Figure 3.3
Comparison of Social Security Tax Receipts and Benefit Expenditures: DEMSIM Baseline and Trustees' (2006) Intermediate Projections, 2006–2080.
Source: Gokhale (2010).

2080.[21] However, DEMSIM's total-benefit trajectory surges initially, at a faster pace compared to the trustees' trajectory. The rate of increase matches that of the trustees after the 2030s—which is not surprising because the rate of longevity increases in the long term is similar to that of the trustees.

DEMSIM's payroll taxes and OASI benefit expenditure estimates for 2006 turn out to be quite close to the trustees' estimates (within 6 percentage points). But DEMSIM's and the trustees' projections diverge in future years, as shown in figure 3.3. Compared to the trustees' 2006 projections of OASI taxes and benefits, DEMSIM produces a larger future gap between the two. Table 3.1 shows that the seventy-five-year open group liability (OGL) equals almost $7.0 trillion under DEMSIM's projections—70 percent larger than the trustees' estimate of $4.1 trillion.[22] Note also that the trustees' total benefit expenditure profile exhibits a much smaller surge in benefits from the retirement of the baby boom generation compared to DEMSIM's profile—probably a result of insufficient detail and modeling of underlying demographic and economic processes. As is evident from figure 3.3, a larger share of the Social Security's imbalance arises before 2050 under DEMSIM's compared to the trustees' projections.

Table 3.1 shows that Social Security's seventy-five-year OGL equals $7.0 trillion under DEMSIM—or 3.4 percent of the present value of payrolls from 2006 to 2080. This is much larger than the trustees' 2006

Table 3.1
DEMSIM's Optimistic, Baseline, and Pessimistic Projections of Social Security's Financial Condition, 2006–2080

		Optimistic	Baseline	Pessimistic
Long-term discount rate assumption (percent)		3.6	2.9	2.1
		Billions of Constant 2006 Dollars Present Values over Seventy-Five Years		
1	OASI projected benefits	27,795	31,231	36,338
2	OASI projected tax receipts	25,454	22,836	21,372
3	OASI total projected imbalance (1 – 2)	2,341	8,395	14,966
4	Current OASI trust fund	1,663	1,663	1,663
5	Present value of OASI trust fund in 2080	290	253	375
6	Open group liability (OGL; 3 – 4 + 5)	968	6,985	13,678
7	Total future payrolls	232,434	208,495	195,096
		Percent		
8	OGL/Payrolls ([6/7] × 100)	0.42	3.35	7.01
9	OGL/Tax Receipts ([6/2] × 100)	3.80	30.59	64.00
10	OGL/Benefits ([6/1] × 100)	3.48	22.37	37.64

Source: Gokhale (2010) and author's calculations.

estimate of 1.9 percent. DEMSIM's estimate implies that maintaining Social Security solvency over the seventy-five-year time horizon requires policymakers to either increase OASI payroll taxes by 3.4 percentage points—that is, increase OASI tax receipts by 31 percent—immediately and permanently. Alternatively, benefits would have to be reduced by 22 percent immediately and permanently.[23]

DEMSIM estimates Social Security's trust fund exhaustion date to be 2029, much sooner than the trustees' (2006) date of 2042. The trustees' most recent estimate of the trust fund exhaustion date (2014) is 2034. It remains later than DEMSIM's estimate of 2029, but is approaching closer to the latter over time. The earlier trust fund exhaustion date under DEMSIM may be the result of a more pronounced effect of baby boomer retirements on the path of projected benefits. I conjecture that because the trustees' intermediate projections are optimistic relative to DEMSIM's baseline projections, the trust fund's official exhaustion date will continue to move closer DEMSIM's projected date of 2029 as official estimates are updated each year.[24]

Social Security's Financial Condition Calculated in Perpetuity

Although seventy-five years is considered to be the standard budget window for assessing Social Security's financial condition, the trustees have begun publishing the infinite-horizon OGL estimate of the program's unfunded obligation since 2003—one that calculates the present value of future financial shortfalls in perpetuity.[25] The infinite-horizon OGL has many advantages and disadvantages over its seventy-five-year counterpart. The advantages are that it comprehensively reflects the implications of the current rules for a program that in principle is intended to last forever. It also avoids underestimation of the program's total obligation under the seventy-five-year OGL estimate, which includes payroll taxes during the seventy-five-year window but excludes the post-seventy-fifth-year benefit obligations created for those taxpayers. Ignoring the program's financial shortfalls after seventy-five years is tantamount to implicitly—but inappropriately—assuming a balanced outlook after the seventy-fifth year. Alternatively, truncating the estimates after-seventy-five years implies an infinite discount rate on post-seventy-fifth year benefits, whereas a more gradual reduction in the weight attached to out-year net obligations—by simply continuing to compound the discount factor—seems to be more appropriate. The disadvantages of the infinite-horizon imbalance calculations are that many people do not comprehend the relevance of such a long time horizon and believe that uncertainty about the future is so large as to render that estimate useless for policymaking. However, the key and policy-relevant advantage of the infinite-horizon metric is that it avoids underrepresentation of the program's total imbalance and enables an apples-to-apples comparison of alternative reform plans, because some plans may shift more of the program underfunding beyond the seventy-fifth year than others. The best solution, then, is to report both the seventy-five-year and the infinite-horizon metrics.[26]

As I have argued elsewhere, the infinite-horizon open-group metric alone is insufficient to fully reflect Social Security's financial condition.[27] The addition of the complementary closed-group liability (CGL) measure is necessary. The CGL is the contribution to the OGL obligation by past generations and all currently alive individuals—that is, it excludes Social Security's transactions (payroll taxes and benefit payments) with future generations. Since OGL encompasses the net contribution of all generations (past, present, and future) and the CGL encompasses the net contribution of only the past and current

Table 3.2
DEMSIM's Optimistic, Baseline, and Pessimistic Projections of Social Security's Financial Condition through Perpetuity

		Optimistic	Baseline	Pessimistic
Long-term discount rate assumption (percent)		3.6	2.9	2.1
		Billions of Constant 2006 Dollars Present Values over Seventy-Five Years		
1	OASI projected benefits	50,691	45,805	48,840
2	OASI projected tax receipts	41,463	30,778	26,605
3	OASI total projected imbalance (1 – 2)	9,228	15,027	22,235
4	Current OASI trust fund	1,663	1,663	1,663
6	Open group liability (OGL; 3 - 4 + 5)	7,565	13,364	20,572
7	Total future payrolls	378,682	281,064	242,943
8	Closed group liability	9,540	14,172	20,179
		Percent		
9	OGL/Payrolls ([6/7] × 100)	2.00	4.75	8.47
10	OGL/Tax Receipts ([6/2] × 100)	18.25	43.42	77.32
11	OGL/Benefits ([6/1] × 100)	14.92	29.18	42.12

Source: Gokhale (2010) and author's calculations.

generations, the difference between them isolates the net contribution of future generations. Thus, the two metrics reflect the program's total fiscal imbalance (OGL) and its distribution along broad generational lines (CGL and OGL–CGL).

Table 3.2 shows that OASI's baseline infinite-horizon OGL is 4.8 percent as of the base year of DEMSIM's projections (2006). Eliminating the infinite-horizon OGL therefore requires an immediate and permanent increase in payroll taxes of 4.8 percent, or by 43 percent of all future OASI tax receipts (including future income taxes on OASI benefits). Alternatively, OASI benefits would have to be reduced, immediately and permanently, by 29 percent.

Table 3.2 also shows OASI's closed-group liability. At $14.2 trillion, the CGL is larger than the infinite-horizon OGL ($13.4 trillion). That means DEMSIM estimates that past and currently alive generations (as of 2006) would receive OASI benefits in excess of their Social Security tax payments during their lifetimes to the tune of $14.2 trillion. Because this amount is more than total excess OASI benefits being promised to all generations (past, present, and future)—the OGL of $13.4 trillion—it implies that future generations will collectively pay $0.8 trillion more in payroll taxes over their lifetimes than they would receive in lifetime OASI benefits (both measured in constant 2006 dollars as a present discounted value as of 2006).

If preserving current Social Security tax and benefit rules for those now alive promises to award excess benefits of $14.2 trillion to past and living generations, that excess must be paid for by future generations. That is, preserving current Social Security rules for current generations promises to bequeath an additional fiscal burden of $13.4 trillion to future generations, increasing their total fiscal burden on account of OASI from $0.8 trillion to $14.2 trillion.

Finally, at $14.2 trillion, the CGL is also much larger than the OASI trust fund, which equaled $1.7 trillion in 2006. Thus, public policy pronouncements frequently aired by Social Security's political supporters—that the "many billions" in the program's trust fund means that its finances are "secure"—ring rather hollow when the trust fund is juxtaposed against the amount required to fully fund the program's benefit obligations to today's generations—an additional $12.5 trillion. Continuing the status quo in Social Security policies would make the program's obligations to current generations firmer. Hence, it would also make the imposition of larger fiscal burdens on future generations more certain.

Projections of Social Security's Annual Cash Flow Imbalances

Present value imbalances between projected revenues and expenditures inform us about the program's overall financial condition but do not reveal the time profile of annual deficits. Obviously, the closer in time that annual imbalances are projected to emerge, the more urgent would be the need to restore financial solvency through policy changes. Social Security's seventy-five-year annual imbalances profile—the difference in annual noninterest expenditures and annual tax receipts under DEMSIM's baseline projections—is shown in figure 3.4. Annual imbalances increase rapidly through about 2040, but the rate of growth slows and becomes negative as reductions in benefit expenditures from dying baby boomers outpaces expenditure increases from progressively longer-lived retirees.

Once the boomers pass away, however, annual imbalances resume an upward trajectory because of continuing increases in longevity that are built into the Social Security Administration's mortality projections. Around 2035, when most retirees are baby boomers, annual imbalances are projected to rise to almost 6 percent of annual payrolls. Toward the

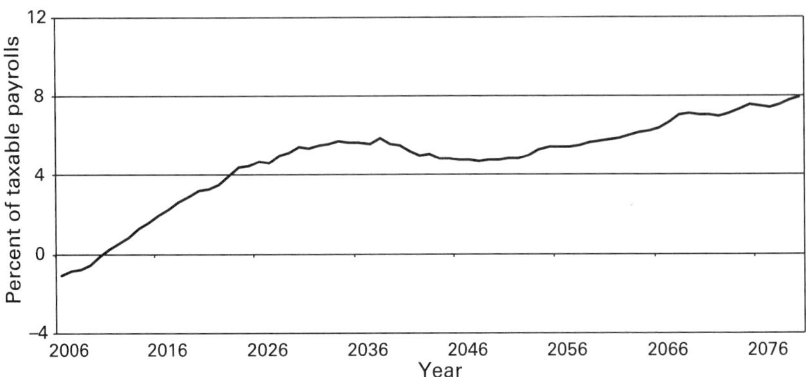

Figure 3.4
Social Security's Annual Cash Flow Imbalances under DEMSIM's Baseline Projections.
Source: Gokhale (2010).

end of the seventy-five-year horizon, DEMSIM projects annual imbalances to be 8 percent of annual payrolls. As table 3.1 shows, however, the average tax rate increase required to close the seventy-five-year funding gap equals 3.4 percent of payrolls.

Micromeasures of Social Security's Fiscal Burdens

Social Security's taxes and benefits affect individuals' budgets each year. Because it is a lifetime program, affecting disposable incomes for those working and those retired, it is important to evaluate those effects under current Social Security policies and under alternative reforms. The two key micrometrics employed here are the Social Security lifetime net tax rate and its retirement wealth metric. The lifetime net tax rate is the excess of lifetime payroll taxes paid over lifetime benefits received, calculated as a share of a person's lifetime earnings. This is the pure tax component of payroll taxes surrendered to the government through (forced) participation in Social Security. The term *lifetime* summarizes the fact that all items are calculated as present discount values as of each person's year of birth.[28]

The retirement wealth metric equals lifetime Social Security benefits received as a share of lifetime earnings. It is the amount of lifetime earnings projected to be devoted through Social Security to pay for retirees' and survivors' expenses under current laws. The two micrometrics under DEMSIM's baseline projections are shown in table 3.3 for fifteen-year birth cohorts among post–World War II (postwar)

Table 3.3
Lifetime Net Tax Rate and Retirement Wealth under Scheduled and Payable Benefits by Fifteen-Year Birth Cohorts

Fifteen-Year Cohort Birth Years	Lifetime Net Tax Rate	Lifetime Scheduled Benefit Rate	Lifetime Payable Benefit Rate
1946–60	5.08	4.08	3.81
1961–75	6.10	3.93	2.87
1976–90	6.11	3.85	2.48
1991–2005	6.14	3.77	2.24
2006–20	6.06	3.81	2.10
2021–35	5.93	3.86	2.07
2036–50	5.78	3.92	2.11

Source: Gokhale (2010).

generations.[29] Because future benefits are not fully funded out of the existing trust fund plus projected tax receipts, two versions of the retirement wealth metric are shown: one under present-law scheduled benefits and one under payable benefits, given projected tax receipts.

Table 3.3 shows that participation in Social Security imposes a significant fiscal burden on postwar generations. Those born before 1960 (most of the baby boomers) are projected to pay the smallest lifetime net tax rates—just over 5 percent of the present value of lifetime earnings calculated as of their years of birth. Lifetime net tax rates are projected to increase for those born after 1960 through the 1991–2005 birth cohort, peaking at 6.14 percent. These generations paid—and will pay—higher payroll taxes than their predecessors, but their benefit increases will be considerably less rapid than those of the first postwar cohort shown. Under current tax and benefit schedules that are incorporated in DEMSIM's baseline projections, most of those born in this century (2006 and later) will experience declining lifetime net tax rates as they enjoy successively longer retirement and benefit collection life spans.

In table 3.3, the retirement wealth metrics show that for successive generations, the gap between retirement wealth on a scheduled basis and that on a payable basis grows wider. This is consistent with figure 3.4, which shows an increasing gap between annual revenues and expenditures except for a brief period of decline during the 2040s. It shows that payable retirement wealth is a smaller fraction of lifetime earnings for those born later in time. Indeed, the gap between scheduled and payable retirement wealth increases consistently for successive birth cohorts. On a payable basis, Social Security sets aside about

3 percent of lifetime earnings for retirement for those born shortly after 1960, but that share declines to 2 percent for those born after 2005.

Evaluating Social Security Reforms

Given that Social Security policy changes are unavoidable, how should we choose between the myriad Social Security reform proposals that have been proposed? Each such reform proposal includes several reform elements encompassing changes to both Social Security taxes and benefits. And all such proposals affect the future finances of retirees, workers, and future generations; men and women; high and low earners; whites and minorities; and recipients of different types of Social Security benefits differently.

Social Security reform elements are of two major types—those primarily seeking to improve the program's financial solvency and those focused on alternative goals—to achieve a better distribution of taxes and benefits, reduce government control over retirement saving through privatization, secure greater benefits for survivors to avoid poverty among the very old, improve work incentives, and so on. Policy changes that are primarily motivated by nonsolvency-related objectives seek to exploit the opportunity presented by the fact that the program must be reformed because it is approaching insolvency quite rapidly. Including both types of policy changes in reform proposals, as is done in all of the reform proposals evaluated using DEMSIM, is justified because although the program's proponents tout its social insurance benefits and poverty reduction among retirees, it also exerts ancillary effects that are economically undesirable.[30]

Six Social Security reform proposals are selected for evaluation using DEMSIM's simulation and projection of future U.S. demographic and economic features. They are among the most frequently cited reform proposals from across the political spectrum—two of them popular among political liberals, two among centrists, and two by politically conservative analysts. Taken together, the proposals cover almost all specific reform options that have been proposed to date, ranging from dedicating new revenues to Social Security to diverting ("carving out") existing payroll taxes to create personal Social Security accounts.

Social Security's actuaries regularly score program reforms proposed by lawmakers and others. Their evaluations, which are publicly available, are based on the trustees' cell-based methodology.[31] The six reform proposals considered here are evaluated under DEMSIM in a detailed manner, closely incorporating all of the features included in each proposal. Ancillary calculations are implemented as required to estimate the parameters controlling changes to Social Security's tax and benefit rules as specified in the proposals.[32]

Closer examination of these six Social Security reform proposals using DEMSIM reveals many interesting features and effects, in both the aggregate and by population subgroups. Some proposals that are touted to restore financial solvency to Social Security actually change the program's financial shortfalls by very little. Others touted to be "balanced" turn out to be significantly liberal leaning in their effects and involve steep increases in fiscal burdens on future generations. Only two of the proposals deliver what their proponents claim: one offers a reasonably balanced outcome despite introducing individual accounts, and the other offers a sizable reduction in the program's financial shortfalls, mostly through staggered future reductions in benefit growth.

Features of Reform Proposals Evaluated

The reform proposals selected for evaluation include two by politically liberal proponents. I report only the macro long-range solvency outcomes from DEMSIM's evaluation.[33] The first proposal, by Robert Ball (commissioner of Social Security during the Kennedy, Johnson, and Nixon administrations), operates exclusively on the system's revenues and asset income. Its features include increasing Social Security's taxable maximum earnings limit so that 90 percent of wage earnings are subject to the OASI payroll tax; dedicating all estate tax revenues to Social Security; and investing the Social Security trust fund in private securities to continually increase it, thereby avoiding large future increases in payroll tax rates.

The second liberal proposal, by Peter Diamond and Peter Orszag, targets four main objectives: to counter forces such as increasing longevity that are pushing the system toward insolvency; combat increasing economic inequality; distribute equitably the "legacy debt" generated by generous benefit awards to Social Security's early participants; and strengthen the program's social insurance functions.

Centrist proposals combine reform elements from liberal and conservative proposals in a reasonably balanced manner. One of the centrist proposals evaluated here is by former members of the U.S. House of Representatives, Jim Kolbe (R-AZ), Charles Stenholm (D-TX), and Allen Boyd (D-FL). It has the primary objective of achieving financial solvency for Social Security through a balanced collection of tax- and benefit-side reform measures. The proposal contains fourteen reform elements that alter the program's tax and benefit rules and introduces Social Security personal accounts.

The second centrist proposal evaluated is by academic economists and think-tank analysts Jeffrey Liebman, Maya MacGuineas, and Andrew Samwick, who have (separately) served in both Democratic and Republican administrations. Their proposal also aims to achieve program solvency over-seventy-five years by seeking compromise between liberal and conservative principles in reforming Social Security. It contains four elements: two for increasing the program's revenues, one to reduce future scheduled benefits, and one that introduces Social Security personal accounts.

Among conservative proposals, the first is by President George W. Bush's Commission to Strengthen Social Security. Its primary objective is to partially change the program's structure by introducing voluntary personal Social Security accounts—to move the program away from a government-operated system to one that enables citizens to own and self-direct investments for retirement financing according to their individual preferences and risk tolerances. The financial quid pro quo for diverting a part of payroll taxes into personal accounts would be an actuarially determined reduction in future benefits from the traditional Social Security system. Because the short-term cost increases are paid for during future decades, its financial effects continue well beyond seventy-five years, making the infinite-horizon OGL more suitable for a comprehensive evaluation of its financial implications—especially for ensuring an apples-to-apples comparison with other reform plans.

The second conservative plan evaluated here is by Congressman Paul Ryan, whose "Roadmap for America's Future" contains a detailed Social Security reform proposal. The Ryan proposal builds on the Bush commission's proposal by also introducing voluntary carve-out personal security accounts (PSA) for those younger than age fifty-five in 2009. It also adopts several measures to reduce the traditional system's scheduled benefits. PSA participants are guaranteed benefits equal to those they would receive under the reformed traditional system. This provision sets up a tension between providing a generous guarantee level to encourage participation in PSAs, but higher taxpayer costs if PSA returns turn out to be low for many participants. The evaluation of the Ryan reform proposal is implemented on the basis of average capital market returns, using the metrics described earlier, and does not tackle the difficult problem of estimating the cost of the proposal's PSA benefit guarantee.

Recall that DEMSIM's evaluation of these alternative Social Security reform proposals is executed under static projections—which is also true about the Social Security actuaries' evaluations of Social Security reform proposals. An evaluation under static projections implies that any behavioral responses by program participants to changes to Social Security's tax and benefit policies are not incorporated into the estimates. The reason for excluding such behavioral responses (even though they occur in reality) is that there is no consensus among economists on how to estimate and calibrate projection models to include behavioral feedbacks by the model's agents.[34]

Macrosolvency Effects: Seventy-Five-Year and Infinite-Horizon Measures

Long-term system solvency effects flowing from the six Social Security reform proposals are shown in table 3.4. The first row of the table shows estimates of the seventy-five-year and infinite-horizon open group imbalance estimates (as present discounted values in constant 2006 dollars) under DEMSIM's baseline. These two estimates show that limiting projections to just seventy-five years into the future would ignore about half of the total imbalance, much of it obligated by participants' payroll tax payments under Social Security–covered employment during the initial seventy-five years. The first row also shows the closed-group imbalance under current laws, indicating that past and current generations together account for more than the total projected financial imbalance.

Rows 2 through 7 of table 3.4 show those three metrics calculated for each of the six reform proposals in constant 2006 dollars. More informative, however, are the percent changes from DEMSIM's baseline values shown in columns 4 through 6 of table 3.4. Column 4 of the table shows the percentage change in the infinite-horizon imbalance achieved under each proposal, and column 5 shows the reduction in the infinite-horizon OGL accomplished within the first-seventy-five years. The last column of the table shows the reduction of the closed-group imbalance achieved by each reform proposal as a share of the infinite-horizon OGL under prereform (current) policies.[35] It shows the amount of the existing imbalance that will be eliminated by reducing the net excess benefits of past and current generations under prereform Social Security policies.

Table 3.4
Aggregate Effects of Alternative Social Security Reform Proposals on Program Solvency

			Seventy-Five-Year Open Group Imbalance	Infinite-Horizon Open Group Imbalance	Closed Group Imbalance	Change in ∞-Horizon Open Group Imbalance from Baseline	Change in 75-year Open Group Imbalance as a Percent of Baseline ∞-Horizon Imbalance	Change in Closed Group Imbalance as a Percent of Baseline ∞-Horizon Imbalance
			Billions of Constant 2006 Dollars[a]			Percent		
			1	2	3	4	5	6
1	DEMSIM baseline		6,985	13,364	14,172	..	..	..
	Present Value of Payrolls		208,495	281,064	145,572	..	..	..
	DEMSIM baseline as a percent of the present value of payrolls		3.4	4.8	9.7	..	..	..
2	Liberal	Ball	5,832	11415	14,046	−14.6	−8.7	−0.9
3		D-O	1,386	1,610	10,889	−88.0	−41.9	−24.6
4	Centrist	KSB	3,369	1,841	10,498	−86.2	−27.1	−27.5
5		LMS	2,120	2,446	9,364	−81.7	−36.4	−36.0
6	Conservative	Model 2	7,851	5,247	12,233	−60.7	6.5	−14.5
7		Ryan	4,661	-983	9,152	−107.4	−17.4	−37.6

a. Except when indicated in row heading.
Source: Gokhale (2010).

These three metrics show that Robert Ball's proposal achieves very little progress toward eliminating the program's total imbalance: it reduces the infinite-horizon imbalance by only 14.6 percent, with a little more than half of the change accomplished during the first seventy-five years. This result arises because the two revenue-increasing proposals—increasing the taxable ceiling to subject 90 percent of all wages to payroll taxes and dedicating estate taxes to Social Security—produce only small increases in revenues in the short term. Hence, the intended sustained expansion of the Social Security trust fund from investments in private capital markets does not occur: The small trust fund increase from additional revenues cannot leverage much additional asset earnings through investments in private capital markets. The failure to increase Social Security's revenues is traced to the meager contributions expected from estate taxes and to DEMSIM's baseline, which itself incorporates an increase in the share of total wages subject to payroll taxes in future years. Under DEMSIM, the prospective retirement of the baby boomers—the exit of such a large cohort from the highest-earning stage of their life cycle—reduces earnings inequality and induces an increase in the taxable share of earnings—from 85.6 percent to 88 percent. This leaves little additional space for further increases under the Ball proposal's 90 percent target for the taxable-to-total-earnings ratio. Hence, this policy generates little additional revenue in the short term. The Ball proposal also imposes a negligibly small cost on current generations: under it, the reduction of CGL is just 0.9 percent of the infinite-horizon OGL. These results suggest that the Ball proposal would mostly preserve the program's structural and financial status quo rather than move the program significantly toward financial solvency.

The Diamond-Orszag (D-O) proposal, in contrast, would cause a significant change in Social Security's infinite-horizon OGL: it would reduce it by 88 percent. However, less than half of that reduction would be achieved within the first seventy-five years.[36] Moreover, the CGL would be reduced by even less: just 25 percent of the infinite-horizon OGL. This proposal's good performance in reducing the infinite-horizon OGL but relatively poor performance on reducing it quickly, and its imposition of only a small reduction in present-law net excess benefits of today's older generations, arises because it predominantly operates on the tax rather than on the benefit side of the program's finances. The authors of the D-O proposal divide adjustments to counter increased longevity equally between increases in payroll taxes and reductions in scheduled benefits, but most of the adjustments relating to inequality and Social Security's legacy costs are implemented through tax increases. The D-O proposal implies steeply escalating lifetime net tax rates on today's young workers and future generations—those born after 1975. This reform approach therefore leaves current older generations relatively unharmed from policy changes for improving Social Security's financial condition.

When it was first publicized, the Kolbe-Stenholm-Boyd (KSB) proposal was viewed as a bipartisan approach to Social Security reform. Its authors are from the two major political parties with divergent views on Social Security policy and their reform proposal incorporates elements from across the political spectrum. The KSB reform proposal introduces carve-out Social Security personal accounts, which increase the program's deficits during early postreform years. Those deficits are offset, however, through reductions in scheduled benefits that become progressively larger for successive retiree generations. As a result, although these reforms achieve a significant reduction in the infinite-horizon OGL, only 27 percent of the reduction is achieved during the first seventy-five years. Moreover, the KSB proposal reduces the excess benefits of past and current generations by just 28 percent of the infinite-horizon OGL, only slightly larger than under the D-O proposal.

The Liebman-MacGuineas-Samwick (LMS) "nonpartisan" proposal also seeks to compromise between liberal and conservative reform principles by splitting the difference between tax increases and scheduled benefit reductions to improve Social Security's financial solvency. The personal accounts system introduced under this proposal includes equal measures of carve-out and add-on elements. The proposal's reform elements—increasing the taxable maximum earnings ceiling, accelerating increases in Social Security's normal retirement age, and altering benefit formulas to reduce scheduled benefits under the traditional Social Security system—yields an 82 percent reduction in the infinite-horizon imbalance. The LMS proposal also achieves 36 percent of the total change within the seventy-five-year time horizon and imposes 36 percent of the total OGL as an adjustment cost on current generations—larger than the D-O and KSB proposals. Thus, compared to the other reform proposals (Ball, D-O, and KSB). the LMS proposal is more balanced in its distribution of adjustment costs on current and future generations.

The. Bush commission's model 2 proposal is a quintessentially conservative Social Security reform proposal, serving as the basis for building many other conservative proposals. Like the centrist proposals (KSB and LMS), its personal accounts are voluntary. However, unlike the centrist plans, model 2 includes individual-specific offsets of future traditional benefits in exchange for participation in its exclusively carve-out personal accounts system. Usually proponents of Social Security personal accounts characterize the diversion of payroll taxes into personal accounts and of owning, directing, and potentially bequeathing one's own retirement assets as desirable features that participants would be willing to pay for. That presents an opportunity to improve Social Security's financial solvency by imposing a "haircut": a larger than actuarially fair offset of future traditional benefits in lieu of diverting payroll taxes into personal accounts. However, model 2 does the opposite: its benefit offset is designed to be smaller than actuarially fair through the use of an interest rate of 2 percent per year—smaller than the interest rate on long-term Treasury securities. The accumulated value of diverted payroll taxes through retirement—to be equated to the present value of future benefit offsets—would be smaller under a 2 percent accumulation rate than their actual accumulation even when invested in the least risky financial assets, such as U.S. Treasury securities. However, this transparent subsidy to personal account participants, designed to attract greater participation, retards progress toward making the Social Security system solvent.

Together with its other reform elements—reductions in scheduled Social Security benefits and benefit enhancements for certain low-income and vulnerable groups, model 2's reduction in the infinite-horizon OGL is smaller than under other reform proposals (except the Ball proposal)—61 percent. Indeed, assuming 100 percent participation in model 2's sizable and actuarially advantageous personal accounts generates large short-term deficits and a larger seventy-five-year OGL—by 6.5 percent of DEMSIM's baseline infinite-horizon OGL. Model 2 also performs relatively poorly on the fiscal discipline metric: its adjustment cost on current generations is just 15 percent of baseline infinite horizon OGL—mostly by way of reductions in traditional benefits imposed on those alive near the end of the seventy-five-year projection horizon.

The Ryan reform proposal is even more ambitious than model 2 in implementing voluntary Social Security personal accounts—starting small but gradually increasing the share of current law payroll taxes that would be diverted into personal accounts. The payroll taxes that are diverted to personal accounts would be offset on an actuarially fair basis by reducing participants' traditional benefits. Under the Ryan proposal, participants who accrue very low or negative cumulative returns on their personal accounts by their desired retirement age are guaranteed to receive at least the benefits provided by the postreform traditional Social Security system. The benefit guarantee would be based on the presumption that such beneficiaries never participated in personal accounts. For those choosing not to participate in the personal accounts system, traditional benefits would be reduced gradually by shifting to a consumer-price-indexed rather than a wage-indexed benefit formula—implying progressively larger cuts to current law scheduled benefits for successive retiree cohorts. The proposal also broadens Social Security's payroll tax base by subjecting employer health insurance payments to payroll taxes.

The gradual but eventually substantial reduction in traditional benefits and large size of personal accounts implies that the Ryan proposal would more than eliminate the program's total financial imbalance calculated in perpetuity. Indeed, assuming 100 percent participation in personal accounts, the proposal, if sustained over many decades, would eliminate Social Security's OGL. But a very small portion of the reduction—just 17 percent—would be achieved during the first seventy-five years.

However, the Ryan reform is the most fiscally responsible among those evaluated here—its reduction of the CGL equals 38 percent of the infinite horizon OGL. The key factor that explains the difference in the effect under the seventy-five-year open-group imbalance versus the closed-group imbalance is the diversion of payroll taxes by future generations among those alive within the first seventy-five years. Their benefit reductions occur mostly outside the seventy-five-year horizon, but their payroll tax diversions, which are larger than those of currently alive generations, dampen the imbalance-reducing effect under the seventy-five-year OGL measure. Note that future generations' payroll tax diversions are not included under the closed-group imbalance calculation.[37]

Macrosolvency Effects: Annual Imbalance Ratios

As noted above, seventy-five-year and infinite-horizon OGL measures inform about the program's financial condition, but do not reveal the timing of when or how rapidly deficits would emerge in the future.

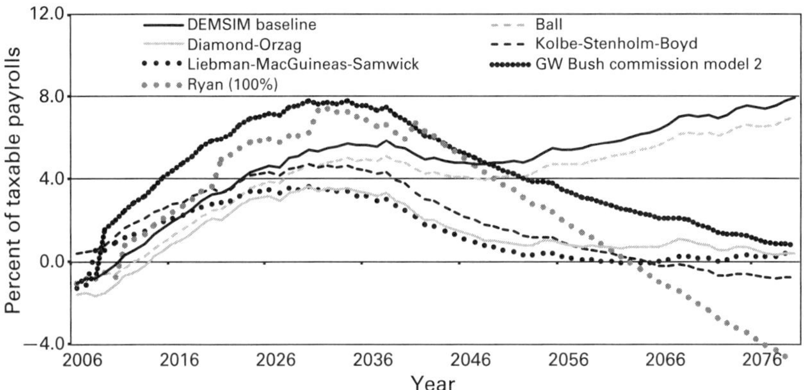

Figure 3.5
Annual Imbalance Ratios: DEMSIM Baseline and Alternative Reform Proposals.
Source: Gokhale (2010).

Figure 3.5 shows the trajectory of Social Security's annual noninterest cash flow deficits—the excess of benefit expenditures over noninterest receipts—for DEMSIM's baseline and the six alternative reform proposals. Comparison across the alternative trajectories reveals several noteworthy features: the proposals that create carve-out personal accounts (KSB, LMS, model 2, and Ryan) produce larger deficits during the initial years after the reforms are implemented. The Ryan proposal's expansion of the payroll tax base to employer health insurance premium payments causes short-term surpluses, increasing medium-term deficits as the proposal's personal account system grows larger and more payroll taxes are diverted from the traditional system during the 2030s, but much smaller longer-term deficits than under DEMSIM's baseline annual deficit trajectory. The projections show that larger annual deficits under model 2 and Ryan proposals from sizable payroll tax diversions into personal accounts would last through the middle of this century. All proposals generate smaller long-term Social Security deficits compared to DEMSIM's baseline, and annual deficits are eventually significantly smaller under all but the Ball proposal.

The Ball and Ryan proposals are polar opposites. Under the Ryan personal accounts proposal, assuming 100 percent participation, Social Security's annual imbalances are eliminated by 2060. Annual imbalances under the Ball proposal, however, are only slightly smaller compared to the DEMSIM's baseline, showing that it does relatively little to improve the system's short- and long-term solvency.

An interesting feature of figure 3.5 is that annual imbalance trajectories under the Liebman-MacGuineas-Samwick and Diamond-Orszag proposals are quite close to each other, reflecting similarity in their reductions to the OGL. However, the two proposals are very different in their impact on current and future generations—as discussed in the next section.

Microeffects: Lifetime Net Tax Rates and Social Security Retirement Wealth

One of the important issues relating to Social Security reform is the impact of alternative policies on population subgroups. The subgroups can be constructed along many dimensions—gender, race, earnings levels, birth-cohort affiliation, and so on. Comparing the lifetime net tax rate and retirement wealth metrics for population subgroups under continuation of baseline policies and under alternative reforms can inform policymakers about key trade-offs—how those groups would be affected under a policy of maintaining the status quo versus implementing a particular reform.

The traditional micrometric used in such evaluations is the annual replacement rate, which measures the percentage of annual preretirement earnings replaced by Social Security benefits each year. Unfortunately, the replacement rate is not as relevant or important today because retirement life spans have lengthened differentially for different population groups. People with different attributes—race, gender, education, and career earning levels—now experience systematic differences in retirement and survival rates, implying that their lifetime treatment under Social Security should be the primary focus when evaluating the program's microlevel effects. Unfortunately, lifetime micromeasures are not reported by Social Security's trustees. Their micrometrics are limited to replacement rates calculated for stylized low, median, average, and maximum earners—with career-earning profiles that are not necessarily representative of any particular population group.

The discussion here is limited to the effects of five alternative proposals on a fifteen-year birth-cohort basis—the Ball proposal is dropped because it includes no changes to Social Security's current tax and benefit policies. Table 3.5 shows the results, beginning with the postwar birth cohort (those born in the years 1946 to 1960) through those born toward the middle of this century (2036 to 2050). The first panel of table 3.5 reports lifetime net tax rates under DEMSIM's baseline and under five alternative reform proposals.

Table 3.5
Financial Effects of Implementing Social Security Reforms by Fifteen-Year Birth Cohorts

Birth Cohort	DEMSIM Baseline	D-O	KSB	LMS	Model 2	Ryan
Panel 1	Lifetime net tax rate (%)					
1946–60	5.1	5.1	5.2	5.5	5.0	5.2
1961–75	6.1	6.5	5.9	6.6	5.9	6.6
1976–90	6.1	7.0	5.6	6.6	5.3	7.0
1991–2005	6.1	7.8	5.7	6.5	4.8	6.8
2006–20	6.1	8.7	5.8	6.5	4.7	6.5
2021–35	5.9	9.5	5.8	6.4	4.8	6.5
2036–50	5.8	10.1	5.8	6.4	5.0	6.8
Panel 2	Total Social Security (payable + IA) Wealth as a Share of Lifetime Earnings (%)[a]					
1946–60	3.4	4.0	3.1	3.3	2.6	3.0
1961–75	2.7	3.4	3.0	3.2	2.4	2.3
1976–90	2.6	3.3	3.3	3.8	2.9	2.7
1991–2005	2.3	3.2	3.2	3.8	3.3	2.9
2006–20	2.2	3.1	3.1	3.7	3.4	2.9
2021–35	2.1	3.1	3.1	3.7	3.3	3.0
2036–50	2.1	3.2	3.1	3.7	3.1	3.1
Panel 3	Share of Traditional Benefits in Social Security Wealth (%)[a]					
1946–60	100.0	100.0	94.0	93.8	94.7	98.0
1961–75	100.0	100.0	78.0	76.3	73.8	82.4
1976–90	100.0	100.0	65.3	61.7	52.8	57.4
1991–2005	100.0	100.0	60.7	57.2	41.8	29.3
2006–20	100.0	100.0	61.0	56.9	38.2	6.7
2021–35	100.0	100.0	61.0	56.9	35.7	0.1
2036–50	100.0	100.0	61.4	57.5	32.0	0.0
Panel 4	Total Payable Retirement Wealth as a Share of Current Law Scheduled Benefit (%)[a]					
1946–60	82.7	96.4	73.6	80.9	61.2	98.3
1961–75	68.3	86.3	74.5	82.9	59.3	91.9
1976–90	66.0	85.2	83.9	97.3	75.4	81.7
1991–2005	60.7	83.5	81.4	100.0	85.6	76.8
2006–20	56.9	81.2	80.0	97.0	87.8	76.2
2021–35	54.8	79.6	78.3	94.3	84.8	77.3
2036–50	54.7	80.4	77.9	93.8	78.7	78.2

a. Percent as of each person's benefit collection year. Assumes 100 percent participation in personal accounts systems under KSB, LMS, model 2, and Ryan reform proposals.
Source: Gokhale (2010).

The most salient feature of the first panel of table 3.5 is the rapid and significant increases in lifetime net tax rates for successive birth cohorts under the D-O reform proposal compared with DEMSIM's baseline and the remaining four reform proposals. Under the D-O proposal, those born during the middle of this century would face net tax rates equaling more than 10 percent of their lifetime earnings—the result of closing Social Security's financial imbalance mainly through tax increases on future generations. Indeed, the extension of additional retirement support while emphasizing tax-side changes to improve the system's finances enables increases in payable retirement wealth of early-born generations under the D-O reform compared with DEMSIM's baseline, as shown in the second panel of table 3.5. The retirement wealth of even early postwar birth cohorts is increased under the D-O proposal from its benefit enhancements to "strengthen social insurance" objective. These results confirm the strong politically liberal orientation of the D-O reform proposal.

In contrast, the other four proposals do not show significant deviations from DEMSIM's baseline lifetime net tax rates. Among the two centrist proposals, the KSB proposal imposes a smaller lifetime net tax rate than the LMS proposal, because the former predominantly relies on both benefit and tax-side changes to reduce Social Security's financial imbalance, whereas the latter partially funds personal accounts through additional contributions. Among the two conservative proposals, model 2 reduces lifetime tax rates by more than all of the five proposals considered here because of its significant diversion of payroll taxes into personal accounts. The Ryan proposal also includes a large personal accounts system, but those accounts are introduced gradually and the proposal broadens the payroll tax base to increase lifetime net tax rates, especially for those born toward the middle of this century.

It is noteworthy that lifetime net tax rates are significantly higher under the D-O proposal compared with the LMS proposal, despite the roughly similar trajectories of annual imbalances that these two proposals generate (see figure 3.5). This means that depending exclusively on aggregative measures to compare reform proposals—for example, the amounts by which OGLs and annual imbalances are reduced through particular reforms—would be inadequate for comprehensively assessing their effects.

All of the five reform proposals analyzed in table 3.5 have higher levels of "payable" retirement wealth from Social Security compared to DEMSIM's baseline. It is also noteworthy that reforms involving personal accounts result in comparable levels of retirement wealth levels, on average, compared to those under the D-O proposal, which does not create personal accounts. Indeed, retirement wealth levels are consistently larger for those born after 1975 under the LMS proposal compared to the D-O proposal.

The third panel of table 3.5 shows the percentage share of retirement wealth arising from traditional Social Security benefits, with the remainder provided out of personal accounts. Of course, traditional system benefits account for 100 percent of benefits under DEMSIM's baseline and under the D-O reform proposal. Among the other four reform proposals shown in table 3.5, each of which involves personal accounts, the two centrist proposals generate approximately 60 percent of Social Security benefits (including retirement, survivor, dependent, and children's benefits) from the traditional system, on average, for successive birth cohorts through the mid-twenty-first century. The share of traditional benefits is much smaller under model 2's reforms, approaching 30 percent for those born during the middle of this century. The traditional benefit share declines rapidly for those born after 2006 under the Ryan proposal, becoming zero for those born after 2035. Thus, in terms of changing the structure of Social Security through personal accounts, the reform proposals analyzed here broadly adhere to their political labels as liberal, centrist, and conservative.

The last panel of table 3.5 shows the extent to which the five reform proposals strengthen Social Security. The metric for this is the amount by which retirement wealth is increased from the payable level under DEMSIM's baseline and moved closer toward its scheduled level. The first column of this panel shows the gap between the payable and scheduled retirement wealth levels under DEMSIM's baseline projections. For those born during the mid-twenty-first century, current payroll tax rules would finance only slightly more than 50 percent of current law scheduled benefits. The other columns show that all five reform proposals increase retirement security by increasing the payable levels of retirement wealth for successive cohorts under their rules. The results show that all proposals involving personal accounts provide similar increases in retirement wealth as under the D-O reform proposal. Indeed, among the five reform proposals, the LMS proposal's average payable retirement wealth comes closest to the scheduled level under today's Social Security rules.[38]

Conclusion

Social Security's finances have been worsening for two decades, and this trend appears to have been accelerated by the recession of 2007–2009. The 2012 annual report of the Social Security trustees showed acceleration in the worsening of the program's financial condition. Social Security's finances may improve once the economy and tax collections recover, but chances that we will witness economic growth rapid enough to eliminate the need to reform the program appear to be very small. Policymakers should have available accurate information about the program's financial future under current laws and under alternative reforms. Providing such information is a key duty of the program's trustees, but their reports are based on decades-old methods for projecting the system's finances. Program officials have been extremely slow in developing and incorporating recent advances in making future budget projections, especially in adopting microsimulation methods for broadening our understanding of how current demographic and economic trends will evolve. Indeed, even those charged with the responsibility of evaluating and recommending the adoption of better projection methods—such as the 2011 Technical Panel on Assumptions and Methods—have not made a critical assessment of the trustees' current projection methods.

The most serious shortcoming in the trustees' methodology is the independent derivation of assumptions prior to combining them to derive outcomes. That means that assumptions on key variables—labor productivity, payrolls, benefits, and so on—are based almost exclusively on historical averages and not conditioned on projected demographic outcomes. That introduces a significant potential for the trustees' prior economic assumptions to be incongruous with features of the future U.S. population, leading to a high likelihood of making nontrivial errors in projecting Social Security's financial condition under given tax and benefit policies—whether the current ones or those specified under a particular reform proposal. A simple example is the assumption by the trustees of constant labor productivity growth over seventy-five years into the future (after a short initial adjustment period between observed rates and their "ultimate assumption")—which is obviously divorced from the likely evolution of the population's future attributes, especially those closely associated with labor productivity growth. Newer techniques involving microsimulation methods organized under an economic growth model framework allow a more coherent specification and development of assumptions and outcomes. Such methods, far from being a black box, can help illuminate key aspects of demographic and economic projections that carry forward the momentum of demographic and economic forces built into the current population and economy.

Implementation of an independent microsimulation, DEMSIM, to capture and project U.S. demographic and economic forces into the future reveals several interesting features. In particular, it shows that the future evolution of many individual attributes, such as education, marital status, labor force attachments, and education, on balance are likely to reduce future labor quality. Thus, although future technological improvements and increases in capital per worker will increase labor productivity, a decline in labor quality is likely to impose a significant drag on future labor productivity growth. DEMSIM's simulations also show that although earning inequality will increase secularly in the long term, it may increase slowly, and perhaps even decline initially, as the baby boomers transition from their years of highest life cycle productivity and earnings into retirement. This could increase the share of Social Security's taxable-to-total-earnings ratio and would accelerate the trajectory of Social Security benefit expenditures relative to its tax receipts during the next few years.

Using DEMSIM to evaluate selected Social Security reforms from across the political spectrum—liberal, centrist, and conservative—reveals significant differences in their impact on the program's seventy-five-year solvency and long-term sustainability. The plans that are evaluated using DEMSIM also differ in the extent to which they impose adjustment costs on living generations as opposed to future ones, the amount by which they increase lifetime net tax rates on various cohorts by birth, and the amount of retirement wealth and security that they would provide compared to the program's current rules. Reporting on Social Security's financial condition and on the impact of alternative reforms using such comprehensive long-term macrometrics and lifetime micromeasures should be standard practice adopted by the program's trustees and actuaries, but for some unfathomable reason, it is not.

References

Biggs, Andrew, and Jagadeesh Gokhale. 2007. Wage Growth and the Measurement of Social Security's Financial Condition. In *Government Spending on the Elderly*, edited by Dimitri B. Papadimitriou, 272–306. New York: Palgrave Macmillan.

Crippen, Dan L. 2002. *Federal Budget Estimating. Testimony, May 9.* Washington, DC: U.S. House of Representatives, Subcommittee on Legislative and Budget Process Committee on Rules.

Danziger, Sheldon, Robert H. Haveman, and Robert Plotnick. 1981. How Income Transfer Programs Affect Work, Savings and Income Distribution: A Critical Review. *Journal of Economic Literature* 19 (3): 975–1014.

Gokhale, Jagadesesh. 2010. *Social Security: A Fresh Look at Policy Alternatives.* Chicago: University of Chicago Press.

Gokhale, Jagadeesh, Laurence J. Kotlikoff, and John Sabelhaus. 1996. Understanding the Decline in National Saving: A Cohort Analysis. *Brookings Papers on Economic Activity* (Winter): 315–407.

Gokhale, Jagadeesh, and Kent Smetters. 2003. *Fiscal and Generational Imbalances: New Budget Measures for New Budget Priorities.* Washington, DC: AEI Press.

Gokhale, Jagadeesh, and Kent Smetters, 2006. *Measuring Social Security's Financial Outlook within an Aging Society.* Dœdalus (Winter): *91–104.*

Gruber, Jonathan, and David A. Wise, eds. 2007. *Social Security Programs and Retirement around the World: Fiscal Implications of Reform.* Chicago: University of Chicago Press.

Jorgenson, Dale W., Mun S. Ho, and Kevin J. Stiroh. 2007. *A Retrospective Look at U.S. Productivity Growth Resurgence.* New York: Federal Reserve Bank of New York. http://www.newyorkfed.org/research/staff_reports/sr277.pdf.

Social Security Administration. 2011. *Long-Range OASDI Projection Methodology.* Washington, DC: Office of the Chief Actuary, Social Security Administration. http://www.ssa.gov/OACT/TR/2011/documentation_2011

Social Security Administration. 2013a. *Social Security Basic Facts.* Washington, DC: Social Security Administration, http://www.ssa.gov/pressoffice/basicfact.htm.

Social Security Administration. 2013b. *The 2013 Annual Report of the Board of Trustees of the Federal Old-Age and Survivors Insurance and Federal Disability Insurance Trust Funds.* Washington, DC: Social Security Administration. http://www.ssa.gov/OACT/TR/2013/tr2013.pdf.

Discussion

Henry J. Aaron

Jagadeesh Gokhale is a member of the small band of scholars who devote themselves in a serious way to the economic analysis of Social Security. He has developed a detailed empirical model for analyzing the long-term effects of the current system and of various alternatives. His goal as expressed through this model is to avoid what he contends are serious analytic shortcomings of the methods used by the Office of the Actuary (OACT). His alternative projections of Social Security's future differ in important ways from OACT's. He then uses the model to compare the effectiveness of six reform proposals in closing the long-term funding gap, measured in alternative ways. He also estimates the impacts on successive age cohorts of the current system and of the alternative plans. His discussion joins a lengthy list of serious papers that Gokhale has written alone and with coauthors on a difficult and important subject. As such, it merits respectful attention and careful review.

As we all know, the results generated by complex models can—and do—depend, often quite sensitively, on specifications about which there is no single indisputably correct approach and no growth rate that can be projected without error. That means that however, much faith the author may have in the rightness of the simulation results, the rest of us may be excused if we take the results less seriously. The results that Gokhale reports differ in major ways not only from those of OACT but also from those generated by other econometric models.

That brings me to Gokhale's quite severe critique of the methods employed by the Office of the Actuary. I believe that those criticisms are seriously unfair in two ways—one procedural and one substantive. First, OACT's methods have for decades been subject to careful review by technical panels similar to the one he helped select. Previous panels,

Table 3.6
Projection Errors, 1983–2012

Type of Assumption	Contribution to Balance	Balance
Projected balance in 1983 (1983–2058)		+0.02
Legislation	+0.16	
Demographic assumptions	+0.23`	
Disability assumptions	–0.78	
Economic assumptions	–0.75	
Methods and all other	+0.18	
Subtotal of effects	–0.94	–0.92
Valuation period	–1.78	
Total effect	–2.72	
Projected balance in 2013 (2013–2088)		–2.72

not just this one, have included leading economists, actuaries, and demographers. OACT has responded to many of their comments, although not to all. On balance, all of the technical panels, including the one that Gokhale helped select, have concluded that OACT has done a responsible job. It should not be a source of concern that the actuaries have stuck to the approaches used by actuaries and have not shifted to methods taught in graduate economics departments.

In support of his charge that the methods used by the Office of the Actuary are flawed, Gokhale notes that projected balance has deteriorated since 1983. The 1983 projections showed that the system would be in balance for seventy-five years. Projections in 2013 now show a deficit of 2.72 percent of payroll and indicate that the trust fund will be exhausted by 2033. There is something to this criticism; but not much, as indicated in table 3.6. It shows that nearly two-thirds of the change in the trust fund balance results from the way the law was designed in 1983, not from substantive revisions.

In 1983, Congress set in place a tax and benefit schedule that generated surpluses in the early years of the seventy-five-year projection period. These early surpluses were almost precisely offset by deficits in the later years. Succeeding seventy-five-year projection windows contained successively fewer surplus years and successively more deficit years. The year in which the combined OASDI trust funds are projected to be exhausted has actually been pushed back over the past eighteen years, from 2030 to 2033.

The design of the legislation enacted in 1983 was flawed, in my view, and should not be repeated in future legislation. But Gokhale is criticizing the actuaries' estimates, not program design. He says that their methods doom them to large errors. Maybe, but the past record is not bad. As the table shows, the economic and disability assumptions made in 1983 were a bit too optimistic. But whose economic assumptions weren't? The actuaries' legislative assumptions were not far off. Their demographic assumptions were a bit too pessimistic because they did not anticipate that increases in female longevity would stop, a continuing puzzlement to demographers.

It is true that the Great Recession worsened Social Security's projected imbalance. But the long-term funding gap projected in 1997 was only a bit smaller than the gap projected today, and the trust fund was projected to be exhausted three years earlier than it is today. Projections since then have shown no trend, despite the steady drag of the worsening projection period. In other words, for better or for worse, according to the cash-in/cash-out methods used by the Social Security actuaries, things have not changed much in seventeen years. The most striking feature of projections over the past seventeen years is not that things have gotten worse, but that they have not gotten worse.

One minor point: Gokhale says that OASI revenues began to fall short of benefit expenditures in 2010. That is false. Social Security revenue includes interest earnings on accumulated reserves. In 2010 the OASI system ran a surplus of $122.6 billion, which is shown by the fact that reserves rose by that amount. Social Security revenues are projected to continue to exceed outlays until 2020, which is why Social Security reserves are projected to rise an additional $159 billion between 2013 and 2020.

Let me turn now to Gokhale's specific criticisms of estimation methods. Some are matters of style—the difference between methods routinely used by actuaries and by economists. More substantively, Gokhale severely criticizes the methods that Social Security actuaries use for what boils down to insufficient disaggregation and excessive attention to history. The actuaries use single values in their long-run projections for several key variables—such as fertility, labor force participation by sex, and so on. Deciding on whether the assumed levels should be changed is a major focus of the technical panels. This approach is wrong, Gokhale argues. Aggregates consist of subgroups. When the subgroups can be expected to behave differently and their relative weights change, projecting a constant, even one well grounded in history, will be wrong, Gokhale argues.

As a general principle, this criticism is certainly correct. The actuaries recognize some differences explicitly, particularly those relevant to variations in the Social Security benefit formula, such as labor force participation for men and women and for different age groups. These rates differ and change over time. But Gokhale calls for more and goes way too far.

Consider fertility. The actuaries assume a single, constant fertility rate that differs in their "optimistic," "intermediate," and "pessimistic" projections. Gokhale points out that fertility differs among population subgroups by education, ethnic group, and race. The share of the population that he designates as Hispanic, for instance, is increasing. Many of the ethnic groups included as Hispanic have higher-than-average fertility rates. Therefore, he argues, it is wrong to assume a constant fertility rate. I think that attempting to disaggregate the projected fertility is largely a waste of time. The comparatively high birth rate of recent immigrants from Latin America will almost certainly fall as they and their offspring become acculturated and as their education and income increase. That is just what happened with other immigrant groups. How fast that happens is anyone's guess, and the record of those guesses is pretty lousy. The one guess that is quite likely to be wrong is the one that Gokhale urges—that relative birth rates of various ethnic or racial groups will not change.

In other cases, disaggregation is also politically unacceptable. African Americans and Hispanics have lower productivity today than do native-born whites. Those gaps stem from numerous factors, including education and past or present discrimination. They are likely to narrow, but no one is sure how fast. Furthermore, no government agency can, or should, be in the business of taking a stand on how much the productivity of particular groups will differ ten, twenty, or seventy-five years in the future. For that reason, Gokhale's approach, whatever its classroom appeal, is impracticable.

Gokhale makes similar arguments for other variables. But not much, if anything, is lost from a projection standpoint by using single numbers that are carefully vetted by technical panels whose members weigh the considerations he emphasizes. A great deal is gained in comparative transparency from using a single number. Even more is gained in avoiding political mine fields, for a government agency to officially project that productivity of one ethnic group or another will remain below average for decades would create a justifiable furor.

I turn now to the projections of the impact of Social Security and the reform plans on various age groups. My first comment is that the story is seriously incomplete. There are two facts about Social Security, viewed through the lens of the trust fund, that define the results. The first fact is that initial beneficiaries received benefits worth much more than the taxes paid on their behalf, discounted at any plausible interest rate. The second is that the trust fund is a closed system, in the sense that whenever the system ends, now or centuries hence, total benefit payments cannot exceed total revenues, including interest. That means that Social Security cannot be in cumulative deficit and cannot add to government debt.

From these two facts it follows, by the laws of arithmetic, that age groups born after any particular date must receive benefits worth less than taxes paid discounted at whatever interest rate trust fund balances earn. No one born before 1946 is included in any of the analyses shown in this essay. As it happens, Dean Leimer (2007) has shown, in an invaluable but little-known paper, that all age cohorts born before about 1935 received internal rates of return greater than the interest rate earned on Social Security reserves. It follows that all age cohorts born in 1936 or later receive internal rates of return lower than the interest rate earned on Social Security reserves. One can present this fact in various ways—through internal rates of return, negative present discounted value, or lifetime taxes.

I ask you to hold that thought for a moment. Now juxtapose it to another finding. This finding, shown for the baseline in table 3.2, lines 6 and 8, is that open-group liability is smaller than the closed-group liability. This implies that future enrollees are more than paying for their benefits.[38] That is the same fact that I asked you to hold in mind, expressed a different way. It follows that the trust fund deficits are attributable completely to people who have already reached retirement age, whose taxpaying days are over, and whose benefits cannot as a practical matter be cut. Quite simply, currently active and future age cohorts are paying fully for the benefits they will receive.

In other words, the projected gap between projected Social Security benefits and revenues is a gap that legally cannot occur. The reason is that when the trust fund balance falls to zero, either benefits must be cut or revenues increased, in which case the gap will not occur. The gap can be viewed in another way—as a measure of the amount by which benefits paid to age groups early in the life of Social Security, whose benefits exceeded the taxes they paid (in present value). Diamond and Orszag christened this gap "the legacy 'debt.'" Trust fund accounting commits the nation to close the gap by boosting earmarked taxes or cutting benefits. Viewed in this light, the gap is indistinguishable from the national debt, which also reflects past expenditures in excess of revenues. In the case of Social Security, the past expenditures have mostly, but not entirely, been made already because some members of those pre-1936 cohorts remain alive and are still collecting benefits. But from both a trust fund and a budget perspective, currently active and future workers under current law are paying fully for their Social Security and imposing no burden on anyone.

References

Board of Trustees of the Social Security Administration. 2011. *The 2013 Annual Report of the Board of Trustees of the Federal Old-Age and Survivors Insurance and Federal Disability Insurance Trust Funds.* Washington, DC: U.S. Government Printing Office.

Leimer, Dean. 2007. Cohort-Specific Measures of Lifetime Social Security Taxes and Benefits. ORES Working Paper 110, Social Security Administration, Woodland, MD.

Discussion

James Alm

The Old-Age Survivors Insurance (OASI) program, popularly known as Social Security, is one of the major social insurance programs in the United States. It is in fact because of this importance that its finances are an essential part of any discussion of the long-run budget outlook for the federal government. At present, these long-run prospects appear somewhat bleak. Such factors as the retirement of the baby boom generation, their extended life expectancies, the recent Great Recession, and the uncertain longer-term economic growth prospects have all combined to suggest that expected future outlays will significantly exceed future revenues. Indeed, in the most recent annual report of the Social Security system (Board of Trustees of the Social Security Administration, 2013), the trustees estimate that the OASI program's trust fund will be exhausted by 2035. Annual OASI revenues began to fall short of program expenditures in 2010, and it is hard to imagine a scenario in which surpluses will reemerge any time soon. Given the importance of Social Security in overall federal government finances, together with the use of consolidated budgetary accounting, large and growing deficits for OASI imply similar budgetary implications for the overall federal budget.

A central issue in this discussion is the accuracy of the Social Security projections by the trustees of Social Security. It is here where Jagadeesh Gokhale's piece enters the debate. He argues that the basic methodology used by the Social Security system in making its projections is flawed in several crucial respects. As a result, he says, its projections are unlikely to give an accurate picture of future finances. Finally, he suggests a methodology of his own, one that is not subject to these same flaws and so one that will give more accurate projections.

What are the flaws Gokhale sees in the current Social Security methodology? First, he says that the current methodology is based on old assumptions about many key variables, assumptions that rely on historical data that are no longer accurate. These variables include assumptions about fertility rates, mortality rates, labor force participation, productivity growth, interest rates, and many other variables, which Gokhale argues are based exclusively on historical data that are not "adequate" for making accurate projections. Second, he says that the current methodology does not have a "coherent" framework for integrating and aggregating factors at the micro-level. Third, he argues that the current methods are based on an "arbitrary decision" about the degree of detail to incorporate in estimating the assumptions to be applied to the population in future years. These various shortcomings also mean that the current methodology is unable to analyze in sufficient detail the distributional effects of Social Security and its evolution over time. Again, the implication of these flaws is that the projections of the trustees cannot be taken very seriously.

For example, Gokhale argues that the current methodology takes basic assumptions about specific variables and applies them mechanically to the existing population using a cell-based method in order to estimate the evolution over time of the variables, regardless of whether the assumption applies any longer to the population. As one specific example, Gokhale mentions female fertility rates. The current methodology does not distinguish female fertility rates by race or education level, despite compelling historical evidence that fertility rates differ by these categories. Applying such unrealistic and inaccurate assumptions to individual cells will, he suggests, necessarily lead to large—and increasingly large—errors in future projections of fertility rates. These errors in fertility rates will also be reflected in other variables that are influenced by fertility rates, such as the composition of the population, mortality rates, labor force participation rates, even labor productivity and earnings growth. These and many other variables are estimated by the trustees almost exclusively on the basis of historical data, and so they will become increasingly outdated and inaccurate over time.

After critiquing the current methodology of the Social Security trustees, Gohkale then presents his own detailed microsimulation model that addresses these flaws, the Demographic and Economic Micro Simulation (DEMSIM) model. This model builds on his own earlier work on generational accounting and especially on his previously published book on Social Security (Gohkale, 2010). He then compares DEMSIM simulations to the trustees' simulations and also simulates the effects of six prominent reforms with his DEMSIM model.

There are several main features of the DEMSIM microsimulation model:

- It is calibrated to U.S. microdata beginning in 1970 by creating a population of about 45,000 families whose demographic characteristics match those of the overall U.S. population in 1970 using conditional distributions of the U.S. population according to various attributes (e.g., age, gender, race, family size and composition, education, labor force status, disability status) as determined by Current Population Survey samples from the late 1960s and early 1970s.
- It uses data from the Panel Survey of Income Dynamics to match earnings to the simulated population.
- It allows the simulated population to evolve over time by applying historical mortality, fertility, and immigration rates to generate a new population for each year from 1971 to 2006 (or the last year of the historical simulation).
- From 2006 and onward, it uses the Social Security Administration's assumptions on demographic driver parameters (e.g., mortality, fertility, and immigration rates) to carry the demographic and economic simulation forward in time. However, DEMSIM disaggregates those parameters along dimensions whose interactions with other population attributes are important to capture when making Social Security's financial projections. For example, DEMSIM disaggregates the trustees' overall fertility rates by female race and education levels using data from the National Center for Health Statistics (NCHS); it disaggregates the trustees' overall mortality rates by age, gender, and race (also with NCHS data); it decomposes labor force participation rates by race and education; it allows education levels and education attainment to vary by age, gender, and race (unlike the trustees' estimates); and so on.

Overall, Gokhale argues that his "detailed projection method captures key determinants of items such as future family formation and dissolution, labor productivity, wage earnings, the payroll tax base, the degree of wage inequality, total Social Security benefits, and so on—factors that significantly influence Social Security's revenue and expenditure projections." Importantly, of course, Gokhale argues that his resulting projections will be more accurate than those of the trustees.

The end result is, I believe, a plausible and convincing critique of the current methodology used for making projections of Social Security and a plausible and convincing alternative to the current methodology.

It is certainly hard to argue that basing projections on outdated and unrealistic assumptions and methods is an appropriate way to make projections. Gokhale makes a strong case that the methods of the trustees are likely to give inaccurate projections and that his methods are a significant improvement.

Having said this, there are some obvious questions. The first is whether Gokhale's—or anyone else's—efforts to improve the projection methods for Social Security are a worthwhile exercise. The answer to this question is, I believe, clear: one should always attempt to improve estimation methods using the latest tools and methods. Relatedly, it seems equally obvious that the trustees' current method is outdated. Any attempt to improve estimation methods and results must be applauded.

A second question then emerges: Is Gokhale's microsimulation model of a better alternative than the current methodology? My answer to this question is less definitive but still relatively clear. Gokhale has established over the years a well-deserved reputation as one of the preeminent scholars in this area of research.

Now microsimulation models, like the Social Security and the DEMSIM models, have a long history in policy analysis. The early models from the 1950s envisioned a dynamic element in modeling where the base data were microfiles of households, individuals, or companies that were often allowed to change over time. However, these early models did not live up to their promise, in large part because of data constraints—public use microdata were hard to come by in the 1950s and early 1960s. The model development then took a step backward in a sense in that models of the 1980s tended to be entirely static in nature. In the 1980s, substantial gains were being made on the data front through the expansion of publicly available household surveys and other data sets (e.g., the Internal Revenue Statistics of Income). As the availability of microdata became less of an issue, focus turned again to the dynamic nature of the microsimulation methodology, and attempts to incorporate the macroeconomic impacts of policy changes emerged.

Today there is no one unique approach to microsimulation modeling. However, I believe that one can classify microsimulation models into (at least) three basic types: static, microdynamic/macrostatic, and dynamic models. Static models are used most often to simulate the short-term distributional and revenue impacts of detailed changes to tax and transfer programs. Microdynamic/macrostatic models allow behavior to change, but with the overall constraint that GDP remains the same. Dynamic models are typically used to simulate the impact of changes in policy on macro-aggregates; in some cases, the data are endogenously aged for population growth and other demographic changes.

Gokhale's DEMSIM model fits most closely the microdynamic/macrostatic modeling form, as he acknowledges, given the "significant uncertainty" that is currently associated with estimating such dynamic behavior. This approach may well be the best that is currently available. However, it seems likely that more explicitly dynamic considerations will become feasible as our methods continue to advance. Put differently, DEMSIM should not be taken as the last word on microsimulation modeling, as I am confident Gokhale would acknowledge himself.

Of perhaps more importance is the question of whether DEMSIM gives different projections than the trustees' methods do. The answer to this is clearly yes, at least in some cases. For example, the trustees' and DEMSIM's projected worker-to-beneficiary ratios are in fact very similar over time. However, in many other cases, there are significant differences. DEMSIM adjusts labor productivity growth by "labor quality," and projects annual average labor productivity growth of just 0.71 percent per year through the year 2080; the trustees' methods do not adjust for labor quality, leading to a substantially higher rate of 1.10 percent per year.

There are also significant differences in the projected paths of revenues and benefits, especially in distant and future years. In particular, DEMSIM projects a significantly larger future gap between revenues and expenditures than do the trustees. The seventy-five-year difference (the open group liability, OGL) equals nearly $7.0 trillion under DEMSIM's projections, which is 70 percent larger than the trustees' estimate of $4.1 trillion. The trustees' total benefit expenditures profile also exhibits a much smaller increase in benefits from the retirement of the baby boom generation relative to DEMSIM. The DEMSIM projection of $7.0 trillion equals 3.4 percent of the present value of payrolls through 2080, which is much larger than the trustees' (2006) estimate of 1.9 percent. Overall, then, DEMSIM estimates the trust fund exhaustion date to occur in 2029, much sooner than the trustees' projection.

Of most importance is the question of whether DEMSIM gives better (or more accurate) projections than the trustees' methods. Unfortunately, there is no real answer to this question. Despite what seem to be obvious improvements in methodology in DEMSIM over the current methodology, despite what are in many cases different projections by DEMSIM versus the trustees' projections, and despite what are reasonable attempts at historical validation for DEMSIM, it is simply unknowable whether DEMSIM gives better projections. Perhaps the "simpler" method of the trustees is justified on benefit-cost grounds; indeed, this method has been subject to many reviews over many years by competent technical panels. In any event, although it is certainly plausible that DEMSIM's projections are more accurate, especially over time, we do not know whether this is in fact the case.

It would be possible to get at least some indication of the answer to this question by making out-of-sample comparisons that start sometime in the recent past. Suppose that we go back in time to the year 2000. At that time, the trustees made projections for future years based on their methodology through the current fiscal year. Now suppose that Gokhale takes his DEMSIM model, but uses his model based on assumptions and methods that apply only through the year 2000. He could then make his own projections for future years based on his own methodology as it would have existed in the year 2000. Comparisons of the trustees' versus Gokhale's DEMSIM projections would give an indication of which approach gives more accurate out-of-sample projections, at least at this earlier point in time. This exercise was not done, but it certainly could be.

Having said all of this, I have to say finally that it is not entirely clear to me whether more accurate projections of the finances of Social Security are all that crucial inputs into any reforms of this program. There seem to be very few issues in Social Security on which there is any real consensus right now. My own (shrinking) list of some aspects that might have general agreement includes such items as the following:

- The existence of the trust fund is largely meaningless.
- Social Security redistributes income in many ways, intended and unintended.
- Any reforms should not affect current retirees.
- Any reforms should protect lower-income workers.
- The demographics upon which Social Security was established have changed dramatically, mainly because of lower birth rates and longer life expectancies.

As for important areas of disagreement, my (expanding) list includes the following questions on which I do not believe that there is any current consensus:

- Is Social Security a Ponzi scheme?
- Should solvency be achieved mainly by tax increases or benefit reductions?
- Should indexation of benefits be changed (e.g., chained CPI indexation)?
- Should private accounts be allowed?
- Is there even a significant fiscal imbalance, in the immediate future or in the distant future?

At one time I would have suggested that there was agreement on policies like increasing revenues by raising the wage ceiling or investing in higher-yield assets, raising (gradually) the retirement age, and subjecting benefits to means tests. However, recent commentary suggests that even these reforms will be contentious.

Indeed, when does real reform—of any type—occur? My own experience with (tax) reforms around the world suggests that reform occurs only when several conditions are met: the system is widely seen as broken, there is a consensus on how to fix it, and there is a strong champion who can generate political support for reform. Do these conditions apply to Social Security? Almost certainly not. Indeed, it is difficult to be very optimistic about any reform possibilities in the current environment. My own assessment is that the chances of a comprehensive reform, a "grand bargain" that would encompass both entitlement reform and tax reform, seem remote right now because none of my three conditions is met.

Where does this leave us? I believe that Gokhale's work is a crucial component of any reform discussion. I also believe that something will happen. Remember Herb Stein's maxim: "Something that can't go on forever won't." But to the extent that any change to Social Security emerges, my guess is that it will be a set of small and piecemeal reforms. The prospect of the grand bargain that not so long ago seemed promising appears to have vanished from the landscape.

Indeed, a particularly sobering possibility is that Gokhale's work may make reform less likely. Why? In large part, my pessimism stems from a suspicion that perhaps we now know "too much." Specifically, I suspect that our increased knowledge about the effects of any potential reforms—increased knowledge typified by such analyses as that performed by Gokhale—serves mainly to paralyze the political process. When we are better able to identify the many effects of reform, as does Gokhale, we energize the losers, and the political process then becomes increasingly immobilized because the losers from any potential change (no matter how small) lobby to prevent the change from occurring. And as our research has advanced, we are better able to identify the losers (and the winners) from any changes. Of course, from an academic perspective, being able to identify the winners and the losers is obviously a plus, and I do not believe that we should ever abandon our efforts to examine and quantify these effects. However, from the broader public policy perspective, I am not so sure whether we are making things better or worse because, when we identify especially the losers of a policy change, it is often harder to assemble the coalition necessary to pass the reforms.

In this regard, Gokhale's DEMSIM model adds to the already large number of models at our disposal, so that, if some group asks, "Might we lose under this plan?" his works increases the odds that someone can find some model under which this will be the case. Since the potential losers are the ones who will make the loudest noise, we may just be expanding the class of protesters.

Regardless, however, these types of considerations must be identified and quantified. Gokhale makes an important contribution to these debates, and his work provides a solid framework in which additional work can be conducted in the future, including work by the Social Security system itself.

References

Board of Trustees of the Social Security Administration. 2013. *The 2013 Annual Report of the Board of Trustees of the Federal Old-Age and Survivors Insurance and Federal Disability Insurance Trust Funds.* Washington, DC: U.S. Government Printing Office.

Gokhale, Jagadeesh. 2010. *Social Security: A Fresh Look at Policy Alternatives.* Chicago: University of Chicago Press.

Acknowledgments

This paper was prepared for a conference at Rice University's James A. Baker III Institute for Public Policy: "Defusing the Debt Bomb: Economic and Fiscal Reform—The Autumn of Our Fiscal Discontent," held October 5–6, 2011. It draws heavily from my book *Social Security: A Fresh Look at Policy Alternative* (University of Chicago Press, 2010). I thank Henry Aaron, James Alm, Matt Fay, Peter Van Doren, and participants at the James Baker III Institute for Public Policy conference at Rice University for helpful comments. The opinions expressed here are my own and not necessarily those of the Social Security Advisory Board.

Notes

1. I use the term *Social Security* refers to the Old-Age and Survivors Insurance (OASI) program.

2. See table II.D1 in Social Security Administration (2014b).

3. The heavy emphasis among policymakers, analysts, and voters—mainly older generations—on the program's overall financial condition derives from their concern about the program's ability to pay benefits as and when they come due. From an analytical perspective, however, because Social Security primarily transfers funds among various population groups—from the young to the old, from the well-off to the poor, from males to females, and on many other dimensions—it appears even more important to assess its distributional effects across clearly defined population groups.

4. See Social Security Administration (2013a). The 94 percent figure on this website was current as of May 17, 2011. Payroll taxes and benefits awarded to retirees, dependents, survivors, and others change participants' trade-offs with respect to key economic decisions—working versus not (especially for secondary earners within families), retiring early versus late, saving less versus saving more for retirement, and so on. Many studies, too numerous to cite here, suggest that such collective decisions substantially influence the course of the economy.

5. See the documentation on the trustees' method at Social Security Administration (2011).

6. This is clear from the flowcharts (charts 1 through 3) in the documentation describing the trustees' methods (Social Security Administration 2011).

7. For race, this is obvious. For education, this would be true if the offspring of educated women are also better educated. Empirical evidence does indicate that parents' and children's education levels (human capital) are positively correlated across successive generations.

8. It is important to recognize that one cannot use an "equilibrium growth model" for making projections of Social Security's finances. The objective is to measure the program's financial imbalance under continuation of the current policies (or laws), but such models cannot be operated without explicitly specifying a policy to close that very imbalance. However, a growth-model framework can guide the integration of various economic and demographic assumptions to derive implications for key elements in the future, especially the impact of the population's evolving demographic and economic attributes for labor productivity growth.

9. See the documentation provided by the Social Security Administration on the projection method used by the trustees (note 3) in Social Security Administration (2011).

10. The Social Security trustees have recently begun reporting results of stochastic analyses that estimate the likelihood of alternative trust fund outcomes within their traditional low- and high-cost scenarios. This introduces random variation over time in underlying "ultimate long-range assumptions"—fertility, mortality, net immigration, inflation, average real wages, and so on. See section VI.E of the trustees' *2013 Annual Report*. Each ultimate assumption's variation is estimated using historical data. Collective

randomization (with assumed or historically calibrated cross-assumption correlations) of assumptions is implemented to simulate the likelihood of various future trust fund outcomes. Unfortunately, because the underlying method of integrating the various assumptions over future time periods is inadequate (for the reasons outlined earlier in the text) one cannot have much confidence in official estimates of the likelihood of different trust fund outcomes—ones that are obtained by simply randomizing the underlying assumptions.

11. The criticism against using perpetuity measures is that there is considerable uncertainty attached to estimation beyond the standard (already quite long) seventy-five-year time horizon. However, the reaction to the existence of long-term uncertainty should not be to ignore it by arbitrarily truncating the projection horizon. For a full discussion of the desirability of calculations in perpetuity, see Gokhale and Smetters (2003). See also Biggs and Gokhale (2007).

12. To increase fidelity, CPS data from 1968 to 1972 are used to calibrate the 1970 U.S. population characteristics.

13. There were about 200 million people in the United States in 1970, so DEMSIM's simulated sample contains one individual for every 5,100 people alive in 1970.

14. Figure 3.5 shows DEMSIM's projection of labor force participation rates. The trustees' projections were not available to me at the time of implementing the project.

15. The parameters of the production function are calculated from historical time series provided by Jorgenson, Ho, and Stiroh (2007).

16. The microdata from the Survey of Consumer Finances (2007) are used to calibrate asset holdings by age and gender in 2006. The capital stock in each future year is based on growing per-person asset holdings by age and gender at the prior year's simulated rate of labor productivity growth and aggregating over the current year's population by age and gender.

17. The earnings regression uses PSID panel data on individual attributes and earnings between 1968 and 1993. To place earnings from different years on par with each other, PSID reported wage earnings that are adjusted by subtracting the effect of (historically known or independently estimated) technological change, capital inputs, and price inflation. For details, see Gokhale (2010, chapter 5).

18. See Gokhale (2010) for details.

19. On the issue of dynamic scoring, see the statement of Crippen (2002).

20. Social Security benefits are calculated by applying a Social Security benefit calculator (SSTBC) to the lifetime wage histories of simulated individuals. The benefit calculator is developed independently by following in detail the rules described in the *Social Security Handbook.* The results of the calculations are compared to Social Security's official benefit calculator to ensure an accurate match. This validation exercise is performed across hundreds of stylized cases with widely divergent attributes on age, race, gender, birth cohort, and earnings levels. SSTBC's benefit calculations are found to be within 1 percent of those of the official calculator. SSTBC calculates retirement, survivor, spousal, divorcee, and child benefits as appropriate under various eligibility configurations applicable to individuals who are members of families with widely varying structures.

21. DEMSIM's projection of Social Security's tax receipts includes revenues from the income taxation of Social Security benefits.

22. Social Security's seventy-five-year OGL equals the present value of projected OASI benefits minus the present value of projected OASI taxes (the "future imbalance"), plus the terminal year's target value of the trust fund (equal to one year's benefit expenditures), and minus the value of the current OASI trust fund. The infinite-horizon estimates are made by continuing projections for a sufficient number of years in the future until present values converge to within an acceptable degree of accuracy. For these estimates, the term involving the terminal year's trust-fund value is zero by construction.

23. Table 3.1 also shows estimates based on optimistic and pessimistic assumptions. The assumptions varied include rates of change in future mortality, fertility, immigration, price inflation, labor productivity, labor force participation, education acquisition, and discount factors. See Gokhale (2010) for a detailed explanation.

24. Social Security's seventy-five-year actuarial deficit has increased from zero in 1983 to 2.22 percent of payrolls today—as reported in the trustees' 2011 annual report. Of this, 1.67 percentage points is attributed to the inclusion of more "deficit" years into the seventy-five-year budget window and the remainder to changes in assumptions and other technical changes after 1983. However, this past "good performance" of the trustees' actuarial methods resulted under relative demographic stability since 1983. It does not invalidate the critique that the trustees' method, which does not condition financial estimates on the projected characteristics of the future population, is likely to undergo much more significant changes than in the past.

25. Note that convergence of present values is guaranteed when the discount rate exceeds the growth rate of the variable being considered (annual benefits or tax receipts). Social Security benefits grow with the size of the retiree population, increases in longevity, and growth in real benefits per beneficiary. Social Security tax receipts grow at the rate of worker population growth plus labor productivity per worker. Both growth rates are projected to be less than the 2.9 percent discount rate applied to future inflation-adjusted dollar flows.

26. A competing metric of "sustainable solvency" proposed by some analysts—whereby the system's unfunded obligation must be smaller than a predetermined threshold and the trust fund must be increasing toward the end of the seventy-five-year horizon—could also be misleading. See Gokhale and Smetters (2006).

27. Gokhale and Smetters (2003).

28. An important issue concerns the discount rate to be used to compute Social Security lifetime net tax rates. Under the reasonable view that the alternative allocation of payroll tax dollars for participants would be to (optimally) consume or invest them in private assets of moderate riskiness—a basket of bonds and stocks—a 5.0 percent inflation adjusted annual discount rate is used. This rate is intermediate to the long-term inflation adjusted annual return on risky stocks (7.0 percent) and the annual return on "riskless" U.S. Treasury bonds of 3.0 percent. Since Social Security's yearly internal rate of return is about 1.0 percent on payroll taxes for today's young workers, a discount rate larger than 1.0 percent applied to OASI taxes and benefits makes the present value of taxes (that occur earlier in the lifetime) larger than the present value of benefits. This implies a positive lifetime net tax rate for those generations, notwithstanding the fact that the Social Security internal rate of return is also positive for them under the program's current rules. It bears emphasizing, however, that the point of the exercise is to compare outcomes under current program rules and under alternative reforms using the selected metric. Whether the metric selected is the internal rate of return or the lifetime net tax rate, a comparative assessment of the fiscal treatment of different population groups—by

birth year, age, gender, race, and so on—under current Social Security laws and under alternative reforms would be quantitatively and qualitatively unchanged.

29. Gokhale (2010) contains more detailed information on both micrometrics distinguished additionally by gender, race, and lifetime-earnings levels.

30. In a paper forthcoming in the Harvard Law School's *Journal on Legislation,* Volume 49, I argue that Social Security's insurance provision function has become significantly diluted as a result of economic and demographic changes that we have witnessed since the program's inception during the mid-1930s. Academic studies have documented the program's negative effects on work effort and national saving since the 1980s. National saving is reduced because the program transfers resources from young and future resources toward retirees who consume a larger share of resources available to them. See Gokhale, Kotlikoff, and Sabelhaus (1996). In addition, the program's negative effects on work effort, especially through earlier retirement, is documented in Danziger, Haveman, and Plotnick (1981). See also Gruber and Wise (2007).

31. The Office of the Chief Actuary website provides official scores for Social Security reforms at "Proposals Affecting Trust Fund Solvency." Social Security Administration, http://www.ssa.gov/OACT/solvency/index.html. The 2007 Technical Panel on Assumptions and Methods made strong recommendations for updating the Social Security trustees' methods, especially by adopting a primarily microsimulation approach, but the actuaries' progress has been extremely slow in this regard.

32. For details, see Gokhale (2010).

33. The results of separately evaluating the individual reform elements of each reform proposal are available in Gokhale (2010).

34. See the statement of Crippen (2002).

35. Note that the denominator is the infinite-horizon imbalance, not the closed-group imbalance as in Gokhale (2010).

36. How much of the total adjustment cost is postponed beyond the seventy-fifth year under any given reform is information that we would not know without the infinite horizon OGL metric.

37. The same explanation applies to the seventy-five-year open-group and the closed-group imbalances under the G. W. Bush Commission's model 2 proposal.

38. The retirement wealth-to-lifetime-earnings ratios shown in table 3.5 are averages for the birth cohorts defined in the first column of the table.

39. The annual trustees' reports prepared by the Social Security actuaries contain a table (IV.B.7) that reaches the same result. In the 2011 report, the gap for all current and past workers is $18.8 trillion. The gap for current, past, and future workers is $17.9 trillion.

II Budgetary Issues and Processes

4 Federal Budget Reform: Lessons from State and Local Governments

Shanna Rose and Daniel L. Smith

While the national deficit and debt of the United States have long inspired widespread hand-wringing, there is currently a renewed sense of urgency to put the nation on a path toward fiscal sustainability. Deficit and debt reduction took center stage in mid-2011, when congressional lawmakers refused to raise the nation's statutory debt limit—effectively threatening to cut off the federal government's cash flow—unless the president agreed to cut federal expenditures by at least as much as the debt limit increase. After a protracted stalemate, Congress and the president reached an eleventh-hour agreement to raise the debt ceiling and cut the budget by up to $2.4 trillion over ten years. Despite having averted default on the national debt, the impasse was a factor in Standard & Poor's decision to downgrade the United States' sovereign long-term credit rating from AAA to AA+ for the first time in the nation's history. The decision reflected mounting concern that "the effectiveness, stability, and predictability of American policymaking and political institutions have weakened at a time of ongoing fiscal and economic challenges" (Standard and Poor's 2011).

As "laboratories of democracy," U.S. state and local governments have experimented with a wide variety of fiscal institutions designed to constrain public expenditures and indebtedness, yielding a myriad of institutional arrangements the federal government might consider—or is already considering—adopting to improve its long-term fiscal outlook. A large empirical literature exploits this institutional variation within and across state and local governments to estimate the effects of fiscal constraints on spending, taxes, deficits, and debt. This chapter, which draws on Rose (2010), synthesizes the literature, summarizing lessons for the federal government about the effectiveness of various institutions in promoting fiscal sustainability.

Before discussing the potential role for fiscal institutions in helping to rein in federal deficits and debt, the next section provides a brief overview of federal deficits and debt over the past several decades, comparing and contrasting the federal experience with that of state and local governments as well as households and businesses.

Deficits and Debt

For the seventy fiscal years spanning 1944 to 2013, the federal government has ended the year in deficit fifty-eight times. Total outlays have exceeded total receipts over 80 percent of the time, despite substantial surpluses in off-budget programs, most notably Social Security. As shown in figure 4.1, federal deficits have historically represented a fairly small share of gross domestic product (GDP)—an average of 2.8 percent over this time period. However, the deficit eclipsed $1 trillion—more than 10 percent of GDP—for the first time in fiscal year (FY) 2009.

By contrast, budgetary balance is the norm for state governments. Figure 4.2 shows that as a share of state GDP, state governments have averaged a small surplus over the past half-century, though most state

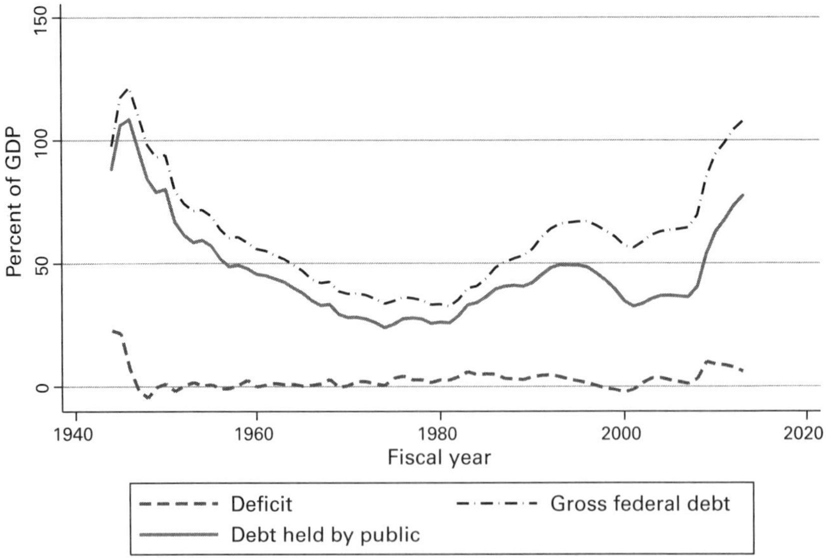

Figure 4.1
Federal Deficits and Debt as a Percent of GDP, Fiscal Years 1944–2013. (Note: FY 2012 and 2013 data are estimates.)

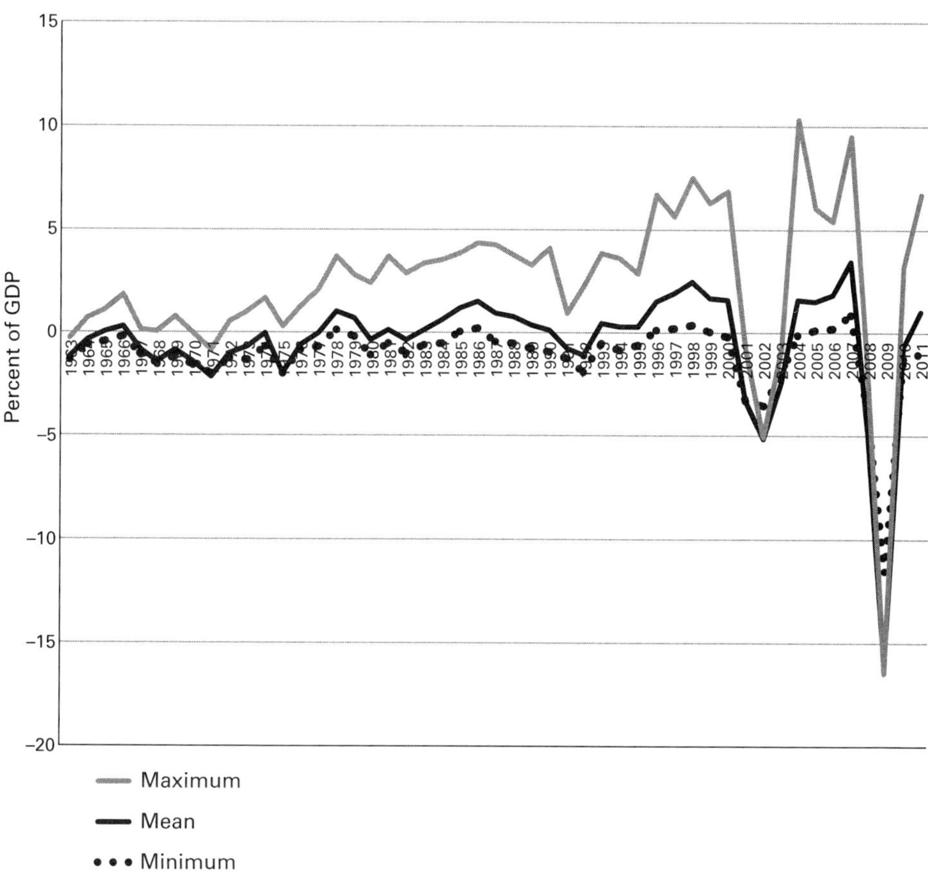

Figure 4.2
State Surplus/Deficit as a Percent of State GDP, 1963–2011. (Note: Excludes Alaska and Wyoming.)
Source: U.S. Census Bureau (1963–2011).

averages are not substantively different from zero.[1] Excluding Alaska and Wyoming, both of which receive large royalties in exchange for leasing public land for oil and gas extraction, the largest state surplus over the period from 1963 to 2011 was achieved in North Dakota at approximately 9 percent of state GDP. Only two states, Oregon and Wisconsin, have experienced deficits in excess of 10 percent of state GDP over the past five decades (both in 2009). Despite the severe economic downturn, the average state deficit in 2009 (excluding outliers Alaska, Wyoming, Oregon, and Wisconsin) was only about 4 percent of state GDP.

Turning to debt, figure 4.1 and subsequent figures demonstrate the challenge that indebtedness poses to the nation's fiscal sustainability. Figure 4.1 shows that after steadily declining following the conclusion of World War II through 1981, the gross federal debt took an upward trajectory, with only a brief period of reduction due to the economic expansion of the late 1990s. The debt held by the public, which includes debt sold on capital markets—namely, Treasury bills and notes—but excludes intragovernmental holdings, follows the same pattern. By the end of FY 2013, the gross federal debt exceeded 100 percent of GDP, the highest level since FY 1947. By contrast, figure 4.3 shows that state debt has averaged less than 10 percent of state GDP over the past fifty years, and the maximum state's debt in any given year has rarely exceeded 30 percent of GDP.

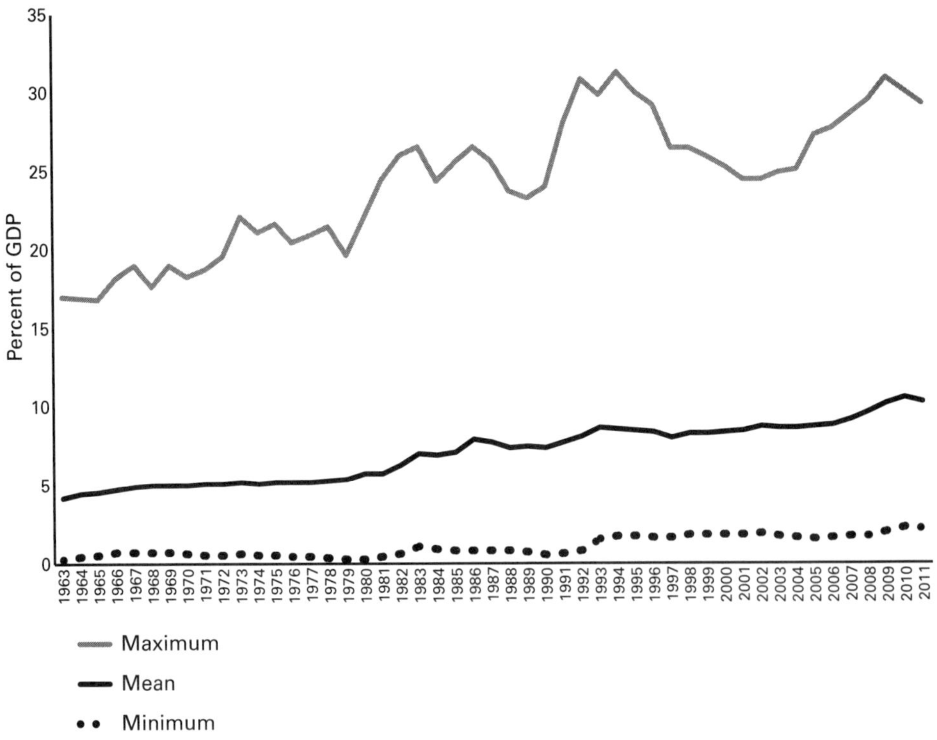

Figure 4.3
State Debt as a Percent of State GDP, 1963–2011. (Note: Excludes Alaska and Wyoming.)
Source: U.S. Census Bureau (1963–2011).

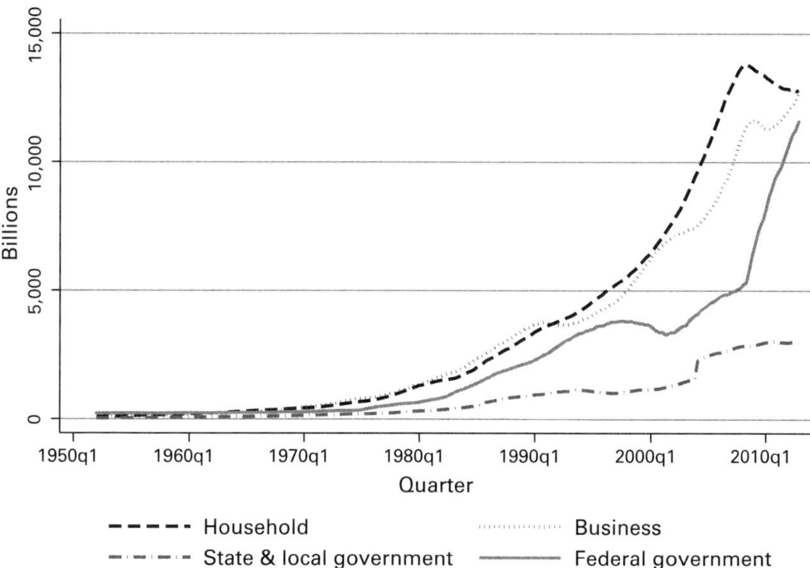

Figure 4.4
Credit Market Debt Outstanding by Selected Sectors, 1952–2012. (Note: Quarterly data are seasonally adjusted.)
Sources: Borrowing data from Board of Governors of the Federal Reserve System (1952–2012). Historical data: Credit market debt outstanding by sector.

Figure 4.4 compares credit market debt outstanding across four sectors—federal government, state and local governments, households, and businesses—over the time period of 1952 through 2012. The long-term trend is much flatter for state and local governments than for the other sectors, as subnational governments borrow primarily for capital investment and are subject to a combination of debt limitations, balanced budget requirements, and tax and expenditure limitations. The sharp upturn in the trajectory of federal debt that began in the third quarter of 2008 illustrates what many consider to be government's primary challenge to fiscal sustainability and has sparked not only the recent debt ceiling showdown but also a renewed call for a federal balanced budget amendment.

Figure 4.5 shows that credit market borrowing by the federal government has been more volatile than that by households, businesses, and state and local governments over the same time period.[2] The effects of the collapse of the housing bubble and ensuing financial crisis are obvious, resulting in a precipitous drop in household and business

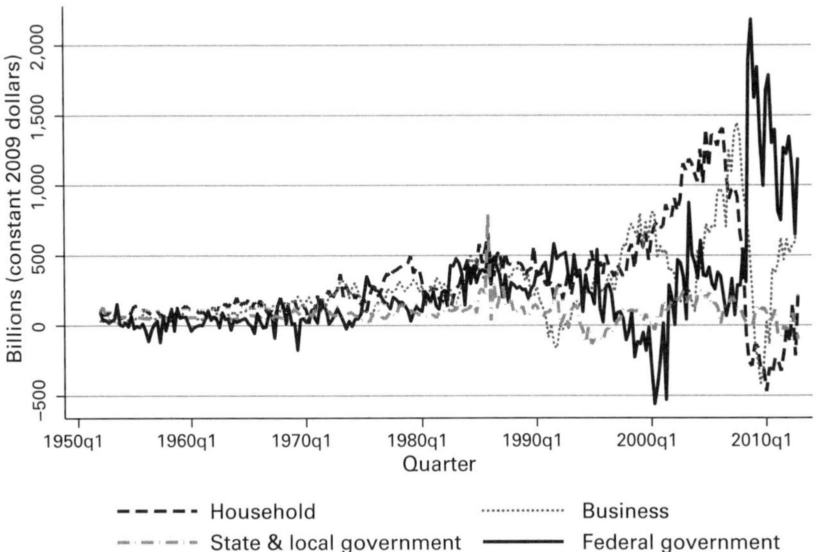

Figure 4.5
Credit Market Borrowing by Selected Sectors, 1952–2012. (Note: Quarterly data are seasonally adjusted.)
Sources: Borrowing data from Board of Governors of the Federal Reserve System (1952–2012). Historical data: Credit market borrowing by sector. Sector-specific price deflator data obtained from U.S. Department of Commerce, Bureau of Economic Analysis (1952–2012, table 1.1.9: Implicit price deflators for gross domestic product.

borrowing, and an even sharper increase in federal borrowing starting in the third quarter of 2008.

Finally, figures 4.6 and 4.7 compare total debt and interest payments for the federal government and the average state over the years 1950 to 2011. The figures are expressed as a percentage of total outlays for the federal government and as a percentage of total expenditures for states. To ensure the figures are comparable, federal debt is measured as debt owned by the public; intragovernmental holdings are excluded.[3]

The federal government's annual debt load is approximately four times the state mean; whereas the average debt load at the federal level is twice total outlays, it is approximately half of total expenditures in the states. An even starker contrast is seen in comparing interest payments. While interest payments average to just over 2 percent of the budget in the states, federal interest payments have averaged nearly 10 percent of outlays. The potential that interest payments will grow as a share of the budget, crowding out more productive pursuits, is widely cited as one of the main reasons for reining in the federal debt.

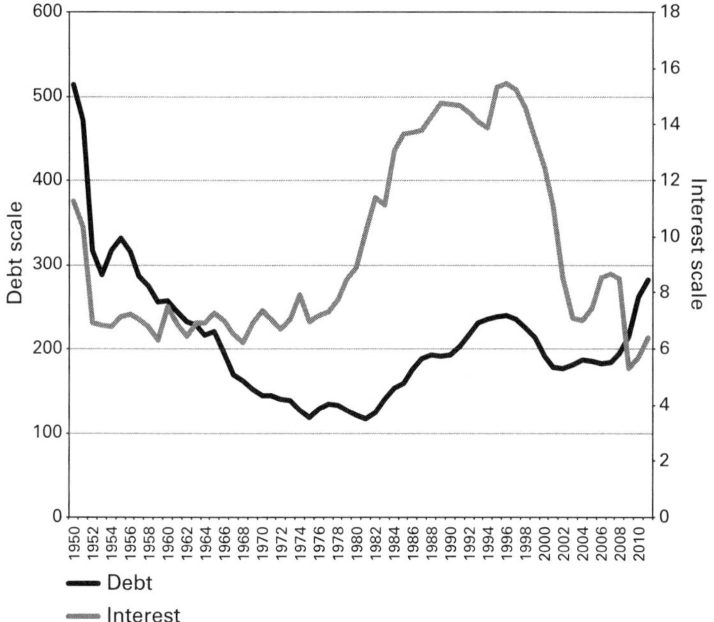

Figure 4.6
Federal Debt and Interest Payments as a Percent of Outlays, 1950–2011.
Source: U.S. Council of Economic Advisers (2013, tables B-78 and B-80).

Of course, it is not possible to make causal inferences about the effectiveness of state budget rules based on these simple comparisons. Nor do the states have a perfect record when it comes to sound financial management. Nonetheless, the states' relatively low deficits and debt have led to considerable interest in the potential federal adoption of fiscal restraints commonly found at the subnational level, such as balanced budget rules, debt limitations, tax and expenditure limits, and the line-item veto. The remainder of this essay summarizes the empirical literature on the effectiveness of each of these four institutions and discusses the likely effects—and challenges—of implementing such institutions at the federal level.

Before we review the literature, a caveat about empirical methodology is in order. The adoption of budget institutions clearly does not occur in a vacuum. Indeed, institutions may be thought of as the "congealed preferences" of voters and their elected representatives (Riker 1980). From an empirical standpoint, institutional endogeneity complicates the task of estimating causal relationships. In particular, endogeneity means that institutions are correlated with unobservable

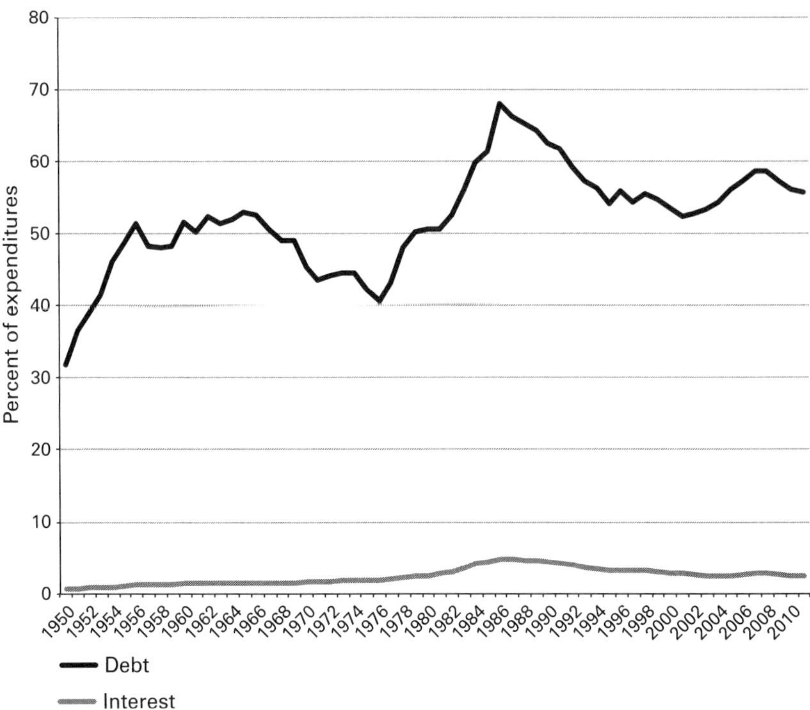

Figure 4.7
State Debt and Interest Payments as a Percent of Expenditures, 1950–2011.
Source: U.S. Census Bureau (1950–2011).

independent variables (voters' and lawmakers' preferences), which may lead to biased estimates of institutions' effectiveness. For example, as Kiewiet and Szakaly (1996) explain in their study of debt limitations, the presence of borrowing constraints in a given state may reflect voters' intolerance of large amounts of debt, while the absence of such constraints may simply reflect the fact that the state's elected officials historically have had little appetite for debt.

Such concerns are somewhat mitigated by the fact that many state budget rules were adopted more than a century ago and thus likely exert independent effects apart from legislator and voter preferences (Poterba 1995). Nonetheless, researchers who study institutions must be careful to choose appropriate empirical strategies—namely, panel data with fixed effects to control for time-invariant state characteristics. Thus, we focus on work that uses this empirical approach, to the exclusion of many early papers that relied on cross-section data from a single year. Ideally researchers will also use instrumental variables to address potential endogeneity bias, although only a handful of studies have done so thus far. A closely related problem is that some institutions have changed very little over time, making it difficult to distinguish the institution's effect from a state fixed effect. Some researchers have found creative ways around this problem, as we discuss.

Balanced Budget Rules

The 2011 showdown over the federal debt ceiling brought special attention to a decades-old idea: a balanced budget amendment to the U.S. Constitution. A balanced budget amendment was first proposed in the House of Representatives in 1936, but neither chamber of Congress passed a balanced budget amendment until 1982, when the Senate mustered the requisite two-thirds majority; however, the House vote on a companion measure fell short of passage. In 1995, House Speaker Newt Gingrich resurrected the proposal as part of the "Contract with America." This time the House had enough votes to secure passage, but the Senate narrowly failed to pass the measure. Since 1975, thirty-two state legislatures have petitioned Congress for the adoption of a federal balanced budget amendment, falling just short of the two-thirds threshold that would require Congress to convene a constitutional convention on the proposal to adopt an amendment.

Although efforts to adopt a balanced budget amendment have failed thus far, Congress has experimented with several legislative approaches to reining in deficit spending. One of the earliest of these efforts was the Balanced Budget and Emergency Deficit Control Act of 1985, often referred to as the Gramm-Rudman-Hollings Act (GRH) after its sponsors. As its name suggests, GRH was enacted in response to the perception that growing federal deficits constituted a fiscal emergency. This legislation established deficit targets and automatic across-the-board budget cuts (or "sequestrations") to enforce those targets. However, policymakers routinely evaded the targets through the use of overly optimistic revenue forecasts and postponements before repealing the measure entirely in 1990 (Lee, Johnson, and Joyce 2008; Rubin 2006).

The Budget Enforcement Act (BEA) of 1990 later took a spending control approach to deficit reduction. Specifically, BEA implemented spending caps and pay-as-you-go (PAYGO) financing, which required policies that would increase direct spending or decrease revenues to be offset by revenue increases or spending decreases elsewhere in the budget in order to achieve deficit neutrality. While BEA was more successful than GRH, it was still subject to evasion and manipulation; moreover, following the economic boom of the late 1990s, large on-budget surpluses weakened federal policymakers' commitment to budget discipline, and Congress allowed BEA to expire in 2002 (Rubin 2006). The Statutory Pay-as-You-Go Act of 2010 restored PAYGO, but does not cap spending and features a long list of exemptions including Social Security, Medicaid, and interest on the federal debt (U.S. Office of Management and Budget 2011).

At the subnational level, virtually all states and many local governments have some form of balanced budget requirement (BBR). In contrast with the federal government, most of these rules were born with the states or were passed shortly after statehood, making them an important part of state governance for centuries. There is considerable variation in the institutional design of these rules. In most states, the governor must submit a balanced budget to the legislature, the legislature must pass a balanced budget, or the governor must sign a balanced budget. Nearly all states have one or more of these three rules, which are sometimes known as prospective or ex ante balanced budget rules. A stricter form of balanced budget rule is a prohibition on carrying forward a deficit—sometimes called a no-carry-over or ex post rule—which exists in approximately half of the states.

There is an enormous empirical literature on the estimated effects of state balanced budget rules. In an early and widely cited paper, the Advisory Commission on Intergovernmental Relations (1987) constructed an index of the stringency of balanced budget requirements, with no-carry-over rules receiving the highest score. Using this index and panel data from 1965 to 1992, Alesina and Bayoumi (1996) find that strict balanced budget rules are associated with larger average surpluses as a share of state product and that moving from no rule to the most stringent rule reduces the cyclical variance of fiscal balance by about 40 percent. Instead of an index, Bohn and Inman (1996) use separate dummy variables for each type of balanced budget rule and find that no-carry-over rules were associated with smaller deficits from 1970 to 1991; however, this effect holds only for constitutional (as opposed to statutory) rules enforced by an elected (as opposed to politically appointed) state supreme court.

Hou and Smith (2006) have developed an alternative typology of balanced budget rules, based on a close reading of state constitutions and statues, which distinguishes "political" rules, such as those requiring the governor or legislature to prepare a balanced budget, from "technical" requirements, including no-carry-over rules as well as within-year fiscal controls to avoid a deficit and limits on the amount of debt that can be assumed for deficit reduction, among others. In their study of fifty states over the period 1950 to 2004, Hou and Smith (2010) find that technical rules are more effective than political rules in restraining deficits; this result is perhaps not surprising, since political rules typically permit unexpected deficits to emerge during the year and thus are relatively easy to circumvent through forecast manipulation and accounting gimmicks. Hou and Smith do not find a statistically significant difference between constitutional and statutory rules, however.

Scholars have also examined the effect of balanced budget rules on variables other than deficits, such as spending, pension fund contributions, and debt. Primo (2006) finds that no-carry-over rules are associated with lower per capita spending. Chaney, Copley, and Stone (2002) find that rules requiring the budget to be balanced at year end are associated with reduced funding of public employee pension systems. Von Hagen (1991) finds that per capita debt is significantly lower in states with stringent balanced budget rules than in states with the weakest form of balanced budget rule.

In addition to reducing deficits, spending, and debt, evidence suggests that stringent balanced budget rules increase the speed with which governments adjust spending and taxes in response to unexpected fiscal shocks. Poterba (1994) finds that among states with annual budget cycles, those with strict balanced budget rules as measured by the ACIR index cut spending and raised taxes more rapidly following an unexpected shock. Similarly, Alt and Lowry (1994) find that no-carry-over rules are associated with more rapid adjustment to deficits, but only when Republicans control both branches of government.

A related question is whether this rapid adjustment to fiscal shocks translates into better credit ratings, and thus lower borrowing costs. Lowry and Alt (2001) find that deficits depress a state's credit rating by less when the state has a strict balanced budget rule. Poterba and Rueben (2001) find a similar result: unexpected deficits are correlated with higher borrowing costs, but this effect is smaller for states with strict antideficit rules than for states without these rules.

Rapid adjustment to fiscal shocks also has a potential downside, however. According to the tax smoothing theory, it is optimal for governments to run budget deficits during downturns to smooth temporary fluctuations in revenues and spending and avoid excess volatility in tax rates (Barro 1979; Lucas and Stokey 1983). Evidence suggests that states operating under relatively stringent balanced budget rules undertake considerably less fiscal stabilization than those with weaker rules (Bayoumi and Eichengreen1995; Fatás and Mihov 2006). Similarly, states with strict balanced budget rules seem to experience greater cyclical variability (Levinson 1998).

A final question is whether balanced budget rules reduce the scope for volatility-increasing manipulation of spending, taxes, deficits, and debt. Rose (2006) finds that states with no-carry-over rules do not experience election-induced "political business cycles" in spending and deficits, whereas states with weaker rules do. In a similar vein, Fatás and Mihov (2006, 101) find that balanced budget rules are associated with "less aggressive use of discretion in conducting fiscal policy and thus less volatility in budgetary outcomes.

In summary, balanced budget rules have the potential to improve fiscal sustainability: they are associated with smaller deficits, lower debt, better credit ratings, more rapid adjustment to fiscal shocks, and less political manipulation of budget policy. However, the devil is in the details: these effects typically hold only for states with no-carry-over rules, not the weaker ex ante balanced budget rules. In some studies, the distinction between constitutional and statutory rules seems to matter. Finally, balanced budget rules appear to impede the use of fiscal policy for macroeconomic stabilization, which is particularly problematic when contemplating adoption at the federal level.

Moreover, there are several practical limitations to the feasibility of a balanced budget amendment steering the federal government toward a path of fiscal sustainability. First, enactment would require passage by two-thirds votes in the U.S. House and Senate and three-quarters of state legislatures, which has proven elusive despite numerous attempts spanning nearly a century. Although a number of state legislatures have petitioned for a federal balanced budget amendment in the past, only two have done so since 1980. In light of the states' increased reliance on federal financial assistance, particularly for the ballooning Medicaid program (not to mention the occasional stimulus package), it seems the states have little incentive to approve a federal balanced budget amendment. Second, in the case of the states, constitutional rules tend to be less stringent precisely because it is more difficult to amend them (Hou and Smith 2006). Given the divisive politics that define the current federal deficit and debt debate, any federal balanced budget amendment that survives a two-thirds vote in both houses would most likely be easy to work around with budget gimmickry, as was the case for past reforms such as GRH.

Two additional considerations are *when* the federal budget is to be balanced and *which* budget is to be balanced. The Congressional Budget Office (CBO) projects the government's budget baseline as well as the long-term budgetary implications of budgetary proposals. These CBO scores have assumed a prominent role in recent major policy debates, including the Iraq War and the Patient Protection and Affordable Care Act of 2010. Given the inherent long-range perspective of most federal programs—and their attendant costs and revenues—any requirement that the federal budget be balanced annually (as is required in most states) is necessarily at variance with the nature of the goods and services provided, especially given that the federal government does not have a separate capital budget. As Joyce (1993, 43) argues, a federal balanced budget amendment "would make annual budgetary balance the most important goal of federal budgeting" and this approach "has already been tried and failed" under GRH.

As for which budget is to be balanced, in recent fiscal years over 25 percent of total federal receipts and 15 percent of total outlays have been off-budget, including those for Social Security and, until FY 2010, the Iraq War. Unless a balanced budget amendment were coupled with substantial budgetary reform at the federal level, at most about 75 percent of receipts and 85 percent of outlays would be constrained, and these figures make the unrealistic assumption that all on-budget items could feasibly be cut. While a constitutional amendment that addresses both when and how to balance the budget certainly could be designed, these issues of institutional design are far from trivial.

Debt Limits

The federal debt ceiling was instituted in 1917. The 2011 debt crisis notwithstanding, the debt ceiling has been a soft constraint in the past, as Congresses have raised it dozens of times in preceding decades with minimal debate. Moreover, any federal debt limit is inherently soft, as the federal government has the authority to simply print money if it deems necessary.

As in the case of balanced budget rules, state and local debt limits vary, but in general they are harder constraints than the federal debt ceiling. Many states adopted debt limits (along with balanced budget rules) in the nineteenth century due to mounting concern about excessive borrowing, scandals, and even a few cases of default (Nice 1991). U.S. state and local governments face four main types of restrictions on public debt. The most stringent and least common variety is an outright prohibition on guaranteed debt. Less stringent debt limits include debt ceilings and voter referendum requirements. Debt ceilings are expressed as either a percentage of the tax base or a dollar limit. Some have provisions for exceeding the limit for certain purposes (such as roads or sewers) or for certain types of jurisdictions (such as home rule municipalities). Voter referendum requirements may require either a simple majority or a supermajority of voters to approve new bond issues. The fourth and least stringent type of limit is a legislative supermajority requirement. In fact, Kiewiet and Szakaly (1996) argue that in theory, legislative supermajority requirements may even increase debt by expanding the size of the "logroll" necessary for passage. Most debt limits apply only to "guaranteed" general obligation debt.

Several early studies that use cross-section data from a collection of states or localities in a single year find evidence of a negative relationship between debt-limit restrictiveness and government borrowing (Advisory Commission on Intergovernmental Relations 1961; Pogue 1970; McEachern 1978). However, more recent studies using more sophisticated panel data models suggest that debt limits are not effective. For instance, using panel data from forty-eight states over three decades, Clingermayer and Wood (1995) find that debt ceilings, public referenda, and legislative supermajority requirements have no impact on the growth of long-term state debt. One potential explanation is that since debt limits typically apply only to guaranteed debt—thereby excluding revenue bonds as well as bonds issued by special districts, authorities, or commissions—these rules can be evaded through heavier reliance on revenue bonds or the creation of separate entities with borrowing power. Bunch (1991) finds that even when a state has debt limits that apply to both general obligation and revenue debt, politicians can circumvent these rules by creating more public authorities or relying more heavily on existing authorities. Stringent debt limits are also associated with the proliferation of special-purpose governments (MacManus 1981).

Over the years a consensus has emerged that debt limits may reduce guaranteed debt, but they do so at least partly through substitution of nonguaranteed debt, so the effect on total debt is less than dollar-for-dollar—and, according to some estimates, it is negligible. Farnham (1985) evaluates the experience of two thousand large municipalities and finds evidence that although the most stringent debt limits have a "depressing effect" on overall debt per capita, they also increase reliance on nonguaranteed debt. Similarly, Von Hagen (1991) finds that median per capita state debt is significantly lower among states with stringent limits, but that these limits also appear to induce substitution into nonrestricted debt instruments. Such findings may help explain Bahl and Duncombe's (1993) observation that states with limits on both general-obligation debt and revenue bonds have lower state and local government debt burdens than those with general-obligation limits alone. Finally, Kiewiet and Szakaly (1996) find that states with debt ceilings and referendum requirements have less guaranteed debt than those with legislative supermajority requirements, but that debt limits are "not insurmountable obstacles" and, among other things, promote the devolution of debt to lower levels of government.

In summary, debt limits have the potential to improve fiscal sustainability, depending on their specific provisions. Debt ceilings and referendum requirements are associated with lower levels of guaranteed debt, while the evidence on legislative supermajority requirements is more mixed. The potential to evade debt limits by issuing revenue bonds means that the combination of general obligation and revenue debt limits is more effective than limits on general obligation bonds alone. Bunch (1991) notes that revising the legal language so that debt limits also clearly apply to debt issued by public authorities could increase their effectiveness.

In addition to adopting a no-deficit-carry-over balanced budget rule or other strict antideficit mechanism—challenges notwithstanding—the federal government might consider making the debt ceiling a hard constraint as opposed to a soft constraint. In some ways, this approach has already begun. The biggest challenge is that this change will also require a fundamental change in the relationship between federal revenues and expenditures. The federal government's accumulated debt is a direct function of the structural gap between revenues and expenditures, and imposing a hard constraint on debt will require reducing or even eliminating this gap. In addition to the political pyrotechnics this likely would inspire among policymakers, it is not clear that the American public is truly ready for an austerity program, particularly as the U.S. economy struggles to recover from the Great Recession.

Moreover, it may well be that the nature of the borrowing function at the federal level is unique and defies traditional mechanisms of fiscal discipline. While at the state and local level debt has primarily been used to finance infrastructure, including roads, bridges, dams, and water sewer systems, the federal government has sold, and continues to sell, debt to accelerate cash flow and supplement tax revenues. Given that debt proceeds are used to finance entitlement programs (which themselves ultimately will be in deficit), principal and interest payments, and a host of other programs that for political intents and purposes are often shielded from budget cuts, a hard debt limit might simply yield an even more severe brand of the interbranch warfare demonstrated during the 2011 debt ceiling debate.

Tax and Expenditure Limitations

Though previous federal attempts to legislate balanced budgets—such as the Budget Enforcement Act of 1990—have incorporated spending caps, tax and expenditure limitations (TELs) have not been a major focus of federal debate. This may be due to the fact that they are relatively new compared to other fiscal institutions. Many state debt limitations and balanced budget requirements, for instance, predated the first federal attempts to adopt these mechanisms by well over one hundred years.

State and local TELs were introduced through the direct democracy process during the tax revolt of the 1970s. In 1976, New Jersey became the first state to adopt a TEL; today thirty states have them. These rules fall into five broad categories: (1) limits on revenue based on an index of income, inflation, or population growth; (2) limits on expenditures based on an index of income, inflation, or population growth (the most common form of tax and expenditure limit); (3) limits that restrict appropriations to 95 to 99 percent of the official revenue forecast; (4) requirements that voters to approve tax increases; and (5) legislative supermajority requirements for tax increases.

The majority of evidence on state TELs suggests that these institutions have not been effective in slowing the growth of the public sector. Kenyon and Benker (1984) and Bails (1990) examine state panel data from the early 1980s and find no significant difference in expenditure or revenue growth between TEL and non-TEL states. Cox and Lowery (1990), Joyce and Mullins (1991), and Shadbegian (1996) examine longer panels of data and similarly find that state TELs have had little to no effect on spending or revenues. Kousser, McCubbins, and Moule (2008) use a quasi-experimental approach in which they examine changes within a given state following the adoption of TELs instead of comparing TEL to non-TEL states—an approach that helps mitigate the potential omitted variables bias that arises in cross-state comparisons. However, like most of the previous literature, they find little impact of state TELs.

A few studies that use alternative methodologies do find evidence suggesting that state TELs are modestly effective in slowing the growth of government, however. Rueben (1996) uses direct democracy as an instrumental variable and estimates a two-stage least-squares model; she finds that the ratio of taxes to personal income is 2 percent lower in states with TELs. Bails and Tieslau (2000) use a random-effects model—rather than the typical fixed-effects model—to estimate that real per capita state and local spending is $41 lower in states with TELs than in states without TELs.

What might explain the modest to negligible effect of state TELs? Kenyon and Benker (1984) note that state TELs typically cover only about 60 percent of a state's revenues, leaving plenty of avenues for evasion. Specifically, state officials might respond to TELs by simply relying more heavily on user charges (Mullins and Joyce 1996), adopting or expanding state lotteries (Glickman and Painter, 2004), or borrowing more (Bahl and Duncombe 1993; Clingermayer and Wood 1995). Another possibility is that state TELs lead state officials to shift responsibility for spending to lower levels of government (Martell and Teske 2007; Skidmore 1999).

Evasion of TELs also seems to occur at the municipal level, although municipal limits appear to be somewhat more effective than state TELs in slowing the growth of government. Lowery (1983) finds that local TELs have reduced local governments' reliance on property tax revenues and increased their reliance on state aid and other revenue sources. Preston and Ichniowski (1991) find that the growth of municipal property tax revenues in states with TELs is lower than the growth observed in municipalities in states without them. Shadbegian (1999) finds that TELs induce counties to shift from taxes to user fees. In two studies of municipalities in Illinois, Dye and McGuire (1997) and Dye, McGuire, and McMillen (2005) find that TELs are associated with lower property taxes and school expenditures. Similarly, Blankenau and Skidmore (2004) present evidence that TELs lead to lower own-source spending on education by localities. Shadbegian (2003) similarly finds a reduction in local education spending—along with a corresponding increase in the state's education funding burden. Poterba and Rueben (1995) find that TELs are associated with slower growth in a major item of government expenditures: government employee salaries.

Other studies have uncovered several potential disadvantages of tax and expenditure limits. Poterba and Rueben (2001) find that unexpected deficits lead to larger increases in a state's borrowing costs when the state has a TEL, which compromises the state's capacity to eliminate deficits by raising taxes. Figlio and Rueben (2001) find evidence suggesting that TELs reduce the average quality of new public school teachers. And James and Wallis (2004) note that highly restrictive TELs can curtail a government's ability to perform even the most basic duties in the event of an economic downturn. In the case of Colorado's infamous Taxpayer Bill of Rights (TABOR) experiment, multiple legal remedies were required to restore adequate funding for basic government services such as K–12 education.

Whereas most of the literature has focused on the most common form of TELs—numerical limits on spending or revenue—a handful of studies investigate the effect of legislative supermajority requirements for tax increases. For instance, following an instrumental variables approach similar to that used by Rueben (1996), Knight (2000) uses direct democracy as well as the legislative vote required to pass a constitutional amendment as instrumental variables. He finds that supermajority requirements decrease the tax rate by between 8 and 23 percent, and reduce tax revenues as a percent of personal income by 1.7 to 3.6 percentage points.

In summary, most types of state tax and expenditure limits appear to be minimally effective in slowing the growth of government, although supermajority requirements and municipal-level TELs appear to be somewhat more effectual. The effectiveness of TELs seems to be diminished by the substitutability of tax and nontax revenues as well as the substitutability of state and local spending. However, to the extent that they are effective, TELs may have potentially negative consequences, including limiting both resources for basic government services and flexibility to respond to fiscal shocks.

As noted above, the notion of a federal expenditure limitation is relatively new compared to discussions of balanced budget amendments and federal debt limits. A federal expenditure limitation did, however, appear in a version of House Republicans' 2011 deficit and debt reduction plan: The Cut, Cap, and Balance Act of 2011, a bill which would have limited spending to a specific percentage of GDP each year. The literature suggests that a federal tax or expenditure limitation modeled on state TELs might not do much to constrain spending or—if it did—might come at a high cost. Moreover, the most common type of expenditure limitation—one that restricts spending to a percentage of some exogenous economic or demographic variable—would in many cases be incongruent with the nature of the goods and services provided. Indexing expenditures to inflation, for instance, ignores the fact that the federal government finances many things, especially health care, that become more costly at a rate that exceeds inflation. (If policymakers want to slow the growth of medical cost inflation, intervention in the health care market, not a blunt cap on total government expenditures, is the answer.) Furthermore, indexing spending to inflation leaves no room for net spending increases without forcing a zero-sum game with existing programs. Although there is some recent political support for a zero-sum approach to government spending, it defies the reality of federal budgeting over the past several decades.

Line-Item Veto

The ongoing national debate over presidential veto authority has generated considerable interest in the state experience; in particular, Ronald Reagan's repeated requests for a line-item veto set off a flurry of state-level empirical studies in the late 1980s. Although Congress denied Reagan's request, a decade later it passed the Line Item Veto Act of 1996, granting the president of the United States broad rescission power over new discretionary spending, new entitlements or enhancements to entitlements, and taxes that benefited one hundred or fewer individuals or corporations (Lee et al. 2008; Rubin 2006). Though in this sense it was not a true item veto, its legitimacy was immediately challenged, and the law ultimately was ruled unconstitutional in 1998 on the basis that it violated the presentment clause of the U.S. Constitution. Subsequent attempts to empower the executive with line-item veto authority include a 2006 proposal that would have subjected presidential item vetoes to congressional approval and a more limited 2009 proposal that would allow the president to remove earmarks, again subject to congressional approval.

In 2011, two longstanding champions of the line-item veto. Senators John McCain (R-AZ) and Tom Carper (D-DE) resurrected the proposal. In a letter to the debt supercommittee, they argued that the president should have a "budget scalpel" for eliminating wasteful spending. Their proposal would authorize the president to cut earmarks and other nonentitlement spending from appropriation bills; Congress would then hold an up-or-down vote on the president's proposed cuts. Although they acknowledged that the line-item veto is "not a silver bullet for eliminating the entirety of federal deficits," McCain and Carper called the institution "an important addition to our toolbox."[4] However, the states' experience with the line-item veto does not provide much support for this argument.

In virtually all states and most municipal governments, the executive has the authority to veto appropriations bills in their entirety. This all-or-nothing veto is a blunt and often useless instrument because governors rarely wish to reject the budget as a whole. However, the majority of governors (forty-three) have the authority to veto individual line items within appropriations bills. In addition, governors in fourteen states have the item-reduction veto, allowing them to reduce the amounts of items within appropriations bills. Since the item-reduction veto can—but need not—be used to reduce the amounts of items all the way to zero, it has the potential to provide the governor with more flexibility than the item veto.

Most states adopted the item veto between 1870 and 1900, although others have adopted the institution more recently. In most cases the legislature rather than voters proposed the item veto. Yet even when politicians have an incentive to tie their own hands ex ante, they may have an incentive to evade the rules. Indeed, legislators in some states responded to the imposition of the item veto by combining multiple unrelated appropriations into a single budget item to prevent the governor from using the item veto (Baker 2000). Thus, in 1885, Pennsylvania became the first state to adopt an item-reduction veto, allowing the governor to reduce the dollar amounts of individual line items, and soon many other states followed suit (Benjamin 1982).

Unfortunately most empirical studies of the item veto use cross-section data due to the lack of time-series variation in this variable, so their results must be interpreted with caution. All of these studies find negligible effects of the item veto on spending and other fiscal variables. Abrams and Dougan (1986), the Advisory Commission on Intergovernmental Relations (1987), and Rowley, Shughart, and Tollison (1986) find no evidence that the item veto is associated with lower per capita state spending, slower spending growth, or lower debt, respectively (see Carter and Schap 1990 for a review of this literature).

However, Crain and Miller (1990) find that possession of the item-reduction veto—but not the item veto—is associated with slightly slower growth in per capita spending.[5]

Other studies examine the partisan dimension of the item veto, conjecturing that it is likely to have the largest effect under divided government. This approach gets around the limited time-series variation in the item veto by interacting the item veto dummy with partisan variables, which do vary over time. Using panel data from1965 to 1983, Holtz-Eakin (1988) interacts possession of the item veto and item-reduction veto with the party composition of government and finds that these institutions are associated with modestly lower spending under divided government, but only in the short run, leading him to conclude that "in general, the line item veto does not appear to significantly alter, on average, the outcomes of the budgetary process." Reese (1997) studies more than four thousand line-item vetoes cast by sixty-three governors in ten southern states between 1973 and 1992 and finds that although use of the line-item veto is more common under divided party control, it is not associated with lower spending. Similarly, a survey of state budget officials reveals that the item veto is used more frequently under divided than under unified government, but is not significantly associated with fiscal restraint (Abney and Lauth 1985).

In summary, the item veto appears to have a negligible effect on spending. There are several potential explanations for this finding. First, Gosling (1986) notes that the item veto is most frequently used to strike qualifying language rather than dollar amounts, and concludes that governors use the item veto primarily to achieve policy and political goals rather than to restrain spending. Second, in their amusingly titled article, "How to Succeed at Increasing Spending without Really Trying," Gabel and Hager (2000) point out that supermajority requirements to override executive vetoes may simply force a logroll that includes more legislators, resulting in more pork-barrel projects. Third, Schap (1990, p. 240) notes that "strategy complicates prediction": the legislature, anticipating the executive's use of the item veto, may deliberately enact a larger budget than if the executive did not have item-veto authority. Nonetheless, institutional design again seems to play an important role, with at least one study suggesting that the item-reduction veto is somewhat more effective than the item veto in reducing spending.

Taken together, research suggests that the line-item veto holds little promise to curb federal spending and debt accumulation. As a practical matter, the U.S. Supreme Court's ruling in 1998 means that—barring a constitutional amendment—the prospects for a true line-item veto at the federal level are dim.

Conclusion

The challenge before the federal government is not one of balancing the budget this fiscal year or next, but rather stemming the long-term upward trajectory of the federal debt. Putting the nation on a fiscally sustainable path requires decisive action in the immediate term coupled with structural policy changes that will redefine the relationship between revenues and expenditures over the long term. The results of subnational experimentation with fiscal constraints—including balanced budget rules, debt limitations, tax and expenditure limits, and the line-item veto—yield several valuable insights into the current debate over federal budget reform.

The experience of state and local governments suggests that fiscal institutions have the potential to promote long-term fiscal sustainability, as evidenced by their fairly consistently balanced budgets and comparatively low debt levels over the past half-century, as well as the results of a large empirical literature demonstrating the effectiveness of various fiscal constraints. Balanced budget rules, especially provisions requiring that deficits not be carried into the next fiscal year, have been quite effective in helping state governments achieve budgetary balance. Other institutions, including stringent debt limitations and supermajority requirements for revenue increases, also seem to have the potential to promote fiscal restraint.

However, several caveats are in order. First, the devil is in the details: research reveals that the effectiveness of state and local fiscal institutions depends critically on their specific legal provisions. For example, "political" balanced budget rules requiring the executive to propose or the legislature to pass a balanced budget appear to have little effect on deficits; "technical" rules such as no-carry-over provisions are much more effective. Debt ceilings and referendum requirements seem to reduce the level of guaranteed debt while less stringent debt limitations do not. Supermajority requirements for revenue increases appear to do more to constrain the growth of government than do tax and expenditure limits that link spending to economic or demographic variables.

Second, where there is a will to evade fiscal rules, there is a way. State and local policymakers have repeatedly devised creative ways around fiscal constraints, just as federal policymakers did under Gramm-Rudman-Hollings and the Budget Enforcement Act. For example, state policymakers have evaded limitations on guaranteed debt by increasing reliance on nonguaranteed debt and circumvented tax and expenditure limitations by relying more heavily on nontax revenue sources and shifting responsibilities to municipal governments and special-purpose governments. The obvious implication is that rules alone are not sufficient to bring about fiscal sustainability; the political will to make difficult choices is critical.

Third, to the extent that fiscal rules are effective in constraining spending, taxes, deficits, and debt, they may have deleterious consequences. By tying the hands of policymakers, stringent balanced budget rules and tax and expenditure limits have demonstrably reduced the states' scope for macroeconomic stabilization. Clearly the consequences would be even more dire at the federal level, where macroeconomic stabilization is a particularly important government function. Moreover, the state and local experience suggests fiscal rules may lead policymakers to slash basic public services, such as K–12 education, or to make fiscally irresponsible decisions, such as underfunding pension plans.

That most state and local pension systems are underfunded to varying degrees and by various measures presents a cautionary tale to the federal government: on-budget deficit management is necessary to achieve fiscal sustainability, but it is not sufficient. While off-budget liabilities have outpaced assets for decades, only recently have state and local governments begun implementing structural and institutional reforms to realign their government-wide balance sheets. Given legal restrictions and practical limitations on increasing employee contributions or reducing retiree benefits, much of the reform in the area of state and local pensions will be driven by accounting conventions. Beginning with FY 2014, state and local governments will report liabilities as they accrue with employee tenure, making the magnitude of postemployment benefits more transparent and therefore more salient.

The lessons offered to federal policymakers by state and local governments are mixed and in many cases entail substantial political and institutional barriers. Many of the fiscal constraints that are commonplace at the state and local levels are centuries old and part of subnational governments' very fabric, and they cannot easily be superimposed on the federal government. The challenge, however, is not insurmountable in light of the renewed and demonstrated sense of urgency to put the federal government on a fiscally sustainable path.

References

Abney, Glenn, and Thomas P. Lauth. 1985. The Line-Item Veto in the States: An Instrument for Fiscal Restraint or an Instrument for Partisanship? *Public Administration Review* 45 (3): 372–77.

Abrams, Burton A., and William R. Dougan. 1986. The Effects of Constitutional Restraints on Governmental Spending. *Public Choice* 49 (2): 101–16.

Advisory Commission on Intergovernmental Relations. 1961. *State Constitutional and Statutory Restrictions on Local Government*. Washington, DC: U.S. Government Printing Office.

Advisory Commission on Intergovernmental Relations. 1987. *Fiscal Discipline in the Federal System: National Reform and the Experience of States*. Washington, DC: U.S. Government Printing Office.

Alesina, Alberto, and Tamim Bayoumi. 1996. The Costs and Benefits of Fiscal Rules: Evidence from U.S. States. NBER Working Paper 5614, National Bureau of Economic Research, Cambridge, MA.

Alt, James E., and Robert C. Lowry. 1994. Divided Government, Fiscal Institutions, and Budget Deficits: Evidence from the States. *American Political Science Review* 88 (4): 811–28.

Bahl, Roy, and William Duncombe. 1993. State and Local Debt Burdens in the 1980s: A Study in Contrast. *Public Administration Review* 53 (1): 31–40.

Bails, Dale G. 1990. The Effectiveness of Tax-Expenditure Limitations: A Re-Evaluation: In 19 States They Resulted in Virtually No Success in Limiting Growth in Their Budgets. *American Journal of Economics and Sociology* 49 (2): 223–38.

Bails, Dale G., and Margie A. Tieslau. 2000. The Impact of Fiscal Constitutions on State and Local Expenditures. *Cato Journal* 20 (2): 255–77.

Baker, Samuel H. 2000. Does Enhanced Veto Power Centralize Spending? *Public Choice* 104 (1–2): 63–79.

Barrilleaux, Charles, and Michael Berkman. 2003. Do Governors Matter? Budgeting Rules and the Politics of State Policymaking. *Political Research Quarterly* 56 (4): 409–17.

Barro, Robert J. 1979. On the Determination of Public Debt. *Journal of Political Economy* 87 (5): 940–71.

Bayoumi, Tamim, and Barry Eichengreen. 1995. Restraining Yourself: The Implications of Fiscal Rules for Economic Stabilization. *International Monetary Fund Staff Papers* 42 (1): 32–48.

Benjamin, Gerald. 1982. The Diffusion of the Governor's Veto Power. *State Government (Denver, Colo.)* 55: 99–105.

Blankenau, William F., and Mark L. Skidmore. 2004. School Finance Litigation, Tax and Expenditure Limitations, and Education Spending. *Contemporary Economic Policy* 22 (1): 127–43.

Board of Governors of the Federal Reserve System. 1952–2012. *Z.1 Financial Accounts of the United States: Flow of Funds, Balance Sheets, and Integrated Macroeconomic Accounts.*

Washington, DC: Board of Governors of the Federal Reserve System, http://www.federalreserve.gov/releases/z1/Current/data.htm.

Bohn, Henning, and Robert P. Inman. 1996. Balanced Budget Rules and Public Deficits: Evidence from the U.S. States. NBER Working Paper 5533, National Bureau of Economic Research, Cambridge, MA.

Bunch, Beverly S. 1991. The Effect of Constitutional Debt Limits on State Governments' Use of Public Authorities. *Public Choice* 68 (1–3): 57–69.

Carter, John R., and David Schap. 1990. Line-Item Veto: Where Is Thy Sting? *Journal of Economic Perspectives* 4 (2): 103–18.

Chaney, Barbara A., Paul A. Copley, and Mary S. Stone. 2002. The Effect of Fiscal Stress and Balanced Budget Requirements on the Funding and Measurement of State Pension Obligations. *Journal of Accounting and Public Policy* 21 (4–5): 287–313.

Clingermayer, James C., and B. Dan Wood. 1995. Disentangling Patterns of State Debt Financing. *American Political Science Review* 89 (1): 108–20.

Cox, James, and David Lowery. 1990. The Impact of the Tax Revolt Era State Fiscal Caps. *Social Science Quarterly* 71 (3): 492–509.

Crain, W. Mark, and James C. Miller, III. 1990. Budget Process and Spending Growth. *William and Mary Law Review* 31 (4): 1021–46.

Dye, Richard F., and Therese J. McGuire. 1997. The Effect of Property Tax Limitation Measures on Local Government Fiscal Behavior. *Journal of Public Economics* 66 (3): 469–87.

Dye, Richard F., Therese J. McGuire, and Daniel P. McMillen. 2005. Are Property Tax Limitations More Binding over Time? *National Tax Journal* 58 (2): 215–25.

Dye, Thomas R. 1969. Executive Power and Public Policy in the States. *Western Political Quarterly* 22 (4): 926–39.

Farnham, Paul G. 1985. Re-Examining Local Debt Limits: A Disaggregated Analysis. *Southern Economic Journal* 51 (4): 1186–1201.

Fatás, Antonio, and Ilian Mihov. 2006. The Macroeconomic Effects of Fiscal Rules in the U.S. States. *Journal of Public Economics* 90 (1–2): 101–17.

Figlio, David N., and Kim S. Rueben. 2001. Tax Limits and Qualifications of New Teachers. *Journal of Public Economics* 80 (1): 49–71.

Gabel, Matthew J., and Gregory L. Hager. 2000. How to Succeed at Increasing Spending without Really Trying: The Balanced Budget Amendment and the Item Veto. *Public Choice* 102 (1–2): 19–23.

Glickman, Mark M., and Gary D. Painter. 2004. Do Tax and Expenditure Limits Lead to State Lotteries? Evidence from the United States: 1970–1992. *Public Finance Review* 32 (1): 36–64.

Gosling, James J. 1986. Wisconsin Item-Veto Lessons. *Public Administration Review* 46 (4): 292–300.

Holtz-Eakin, Douglas. 1988. The Line Item Veto and Public Sector Budgets: Evidence from the States. *Journal of Public Economics* 36 (3): 269–92.

Hou, Yilin, and Daniel L. Smith. 2006. A Framework for Understanding State Balanced Budget Requirement Systems: Reexamining Distinctive Features and an Operational Definition. *Public Budgeting and Finance* 26 (3): 22–45.

Hou, Yilin, and Daniel L. Smith. 2010. Do State Balanced Budget Requirements Matter? Testing Two Explanatory Frameworks. *Public Choice* 145 (1): 57–79.

James, Franklin J., and Allan Wallis. 2004. Tax and Spending Limits in Colorado. *Public Budgeting and Finance* 24 (4): 16–33.

Joint Committee on Taxation. 1987. *General Explanation of the Tax Reform Act of 1986*. Washington, DC: Joint Committee on Taxation.

Joyce, Philip G. 1993. The Reiterative Nature of Budget Reform: Is There Anything New in Federal Budgeting? *Public Budgeting and Finance* 13 (3): 36–48.

Joyce, Philip G., and Daniel R. Mullins. 1991. The Changing Fiscal Structure of the State and Local Public Sector: The Impact of Tax and Expenditure Limitations. *Public Administration Review* 51 (3): 240–53.

Kenyon, Daphne A., and Karen M. Benker. 1984. Fiscal Discipline: Lessons from the State Experience. *National Tax Journal* 37 (3): 433–46.

Kiewiet, D. Roderick, and Kristin Szakaly. 1996. Constitutional Limitations on Borrowing: An Analysis of State Bonded Indebtedness. *Journal of Law Economics and Organization* 12 (1): 62–97.

Knight, Brian G. 2000. Supermajority Voting Requirements for Tax Increases: Evidence from the States. *Journal of Public Economics* 78 (1): 41–67.

Kousser, Thad, Matthew D. McCubbins, and Ellen Moule. 2008. For Whom the TEL Tolls: Testing the Effects of State Tax and Expenditure Limitations on Revenues and Expenditures. *State Politics and Policy Quarterly* 8 (4): 331–62.

Lee, Robert D., Ronald W. Johnson, and Philip G. Joyce. 2008. *Public Budgeting Systems*. Sudbury, MA: Jones and Bartlett.

Levinson, Arik. 1998. Balanced Budgets and Business Cycles: Evidence from the States. *National Tax Journal* 51 (4): 715–32.

Lowery, David. 1983. Limitations on Taxing and Spending Powers: An Assessment of their Effectiveness. *Social Science Quarterly* 63 (2): 247–63.

Lowry, Robert C., and James E. Alt. 2001. A Visible Hand? Bond Markets, Political Parties, Balanced Budget Laws, and State Government Debt. *Economics and Politics* 13 (1): 49–72.

Lucas, Robert E., Jr., and Nancy L. Stokey. 1983. Optimal Fiscal and Monetary Policy in an Economy without Capital. *Journal of Monetary Economics* 12 (1): 55–93.

MacManus, Susan A. 1981. Special District Governments: A Note on Their Use of Property Tax Relief Mechanisms in the 1970s. *Journal of Politics* 43 (4): 1207–14.

Martell, Christine R., and Paul Teske. 2007. Fiscal Management Implications of the TABOR Bind. *Public Administration Review* 67 (4): 673–87.

McEachern, William A. 1978. Collective Decision Rules and Local Debt Choice: A Test of the Median-Voter Hypothesis. *National Tax Journal* 31 (2): 29–136.

Mullins, Daniel R., and Philip G. Joyce. 1996. Tax and Expenditure Limitations and State and Local Fiscal Structure: An Empirical Analysis. *Public Budgeting and Finance* 16 (1): 75–101.

Nice, David C. 1988. The Item Veto and Expenditure Restraint. *Journal of Politics* 50 (2): 487–99.

Nice, David C. 1991. The Impact of State Policies to Limit Debt Financing. *Publius* 21 (1): 69–82.

Pogue, Thomas S. 1970. The Effects of Debt Limits: Some New Evidence. *National Tax Journal* 23 (1): 36–49.

Poterba, James M. 1994. State Responses to Fiscal Crises: The Effects of Budgetary Institutions and Politics. *Journal of Political Economy* 102 (4): 799–821.

Poterba, James M. 1995. Balanced Budget Rules and Fiscal Policy: Evidence from the States. *National Tax Journal* 48 (3): 329–36.

Poterba, James M., and Kim Rueben. 1995. The Effect of Property-Tax Limits on Wages and Employment in the Local Public Sector. *American Economic Review* 85 (2)384–89.

Poterba, James M., and Kim Rueben. 2001. Fiscal News, State Budget Rules, and Tax-Exempt Bond Yields. *Journal of Urban Economics* 50 (3): 537–62.

Preston, Anne, and Casey Ichniowski. 1991. A National Perspective on the Nature and Effects of the Local Property Tax Revolt, 1976–1986. *National Tax Journal* 44 (2): 123–45.

Primo, David. 2006. Stop Us before We Spend Again: Institutional Constraints on Government Spending. *Economics and Politics* 18 (3): 269–312.

Reese, Catherine C. 1997. The Line-Item Veto in Practice in Ten Southern States. *Public Administration Review* 57 (6): 510–16.

Riker, William H. 1980. Implications for the Disequilibrium of Majority Rule for the Study of Institutions. *American Political Science Review* 74 (2): 432–46.

Rose, Shanna. 2006. Do Fiscal Rules Dampen the Political Business Cycle? *Public Choice* 128 (3): 407–31.

Rose, Shanna. 2010. Institutions and Fiscal Sustainability. *National Tax Journal* 63 (4): 807–38.

Rowley, Charles K., William F. Shughart II, and Robert D. Tollison. 1986. Interest Groups and Deficits. In Deficits, edited by James M. Buchanan, Charles K. Rowley, and Robert D. Tollison, 263–80. New York: Basil Blackwell.

Rubin, Irene S. 2006. *The Politics of Public Budgeting: Getting and Spending, Borrowing and Balancing*. Washington, DC: CQ Press.

Rueben, Kim. 1996. Tax Limitations and Government Growth: The Effect of State Tax and Expenditure Limits on State and Local Government. Unpublished manuscript, Public Policy Institute of California, San Francisco.

Schap, David. 1990. Executive Veto and Spending Limitation: Positive Political Economy with Implications for Institutional Choice. *Public Choice* 65 (3): 239–56.

Shadbegian, Ronald J. 1996. Do Tax and Expenditure Limitations Affect the Size and Growth of State Government? *Contemporary Economic Policy* 14 (1): 22–35.

Shadbegian, Ronald J. 1999. The Effect of Tax and Expenditure Limitations on the Revenue Structure of Local Government, 1962–1987. *National Tax Journal* 52 (2): 221–37.

Shadbegian, Ronald J. 2003. Did the Property Tax Revolt Affect Local Public Education? Evidence from Panel Data. *Public Finance Review* 31 (1): 91–121.

Skidmore, Mark. 1999. Tax and Expenditure Limitations and the Fiscal Relationships between State and Local Governments. *Public Choice* 99 (1–2): 77–102.

Standard and Poor's. 2011. *United States of America Long-Term Rating Lowered to "AA+" due to Political Risks, Rising Debt Burden; Outlook Negative.* New York: Standard & Poor's, http://www.standardandpoors.com/ratings/articles/en/us/?assetID=1245316529563.

U.S. Department of Commerce. Bureau of Economic Analysis, 1952–2012. *National Income and Product Accounts Tables: Implicit Price Deflators for Gross Domestic Product.* Washington, DC: U.S. Department of Commerce. http://bea.gov/iTable/iTableHtml.cfm?reqid=9&step=3&isuri=1&903=13

U.S. Census Bureau. 1950–2011. State Government Finances. Washington, DC: U.S. Government Printing Office.

U.S. Council of Economic Advisers. 2013. *2013 Economic Report of the President.* Washington, DC: U.S. Government Printing Office.

U.S. Office of Management and Budget. 2011. The Statutory Pay-As-You-Go Act of 2010: A Description. Washington, DC: U.S. Office of Management and Budget, http://www.whitehouse.gov/omb/paygo_description

Von Hagen, Jürgen. 1991. A Note on the Empirical Effectiveness of Formal Fiscal Restraints. *Journal of Public Economics* 44 (2): 199–210.

Discussion

Joe Barnes

Shanna Rose and Daniel Smith have summarized a rich literature on the efforts by state and local governments to constrain the growth of debt through institutional constraints and thus provide an important and timely contribution to the debate over how best to address rising U.S. federal debt.

This chapter is in many ways a companion piece to Rose's "Institutions and Fiscal Sustainability" (2010), which features a more extended discussion of how institutional reforms, ranging from referenda to term limits, attempt to bring voters' preferences and legislative decisions more closely into alignment. Nonetheless, Rose and Smith expand significantly on "Institutions and Fiscal Sustainability." In particular, as the title implies, it focuses on the applicability of fiscal lessons from state and local government at the federal level. It also touches on some of the measures, both attempted and proposed, undertaken by the U.S. Congress.

Federal versus State Governments

Rose and Smith stress the relatively low level of debt among states, which have, over the past fifty years, tended to run budget surpluses, although modest ones. In contrast, the federal budget has been in surplus only five times in that same time period: once under President Nixon and four times during the Clinton administration. Moreover, the deficit rose sharply in the aftermath of the recession that struck the United States in December 2007, reaching 10.1 percent of GDP in fiscal year (FY) 2009, the highest level since the end of World War II.

The federal deficit has dropped steadily since then, largely reflecting increased tax receipts associated with economic recovery and budgetary cuts, or sequestrations, mandated by the Budget Control Act of

2011. According to the CBO, the deficit was 8.8 percent of GDP in FY 2010, 8.4 percent in FY 2011, 6.8 percent in FY 2012, and 4.1 percent in FY 2013. Despite this decline, many in the political and academic spheres alike stress the need to address the sustainability of U.S. federal debt, especially given the medium- to long-term challenges associated with funding entitlement programs such as Social Security, Medicare, and Medicaid.

The View from the States

Much of Rose and Smith is devoted to detailing the scale and variety of state procedures to limit deficits and constrain debt. Almost all states have measures in place—some constitutional, some statutory—to impose fiscal discipline on legislators and executives. These include balanced budget rules, tax and expenditure limits, and the line item veto. I examine these various measures in what I take to be Rose and Smith's assessment of them in ascending order of usefulness.

First is the line item veto. After an examination of the literature, Rose and Smith declare that it "appears to have a negligible effect on spending." The evidence on tax and expenditure limits is more mixed. The authors describe their effectiveness as "modest to negligible"—a step up from the line item veto, but not necessarily much of one. In both cases, the authors note that enterprising politicians can always find ways to increase taxes and expenditures if they are inclined to do so. Under the line item veto, legislators may simply pass a larger budget in the expectation that the executive will veto part of it. Under taxes and expenditure limits, legislatures can respond by relying more on user charges, expanding states lotteries, or simply borrowing.

Rose and Smith are most hopeful about the effectiveness of balanced budget rules, which they say are "associated with smaller deficits, lower debt, better credit ratings, more rapid adjustment to fiscal shocks and less political manipulation of budget policy." In particular, balanced budget rules that prohibit states from carrying forward deficits appear effective. Nonetheless, Rose and Smith remind us that the devil is in the details. Again, adept legislators can find ways around what appear to be the strictest of limitations.

The View from Washington

What of balanced budget rules that the U.S. Congress has adopted?

Rose and Smith are unimpressed. They judge the Balanced Budget and Emergency Deficit Control Act of 1985 (commonly called Gramm-Rudman-Hollings) to have been a failure. Congress got around the act's requirements by inflating revenue forecasts and deferring enforcement. Rose and Smith are also less than enthusiastic about the Budget Enforcement of 1990, which instituted a PAYGO system that, at least theoretically, compelled the Congress to find budgetary offsets when it increased certain categories of expenditures. On balance, the authors believe that the 1990 PAYGO performed more effectively than Gramm-Rudman-Hollings but was subject to legislative manipulation. According to Rose and Smith, the newest PAYGO rules, passed in 2010, exempt large swaths of the federal budget from their provisions.

Rose and Smith briefly review the long history of efforts to enact a balanced budget amendment to the U.S. Constitution though do not discuss recent congressional efforts to pass a balanced budget amendment. Significant Republican support has coalesced around two proposals: one is fairly straightforward, mandating a balanced budget every fiscal year unless the requirement is waived by a supermajority of both houses of the Congress; a second version is similar, but also includes a federal expenditure cap of 18 percent of GDP.

Rose and Smith do not address these proposed amendments, perhaps because their chance of passage approaches zero given current partisan alignments. Still, a constitutional amendment to balance the budget retains strong support among congressional Republicans; it also polls well with the general public. But the current proposals, with or without the expenditure cap, have been criticized for their inflexibility, particularly during economic downturns. Glenn Hubbard, chairman of George W. Bush's Council of Economic Advisors from 2001 to 2003, has proposed his own balanced budget amendment in an effort to address these concerns. His proposal, cowritten with economist Tim Kane, laid out in the article "In Pursuit of a Balanced Budget" (Hubbard and Kane 2011), would make the constraint on federal expenditures a five-year average and institute escalating supermajorities required to waive limits in times of national crisis. The Hubbard proposal, or something like it, is surely worth considering. But it is still open to the legislative manipulation that is endemic at the state and local levels. It is easy to imagine, for instance, the Congress simply finding ways to spend money by terminological sleight of hand; as Rose and Smith point out, sizable federal outlays are already "off-budget." In fact, our wars in Iraq and Afghanistan were largely off-budget until the Obama administration. And any balanced budget amendment raises the prospect of court challenges to budgetary legislation on the grounds of its unconstitutionality, which creates the possibility of budget by court decision. Perhaps such a role for the federal judiciary is necessary or even advisable. But we must surely consider its consequences carefully in any discussion of a balanced budget amendment.

The authors' bottom line, as I take it, when it comes to lessons the federal government might take from the states is that there are no easy solutions, though some variation of a balanced budget rule might be helpful.

Apples and Oranges?

Rose and Smith note that "it may well be that the nature of the borrowing function at the federal level is so unique that it defies traditional mechanisms of fiscal discipline." They stress the extent to which significant parts of the federal budget—entitlements, other popular programs, and debt service—are often shielded from budget cuts.

The authors are right: the federal government is unique. I will touch on three areas of difference between Washington and the states. The first is the prerogative of the federal government to make war, declared or not, thus incurring unexpected and potentially huge costs. Our interventions in Iraq and Afghanistan, for instance, have surely contributed to increased federal debt. Second, the federal government plays a lead role in stabilizing financial markets during emergencies. The Troubled Asset Relief Program passed by the Congress in 2008 and originally budgeted at $700 billion (though later reduced to $475 billon) represented a commitment of a scope simply unimaginable at the state level, although most of the loans were ultimately repaid. A last difference between the mandates of the state and federal government is the critical role played by U.S. debt instruments in domestic and international financial markets. Rose and Smith note S&P's mid-2011 downgrade of the U.S. federal credit rating. Ironically, investors moved into U.S. bonds in the aftermath of the downgrade. This reflected in part a flight to safety by domestic investors worried about poor overall U.S. economic performance and by foreign investors rattled by market turbulence associated with the ongoing eurozone sovereign debt crisis. The bottom line is that Washington and the states are very different fiscal beasts indeed.

The Federal Role in Macroeconomic Stabilization

I now turn to perhaps the most significant, and surely the most controversial, difference between the states and Washington: the federal government's role in macroeconomic stabilization. Rose and Smith mention the difficulty of reconciling mandatory balanced budgets with macroeconomic management. "Balanced budget rules," they write, "appear to impede the use of fiscal policy for macroeconomic stabilization, which is particularly problematic when contemplating adopting at the federal level." This is, to put it mildly, an understatement. Indeed, this precise issue is perhaps the difficult and important one surrounding federal budget rules.

The recent economic downturn, now called the Great Recession, has thrown this difficulty into sharp relief. For instance, had either currently proposed form of constitutional amendment (with or without the spending cap) been in effect when the recession struck, it would have required, absent supermajority votes by both houses of Congress, budget cuts or tax increases of over $1 trillion in FY 2009. This was not, it should stressed, because of the Obama's administration controversial stimulus package; the Congressional Budget Office (CBO) was projecting an FY 2009 deficit of over 8 percent of GDP before Obama was inaugurated. One need not be a doctrinaire Keynesian to believe that fiscal consolidation of such a magnitude, putting aside the impact of huge cuts on the normal functioning of government, would have been potentially catastrophic in terms of output and employment. Joel Prakken of Macroeconomic Advisors suggests that balancing the budget at the height of the Great Recession could have driven unemployment up to 18 to 20 percent, a level not seen since the 1930s (Prakken 2011).

The question of federal balanced budget rules and economic stabilization leads to another question: To what extent have balanced budget rules at the state level contributed to the ongoing weakness of the U.S. economy? Because of these rules, states responded to lower tax revenues associated with the recession by cutting back on expenditures. Rose and Smith note that the various budget rules of the states on balance permit a rapid adjustment to fiscal shocks. From the narrow point of view of state finances, this may indeed be welcome. But the effect on the national economy can be both negative and severe, as states move to cut spending by reducing outlays and shedding employees. Indeed, during the Great Recession and its immediate aftermath, states represented a substantial fiscal drag on the economy, becoming, in Paul Krugman's much-quoted phrase, "50 Herbert Hoovers" (Krugman 2008).

Perhaps state governments have grown too large and should be reduced in size; perhaps state payrolls have become bloated and need to be trimmed. But surely doing so during a period of feeble economic growth, struggling consumer demand, and high unemployment merely increases the task confronting the federal government as it seeks to stabilize the economy. The idea of reproducing state rules at the federal level should certainly give pause to policymakers who believe that fiscal policy can and should play a role during economic downturns.

More broadly, we should be aware of the macroeconomic cost of efforts to constrain the federal short-term budget deficit. We have an illustrative case in point: the Budget Control Act of 2011. Mandatory budget cuts, or sequestrations, under the act have clearly helped reduce the deficit. But they have also, according to many analysts, contributed to weaker economic growth; the International Monetary Fund (2013) , for instance, has criticized the United States for its "excessively rapid" debt reduction. I lack the competence (and the courage!) to take sides in the contentious debate between advocates of stimulus and austerity. But at a minimum, any consideration of budgetary rules must take into account potential trade-offs, at least in the short term, between fiscal consolidation on the one hand and economic growth and employment on the other.

Conclusion: The Primacy of Politics

I conclude with a discussion of a subject that Rose and Smith in general, and perhaps wisely, avoid: the highly partisan nature of our federal budget debate. Since the elections of 2010, which returned the House of Representatives to Republican control and reduced the Democratic majority in the Senate, we have been presented with the spectacle of what could be called fiscal policy by crisis. The Budget Control Act of 2011 was a last-minute compromise to avoid hitting the statutory debt limit. The American Tax Payer Relief Act of 2012 was a similarly hurried deal to avert an across-the-board increase in federal tax rates. Efforts to strike a bipartisan fiscal grand bargain that would include both revenue increases and expenditure cuts have thus far failed.

It is interesting to compare today with another period of budgetary brinksmanship: the mid-1990s, when conflict between the Clinton administration and a Republican Congress led to two dramatic, if brief, government shutdowns in late 1995 and early 1996.

What do these two periods have in common? Certainly not an imminent budget crisis. The deficit may indeed have been extremely high–—at nearly 9 percent of GDP—in 2011. But the federal deficit was, in contrast, modest and shrinking in 1995 and 1996, at 2.2 and 1.4 percent of GDP, respectively. No, the similarity between the periods is political. It is to be found in a Democratic president in the White House and a highly mobilized Republican congressional caucus. The earlier period of fiscal agitation was marked by the Contract with America and Republican capture of the U.S. House of Representatives for the first time in forty years. The latter period was shaped by the sweeping Republican gains in the 2010 congressional elections, driven in large part by the rise of the so-called Tea Party.

Let me stress that the partisanship of the 1990s like that of today reflects much more than simple enmity between political rivals. Fiscal differences between congressional Republicans and the Obama administration transcend their approaches to deficit reduction. They partake of a broader disagreement, driven by important constituencies and deeply held ideology, on the appropriate size and role of the federal government.

Faced with today's gridlock, it is understandable that we would seek some procedural mechanism to help us beyond the partisan impasse that fosters it. Still, one wonders if further rules, particularly those requiring supermajorities, make any sense for an already nearly paralyzed political system. Today forty-one U.S. senators can plunge the country into default by refusing to vote for cloture on a bill raising the debt ceiling. Ours is a system rife with many veto points. Some—the separation of powers, for instance, as well as a bicameral legislature–—are part of our constitutional plan. Others, like the Senate filibuster, have grown up over time. Do we really want to create more veto points, especially those involving supermajorities? We have seen what can happen when just one requirement, the necessity of Congress's approving an increase in the debt limit, becomes the proximate cause of partisan conflict and fiscal crisis.

I suspect that our debt problem, such as it is, will be solved by politics. Rose and Smith are, admirably, modest about the usefulness of state experience in federal budget reform. We should share their modesty. Perhaps it is time to give a strengthened PAYGO another chance, though even this will require bipartisan cooperation. The short-term improvement in the federal deficit creates a mixed blessing for supporters of budgetary reform. It surely reduces the urgency of such reform. But it also creates some breathing space as we consider ways to tackle longer-term problems associated with federal debt. We may need this reprieve to allow politics to take its course through one or more election cycles.

Acknowledgments

I extend my thanks to Emilio Longoria, my research assistant, for his help in preparing this response.

References

Congressional Budget Office. 2009. *The Budget and Economic Outlook: Fiscal Years 2009 to 2019*. Washington, DC: Congressional Budget Office.

Congressional Budget Office. 2014. *The Budget and Economic Outlook: Fiscal Years 2014 to 2024*. Washington, DC: Congressional Budget Office.

Hubbard, Glenn, and Tim Kane. 2011. In Pursuit of a Balanced Budget. (July 28). http://www.politico.com/news/stories/0711/60103.html.

International Monetary Fund. 2013. *Concluding Statement of the 2013 Article IV Mission to the United States of America*. Washington, DC: International Monetary Fund.

Krugman, Paul. 2008. Fifty Herbert Hoovers. *New York Times*, December 29.

Prakken, Joel. 2011. Defusing the Debt Bomb Economic and Fiscal Reform. Oral presentation, October 5, Houston, TX: Baker Institute for Public Policy.

Rose, Shanna. 2010. Institutions and Fiscal Responsibility. *National Tax Journal* 63 (1): 807–38.

Discussion

Rudolph G. Penner

Rose and Smith provide a useful survey of the role of fiscal limits at state and local levels. They find that the strictest balanced budget amendments may have some impact, but otherwise, constitutional or legal limits on deficits, tax burdens, and spending do not seem very effective in bolstering fiscal responsibility.

I feel a lot of sympathy for anyone doing empirical work in this field, which presents several major problems:

1. The first resort of the scoundrels when confronted by a constitutional or legal fiscal restraint is to engage in budget gimmickry. Unfortunately the gimmickry usually shows up in the historical record in the same way as real policy choices. A good example comes from the federal level. I would argue that the Republican Congress went on something of a spending binge soon after they were totally surprised by a budget surplus in 1998. However, they cheated outrageously, artificially moving some spending back into the previous fiscal year and some forward to future years. You can do a lot at the federal level moving outlays by one day forward or back at the end or beginning of fiscal years. The end result was that they smoothed out spending, and the historical record shows no significant bump. Empirical researchers have little choice but to rely on the historical record, and it can be very misleading.
2. The longer-run resort of the scoundrels is to move activity to off-budget independent agencies and other off-budget accounts. There is some mention of this in Rose and Smith's discussion of debt limits, but I wished for a more detailed analysis in the discussion of balanced budget constraints. Off-budget activity is extremely important at the state and local levels. There are over thirty-five thousand independent

agencies and other off-budget activities at lower levels of government. I have been told, but have not verified, that there are over six hundred off-budget accounts in the Illinois state budget. In addition to allowing blatant violations of constitutional and legal fiscal constraints, this activity makes state budgets very hard to understand. I would like to know more about the history of off-budget activity and how it evolved as constitutional or legal constraints became more common.

3. The last problem bedevils all empirical research. Which way does the causality run? Do more naturally conservative states tend to adopt the most conservative spending, tax, and deficit restrictions? Would they have more conservative budgets anyway without restrictions? Is that why some of the literature finds that states with stricter budget rules tend to get better credit ratings? Rose and Smith discuss this problem and claim to focus on studies that minimize it with fixed-effects analysis. But it has clearly been a problem with much of the literature on fiscal restraints.

My own intuitive view is that credit rating agencies exert far more discipline on state and local budgets than constitutional and legal constraints. In my home, the District of Columbia, we live and die by credit ratings. Too bad it did not work to discipline the federal government when S&P downgraded the federal debt after the debt limit fiasco.

I cannot help but wonder how relevant this discussion is for the federal government. The cut, cap, and balance movement that would like to cap total spending at 18 percent of GDP and pass a balanced budget amendment may be quite sincere, but as Rose and Smith imply, I do not think that it really understands budget arithmetic. With health and Social Security programs constituting almost half of noninterest spending; with most of those programs being retirement programs; with the baby boomers retiring in greater and greater numbers and causing a spending explosion, the notion of capping federal spending at 18 percent of GDP is totally unrealistic. It would take profound reforms in Social Security and Medicare to attain this goal. The programs would become shadows of their current selves, and given their extreme political popularity, anyone implementing such reforms would never be elected again.

I know of no carefully formulated budget plan that would balance the federal budget before the 2030s: not the House Republican budget, not the presidents' fiscal commission, not the Domenici-Rivlin commission, or the four fiscal packages formulated by a committee that I cochaired for the National Academies of Science and Public Administration. The best that one can hope for, and Rose and Smith note this point, is to stabilize the debt-to-GDP ratio. Sixty percent is a common goal. The president's proposals would take it higher than that.

The basic reasons that we are not making progress toward stabilizing the debt are twofold. First, the public and more than a few legislators are not aware of the basic arithmetic of the spending side of the budget that I already described. There is a great reluctance to believe that those two wonderful programs, Social Security and Medicare along with Medicaid, lie at the root of our budget problems.

Even if people knew, it is not clear that we would make progress. The two political parties have become purer ideologically than they used to be, and the population has as well. In other words, there is a bimodal distribution across the ideological spectrum and not enough people in the center or at the two ideological extremes to form a majority for anything. So with most Democrats strongly against reforming Social Security and Medicare and most Republicans adamantly against raising taxes, there is nowhere we can go.

As a result, the budget process is totally broken. The problem is not a lack of rules. We have plenty of rules. The problem is that the Congress does not follow the rules that they have. The Senate has not passed a budget for two years, and the House failed to pass one the year before. The House Republicans passed one this year, and I give them considerable credit for that whether you like their budget or not. It has become widely accepted that the Congress will never pass appropriations on time, and as a result, they waste an enormous amount of effort passing continuing resolutions, sometimes for a month, a week, or just a few days. The bureaucracy is often criticized for being inefficient, but it is hard to see how administrators can rationally plan their activities when they usually do not know how much they will have to spend until after the fiscal year begins.

One could not have a better symbol that the process is broken than the debt limit debate of July 2011. The Budget Control Act that emerged from that chaos totally bypassed the budget committees of the Congress by creating a supercommittee. I find it astonishing that neither the Senate nor the House budget committee chairman was put on that committee. The rules stated that if the supercommittee did not come up with at least $1.2 trillion in deficit reductions over ten years, we would have a totally mindless across-the-board reduction (sequester) in spending that cuts defense 10 percent starting in 2013 and cuts domestic programs that are not exempted by 7.5 percent. The supercommittee failed, and the sequester went into effect. The rules were made less stringent in a number of respects, but the sequester remains a totally irrational way to cut spending.

It would be nice if a few extra rules could fix the federal budget process, but at this point, the problem goes far beyond anything that could be fixed by changes in the rules. I do not see a complete resolution of our budget problems until we are faced with a sovereign debt crisis similar to that now afflicting Greece.

Rose and Smith end with a discussion of the line item veto. This is something that would work very differently at the federal level than it does at the state and local levels. Indeed, few understand how little relevance the notion of an item veto has for the federal budget. The problem is that the typical federal appropriation bill has very few line items. Money is not allocated to things like the bridge to nowhere and other specific items in typical appropriations bills. The money devoted to specific items is more often allocated using reports on bills. Those reports have no legal standing and therefore cannot be vetoed by the president. However, the executive branch ignores them at its peril. As a result, reports are followed to the letter.

A most minor budget reform would be to reform what is known as the rescission process. It now allows the president to define a line item in a spending program according to his wishes and to suggest canceling its budget authority. The cancellation does not go into effect unless it is approved by the Congress. If the Congress ignores the request, the rescission cannot go into effect. I think that it would be useful to force the Congress to vote on all rescission requests. If they voted against one, they would be saying, "This program that the president thinks is wasteful seems wonderful to us."

No one can guarantee that such a rule, often referred to as enhanced rescission, would actually cut spending. As Rose and Smith point out, such rules are vulnerable to logrolling. A liberal president might say to a legislator, "I won't suggest canceling your favorite program if you vote for my favorite program."

So I am for enhanced rescission not so much because I think it would cut spending, although it might on balance. I am mainly for it because it would enhance the power of the president in the budget process. He has little power now, and as the only elected person representing the whole nation, I believe that the president should play a more important role. But that may be because I was born in a country with a Westminster-style parliament.

Notes

1. Data were obtained from the U.S. Census Bureau (1963–2011) and the U.S. Bureau of Economic Analysis.

2. One notable exception is the spike in state and local municipal debt issues in the fourth quarter of 1985, which likely reflects anticipation of enactment of the Tax Reform Act of 1986, which lowered the top federal marginal income tax rate from 50 percent to 28 percent, reducing the tax advantage of municipal debt.

3. Data were obtained from the U.S. Census Bureau (1950–2011) and the U.S. Council of Economic Advisers (2013).

4. http://www.mccain.senate.gov/public/index.cfm/press-releases?ID=8839f721-0a7b-7367-d4f9-22c406e82c60.

5. Another branch of the literature examines the effect of the item veto on the composition—rather than the level or growth rate—of spending. Some studies find no significant effects (Dye 1969; Nice 1988), while others find that executive budget authority, including not only veto authority but also proposal authority, shifts the composition of spending from localized programs to spending with state wide benefits (Barrilleaux and Berkman 2003).

5 The Challenges of Funding U.S. Deficits and Debt

John Kitchen

The United States and other advanced economies are facing fundamental budget and external imbalances that are unsustainable in the long run under current policies. Large budget deficits in recent years in the United States and sovereign debt concerns in Europe have heightened the attention devoted to public finances and the outlook for public debt. In the face of such challenges, renewed efforts are needed in the United States to undertake fundamental tax and budget reforms. However, with the slow recovery from the recent severe recession and the need to limit short-term economic effects from immediate deficit reduction, successful strategies for reducing U.S. federal budget deficits and projected public debt will likely need to be implemented over an intermediate to longer time horizon. As a result, significant challenges will continue for funding U.S. budget deficits and public debt. My analysis and discussion examine the U.S. federal budget outlook and the associated public debt projections under scenarios identifying alternative potential sources of funding and their economic costs and effects.

The United States must fund its budget deficits and debt from three primary sources: private (domestic and foreign), foreign official, and domestic monetary (Federal Reserve). Funding from all three sources has occurred in the past and will occur in the future; only the relative extent of funding from each source is in question. Nonetheless, the fundamental opportunity cost adage of economics, "There is no such thing as a free lunch," applies regardless of which funding source might predominate. Ultimately costs will be realized from running large budget deficits and debt, and the real question is the nature and extent of the economic effects and costs. This analysis examines how that will depend on the sources of funding. Many forecasters do not explicitly address or account for the funding challenges and their economic and budget effects. Also, under standard budget rules and baselines, published comparisons of alternative budget scenarios usually do not directly include the budget effects of changes to economic variables and assumptions and can therefore understate the extent of the effects on budget deficits, debt, and the economy.

In order to address these issues, I first present information and discussion on current and historical funding relationships for U.S. domestic and international imbalances—for the public debt, the trade deficit, and the U.S. international debt position. General stylized economic effects and relationships associated with the alternative funding sources are examined. Then the analysis explores the implications of the relationships for the economic and budget outlook using economic and budget projections over the next decade that include the continuation of various politically popular policies in alternative scenarios. Three of the alternatives considered are based on the alternative funding sources for federal deficits and debt; a fourth alternative considers the outlook under successful (generic) fundamental budget and tax reform.

In each case, the implied necessary amount from the specific funding source to meet the additional borrowing is determined, and the associated economic and budget effects are included. Under the private funding case, for example, higher interest rates are required to induce the private funding, and the economic effects include the traditional crowding-out effects of lower investment, lower capital stock, and lower gross domestic product (GDP) over time. The estimated budget effects under the private funding case include those effects, as well as higher interest costs. Although the use of increased foreign official holdings to fund the higher deficits and debt would help mitigate increases in domestic U.S. interest rates, the required balancing flows in international markets would result in net export crowding out and associated negative effects on real GDP. If the Federal Reserve were to fund higher deficits and debt ("monetizing the debt"), inflation ultimately would rise with the sustained increase in the Federal Reserve balance sheet, and costs would be realized through real capital losses for holders of Treasury securities and other bonds. The negative wealth effects from those capital losses would adversely affect consumption, investment, and real GDP. In each case, the scenarios examine the resulting implications for the projected public debt relative to gross national product (GNP).[1] Similar magnitudes of increases in the public debt relative to GNP are observed in the case of private funding and foreign official funding cases, rising to over 90 percent of GNP by 2022; the case of monetizing the debt through Federal Reserve funding results in a more modest effect on the public debt relative to GNP (at about 70 percent) as nominal GNP rises with higher inflation and prior issues of debt are diluted in value on a relative basis.

In addition to the effects on the key budget variables and the domestic U.S. economy, the scenarios also examine and include the effects on key international variables for the U.S. economy, including U.S. net exports, net international income flows, and the U.S. net international investment position (U.S. net international debt). The inclusion of the effects on international flows and balances is of fundamental importance to more completely understand the full costs of alternative funding sources. For example, although foreign official funding may initially appear to generate relative benefits for the domestic U.S. economy by keeping U.S. long-term interest rates lower than otherwise (and thereby mitigating investment crowding out), the increased foreign financial flows have the adverse balancing effect of net export crowding out. Furthermore, there would be persisting negative effects of lower net international income flows and a much larger U.S. net international debt position. Adverse effects on net international income flows would reduce U.S. national income for any given level of GDP, reducing U.S. standards of living on a relative basis.

The results and scenarios presented are not forecasts but rather projections that examine the relative economic and budget effects from alternative funding sources over the intermediate horizon. This is based on given baseline projections of economic growth, budget deficits, and interest rates. Although the analysis begins from the short-run economic and budget situation and outlook on which the intermediate- and long-term projections are based, alternative short-run policy and cyclical factors and relationships are not directly considered. The economic and budget situation and outlook once the economy has returned to its long-run trend is the reference for analysis and comparison. Also, as the analysis focuses on federal deficits and debt over an intermediate horizon, it can only serve as an upfront look at the longer-run budget and debt challenges over coming decades that exist under the current set of unsustainable policies. The analysis also does not address other significant challenges beyond the federal budget such as state and local government budgets, public and private pensions, and private debt burdens. Even so, budget and tax reforms and debt mitigation efforts would have to begin somewhere, sometime, and the overall economic and budget effects addressed here would also generally apply to longer-run projections and outlooks for the federal budget as well.

I first present background and explanatory information and then describe the analysis of the base and alternative scenarios. I next examine data and information on U.S. government debt, recent Federal Reserve policies, and U.S. international imbalances. This is followed by a baseline outlook based on projections by the Congressional Budget Office (CBO). The discussion continues with a preliminary look at the stylized economic effects associated with the alternative sources for funding U.S. government deficits and debt, as well as discussion of the empirical basis for analyzing the effects on U.S. Treasury interest rates from budget deficits and alternative funding sources. I examine the scenarios for alternative funding sources for the debt and also provide a scenario for tax and budget reform, with explicit accounting and a description of the economic and budget effects and follow with some additional issues and concerns. I close with summary comments and discussion.

The Context: U.S. Budget and International Imbalances

Historical data on U.S. government debt, the U.S. net export deficit, and the U.S. net international investment position illustrate the ongoing imbalances the United States is facing and help provide a foundation for the analysis.

Treasury Debt and Foreign Official Holdings

U.S. Treasury public debt is held by domestic and foreign holders, and private and official holders:

$$T_{TOT} = (T_{D,P} + T_{D,O}) + (T_{F,P} + T_{F,O}) \tag{5.1}$$

T_{TOT} is the total supply of Treasury debt held by the public. For the other variables, the first subscript represents domestic (D) or foreign (F), and the second subscript is private (P) or official (O).[2]

Historical data show growing U.S. Treasury debt held by the public (T_{TOT}) and growing foreign official ($T_{F,O}$) holdings and shares for U.S. Treasury securities outstanding. This is especially true for the recent period associated with and following the recession and financial crisis (figure 5.1). Particularly noteworthy is the large and growing role of foreign official holdings. They have risen from just over $600 billion

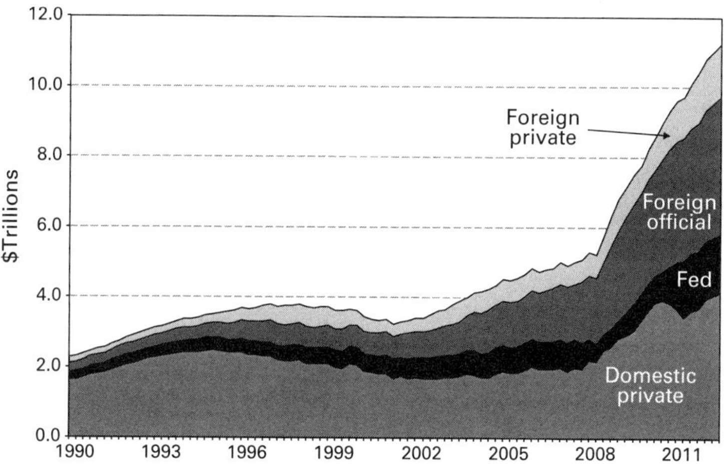

Figure 5.1
Outstanding Treasury Securities by Holder, 1990–2012.

(17 percent of total Treasury debt securities outstanding) at the end of 1999 to over $3.9 trillion (35 percent of total outstanding) by the end of 2012 (figure 5.2). In this application, domestic official ($T_{D,O}$) amounts in equation 5.1 are those held by the Federal Reserve, which over the past twenty-five years generally have accounted for about 10 to 15 percent of total outstanding Treasuries (and also generally in the range of about 4 to 6 percent of GDP). During the financial crisis, however, the Federal Reserve share fell sharply (to as low as 7 percent of Treasuries outstanding) as the Federal Reserve used its portfolio of Treasury securities as part of its implementation of the various lending facilities, and reflecting its portfolio shift (and expansion) to other assets, including government-sponsored enterprise (GSE) debt securities. More recently, the Federal Reserve's share of Treasuries has increased back to about 15 percent of the total outstanding with the extended quantitative easing policies. Figure 5.3 shows foreign official holdings of U.S. Treasury securities as a percent of U.S. potential GDP. The figure shows the rising importance of foreign official holdings as both a source of funding and a share of the U.S. economy as a whole.[3]

GSEs, Fannie and Freddie, and the Fed's "Quantitative Easing" Programs

Following the decline in housing and mortgage markets and the ensuing financial crisis, much attention has been directed at U.S agency

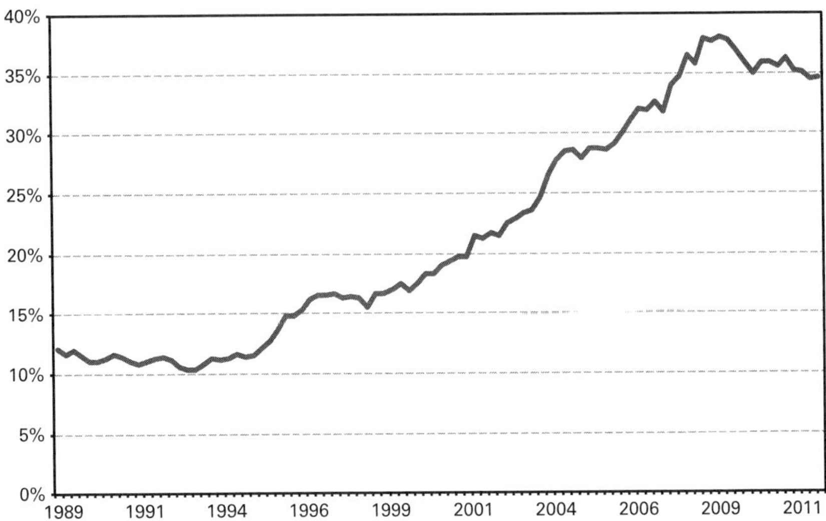

Figure 5.2
Foreign Official Treasury Holdings as Share of Total Outstanding Treasuries.
Source: Federal Reserve Flow of Funds.

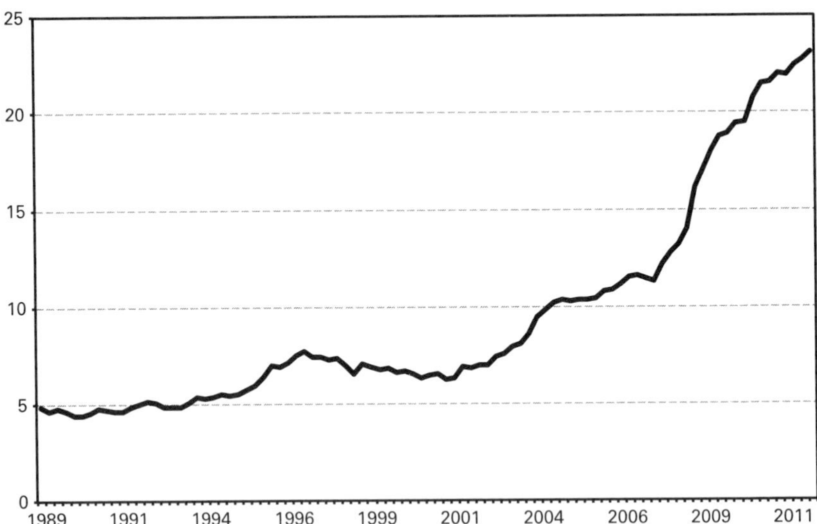

Figure 5.3
Foreign Official Treasury Holdings as a Percent of GDP
Source: Federal Reserve Flow of Funds.

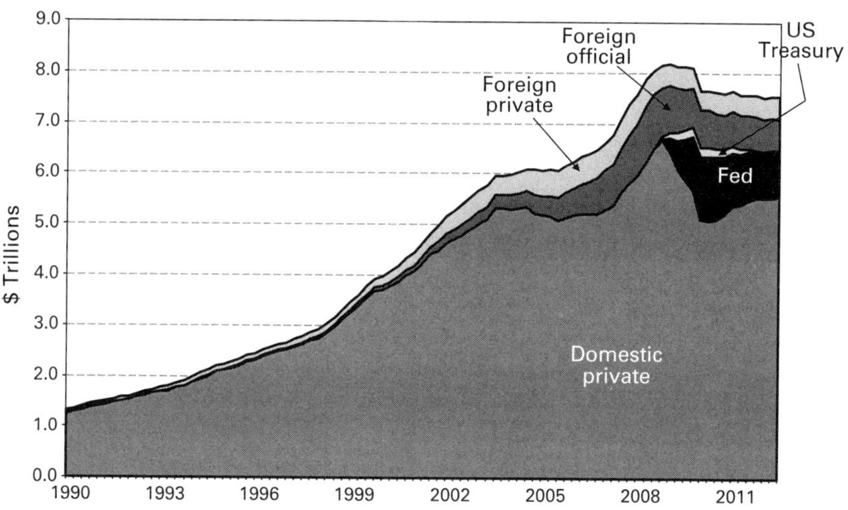

Figure 5.4
Agency, GSE, and GSE-Backed Securities by Holder, 1990–2012.
Source: Federal Reserve Flow of Funds.

and GSE debt and securities, notably the Federal National Mortgage Association (Fannie Mae) and the Federal Mortgage Guarantee Corporation (Freddie Mac). Figure 5.4 shows historical data for agency, GSE, and GSE-backed securities by holder.[4] During the financial crisis, the U.S. government undertook direct actions to provide backing for Fannie Mae and Freddie Mac, including direct purchases of GSE-backed debt.

The Federal Reserve's purchases and holdings of agency and GSE-backed securities, through its balance sheet expansion and purchase of mortgage-backed securities, has attracted much attention because of the tripling of the size of the Fed's balance sheet (and, hence, the monetary base) since the end of 2007, with a significant share of that increase held in GSE-backed debt securities. In early 2009 the Federal Reserve implemented a plan to expand credit and support aggregate demand through purchases of longer-term assets, described by Kohn (2009) as the large-scale asset purchases (LSAP) program. The Fed increased purchases of GSE and agency debt, mortgage-backed securities, and longer-term U.S. Treasury securities. Federal Open Market Committee (FOMC) statements announced that the program would include purchases of up to $200 billion of agency debt, up to $300 billion in longer-term U.S. Treasury securities, and up to $1.25 trillion in agency mortgage-backed securities. In November 2010, the FOMC announced plans "to purchase a further $600 billion of longer-term Treasury securities by the end of the second quarter of 2011." By the end of June 2011, the Federal Reserve's balance sheet stood at $2.9 trillion, with agency and GSE-backed securities accounting for just over $1 trillion, or about 35 percent of the total assets on the Federal Reserve balance sheet, and Treasury securities accounting for $1.6 trillion, or about 40 percent of the total. Additional quantitative easing actions continued in 2012, and Fed policy announced in October and December 2012 specified further quantitative easing through continued purchases of agency mortgage-backed securities and long-term Treasury securities. These policy statements indicate that the Fed anticipates the need to maintain the large balance sheet for an extended period.

For my analysis, I make specific assumptions for the base projections regarding Federal Reserve holdings of longer-term Treasuries and GSE securities and federal budget exposure. These assumptions are that the expanded size of the balance sheet will continue to grow through 2013 and then stabilize in 2014, before gradually unwinding after 2014. The unwinding is assumed to occur in an orderly and benign fashion over a five-year period, consistent with FOMC statements regarding "exit" policy and also similar to the unwinding pattern in prior analyses such as Chung et al. (2011) and as described by Yellen (2011). For the base projection, the assumption is that the Fed will gradually and successfully reduce its expanded portfolio holdings of GSE securities and longer-term Treasuries and return to its precrisis position of a balance sheet primarily of Treasury securities, and at a level relative to GDP consistent with the sustained growth and low inflation of the economic projections. In contrast to the base case assumptions, for the alternative scenario that examines Federal Reserve monetization of the debt, the balance sheet is assumed to be larger relative to the base case as needed to mitigate interest rate term structure effects from the increases in deficits and debt (relative to the base) as implied in the scenario.

International Imbalances: What about China? What about Oil?

In addition to the challenges from budget deficits and debt and an expanded monetary base, the United States faces fundamental international trade and international debt imbalances.

General U.S. International Imbalances

The United States has run large international imbalances over the past decade and a half, with a large net export deficit and large net

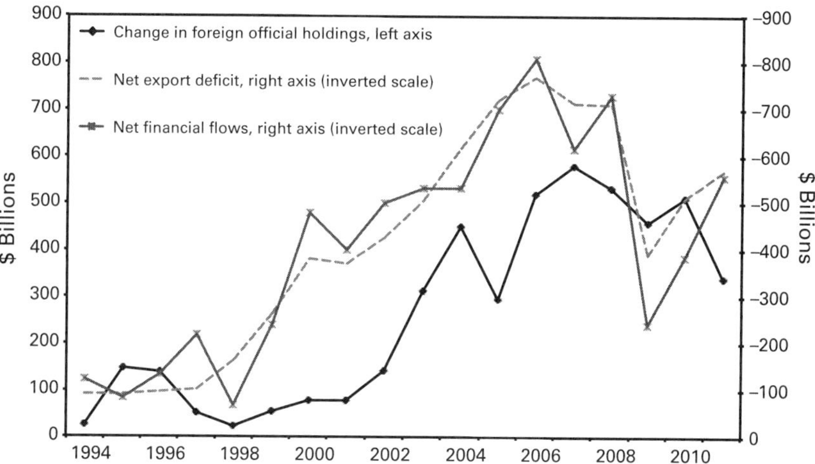

Figure 5.5
U.S. Net Exports Deficit and Change in Foreign Official Holdings.
Source: Bureau of Economic Analysis; Federal Reserve Flow of Funds.

international financial flows from abroad (figure 5.5). These imbalances are not independent of the financing of the U.S. federal budget deficits that has occurred; the foreign official flows into Treasuries are a significant part of the growing net international financial flows. On average from 2003 through 2009, the change in foreign official holdings was two-thirds of the amount of the U.S. net export deficit. Gagnon (2011b, 220) presents a similar chart that shows the close relationship in IMF data for "net official capital outflows (including purchases of foreign exchange reserves) for all developing economies, along with their aggregate current account balances." Gagnon then states, "This level of official capital flows from developing economies to the advanced economies is unprecedented. . . . Official capital flows of this magnitude are not sustainable indefinitely, but they have persisted for quite a while and it is not clear when or how they will eventually subside." For the United States, in particular, large foreign official financial flows have their mirror in large trade deficits.

In addition, the accumulation of ongoing trade deficits and international financial flows has resulted in a large net international debt position for the United States (figure 5.6). Three decades ago, the United States was a significant net creditor in its net international investment position at about 10 percent of GDP, but has since experienced a trend decline in the investment position to being a net debtor at around -20

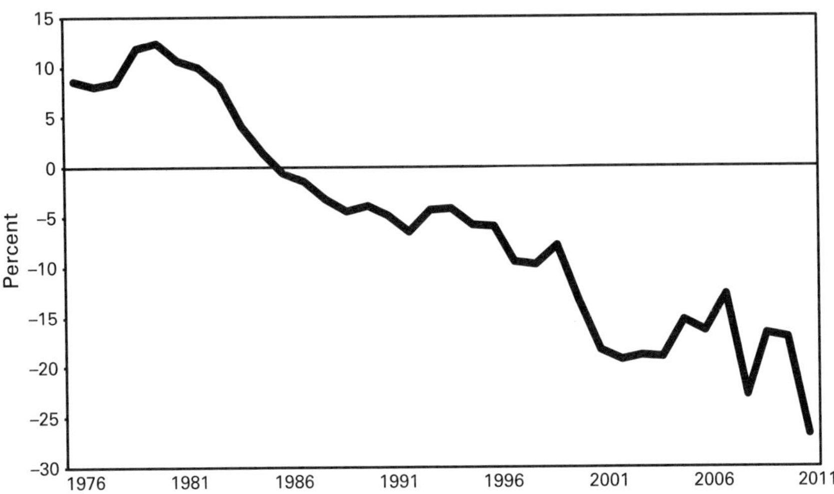

Figure 5.6
U.S. Net International Investment Position as a Percent of GDP.

percent to -25 percent of GDP. Questions of how the United States will finance its debt thus extend beyond issues regarding the federal budget and the public debt to the international dimension.

Specific China and Oil Issues

From looking back over recent years and at the current situation, it is clear that the two major factors in the U.S. international imbalances have been the large dependence of the United States on imported oil and China's policy of maintaining a low exchange value for its currency, through large (foreign official) purchases of U.S. Treasury securities, and the associated large bilateral net export deficit for the United States (figure 5.7).[5] An important part of the financial flows that balance those trade flows are the foreign official purchases of Treasury securities. Table 5.1 shows the foreign official holdings by country for major holders of Treasuries as shown in the Treasury International Capital data. China and East Asia holdings of Treasuries comprise about half of all foreign holdings of Treasuries.

These imbalances also contributed to the financial and economic instability of recent years. China's policies played a role in the financial crisis for the United States. The policy of maintaining a low value of its currency relative to the dollar, implemented through high foreign

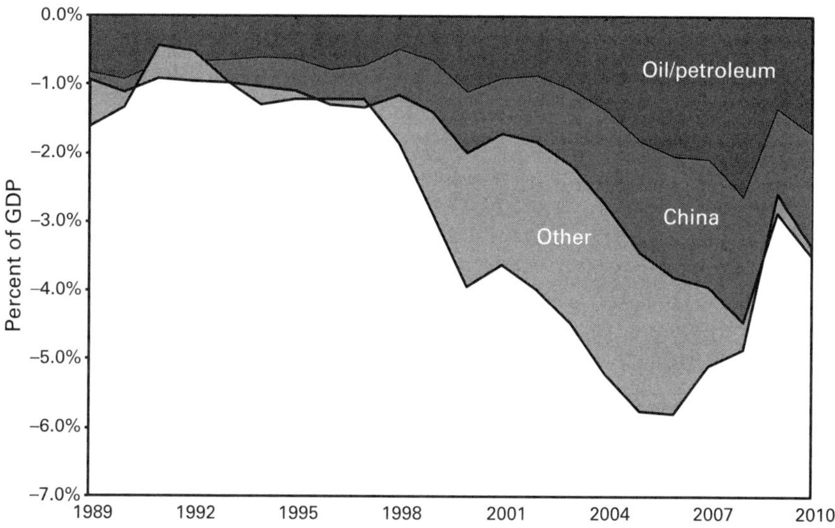

Figure 5.7
U.S. Net Export Deficit by Major Components.

Table 5.1
Foreign Holdings of U.S. Treasury Securities by Country, October 2012 (billions)

China, Mainland	$1,162
Japan	1,135
Oil exporters	266
Caribbean banking centers	259
Brazil	255
Taiwan	202
Switzerland	194
Russia	165
Luxembourg	139
Hong Kong	137
All other	1,568
Total	5,482
Note: Foreign Official Total	3,962

Source: Treasury International Capital data, U.S. Department of the Treasury.

official purchases of U.S. Treasury securities, exacerbated the international trade imbalance and contributed to the lower saving and higher consumption on the part of the United States. As Eichengreen (2011) also describes, China's ongoing and large purchases of U.S. Treasury securities (along with other sovereign wealth funds) contributed to lower long-term interest rates in the United States. At the same time, lower mortgage rates and lax lending standards were contributing to the housing boom and excess funding of mortgages in the lead-up to the financial crisis. These relationships illustrate some of the challenges and costs from having foreign official flows as a predominant funding source for U.S. budget deficits and debt.

Both the full examination of the needed corrections to international policy generally and the needed corrections to the policies of specific foreign nations are beyond my scope here. Nonetheless, these relationships can help to highlight the types of domestic policy reforms that could have obvious benefits to reducing U.S. international imbalances, notably tax policy reforms such as consumption taxes or energy consumption taxes generally, or oil- or carbon-based taxes specifically. Of note among recent reform proposals, the Bipartisan Policy Center's Deficit Reduction Task Force, chaired by Pete Domenici and Alice Rivlin, proposed tax simplification and reform that included a consumption tax—a "debt reduction sales tax" (Bipartisan Policy Center 2010).

The Baseline Outlook

The base case of this first essay in the chapter uses the Congressional Budget Office's baseline economic and budget assumptions and projections (2012b). The CBO economic projections show the U.S. economy ultimately recovering from the Great Recession, returning over about six years to its potential growth path. Output and unemployment gaps are projected to decline, and interest rates and inflation rates are assumed to reflect the return to an environment of sustained real growth at potential with low inflation. The budget projections used in the analysis start with the CBO's baseline budget outlook; the alternative scenarios considered include adjustments to the baseline budget outlook, including the "continuation of certain policies" as identified by CBO, although adjusted for passage of the American Taxpayer Relief Act of 2012 (ATRA).[6] Each of the cases then includes alternative sources of funding for federal budget deficits and the U.S. public debt. Although various alternative policy and budget outlooks are possible, the use of the CBO's base projection and the inclusion of the adjusted "continuation of certain policies" in the alternatives provide reasonable benchmarks to illustrate the budget outlook and the associated funding challenges I address. The projections used are at an intermediate horizon—ten years, through 2022—and serve to illustrate the outlook and challenges over that horizon. Although the longer-term budget outlook beyond ten years is not explicitly addressed, in most cases the longer-term challenges can be viewed as extensions and multiples of those of the intermediate horizon. Absent significant policy changes, the U.S. budget outlook ultimately is unsustainable and even undefined over the longer time horizon.

Regarding the international economic outlook, the CBO (2012a), as well as the administration and private sector forecasters, have had an improving net export outlook in their economic assumptions (Council of Economic Advisers 2010). Such projections are also consistent with an ongoing trend decline in the value of the dollar. To reflect these views and relationships, the base case projection includes a gradual trend improvement in U.S. net exports and a gradual trend decline in the exchange value of the dollar.

Underlying Relationships for Alternative Funding Sources for U.S. Government Debt

In this section, I examine broad-brush, stylized relationships for alternative funding sources and their economic effects. Also, an empirical, estimated equation is introduced for the effects of the budget deficit, foreign official funding, and Federal Reserve holdings on Treasury interest rates. And in considering the underlying economic relationships associated with alternative funding sources for U.S. government deficits and debt, various accounting relationships and constraints must be explicitly included.

Some Accounting Relationships

Injections-Leakages

Consider the standard textbook "injections-leakages" relationship from international macroeconomics:

$$I + G + X = S + T + M, \tag{5.2}$$

where I is private domestic investment, G is government purchases, X is (foreign) expenditures on U.S. exports, S is private domestic saving, T is tax revenues, and M is (domestic) expenditures on imports (from foreign countries). The left-hand side is the injections into the flow of the domestic economy; the right-hand side is the leakages from the domestic economy. Rearranging equation 5.2 yields an equation that more directly shows the considerations we are examining:

$$(G - T) + I = S - (X - M). \tag{5.2'}$$

The left-hand side of equation 5.2′ comprises the domestic uses of funds, and the right-hand side shows sources. In order to fund domestic government budget deficits ($G - T$) and private domestic investment, I, the sources of funding are domestic private saving, S, and foreign financial flows that are the mirror of the net export deficit (note that the foreign flows represented by –[X –M] would include both foreign private and foreign official flows). Two of the alternative cases examined for alternative sources of financing are therefore readily apparent in equation 5.2′: private funding (both domestic and foreign private) and foreign official. The third alternative for Federal Reserve funding, monetizing the debt, requires a more detailed representation beyond the flows of saving and investment associated with current production as in the National Income and Product Accounts (NIPAs). Federal Reserve funding beyond that for money supply growth needed to match real transactions and output growth would occur though additional changes in financial stocks, and effects would occur through monetary and price relationships and through the effects of inflation on nominal variables.

Income Side of the NIPAs

A second set of relationships that must be considered, and often is not explicitly or fully addressed by analysts and forecasters, is the national income accounting for the income side of NIPAs. Table 5.2 shows the income side of the NIPAs with data for calendar year 2011. Of particular note are the international income flows at the top that add income flows from abroad and subtract domestic income payments to foreigners. The net effect of those international income flows is part of the translation from gross domestic product to national income, along with depreciation and statistical discrepancy. Hence, to the extent that the funding source for deficits adversely affects net international income flows, it would then adversely affect domestic incomes and standards

Table 5.2
Income Side of NIPAs, 2011 (billions)

1	**Gross domestic product**		**$15,076**
2	+	Income receipts from rest of world	784
3	-	Income payments to rest of world	532
4	**Equals: Gross national product**		**15,328**
5	-	Consumption of fixed capital	1,937
6	-	Statistical discrepancy	32
7	**Equals: National income**		**13,359**
8		Compensation of employees	8,295
9		Wages and salaries	6,661
10		Supplements to wages and salaries	1,634
11		Proprietors income with IVA and CCAdj	1,157
12		Rental Income of persons with CCAdj	410
13		Corporate profits with IVA and CCAdj	1,827
14		Net interest and miscellaneous payments	527
15		Taxes on production and imports less subsidies	1,036
16		Business current transfer payment (net)	133
17		Current surplus of government enterprises	-27

Source: Bureau of Economic Analysis

of living on a relative basis.[7] Accounting for this relationship will be of particular importance for the case of foreign official funding of budget deficits, but there also will be relative differences to the base case for other funding alternatives. Note there would also be a small offsetting effect in cases where investment is affected, as the consumption of fixed capital (depreciation) would be reduced by a fraction of the investment change, depending on the life of the capital and the associated rate of economic depreciation.

Stylized Effects and Costs for Alternative Funding Sources and Scenarios

In the alternative scenarios examined here—and to illustrate the roles of alternative sources of financing—the analysis examines changes in Treasury debt and holdings relative to the base case. The analysis examines funding for U.S. government borrowing from three alternative sources: private (domestic and foreign), foreign official, and domestic official (monetary/Federal Reserve). Using equation 5.1, expressing in change (Δ) form, and rearranging, we get:

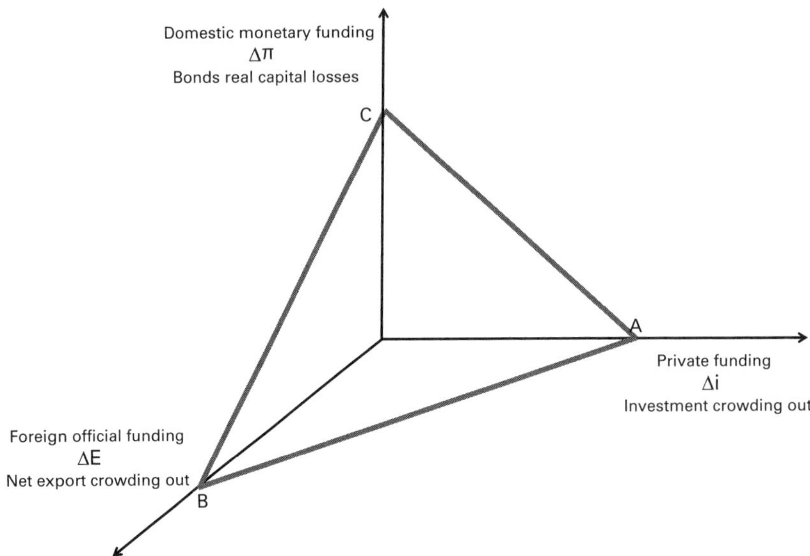

Figure 5.8
Graphical Representation of Alternative Funding Possibilities.

$$\Delta T_{TOT} = (\Delta T_{D,P} + \Delta T_{F,P}) + \Delta T_{F,O} + \Delta T_{D,O.} \tag{5.3}$$

Figure 5.8 shows a stylized, graphical representation of the alternative funding possibilities. The three axes correspond to the three alternative funding sources, as well as the financial variables and the real economic and activity responses associated with each. The distance from the origin on each of the axes represents the amount of additional funding needed to match the increased deficits and debt service costs. The cases examined and the financial and economic responses presented are representative and illustrative of the changes and resulting positions in comparative static equilibriums but would not necessarily account for or represent transitional or cyclical relationships.

Private Funding

Point A on the private funding axis represents a case in which additional funding comes from private sources. In this case, the long-term Treasury interest rate response is at its largest (to induce the increase in private funding), and domestic investment is crowded out to the extent that interest rate increases raise the cost of capital and reduce investment. If the change in private funding is solely from domestic sources, this would then be equivalent to the standard textbook response for the effects in a closed economy of a decrease in national saving from a government budget deficit. For the funding effect to be fully from private domestic sources—and the increase in the domestic interest rate to not induce an increase in foreign private funding flows—would require the international transmission of the domestic interest rate response to foreign interest rates. Note that the interest parity conditions would be maintained in this special case by having no change in the foreign spot exchange rate spread and no difference between domestic and foreign interest rates (with the increase in foreign rates matching that for the domestic rate). The pure application of this stylized case would be limited to the extent foreign private funding could rise with higher U.S. interest rates. If the rise in foreign private holdings of U.S. Treasuries occurs with a reshuffling of the foreign-held asset portfolio and no change in the aggregate size of that portfolio, then the stylized example would still apply. It is limited only to the extent that total foreign financial flows change (relative to the base) with a change in foreign private funding flows for Treasuries. In the end, the analysis and results would be less sensitive to changes in foreign private funding as it represents only about 10 percent of the total, compared to 40 percent each for domestic private funding and foreign official holdings. As such, the stylized presentation here is a representative application.

Foreign Official Funding

Point B on the foreign official funding axis corresponds to the case in which additional funding comes from increases in foreign official holdings of Treasury securities. That increase (with no change relative to the base in private foreign holdings or private financial flows) would result in an increase in total foreign financial flows and would require a balancing increase in the U.S. net export deficit and an associated increase in the exchange value of the dollar. Hence, in contrast to the private funding case that results in crowding out of domestic investment, the case of full foreign official funding results in net export crowding out. International balance accounting identities require that an increase in foreign financial flows to the United States would be mirrored by an increase in the U.S. net export deficit. This position is the full "twin-deficit" relationship, in which the change in the U.S. government budget deficit is mirrored by the change in the U.S. net export deficit (Chinn 2005).

Domestic Monetary Funding

Point C on the domestic monetary funding axis corresponds to the case in which funding comes from increases in purchases of Treasury securities by the Federal Reserve. The increase in the Fed's balance sheet and the increase in reserves in the system—an increase in the monetary base—would result in higher domestic inflation under a monetarist approach, and higher inflation would result in higher nominal short-term and long-term interest rates. The higher domestic inflation also leads to a depreciation of the nominal exchange value of the dollar, preserving purchasing power parity in the long run. Note that in the stylized relationships considered here, the change is in the nominal exchange rate but not in the real exchange rate, so real net exports are not affected. Higher inflation erodes the real value of preexisting bonds.[8] Costs are realized through real capital losses for bondholders, for both Treasuries and other dollar-denominated public and private bonds.

Mixed Funding

Ultimately the result could be a mix of funding outcomes, with a weighted average combination of the separate funding components represented by a point on the surface defined by A-B-C in figure 5.8; a mix of interest rate, exchange rate, and inflation rate responses; and a mix of economic effects of investment crowding out, net export crowding out, or inflation-induced real losses for bond holders. The alternative scenarios I present illustrate the range of outcomes associated with the alternative funding sources, and a mixed outcome would generally lie within those results.

Ultimately an important challenge arises from the fact that the mix of funding is not a "policy choice." Once the policy choice has been made to have budget deficits, the only domestic policy choice is whether the budget deficits and debt would be monetized, but that is a monetary policy decision and not one for fiscal policymakers. Rather, from the perspective of fiscal policymakers, the funding decision is made by others, and a large measure of how fiscal policy affects the economy is surrendered to others, even to foreign actors.

Empirical Specification for Funding Sources Effects on U.S. Treasury Rates

A large and growing literature exists relating interest rates to federal debt and deficits, including Gale and Orszag (2002, 2005) Canzoneri,

Cumby, and Diba (2002), Kitchen (2003), Laubach (2003, 2009), Engen and Hubbard (2005), and Gagnon (2011a). The advent of the conundrum—that is, surprisingly low long-term interest rates relative to short rates in the early 2000s—inspired research introducing an international dimension. Warnock and Warnock (2006) and Chinn and Frankel (2007) augmented conventional bond pricing specifications with international variables, namely, foreign official purchases of U.S. Treasuries.

More recently, Kitchen and Chinn (2011) examined interest rate relationships in a comprehensive analysis that included federal structural budget deficits, Federal Reserve purchases of long-term government securities, and foreign official purchases of U.S. Treasury securities. Notably, Kitchen and Chinn tested constraints on the coefficient estimates for structural budget deficits and alternative exogenous funding sources and were unable to reject the hypothesis that the effects were equal. The preferred equation estimated by Kitchen and Chinn, and a relationship to be used in this analysis, is given by

$$i_{10YR} - i_{3MO} = 1.22 + 0.56\ UNGAP - 0.38\ INFL - 0.33\ (STRSURP + FOREIGN + FED), \quad (5.4)$$

where:

i_{10YR} is the constant-maturity yield on ten-year Treasury notes
i_{3MO} is the secondary market interest rate on three-month Treasury bills
UNGAP is the gap between the unemployment rate and the NAIRU
INFL is the deviation of consumer price inflation from the Fed's target inflation rate
STRSURP is the federal structural budget surplus as a percent of potential GDP
FOREIGN is the change in foreign official holdings of U.S. Treasuries as a percent of potential GDP
FED is the change in the Federal Reserve's holdings of long-term Treasury and government securities as a percent of potential GDP

The Federal Reserve's inflation target was assumed to be 2.0 percent for history in the estimation of equation 5.4, and that assumption applies for the base case of this analysis as well. For the alternative cases (and notably the Federal Reserve funding case), the target inflation rate rises with the growth of the Fed's balance sheet relative to the base case, with the increase in holdings of long-run government securities. The specification in equation 5.4 was derived from a Taylor rule for the determination of short-term rates (discussed in more detail later) and a term-structure relationship positing the role of relative supply, demand factors, and risk for the costs and funding of long-term Treasury borrowing.

The positive coefficient on the *UNGAP* variable and the negative coefficient on the *INFL* variable reflect their roles in the monetary policy rule and the resulting relationship to short-term rates. That is, consistent with the Taylor rule and with well-anchored long-run expected inflation, as output rises relative to potential, and unemployment falls relative to the NAIRU, the Federal Reserve would raise the short-term interest rate relative to the long-term interest rate (ceteris paribus) and the term spread would decline. Similarly, as inflation increased relative to the target level of inflation, the Federal Reserve would raise the short-term interest rate relative to the long-term rate and the term spread would decline. The coefficient on the structural surplus variable is negative, as an increase in the structural budget surplus (a fall in the deficit) would reduce the relative supply of Treasury securities and reduce risk and uncertainty for longer-term Treasury securities, leading to a lower long-term yield relative to short-term (short-run policy-determined) rates. The coefficients on the change in foreign official holdings of U.S. Treasuries, and for Federal Reserve holdings of long-term Treasuries, Mortgage Backed Securities and U.S. agency assets, are also negative. An increase in official/monetary holdings (foreign or domestic) is effectively an exogenous demand shift for Treasury securities (at that point in time) that would lower longer-term yields.

The results in equation 5.4 from Kitchen and Chinn generally conform to prior estimates in the literature for the effects of the budget deficit on long-term Treasury yields—and for the effect of the change in foreign official holdings as well. The estimated effect is 33 basis points on the ten-year yield relative to the short-term yield for each 1 percentage point of GDP for the structural budget deficit.[9] Also, the results confirm the importance of foreign official holdings of Treasuries as a determinant of the long-term Treasury yield (here expressed relative to the short-term yield).[10] For the *FEDLT* variable—the change in Fed holdings of longer-term Treasury, MBS, and U.S. government agency securities as a percent of potential GDP—the constrained coefficient estimate is also roughly consistent (albeit somewhat higher) with other estimates from the literature for the effects of the Fed's purchases of longer-term government assets.[11]

The estimated equation from Kitchen and Chinn conforms to an analytical approach in which short-term rates are generally determined according to a Taylor rule, with budget deficits, foreign official holdings of Treasury securities, and Federal Reserve purchases of longer-term assets affecting long-term yields relative to short-term rates. Notably, the estimated relationships also imply that foreign official flows from abroad kept U.S. long-term rates lower than otherwise would have occurred during the decade of the 2000s (as discussed earlier), contributing to an environment in which foreign financial flows and the effects on interest rates exacerbated the housing and financial boom and bust.[12]

Scenarios for Alternative Funding Sources for U.S. Debt, and the Economic and Budget Effects

This section provides a comparison using estimates and projections for alternative funding sources for U.S. federal budget deficits and debt. The scenarios start from a base projection, and the alternatives then include the budget costs from the "continuation of certain policies" as adjusted post-ATRA. Economic effects on gross domestic product from the additional structural budget deficit effects on national saving are also included by using the estimated effect on output growth as determined in a Solow growth model.[13] Each case considers an alternative funding source, and the estimated budget and economic effects over the next decade are determined and presented. The determination of the amount of funding in each scenario is the amount that maintains the term structure spread, the ten-year Treasury yield to three-month Treasury bill interest rate spread of the base case.[14] Beyond the alternative funding scenarios, an additional scenario is presented to show the illustrative effects under a "generic" fundamental budget and tax reform—reform that would generate significant budget savings and a simplified and more efficient tax structure. Effects on the U.S. international investment position and net international income flows are also presented, based on calculations in a model originally presented in Kitchen (2007).

Some additional notes regarding relationships used in making the estimates and projections are in order. First, the Taylor rule relationship employed is based on Taylor (1993), here having the specification:

$$i = \pi + 0.5\,(\pi - \pi^*) - 1.0\,(U - U_N) + g_T \qquad (5.5)$$

where

i is the short-term interest rate targeted by monetary policy (here the three-month Treasury bill rate in application)
π is the rate of consumer price inflation (here for the NIPA personal consumption expenditures price index)
π^* represents the inflation target
U is the unemployment rate
U_N is the NAIRU or natural rate of unemployment
g_T is the steady-state trend rate of real GDP growth

In the analysis that follows, the Taylor rule equation is applied to calculate changes in the interest rate for differences in the determining variables relative to the base values. One difference in this specification is to use the deviation of the unemployment rate from the NAIRU rather than the output gap as in Taylor's original specification; in most times, they carry roughly the same information through the Okun's law relationship between unemployment and real GDP. Regarding the inflation target, generally the assumed targeted inflation rate π^* is 2 percent; in the Federal Reserve funding scenario, the targeted inflation rate varies with the resulting inflation rate with the funding. The value of g_T changes from the base case to the alternatives depending on how the rate of potential GDP growth changes; hence, the short-term rate will be lower relative to the base if potential real GDP growth is lower relative to the base. This dependence on the trend rate of growth for real GDP was conceptually part of the original Taylor rule, although many users have assumed a hard value of 2 percent given that number expressed in the original equation of the paper. Note that Taylor described it as "the 2-percent `equilibrium' real rate is close to the assumed steady state growth rate of 2.2 percent" (Taylor 1993, 202).

Second, the implicit assumption is that the longer-term interest rate or yield is the interest rate that matters for investment, for debt financing. Third, the ultimate values and relationships in the scenarios are determined endogenously and simultaneously, so that the full effects with feedbacks are accounted for. Fourth, in each of the alternatives, the inclusion of the "continuation of certain policies" accounts for nearly $5 trillion of additional debt relative to the base, including debt service costs. However, to the extent economic effects—interest rates, GDP, or inflation—occur in the scenarios, the additional budget effects are calculated, included endogenously and simultaneously. Also, the budget effects from reductions in national income on the income side of the accounts relative to GDP resulting from lower net international income are also included. Finally, the deficit and debt levels are expressed relative to GNP and not GDP so that the effects of the change in net international income flows can be accounted for in terms of the effects on domestic national income.

Table 5.3 presents the comparisons for the scenario results for various economic and budget variables, including interest and inflation rates,

Table 5.3
Comparison of Scenario Results

	2018	2022
Three-month Treasury bill rate		
Base	3.7	3.8
Private funding	3.3	3.3
Foreign official funding	3.5	3.7
Federal Reserve funding	7.3	7.8
Budget and tax reform	3.9	4.2
Ten-year Treasury yield		
Base	4.9	5.0
Private funding	5.8	6.3
Foreign official funding	4.7	4.8
Federal Reserve funding	8.5	9.1
Budget and tax reform	5.1	5.3
Consumer inflation rate		
Base	2.0	2.0
Private funding	2.0	2.0
Foreign official funding	2.0	2.0
Federal Reserve funding	5.7	6.2
Budget and tax reform	2.0	2.0
Federal deficit as % of GNP		
Base	-0.4	-0.8
Private funding	-4.3	-6.4
Foreign official funding	-4.3	-6.3
Federal Reserve funding	-4.1	-5.2
Budget and tax reform	-0.3	-0.6
Federal debt as % of GNP		
Base	64.1	57.7
Private funding	82.5	93.5

Table 5.3
(continued)

	2018	2022
Foreign official funding	82.9	93.4
Federal Reserve funding	71.9	70.5
Budget and tax reform	63.8	56.1
Real GDP effect, % relative to base		
Private funding	-2.0	-3.8
Foreign official funding	-2.5	-3.1
Federal Reserve funding	-0.5	-1.4
Budget and tax reform	0.6	2.0
Net international income, % of GNP		
Base	0.7	0.5
Private funding	-0.6	-1.0
Foreign official funding	-0.4	-1.9
Federal Reserve funding	0.2	0.0
Budget and tax reform	0.7	0.2
Net international investment position, % of GNP		
Base	-25.3	-28.7
Private funding	-30.6	-39.5
Foreign official funding	-46.8	-73.3
Federal Reserve funding	-18.2	-15.2
Budget and tax reform	-26.4	-33.7

the Federal deficit and public debt, effects on real GDP relative to the base case, and the net international income and net international debt position. Table 5.4 shows comparisons of the resulting funding shares and the share of rest-of-world GDP that foreign holdings of Treasuries would represent under each scenario.[15] Regarding the foreign official share relative to rest-of-world GDP, Kitchen and Chinn (2011) and Mann (2009) address the issue of the extent to which foreign funding would continue to be forthcoming in funding ongoing U.S. budget deficits and debt. Although the conclusion was that technically there could be sufficient funding to yield such portfolio allocations into U.S. assets, the ongoing demand for debt financing internationally and the extent of the demands going forward would mean that it ultimately could not be sustained indefinitely over the long run. The relative magnitude for foreign official funding relative to rest-of-world GDP helps to illustrate the extent of that challenge.

Table 5.4
Funding Shares in Scenarios

Debt funding shares across scenarios	
BASE	
Private	54%
Foreign official	34%
Fed	13%
Private funding	
Private	64%
Foreign official	26%
Fed	10%
Foreign funding	
Private	38%
Foreign official	52%
Fed	10%
Federal Reserve funding	
Private	62%
Foreign official	27%
Fed	11%
Budget and tax reform	
Private	53%
Foreign official	34%
Fed	13%
Foreign Treasuries funding as % of rest of world GDP, 2022	
Base	7%
Private funding	7%
Foreign official funding	17%
Federal Reserve funding	8%
Budget and tax reform	7%

Private Funding Scenario

Under the private funding alternative, the increase in the budget deficit and public debt relative to the base case is assumed to be funded by an increase in domestic private holdings of U.S. Treasury securities. Federal Reserve holdings and foreign official and private holdings are little changed.[16]

Interest Rates

As shown in table 5.3, in order to induce the increase in private funding, under the estimated relationships from equation 5.4, the increase in the structural budget deficit in this alternative relative to the base (without increases in foreign official holdings or Federal Reserve holdings relative to GDP) leads to an increase in the ten-year Treasury yield spread relative to the three-month Treasury bill rate. The scenario results show the ten-year yield increasing to 5.8 percent in 2018 compared to 4.9 percent in the base case and increasing to 6.3 percent in 2022 compared to 5.0 percent in the base case. The three-month Treasury bill rate declines by about a half percentage point relative to the base, reflecting the lower real GDP growth relative to the base.

Budget Deficits and Debts

With the increased budget costs of the extended "certain policies" and the effects on interest rates and GDP, the budget deficit increases from 0.4 percent to 4.3 percent of GNP in 2018 and from 0.8 percent to 6.4 percent of GNP in 2022. Federal debt increases to 82.5 percent of GNP in 2018 compared to the 64.1 percent of the base case, and to 93.5 percent of GNP by 2022 compared to the 57.7 percent for the base case.

Real GDP

Reflecting the increased structural budget deficit and the higher long-term bond yields, real GDP is lower by 3.8 percent relative to the base case by 2022.

International Income Flows and Net Debt

Net international income flows are lower relative to the base, even becoming negative at -1.0 percent of GNP by 2022 compared to the 0.5 percent of GDP of the base. This results from the higher interest rates on U.S. assets, for both the turnover of Treasury holdings and other yields that rise with the long-term Treasury yield. Hence, the cost of servicing the international debt rises. The net international debt position also deteriorates to -39.5 percent of GNP by 2022 compared to -28.7 percent under the base case.

Funding Shares

Table 5.4 shows the resulting funding shares, with the large increase in the private funding share and the declines in the foreign official and Federal Reserve shares compared to the base case. Given the predominance of private domestic funding at 64 percent of total, foreign official holdings remain at a relatively low level at 7 percent of rest-of-world GDP.

Foreign Official Funding Scenario

In the case for which foreign official holdings of Treasuries are assumed to fund the higher budget deficits and debt, U.S. longer-term Treasury rates are held down by that funding, but at the adverse cost of a higher trade deficit and a more negative net international debt position.

Interest Rates

When the estimated relationships from equation 5.4 are used, the increase in foreign official funding is assumed to offset the increase in the structural budget deficit in this alternative relative to the base, so that the ten-year Treasury yield spread relative to the three-month Treasury bill rate is unchanged relative to the base. The three-month Treasury bill rate declines only slightly relative to the base, and the ten-year yield is also only slightly different relative to the base, at 4.7 percent in 2018 compared to 4.9 percent in the base case and at 4.8 percent in 2022 compared to 5.0 percent in the base case.

Budget Deficits and Debts

The budget deficit increase is similar to the private funding alternative, rising relative to the base from 0.4 percent to 4.3 percent of GNP in 2018 and from 0.8 percent to 6.3 percent of GNP in 2022. The public debt increase in the scenario is also similar to the private funding alternative, increasing to 82.9 percent of GNP in 2018 compared to the base case of 64.1 percent and to 93.4 percent of GNP by 2022 compared to the 57.7 percent for the base case.

Real GDP

Reflecting the increased structural budget and net export deficits, real GDP is lower by 3.1 percent relative to the base case by 2022.

International Income Flows and Net Debt

The adverse effect on net international income flows is larger relative to the base than under the private funding case by 2022, at -1.9 percent of GNP compared to the 0.5 percent of GNP of the base case. The increase in the net export deficit and accumulation of greater international debt requires a greater funding cost for servicing the international debt, although those effects are initially offset by the lower interest rates and interest costs from the foreign funding in the earlier years. The decline in the net international debt position is more severe than under the private funding case, deteriorating to -46.8 percent of GNP by 2018 and to -73.3 percent by 2022, compared to -28.7 percent of GNP in 2022 for the base case and -39.5 percent for the private funding case.

Funding Shares

As should be expected for this case, the results from table 5.4 show the large increase in the share of foreign official funding, at 52 percent compared to the base case at 34 percent. In order for foreign official holdings to meet such funding (and keep U.S. interest rates low), the level of foreign official funding would have to rise to 17 percent of rest-of-world GDP by 2022.

Federal Reserve Funding Scenario: Monetizing the Debt

Perhaps one of the more controversial methods for funding the U.S. budget deficit and public debt would be to have the Federal Reserve permanently expand its balance sheet and the monetary base by purchasing Treasury securities, effectively monetizing the debt. Mankiw (2009), for example, argued for a policy that generates significant negative real interest rates, in which

> the Fed commits itself to producing significant inflation. … Having the central bank embrace inflation would shock economists and Fed watchers who view price stability as the foremost goal of monetary policy. … A little more inflation might be preferable to rising unemployment or a series of fiscal measures that pile on debt bequeathed to future generations.

Aizenman and Marion (2009) examine using inflation to reduce the debt-to-GDP ratio and use a stylized theoretical model that predicts that "a moderate inflation rate of 6 percent could reduce the debt/GDP ratio by 20 percent within 4 years," although "history suggests that a modest inflation may increase the risk of an unintended inflation acceleration to double digit levels." Meltzer (2010) in turn views the Fed's increased purchases of Treasuries as only ultimately leading to crisis:

> The current massive volume of excess reserves will melt into greater money supply, and later higher inflation. … History gives many examples of countries with high actual and expected money growth, unsustainable budget deficits, and a currency expected to depreciate. Unless these countries made massive policy changes, they ended in crisis.

Even so, given that the United States previously has in practice reduced its debt burden relative to the size of the economy through higher inflation, it is interesting to examine this alternative scenario in which the Federal Reserve would monetize the debt and accept higher inflation than in the baseline outlook.

In this scenario, nominal prices and values are assumed to ultimately reflect a pure monetarist relationship—in order to demonstrate the most straightforward form of the scenario. The Taylor rule parameter for the targeted inflation rate rises with the increase in inflation that occurs in the scenario—that is, inflation is expected and the Fed targets short-run interest rates accordingly. Inflation increases with money growth, and the exchange value of the dollar declines in accord with a purchasing power parity relationship. Although these assumptions would be restrictive in short-run analyses during which monetary changes can have real effects, in the longer run they reflect the pressures and relationships that would be experienced.[17] As such, they serve to help explain the costs and effects of the monetary funding in the scenario. Even so, the scenario implicitly assumes that inflation is anticipated and does not have real costs beyond the capital losses that bondholders experience.[18]

Inflation

With the higher growth in the Federal Reserve balance sheet from increased purchases of Treasury bills, the results in table 5.3 show that consumer price inflation rises to 5.7 percent by 2018 compared to 2.0 percent in the base and to 6.2 percent by 2022 compared to 2.0 percent in the base. The higher inflation results in higher nominal GDP. Note that the estimated budget effects for this scenario also account for the effects of higher inflation (mostly through indexation effects in the budget other than the nominal interest rate effects discussed next).

Interest Rates

Interest rates reflect the higher inflation rate, with the short-term rate at 7.3 percent in 2018 compared to 3.7 percent of the base and at 7.8 percent in 2022 compared to 3.8 percent in the base. The ten-year yield increases to 8.5 percent in 2018 compared to 4.9 percent of the base and to 9.1 percent by 2022 compared to the 5.0 percent of the base. These increases in interest rates lead to higher budget costs through increases in debt service costs.

Budget Deficits and Debts

With the increased budget costs of the alternative scenarios, the budget deficit and public debt increase substantially in nominal terms but end up exhibiting smaller increases relative to nominal GNP in this Federal Reserve funding scenario compared to the other scenarios because of the increases in the price level and overall nominal GNP. The budget deficit in 2018 is at 4.1 percent of GNP (a similar increase to the other alternatives) but is at a lower relative level by 2022 at 5.2 percent of GNP compared to over 6 percent in the private and foreign official funding scenarios. With the increase in nominal GNP, the relative increase in the public debt is also smaller than in the other alternatives, with the public debt at 71.9 percent of GNP in 2018 and at 70.5 percent in 2022, compared to more than 90 percent of GNP in 2022 in the private and foreign official funding scenarios. Relative to the other alternative funding cases that maintained the level of inflation at the roughly 2 percent level of the base case, the debt ratio relative to GNP is roughly 20 percentage points lower by the end of the scenario. These results appear to be very roughly comparable to those observed by Aizenman and Marion (2009) already discussed. Inflation in the scenario rises steadily and reaches 6.2 percent at the ten-year horizon, averaging about 4.5 percent over the ten years. That is a lower level than the 6 percent assumed by Aizenman and Marion in getting the 10 percent of GDP decline for the debt ratio over a four-year horizon.

Real GDP

The effects on real GDP in this scenario are smaller than for the private funding and the foreign official funding cases. Real capital losses for private domestic bond holders from the higher inflation lead to a decline in real wealth. When typical elasticities assumed for spending effects of wealth changes are employed, the effect on real GDP growth averages just over -0.1 percent per year. Table 5.3 shows the results for the level of GDP being a decline of -0.5 percent relative to the base in 2018 and -1.4 percent relative to the base in 2022. Note also that the negative effects on real GDP are mitigated because a significant part of the capital loss would be borne by foreign holders of U.S. bonds. This illustrates the incentives noted by Aizenman and Marion (2009) that "this large foreign share increases the temptation to inflate away some of the debt."

International Income Flows and Net Debt

Even with the effects of inflation on interest rates and the higher rates of return that would be paid to foreign owners of U.S. assets, the increase in U.S. inflation and the decline in the value of the dollar result in significant valuation changes (increases in the dollar value of U.S. holdings of foreign assets) that reduce the U.S. net international debt position. These relationships help to mitigate adverse effects on net international income flows and the net international debt. Table 5.3 shows net international income flows for the Fed funding case at 0.2 percent of GNP in 2018, a relatively small decline compared to 0.7 percent of the base case; similarly, net international income flows are at 0.0 percent of GNP in 2022 compared to 0.5 percent of the base case. For the U.S. net international debt position, the results show an analogous effect as observed for the public debt for the debt ratio relative to GNP; the higher inflation, valuation changes, and higher level of nominal GNP help to reduce the international debt burden relative to the size of the economy. The results for the scenario show the net international debt at -18.2 percent of GNP in 2018 and -15.2 percent of GNP in 2022, an international debt burden level in 2022 that is even lower than the level at the start of the scenarios in 2012.

Funding Shares

Table 5.4 shows the resulting funding shares, with similar funding shares compared to the base case, albeit with the Fed share somewhat larger. Yet funding would be at higher nominal levels as the nominal debt amounts rise with inflation and as the Fed funding "leans into the wind" of the rising prices.

Fundamental Budget and Tax Reform Scenario

An additional scenario is considered here to provide a rough illustration of how fundamental budget and tax reform could affect the budget and economic outlook and to tie the analysis back into the focus of the conference more generally. The broad assumptions used are for a generic reform plan in which there are cumulative budget deficit reductions of $5 trillion over the next decade and the adoption of fundamental tax reform that results in a simplified and more efficient tax structure. No specifics are assumed regarding the budget deficit reductions, but in order to attain true budget reforms to the current outlook of that magnitude clearly would require some reform of entitlement spending. By comparison, the National Commission on Fiscal Responsibility and Reform (2010) Bowles-Simpson plan for fundamental entitlement and tax reform proposed nearly $4 trillion in deficit reduction through 2020, and the Bipartisan Policy Center (2010) Domenici-Rivlin Debt Reduction Task Force proposal called for debt reduction of $3 trillion over ten years. Consistent with analyses that show fundamental tax reform generates significant economic gains such as shown in Altig et al. (2001), an increase in real GDP is included in the scenario. Altig et al. (2001) showed ultimate long-run gains from various reforms generating national income increases in the range of 1.9 to 9.4 percent, with the lower amounts occurring for a flat tax with transition relief and the higher amounts for a proportional consumption tax. Their long run was a fifty-year horizon; over a shorter horizon of fifteen years, the increases were anywhere from about one-third to 90 percent of the long-run gains, in a range of 0.5 to 6 percent. Here, the assumption is that over the ten-year horizon, an adopted fundamental tax reform would yield increases in GDP of 2 percent by 2022, a result consistent with the lower-middle part of the Altig et al. range. Debate can occur over the exact magnitude, and the results are implicitly determined by the assumptions, but it should be illustrative of the rough magnitudes and thereby allow for useful information from the scenario.

The results for the scenario are presented in table 5.3 and are generally left to the reader. Several points worth noting are that, as expected, the budget deficit and public debt levels as shares of GNP are reduced to manageable levels (reflecting both the assumed budget savings and the beneficial GDP effects). The budget deficit is at 0.6 percent of GNP in 2022 compared to the 0.8 percent of the base case.

Some Additional Concerns

As challenging as the alternative scenarios considered here may be, several additional issues raise further concerns.

First, unresolved imbalances and potential costs occur in the scenarios that are not resolved within the time horizon considered. The foreign official funding and the Federal Reserve funding cases may have aspects that initially appear attractive, for example, the maintained low long-term Treasury yields of the foreign funding case or the low public debt ratio relative to GNP of the Federal Reserve funding case. Yet the unresolved imbalances of persisting trade deficits or excessive inflation would be problematic and could generate unmanageable consequences—in particular, asset price inflation and overshooting that could occur with either the Fed funding or foreign official funding cases. Over the past decade and a half, we have observed that we are not very good at anticipating or identifying persisting asset price anomalies or "bubbles" as they are occurring. The costs of financial crises and correcting financial imbalances can be quite severe. And while some might argue that the United States benefited from inflation in reducing the public debt burden in the decades after World War II, the cost became the high and rising inflation and interest rates of the 1970s and the relatively severe recession of the early 1980s to break that inflation.

The slow recovery following the Great Recession has been another challenge. The U.S. and world economies have experienced slower-than-expected growth following the recession, and the low GDP growth means the budget challenges are greater than what was previously anticipated. If such economic outlook challenges persist and with growth lower than projected, the budget outlook could be even more severe than currently foreseen.

Finally, if the United States were to rely heavily on foreign funding to finance its budget deficits and debt, then in addition to the costs described in the foreign official funding scenario, there is the uncertainty regarding the extent to which such foreign funding would be forthcoming in the future. Although the increase to 17 percent of rest-of-world GDP might be technically feasible, it could become increasingly challenging in a world in which numerous countries are competing for funding of sovereign debt.

Conclusion

The analysis and results presented in this opening essay for the chapter confirm the fundamental challenges associated with funding U.S. deficits and debt, with a specific recognition of the role of—and interactions with—international financial assets and flows. Various scenarios are presented to make broad-brush illustrations of how projected U.S.

deficits and debt could be funded by alternative sources of funding and how they would affect the ultimate economic and budget effects. The results from the cases examined highlight the challenges and potential trade-offs of alternative funding sources, but in the end, all of them have significant costs from persisting deficits, just different ways in which the costs would be realized. If the funding for additional deficits and debt comes from private sources, interest rates would have to be higher than what is typically assumed in public and private projections, and the result would be lower U.S. domestic investment and GDP than otherwise. If foreign funding is the source, then the balancing flows would be larger net export deficits and growing international debt imbalances and higher income payments to foreign holders of dollar-denominated assets. That scenario would exacerbate the international imbalances that already exist and need to be resolved. Alternatively, if the hope is that Federal Reserve funding—monetizing the debt—would work to reduce the debt burden relative to the size of the economy through higher inflation, while the results show how that could technically be accomplished, fundamental challenges would remain from realizing real capital losses for bondholders and having higher sustained inflation in the economy—and having to deal with the potential costs to resolve that higher inflation.

Simply put, there are no simple or relatively lower-cost options for dealing with and funding high budget deficits and growing debt. The costs come in different forms and would be borne by different groups in the economy, but nonetheless the costs would exist. Perhaps one of the more significant problems from having to finance large budget deficits and high levels of debt is that the United States has surrendered a large part of its policy autonomy and has less control over how the economy will be affected and who will bear the burdens. Ultimately the solution to these problems and the way to reduce such costs is through fundamental budget and tax reform that reduces projected deficits and debt and enhances U.S. economic performance.

Acknowledgments

The views contained here are solely my own and do not necessarily represent those of the institutions with which I am associated. My thanks to Craig Johnson and discussants Peter Hartley and John Mutti at the Economic and Fiscal Reform in the United States conference at the James A. Baker III Institute for Public Policy, October 5–6, 2011 for helpful comments.

References

Aizenmen, Joshua, and Nancy Marion. 2009. Using Inflation to Erode the U.S. Public Debt. Working Paper 15562, National Bureau of Economic Research, Cambridge, MA.

Altig, David, Alan J. Auerbach, Laurence T. Kotlikoff, Kent A. Smetters, and Jan Walliser. 2001. Simulating Fundamental Tax Reform in the United States. *American Economic Review* 91 (3): 574–95.

Autor, David, David Dorn, and Gordon Hanson. 2011. The China Syndrome: Local Labor Market Effects of Import Competition in the United States. MIT Working Paper 12–12, MIT, Cambridge, MA.

Bergsten, C. Frederick, 2009. The Long-Term International Economic Position of the United States. Washington, DC: Peterson Institute for International Economics.

Bernanke, Ben. 2005. The Global Saving Glut and the U.S. Current Account Deficit. Paper presented at the Homer Jones Lecture. St. Louis, Missouri, April 14.

Bipartisan Policy Center. 2010. *Restoring America's Future*. Washington, DC: Bipartisan Policy Center.

Canzoneri, Matthew B., Robert E. Cumby, and Behzad T. Diba. 2002. Should the European Central Bank and the Federal Reserve Be Concerned about Fiscal Policy? In *Rethinking Stabilization Policy*. Kansas City, Kansas: The Federal Reserve Bank.

Chinn, Menzie. 2005. *Getting Serious about the Twin Deficits*. New York: Council on Foreign Relations.

Chinn, Menzie, and Jeffrey Frankel. 2007. *Debt and Interest Rates: The U.S. and the Euro Area*. Kiel, Germany: Kiel Institute for the World Economy.

Chung, Hess, Jean-Philippe Laforte, David Reifschneider, and John C. Williams. 2011. Have We Underestimated the Probability of Hitting the Lower Bound? Working Paper 2011–01, Federal Reserve Bank of San Francisco, San Francisco.

Congressional Budget Office. 2012a *The Budget and Economic Outlook: Fiscal Years 2012 to 2022*. Washington, DC: Congressional Budget Office.

Congressional Budget Office. 2012b. *The Budget and Economic Outlook: An Update*. Washington, DC: Congressional Budget Office.

Council of Economic Advisers. 2010. *Economic Report of the President*. Washington, DC: Council of Economic Advisers.

Eichengreen, Barry. 2006. Global Imbalances: The New Economy, the Dark Matter, the Savvy Investor, and the Standard Analysis. *Journal of Policy Modeling* 28 (6): 654–52.

Eichengreen, Barry. 2011. *Exorbitant Privilege: The Rise and Fall of the Dollar and the Future of the International Monetary System*. Oxford: Oxford University Press.

Engen, Eric, and Glen Hubbard. 2005. Federal Government Debt and Interest Rates. In *NBER Macroeconomics Annual 2004*, edited by Mark Gertler and Kenneth Rogoff , vol. 19, 83–138. Cambridge, MA: MIT Press.

Gagnon, Joseph E. 2011a. *The Global Outlook for Government Debt over the Next 25 Years: Implications for the Economy and Public Policy*. Washington, DC: Peterson Institute for International Economics.

Gagnon, Joseph E. 2011b. *Flexible Exchange Rates for a Stable World Economy*. Washington, DC: Peterson Institute for International Economics.

Gagnon, Joseph E., Matthew Raskin, Julie Remache, and Brian P. Sack. 2010. Large-Scale Asset Purchases by the Federal Reserve: Did They Work? FRB of New York Staff Report 441, Federal Reserve Bank of New York, New York.

Gale, William G., and Peter R. Orszag. 2002. The Economic Effects of Long-Term Fiscal Discipline. Urban-Brookings Tax Policy Center Discussion Paper, Urban-Brookings Tax Policy Center.

Gale, William G., and Peter R. Orszag. 2005. Budget Deficits, National Saving, and Interest Rates. *Brookings Papers on Economic Activity* 35 (2): 101–187.

Greenspan, Alan. 2009. The Fed Didn't Cause the Housing Bubble. *Wall Street Journal*, March 11.

Gruber, Joseph, and Steven B. Kamin. 2010. Fiscal Positions and Government Bond Yields in OECD Countries. *Journal of Money, Credit and Banking* 44 (8): 1563–87.

Higgins, Matthew, Thomas Klitgaard, and Cedric Tille. 2005. *The Income Implications of Rising U.S. International Liabilities*. New York: Federal Reserve Bank of New York.

International Monetary Fund. 2013. *Fiscal Monitor: Fiscal Adjustment in an Uncertain World*. Washington, DC: International Monetary Fund.

Kitchen, John. 2003. A Note on Interest Rates and Structural Federal Budget Deficits. MPRA Paper 21069, University Library of Munich, Munich..

Kitchen, John. 2007. Sharecroppers or Shrewd Capitalists? Projections of the U.S. Current Account, International Income Flows, and Net International Debt. *Review of International Economics* 15 (5): 1036–61.

Kitchen, John, and Menzie Chinn. 2011. Financing U.S. Debt: Is There Enough Money in the World—and at What Cost? *International Finance* 14 (3): 373–413.

Kohn, Donald L. 2009. Monetary Policy Research and the Financial Crisis: Strengths and Shortcomings. Speech delivered at the Federal Reserve Conference on Key Developments in Monetary Policy, Washington, DC.

Laubach, Thomas. 2003. New Evidence on the Interest Rate Effects of Budget Deficits and Debt. Finance and Economic Discussion Series Working Paper, Federal Reserve Board of Governors, Washington, DC.

Laubach, Thomas. 2009. New Evidence on the Interest Rate Effects of Budget Deficits and Debt. *Journal of the European Economic Association* 7 (4): 858–85.

Mankiw, N. Gregory. 2009. It May Be Time for the Fed to Go Negative. *New York Times*, April 18.

Mann, Catherine. 2009. International Capital Flows and the Sustainability of the US Current Account Deficit. In The Long-Term International Economic Position of the US, edited by C. Frederick Bergsten, 35–64. Washington, DC: Peterson Institute for International Economics.

Meltzer, Alan. 2010. "The Fed's Anti-Inflation Exit Strategy Will Fail." *Wall Street Journal*, January 27.

National Commission on Fiscal Responsibility and Reform. 2010. *The Moment of Truth: Report of the National Commission on Fiscal Responsibility and Reform*. Washington, DC: National Commission on Fiscal Responsibility and Reform.

Office of Management and Budget. 2010. *Analytical Perspectives, Budget of the United States Government, Fiscal Year 2011*. Washington, DC: Office of Management and Budget.

Pakko, Michael. 1999. The U.S. Trade Deficit and the "New Economy." *Federal Reserve Bank of St. Louis Review* 81 (5): 11–19.

Taylor, John B. 1993. Discretion versus Policy Rules in Practice. *Carnegie Rochester Series on Public Policy* 39 (1): 195–214.

U.S. Bureau of Economic Analysis. 2010. *U.S. International Investment Position at Yearend 2010*. Washington, DC: U.S. Department of Commerce.

Warnock, Francis E., and Veronica Cacdac Warnock. 2006. International Capital Flows and U.S. Interest Rates. NBER Working Paper 12560, National Bureau of Economic Research, Cambridge, MA.

Yellen, Janet. 2011. The Federal Reserve's Asset Purchase Program. Speech to the Allied Social Science Associations Annual Meeting, January 8, Denver, CO.

Discussion

Peter R. Hartley

Kitchen raises some difficult questions about the sustainability of current U.S. fiscal policy. Large deficits have to be financed, and every method of financing them imposes serious costs. Furthermore, the balance of financing is not under the control of the U.S. government but will be determined in the marketplace. Failure to reform the current budgetary imbalance thus exposes the United States to considerable risk of incurring substantial costs of an uncertain nature and size.

Kitchen points out that there are three main sinks for U.S. government debt: private saving, foreign official purchases of Treasuries, and Federal Reserve purchases that amount to monetization of the debt. He illustrates these alternative financing methods in figure 5.1.

The core of the analysis is an equation estimated by Kitchen and Chinn (2011):[19]

$$i_{10YR} - i_{3MO} = 1.22 + 0.56(U - U^*) - 0.38(\pi - \pi^*) - 0.33(STRSURP + FOREIGN + FEDLT).$$

The unemployment and inflation gap terms are motivated by a Federal Reserve policy reaction rule.[20] The negative coefficient on the structural surplus reflects the reduced supply of Treasuries resulting from a higher surplus. On the other side of the market, foreign official and Federal Reserve demand for Treasuries reduce long-term interest rates by raising the demand for Treasuries.

Although the final three terms have a common coefficient, the three forms of funding differ in their impacts. Private funding requires higher interest rates, which crowds out private investment, reducing economic growth. With foreign funding, the increase in *FOREIGN* offsets decline in *STRSURP*, so the yield spread is unaffected, but changes in the exchange rate crowd out net exports and cut growth. Finally, monetization of an increased deficit by the Federal Reserve raises (anticipated) inflation, causing real losses on nominal assets.

Kitchen also illustrates his argument using the simple accounting identity

$$G - T + I = S - (X - M)$$

Thus, a fiscal deficit ($G - T$) has to be funded by savings or net exports. Kitchen remarks that the third alternative, monetization, is not readily apparent in this equation. However, an erosion of wealth through anticipated inflation would reduce real income and thus affect S. Although Kitchen does not note this, anticipated inflation is also likely to affect growth as a result of nonindexation of the tax system, and especially erosion in the real value of depreciation allowances. In fact, I would have thought that this effect of anticipated inflation would dominate the effects of eroding the real value of wealth.

The macroeconomic effects of additional structural deficits are determined from a simple Solow growth model. Effects on the U.S. international investment position (and hence the difference between GDP and GNP) and net international capital flows are based on a model originally presented in Kitchen (2007).[21] Although the details of the time paths for the fiscal policy changes and the macroeconomic effects are presented elsewhere (CBO publications and other papers), I would prefer to see them outlined in Kitchen's essay to make it somewhat more self-contained. At the moment, the basis of the calculations is largely a black box for readers. Without further justification of the calculations that readers can assess for reasonableness, the results will be less convincing.

Recent Funding History

Figure 5.9 illustrates the scope of the problem Kitchen is addressing. Clearly, recent budget deficits have been out of all proportion relative to anything that has been experienced in recent decades. Although figure 5.9 gives the total in current year dollars and does not adjust for growth in "funding capability" by expressing the amounts relative to GDP (or GNP), dividing by GDP would make little difference to the overall impression created by the figure. I also obtained data from the FRED database on gross federal debt outstanding, but for some reason it gives a larger total than the series plotted by Kitchen in his figure 5.1

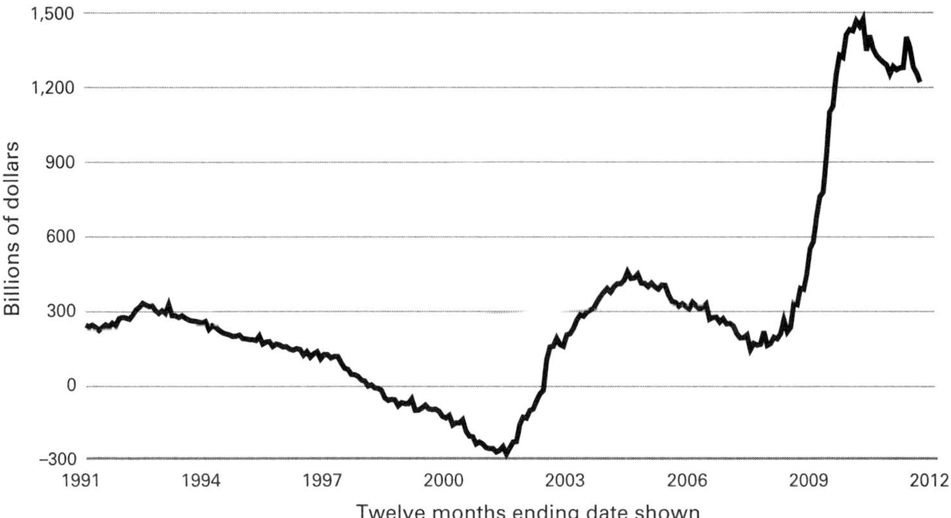

Figure 5.9
Recent Federal Budget Deficits (Surplus If Negative).
Source: Financial Management Service, U.S. Treasury Department.

obtained from the flow-of-funds accounts. I have plotted the series from the FRED database in figure 5.10.

Figure 5.11 shows interest payments on the federal debt. Comparing these with Figure 5.9, we can see that interest payments are already a substantial part of the annual budget deficit. The idea that interest payments may eventually lead to ever-increasing deficits is another notion of "unsustainable" fiscal policy that Kitchen does not address.

Turning more to the issues Kitchen addresses in his opening essay in this chapter, figures 5.12 and 5.13 show recent holdings of U.S. federal debt by international investors and the Federal Reserve banks. The large drop in Federal Reserve holdings in the immediate aftermath of the financial crisis occurred as the Fed purchased GSE and GSE-backed securities, in part swapping them for Treasuries. Nevertheless, the overall balance sheet of the Fed expanded dramatically, with a consequent explosion in the monetary base, as illustrated in figure 5.14.

Interest Rates, Inflation, and the Exchange Rate

Despite the large expansion in federal debt and the monetary base over the last two years, we have not seen a large increase in interest rates or

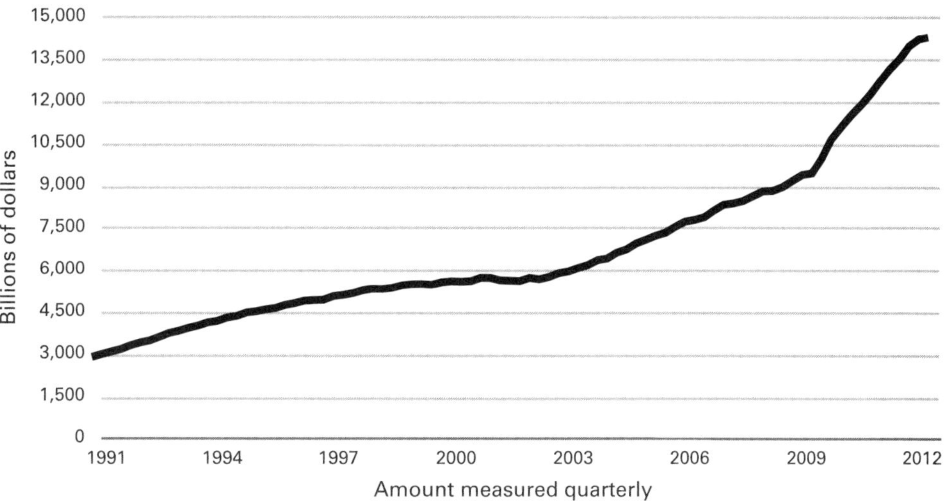

Figure 5.10
Gross Federal Debt Outstanding.
Source: Federal Reserve Bank of St. Louis.

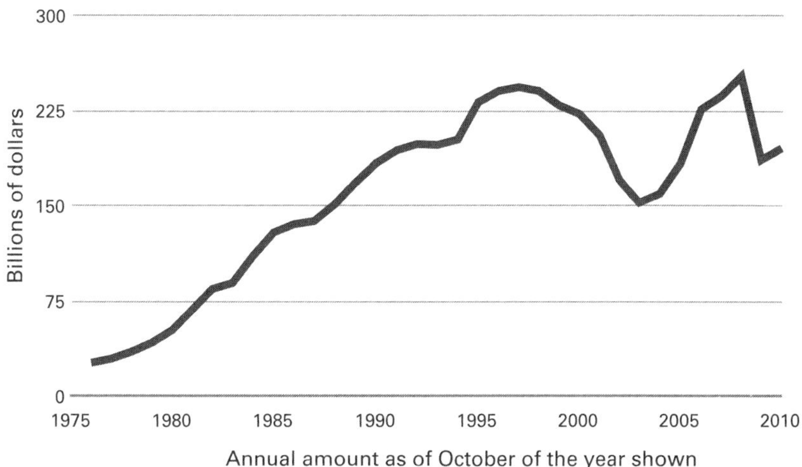

Figure 5.11.
Federal Outlays on Interest.
Source: Federal Reserve Bank of St. Louis.

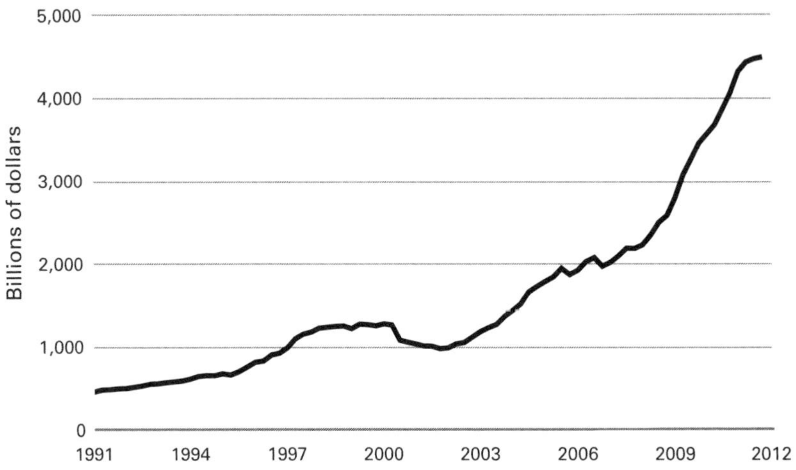

Figure 5.12
U.S. Federal Debt Held by International Investors.
Source: Federal Reserve Bank of St. Louis.

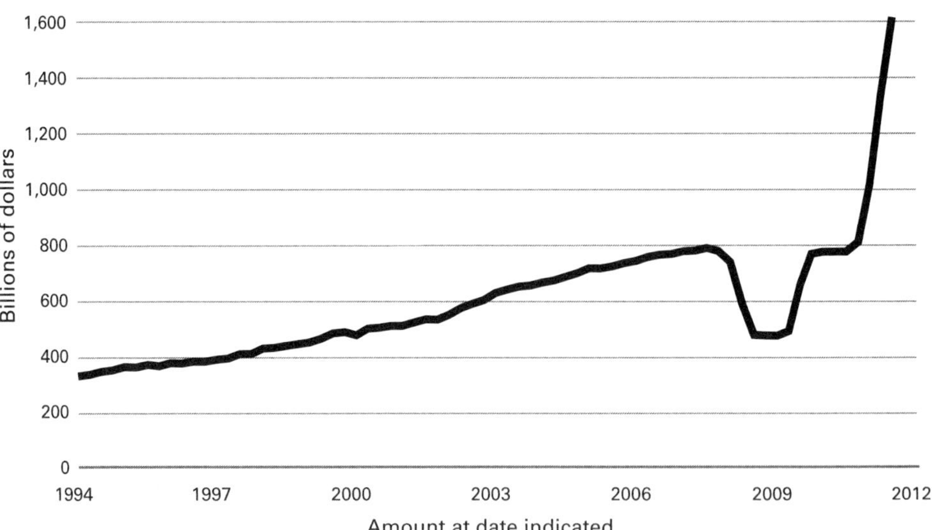

Figure 5.13
Federal Reserve Holdings of Federal Debt.
Source: Federal Reserve Bank of St. Louis.

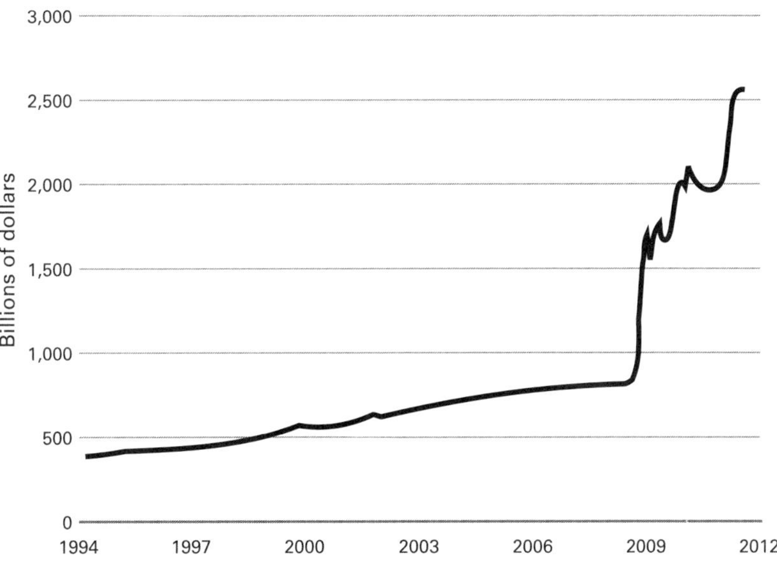

Figure 5.14
U.S. Monetary Base Adjusted for Reserve Requirements.
Source: Federal Reserve Bank of St. Louis.

the inflation rate. On the contrary, figure 5.15 shows that interest rates are extremely low by historical standards. The figure also illustrates that the spread between long-term and short-term yields tended to increase in economic downturns. This is consistent with a Federal Reserve policy reaction rule that results in monetary expansions in business cycle downturns as in the Kitchen and Chinn equation discussed above.

While figure 5.15 suggests that the huge expansion in U.S. debt in recent years graphed in figure 5.10 has not increased interest rates, figure 5.16 also shows that the even more spectacular increase in the monetary base graphed in figure 5.14 has not greatly raised the inflation rate as measured by the CPI. Indeed, in the recent severe recession, the United States experienced annual deflation in prices for the first time in many decades. Since 2010, however, annual inflation at the consumer level has been rising and now exceeds 3 percent.

Figure 5.17, which graphs inflation at the wholesale level, suggests that more inflation at the consumer level may be coming. Comparing figures 5.16 and 5.17, one can see that producer price inflation is much more volatile than consumer price inflation, but the series do tend to

Figure 5.15
Spot Yields on U.S. One-Year and Ten-Year Treasuries.
Source: Federal Reserve Bank of St. Louis.

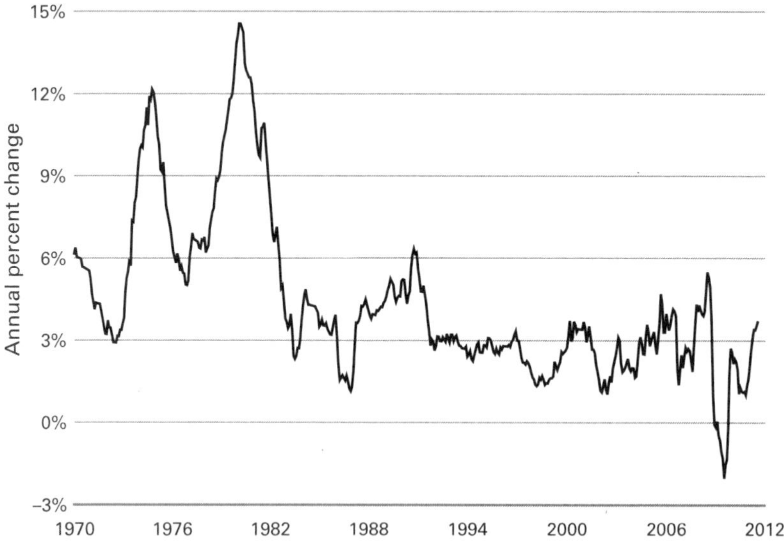

Figure 5.16
Annual CPI All Items Inflation Rate.
Source: Federal Reserve Bank of St. Louis.

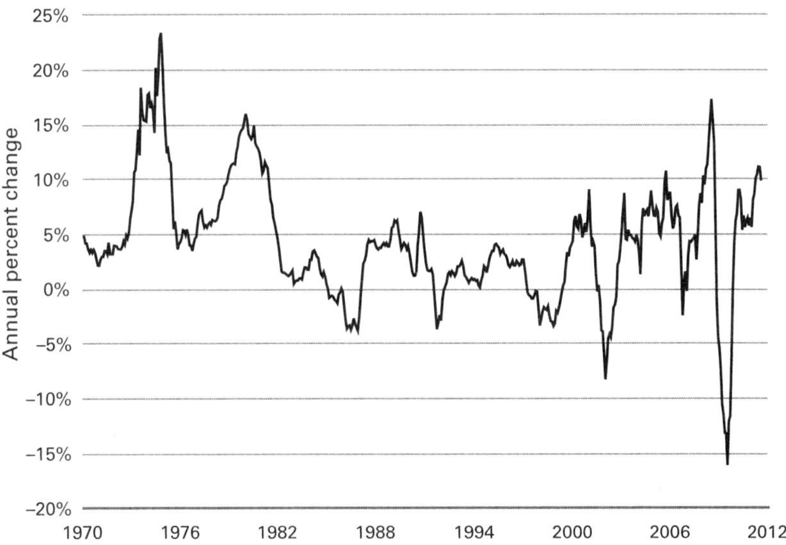

Figure 5.17
Annual Inflation in the Producer Price Index.
Source: Federal Reserve Bank of St. Louis.

move together. Figure 5.17 reveals that recent annual increases in the producer price index have exceeded 10 percent.

Focusing on the period since 1992, the CPI inflation graphed in figure 5.16 can be seen as increasing volatile fluctuations around an average of around 2.5 percent. The maximum rate in this period reached almost 5.5 percent, while the minimum fell to almost -2 percent. Figure 5.15 reveals that the ten-year nominal spot rate followed a declining trend over this period. The implication is that the real interest rate likely fell.[22] More direct evidence on this can be obtained from figure 5.18, which graphs the rate of return on one-year Treasuries along with the rate of return on ten-year Treasury Inflation Protected Securities (TIPS) securities that are indexed for changes in the CPI. The latter can be regarded as a real rate of interest and the difference between the two rates as a measure of expected inflation.[23] Figure 5.18 shows that the real rate of return on TIPS displayed a declining trend for most of 2007 to 2011, although it was relatively constant at a generally higher level of around 2 percent for the early part of this decade.

One way to reconcile the relatively low inflation rates in recent years in the face of extraordinary base money expansion is that the financial crisis simultaneously created a large increase in the demand for

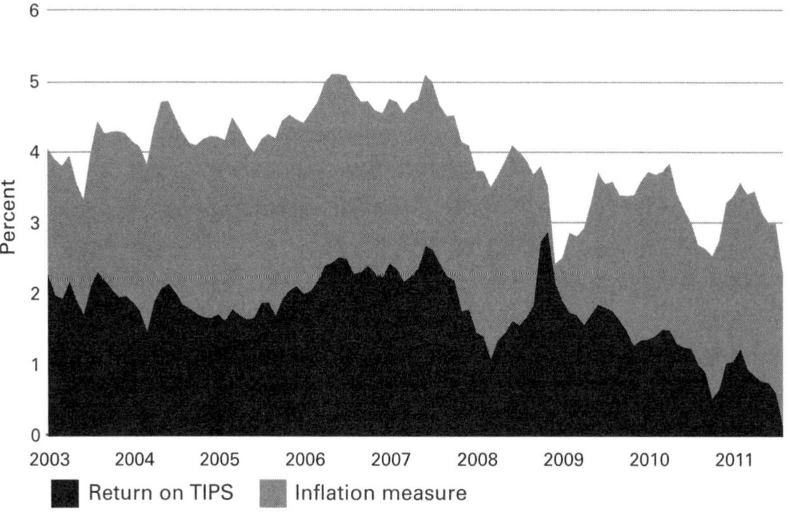

Figure 5.18
Using TIPS to Decompose the Ten-Year Treasury Yield into Real and Expected Inflation Components.
Source: Federal Reserve Bank of St. Louis.

liquidity. As a result, the Fed was able to expand the monetary base without triggering inflation. Indeed, the period of deflation from late 2008 through the third quarter of 2009 suggests that if the Fed had not supplied the additional liquidity that was being demanded at that time, the deflationary contraction in the economy would have been far worse.

Figure 5.19 supports this interpretation. It shows a dramatic shift away from inside money toward base money in 2009. Banks have become more reluctant to lend to each other, let alone to individual or commercial borrowers. With banks holding much higher levels of base money relative to loans and other assets, the size of the money supply that can be supported by a given level of base money has fallen substantially.

Kitchen also mentions foreign purchases of Treasuries as another major source of funding. He argues that this should appreciate the exchange rate, penalizing exports and encouraging imports and thus reducing net exports. Figure 5.20 graphs movements in the trade-weighted exchange rate since 1992. While the exchange rate appreciated for much of the 1990s, for most of the previous decade, it has tended to depreciate relative to the currencies of major trading

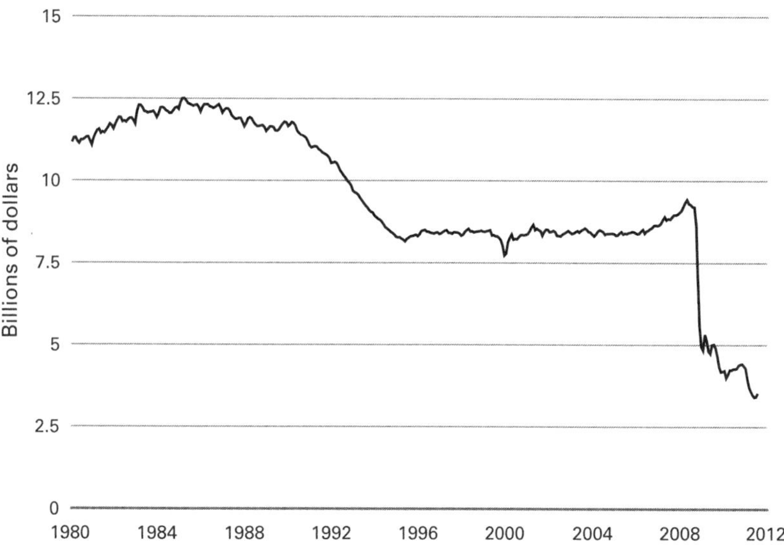

Figure 5.19
The M2 Money Multiplier.
Source: Federal Reserve Bank of St. Louis.

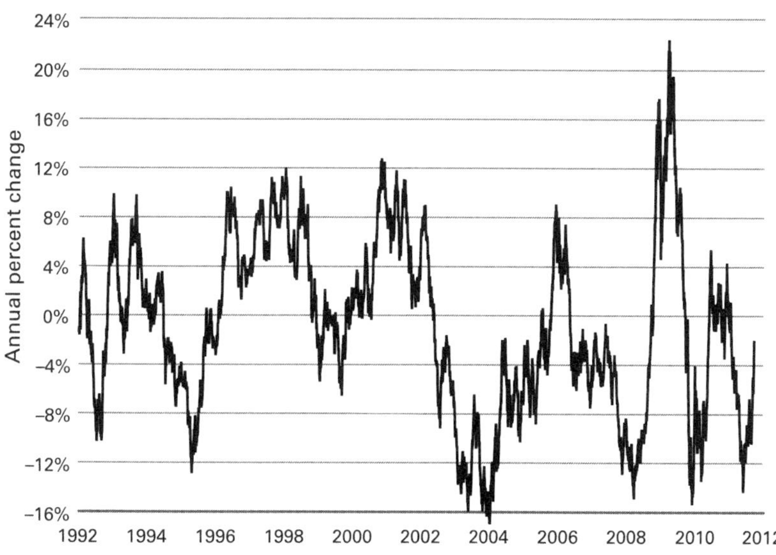

Figure 5.20
Annual Change in Trade-Weighted Exchange Rate.
Source: Federal Reserve Bank of St. Louis.

partners. The main exceptions in the latter case are short periods around 2006, 2009, and early 2011. The U.S. dollar has also appreciated in recent months as a result of the sovereign debt crisis in Europe, but the value of the U.S. dollar is still not back above where it was twelve months previously.

Figure 5.21 focuses more specifically on the sovereign debt crisis in Europe. One reason that the parlous U.S. fiscal situation might not have caused more problems is that the United States is not alone. In particular, many European economies have a very similar trajectory for deficits as a percentage of GDP.

Some Critical Remarks on Kitchen's Essay

Returning to the accounting identity,

$$G - T + I = S - (X - M),$$

there seems to be an implicit assumption in Kitchen's discussion that private saving must take the form of accumulating assets issued by private firms or government debt. However, some saving can take the form of accumulating money balances and, indirectly, the monetary base and Fed assets. Thus, if increases in liquid assets are demanded, monetization would not cause inflation.

Similarly, an increase in official foreign holdings of U.S. assets might be demanded as world economic growth increases, which would expand demand for U.S. assets as the main reserve currency. Foreign asset purchases may then lead to nonzero balance of payments but without affecting the net exports.

In short, Federal Reserve or foreign official asset purchases might reflect seigniorage for the United States. If this is the case, the triangle diagram needs to be amended. Monetization need not lead to inflation, and foreign official purchases need not crowd out net exports.

The critical issue, however, is how long these benefits can continue to accrue to the United States. What happens if the domestic money multiplier returns to more normal levels, and can the United States continue to tax the rest of the world without affecting the reserve currency status of the U.S. dollar? With respect to the latter question, figure 5.22 shows that the role of the U.S. dollar as an international reserve currency has been steadily eroding for at least two decades. For some time, this loss in status was mainly at the expense of the euro. In the last couple of years, however, the fiscal crisis in Europe has stopped

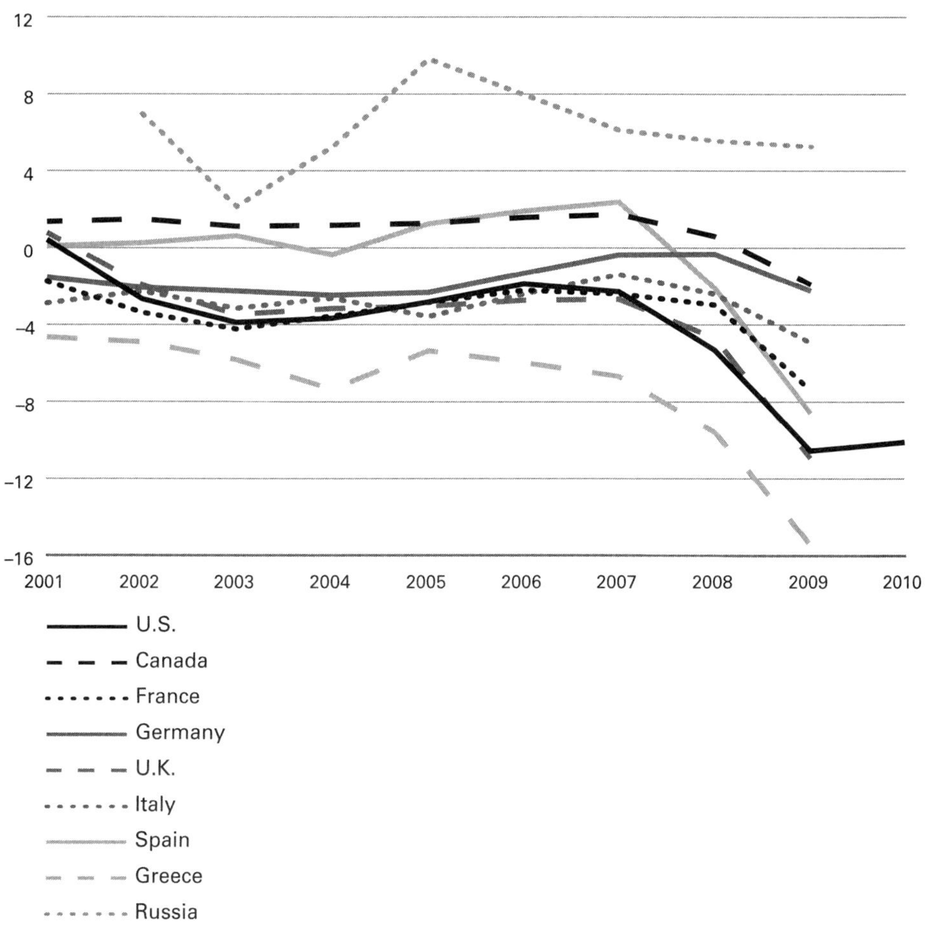

Figure 5.21
Fiscal Surplus and Deficits as a Percent of GDP.
Source: Federal Reserve Bank of St. Louis.

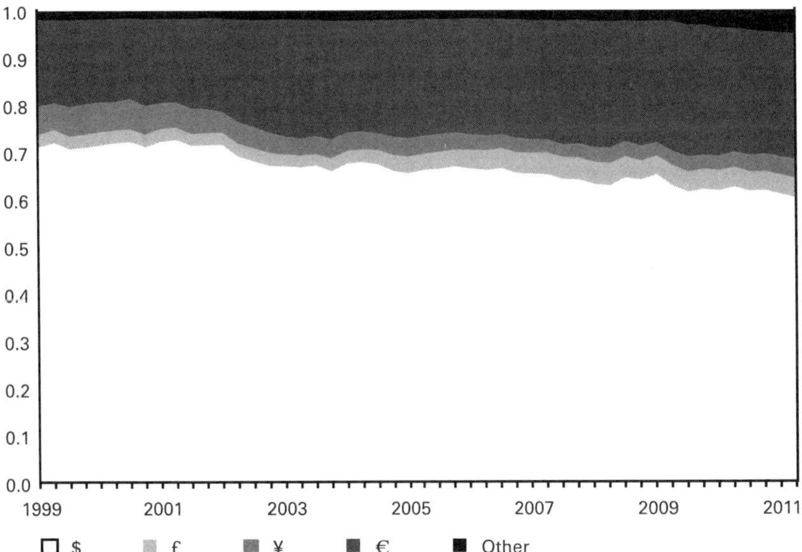

Figure 5.22
Proportions of Currencies in Allocated Foreign Reserves.
Source: International Monetary Fund.

the displacement of the dollar by the euro. Nevertheless, the share of official foreign reserves held as dollars has continued to decline as other third currencies have become more important.

More generally, Kitchen focuses on the longer-term difficulties of financing large on-going deficits. Thus, for example, he considers the effects of anticipated inflation rather than the short-run effects of unanticipated inflation. I do not have a problem with this focus given the issue that he is addressing. However, if we want to consider the effects of the current fiscal imbalance in a more general sense, I worry that we are now in a peculiar situation that is going to create substantial continuing short-run difficulties. We have had an extraordinary liquidity expansion. The extra liquidity has to date been demanded, but how long can that last? Real interest rates as measured from the gap between ten-year bonds and ten-year TIPS yields are unsustainably low. What might happen if much of the rest of the world ceases to abet the United States in abusing its reserve currency status? I suggest that these issues are at least as concerning possible consequences of current U.S. fiscal policy as the longer-run issues that Kitchen focused on in his essay at the start of this chapter.

References

Kitchen, John. 2007. Sharecroppers or Shrewd Capitalists? Projections of the U.S. Current Account, International Income Flows, and Net International Debt. *Review of International Economics* 15 (5): 1036–61.

Kitchen, John, and Menzie Chinn. 2011. Financing U.S. Debt: Is There Enough Money in the World—and at What Cost? *International Finance* 14 (3): 373–413.

Discussion

John Mutti

John Kitchen addresses the consequences of fiscal policy choices over an intermediate time horizon, beyond any debate about the need for Keynesian stimulus during a cyclical downturn. Instead, he projects the effects on U.S. output, capital formation, and debt position after five and ten years, depending on how the federal government finances the continuation of current government programs. His analysis clearly demonstrates that any of three common options that might be considered to fund a budget deficit have repercussions that should not be ignored. Identifying these repercussions within a consistent framework is no small challenge. Because he draws on several separate conceptual and empirical insights from his previous work, it is useful to recognize how all these separate elements are combined in the analysis in the opening essay of this chapter.

A starting point is the CBO's estimate of the effect of current law on the deficit over the next ten years. Based on past actions, Congress is not likely to leave current law in place, but instead will alter it in ways that add to the budget deficit. Kitchen demonstrates how three alternative ways of financing this additional deficit are likely to cause deviations from the CBO's predicted path of interest rates, output, inflation, and international payments. He also applies the same analysis to a deficit reduction and budget reform plan that results in a cumulative reduction in the deficit of $5 trillion.

With respect to the components of the analysis that allow such predictions to be made, several of the important building blocks are worth reviewing at the outset. One key input is a relationship Kitchen and Chinn (2011) estimated to show how the gap between the interest rate on ten-year U.S. government notes and three-month bills will be affected by the budget deficit. Knowing that gap and assuming that the three-month Treasury bill rate is given by a Taylor rule response by the

Federal Reserve to unemployment and inflation deviations from target values, Kitchen can then determine the ten-year yield. That latter value can be used in a Solow growth model approach to predict the change in the capital stock and output in the economy. The new interest rates also allow changes in payments to foreigners to be determined, based on the modeling Kitchen (2007) previously presented. Recognizing the changes in those payments allows the national income that remains for U.S. residents to be determined. In short, there are several independent pieces that are creatively assembled to carry out this analysis, although a reader may be excused for not fully appreciating how all these variables are determined simultaneously and endogenously. An excellent starting point is the empirical relationship from Kitchen and Chinn, which gives the interest gap explained above:

$$i10YR - i3MO = 1.22 + 0.56\ UNGAP - 0.38\ INFL - 0.33(STRSURP + FOREIGN + FEDLT). \quad (5.6)$$

Without repeating the definitions of variables provided in the chapter, I note that this formulation allows a compact representation of the influence of the alternative policy scenarios on this interest rate gap.

Scenario 1

If additional private domestic purchasers must be attracted to finance the deficit and the budget surplus as a share of GDP falls by 1 percentage point, then the interest spread increases by 33 basis points. This relationship was estimated over the 1979–2009 period, and over this time frame, the actual effect on the interest gap was influenced by inflows of private foreign capital too. Therefore, we might expect that those inflows reduced the observed increase in the interest rate as the budget surplus fell. Conversely, if we just allowed for the extra purchases by domestic buyers, we would need a larger increase in long-term interest rates. Kitchen's stylized case rests on foreign interest rates rising at the same time U.S. rates increase, so that no inflow of private foreign capital occurs. Alternatively, if foreigners' holdings of U.S. assets increase but their holdings of other assets decrease, with foreign saving unchanged, neither the foreign nor the U.S. trade balance is affected. More generally, if foreign saving increased and capital flowed into the United States, we would expect the value of the dollar to strengthen internationally and cause a further crowding out of the net export sector. Kitchen wants to rule out this effect and to limit the crowding-out effect to a reduction in gross private domestic investment.

Of the three potential sources for financing the deficit, this is the one that results in the greatest crowding out of domestic investment. Equation 5.6 suggests that an increase in the budget deficit that is not offset by either greater foreign official purchases of U.S. assets or by Federal Reserve purchases of long-term assets will result in an increase in U.S. long-term interest rates. Here is where the Solow growth model story is relevant. Although no details are provided in the text and I am not familiar with the accepted tricks of the trade in making such projections, presumably the standard Cobb-Douglas representation with capital's share equal to one-third serves as the basis for predicting the reduction in the steady-state desired capital stock (Jones 2010). Although the author cites the view that higher interest payments to finance greater government debt also may imply greater reliance on distorting taxes that further reduce output and the capital stock, presumably that aspect of fiscal policy choices is addressed only in the fiscal reform alternative in which a consumption tax is adopted. In scenario 1, the extent of the change in capital that occurs over the ten-year observation period is the relevant factor to determine the decline in GDP. Although readers are not told what proportion of the eventual steady-state change is projected to occur within ten years, any attention to subsequent adjustments is not included in Kitchen's analysis.

Scenario 2

If foreign official entities buy the additional U.S. debt, crowding out instead is likely to occur in the net export sector. A large U.S. budget deficit may result in a large U.S. trade deficit, as occurred with the twin deficits of the 1980s. A key part of that adjustment process was an appreciation of the U.S. dollar. Although a traditional focus of international trade economists is to agonize over the relevant demand elasticities for exports and imports, such values are incidental to the broader recognition that the appreciation must be sufficient to cause the foreign official purchases of U.S. debt to equal the deterioration of U.S. net exports. The equilibrium condition that

$$(G - T) + I = S - (X - M) \tag{5.7}$$

neatly summarizes that outcome, where the right-hand side represents private domestic saving plus the foreign capital inflow. I assume that the sources and uses of funds framework applied to derive this expression includes net international income receipts and net transfers received, and the $X - M$ term refers to the U.S. current account position.

With respect to the choice of foreign central banks to hold more dollar assets, perhaps it is useful to recount some changing historical perspectives over the past decades. In the 1960s under the Bretton Woods system, foreign central bank purchases of U.S. dollar assets were regarded as accommodating transactions, as if the central banks' arms were twisted to buy these assets; those purchases represented a vulnerability that contributed to a larger overall balance-of-payments deficit. In the 1970s, as the Bretton Woods system of pegged exchange rates crumbled and OPEC central banks increased their holdings of dollar assets, balance-of-payments accounting conventions changed. Such dollar purchases by foreign central banks were interpreted as a wise choice that recognized the relative desirability in terms of risk and return from holding those assets. More recently, such risk-and-return characteristics may be tangential to foreign central banks' desires to maintain an undervalued currency and pursue an export-oriented growth strategy. Kitchen and Chinn (2011) raise the perceptive point that foreign central banks are less likely to continue to choose to hold dollar assets if they are not achieving the goal of strong export growth. They cite work by Catherine Mann (2009) suggesting that if foreigners acquired U.S. assets in proportion to U.S. capitalization as a share of total world capital, there would be a sufficient inflow of foreign funds to finance the U.S. deficit in the intermediate run. Whether foreign central banks would choose to pursue such a strategy is unclear, and any choice could be reversed quickly.

The equation from Kitchen and Chinn suggests that greater foreign central bank holdings of U.S. assets to match a greater U.S. budget deficit will leave the U.S. long-term interest gap unchanged. Equation 5.6 also shows that for an unchanged budget deficit, greater foreign central bank holdings of U.S. assets and a comparable reduction of Federal Reserve purchases of long-term assets will not affect the long-term interest gap. As they note, there is considerable multicolinearity among the three bracketed variables in equation 5.6, and the equality of the three effects is a constraint that they impose in their estimates. Beyond the statistical tests that cannot reject such a constraint, Kitchen and Chinn also provide evidence to suggest that there has been an increase in foreign official purchases of longer-term U.S. Treasury securities and agency debt, which could contribute to the neutrality condition noted. How precisely the composition of foreign central bank purchases must be concentrated in long-term assets to have an effect equivalent to the Fed's intervention in that market is a topic for further exploration.

In addition, another potential longer-run result seems possible. When greater official purchases of U.S. assets occur, investors may believe that greater uncertainty is created, because policy changes of foreign central banks may be less predictable than Fed actions. Presumably U.S. interest rates would have to rise to allow a greater risk premium to be earned.

Finally, the impact effect of foreign central bank purchases can be identified from equation 5.6, but additional consequences rest on the foreign central bank's success in sterilizing the tendency for its own money supply to rise. If sterilization is not successful, a possible outcome is that foreign inflation rates rise, foreign trade surpluses fall, and the availability of foreign savings to acquire U.S. government debt will decline.

Scenario 3

If the Federal Reserve purchases the additional government debt, with no particular twist toward the acquisition of long-term assets, such monetization of the debt results in an increase in the U.S. rate of inflation and an offsetting decline in the value of the dollar. The interest gap is not affected, because both short-term and long-term interest rates rise, as can be observed in the simulation results. Purchasing power parity is maintained, so there is no direct price influence on U.S. trade, but the capital loss to current owners of U.S. assets tends to lower U.S. consumption and imports. If foreign holders of U.S. assets also suffer capital losses, they may reduce their consumption and imports from the United States. An unexpected increase in inflation is a tax on those who are holding U.S. government debt, and if one were to extrapolate from the experience of Latin American countries, that would result in a higher risk premium to convince borrowers to hold dollars in the future. Thus, the short-term gain is recognized within the ten-year window examined, but the longer-run cost is not fully represented. Given the shorter maturity of U.S. outstanding debt compared to ten years ago, the potential gain from such a strategy would be smaller because more of the debt must be rolled over within a few years and the capital losses imposed on holders of the debt would be smaller.

The projected results are well summarized in table 5.3. Not surprisingly, the largest crowding out of domestic investment occurs under the first scenario, and the largest decline in output also occurs then. Greater foreign official purchases of the debt result in a slightly smaller decline in GDP, but because net exports improve less and income payments to foreigners rise more, the effect on the current account is less favorable and U.S. indebtedness to foreigners rises. Monetization of the debt results in a smaller reduction in GDP and may appear alluring because more of the cost is borne by foreign holders of U.S. debt. The fundamental fiscal reform, combined with the adoption of a consumption tax, allows for an increase in GNP and an increase in net international income earned by the United States.

As a final comment, these intermediate-run consequences are important inputs into any determination of the effects on U.S. welfare of alternative strategies. That choice would further depend on the way individuals balance the effect of a fall in income and a reduction in risk under the various strategies. Whether a mean-variance utility function is sufficient to address that trade-off is uncertain today, because worries about extreme events and higher moments of the distribution of consequences have become more important.

I congratulate Kitchen on a creative way of combining these separate empirical elements together to characterize deviations from the CBO scenario without having to reinvent the wheel and justify an entirely new forecasting model. The purpose of his essay in this chapter is not to specify the appropriate source of funding a deficit, but it clearly demonstrates the potentially negative consequences of three commonly accepted strategies. Consequently, the case for intermediate-run fiscal reform becomes more compelling.

References

Jones, Charles. 2010. *Macroeconomics*. 2nd ed. New York: Norton.

Kitchen, John. 2007. Sharecroppers or Shrewd Capitalists? Projections of the U.S. Current Account, International Income Flows, and Net International Debt. *Review of International Economics* 15 (5): 1036–61.

Kitchen, John, and Menzie Chinn. 2011. Financing U.S. Debt: Is There Enough Money in the World—and at What Cost? *International Finance* 14 (3): 373–413.

Mann, Catherine. 2009. International Capital Flows and the Sustainability of the US Current Account Deficit. In The Long-Term International Economic Position of the US, edited by C. Frederick Bergsten, 35–64. Washington, DC: Peterson Institute for International Economics.

Notes

1. The comparison relative to GNP rather than GDP for deficit and debt burden ratios is used so as to account for the effects of changes to net international income flows on domestic national income.

2. Treasury debt held by the public is the net debt and does not include the amounts owed within the U.S. government across accounts (e.g., Social Security and other trust fund accounts) that are included in measures of the gross debt.

3. This analysis addresses relationships for the United States, which can be a special case given the special role for the United States and the U.S. dollar in international financial markets, and also for the relative importance for foreign creditors holding government debt. The International Monetary Fund's *Fiscal Monitor* (2013) provides data for nonresident holdings of government debt by country: for example, among advanced economies, Japan (9 percent) and Switzerland (10 percent) are notably at the low end; the United States, Italy, Spain, and the United Kingdom are among those in the middle (around 30 percent held by foreign creditors); and Portugal and Ireland are at higher levels with the foreign share above 60 percent.

4. Beyond Fannie Mae and Freddie Mac, the total amounts in figure 5.4 include the Federal Home Loan Banks and other agencies.

5. See Autor, Dorn, and Hanson (2011) for discussion and evidence on the effects on the U.S. economy from the ongoing trade imbalance with China.

6. The analysis was conducted largely prior to the fiscal cliff resolution that occurred in early January 2013, but estimates for the alternative scenarios were updated to include budget effects of ATRA after its passage, but prior to the CBO economic and budget updates post-ATRA. ATRA permanently extended much of the tax policies assumed in the "continuation of certain policies" in prior estimates, but other spending policies were assumed in the "continuation" as well. As such, the results of the alternative scenarios presented here remain valid representations of the budget and economic relationships and effects since ATRA.

7. It is interesting to note that net international income flows were positive in 2010, continuing an observed outcome for numerous years, even despite the fact that the United States is a net international debtor. A full explanation is beyond the scope of this essay; Eichengreen (2006) and Kitchen (2007) address a number of the factors that have contributed to the ongoing positive net international income flows.

8. To the extent that the further inflation that occurs is not fully anticipated, the real value of bonds issued over time would be eroded as well (i.e., to the extent that the inflation premium included in the nominal interest rate at the time of issue does not fully reflect subsequent inflation).

9. This result lines up with the estimates from Gale and Orszag (2002, 2005) at 25 to 35 basis points and Laubach (2009) at 20 to 30 basis points.

10. Warnock and Warnock (2006), for example, showed estimated effects for the budget deficit (relative to GDP) of 19 to 31 basis points and for foreign official flows (measured relative to GDP) of 24 to 61 basis points; Chinn and Frankel (2007) observe estimates in the range of 52 to 71 basis points (for real and nominal Treasury rates and for a sample extending to September 2004). Most recently, Gruber and Kamin (2010) obtain a coefficient of approximately 15 basis points impact on the ten-year yield.

11. The *FEDLT* variable in the estimation had a value of about 2.8 percentage points of GDP for 2009, so the coefficient value of -0.33 indicates an estimated impact on the term premium of just under 100 basis points for that year. This estimate is somewhat larger than that obtained by Gagnon et al. (2010), who estimated that the effect of the first-round LSAP was in the range of 38 to 82 basis points (although standard errors of the coefficient estimates indicate a degree of imprecision that allows for overlapping confidence intervals at typical levels).

12. These observations are similar to those of Greenspan (2009) regarding foreign financial flows and of Bernanke (2005) regarding a global saving glut, with the observed relationship here pointing to the (foreign) policy-determined flows via foreign official holdings. Warnock and Warnock (2006) also discuss this observation. Bergsten (2009) stated: "The crisis occurred at least partly because the rest of the world was *too* willing to finance US current account deficits rather than becoming unwilling to do so." The interpretation presented here is also remarkably similar to that of Eichengreen (2011, 112–18).

13. The estimated results from the Solow growth model, albeit from a simplified modeling approach, are reasonable estimates compared to others. For example, the International Monetary Fund's WEO (2010, 95) discusses its estimates: "Model simulations suggest that over the long term, reducing debt is likely to be beneficial. In particular, the GIMF simulations considered here suggest that the lower government debt levels reduce real interest rates, which stimulates private investment. Also, the lower burden of interest payments creates fiscal room for cutting distortionary taxes. Both of these effects raise output in the long term. Overall, the simulations imply that for every 10 percentage point fall in the debt-to GDP ratio, output rises by about 1.4 percent in the long term."

14. Budget effects from changing economic assumptions are modeled consistent with the sensitivities identified by the Congressional Budget Office (2012a).

15. IMF projections from the World Economic Outlook were used for rest-of-world GDP.

16. For example, in this scenario, the Federal Reserve holdings change only to the extent that they differ relative to the base case to maintain the ultimate targeted level of holdings relative to GDP with changes to GDP.

17. Gagnon (2011b, 37), for example, states: "There is strong evidence of adjustment toward [purchase power parity (PPP)] over time. Studies indicate that half of any deviation from PPP tends to unwind within two to five years and three quarters of any deviation unwinds within four to ten years. Thus, at any point in time, the best estimate of the [real exchange rate] 10 years into the future will be its PPP value."

18. It is worth reiterating that the analysis focuses on intermediate-run projections and not on the short-run transitions.

19. Although the corresponding equation 5.4 labels the final variable in this equation as *FED*, page 21 refers to it as *FEDLT*.

20. Kitchen refers to the Taylor rule to justify this relationship. As he notes, the original Taylor rule was written in terms of deviations of output from trend rather than deviations of unemployment from its natural rate. However, a positive dependence on the output gap would correspond to a negative dependence on the unemployment gap in equation 5.5 rather than the positive dependence as written.

21. The discussion of international imbalances includes a discussion of the foreign official holdings of U.S. Treasury securities by country. Kitchen's essay in this chapter

presents a table of holdings by country as of July 2011 that gives China's total as $1,174 billion and a total of $4,478 billion, which implies China has about 26 percent of the total. I must have misunderstood something, however, since he comments in the text that China's holdings comprise "about one-half of all foreign holdings of Treasuries."

22. I say "likely" since the real rate would be based on the nominal rate and the expected rather than the actual rate of inflation. However, given the lack of trend in the realized inflation rate over this period, it is unlikely that the expected rate would have displayed as large a declining trend as is evident in the nominal interest rate.

23. This is not completely accurate since the securities are not otherwise identical. In particular, the TIPS market is less liquid than the market for Treasuries denominated in nominal terms.

III Individual and Corporate Income Tax Reform

6 Curbing Tax Expenditures

Daniel Baneman, Joseph Rosenberg, Eric Toder, and Roberton Williams

The nation's persistent budget deficits and rising national debt have driven policymakers to seek politically acceptable ways to cut spending or increase revenue. One recurring proposal would increase federal tax collections by paring back or eliminating tax expenditures—provisions in the tax code that provide special tax benefits for selected taxpayers or activities. President Obama's National Commission on Fiscal Responsibility and Reform called for eliminating or reducing most tax expenditures and using some of the additional revenue to slash tax rates to reduce the economic burden of federal taxes. The Bipartisan Policy Center offered a similar proposal, and members of Congress have shown a willingness to consider reducing at least some tax expenditures in exchange for lower rates.

Tax expenditures are defined as "revenue losses attributable to provisions of the Federal tax laws which allow a special exclusion, exemption, or deduction from gross income or which provide a special credit, a preferential rate of tax, or a deferral of liability" (U.S. Office of Management and Budget, 2013). That definition covers a wide range of tax preferences for individuals and businesses, from excluding municipal bond interest and most Social Security benefits from taxable income to allowing the deduction of mortgage interest payments, providing tax credits for children, imposing reduced tax rates on long-term capital gains, and allowing businesses to claim accelerated write-offs for investments in equipment. The 2014 budget lists 169 tax expenditures.

Tax expenditures have proliferated since the Tax Reform Act of 1986 reduced them sharply (Rogers and Toder 2011). Congress has added or expanded credits for children, workers, college students, health insurance, and retirement saving. New above-the-line deductions—so-called because they are subtracted in calculating adjusted gross income

(AGI)—reduce taxable income, and temporary provisions have been enacted in the hopes of stimulating the economy. The growth of tax expenditures has eroded the tax base, complicated our tax system, and cut revenue substantially.

We take a broad look at tax expenditures in the context of tax reform and increasing revenue. We first review how tax expenditures have changed over the past twenty-five years and provide estimates of the distribution of tax savings resulting from tax expenditures today.[1] We then examine three comprehensive approaches for reducing the impact of tax expenditures: replacing current provisions with fixed-rate tax credits, limiting the value of tax expenditures as a share of income, and proportionally reducing the value of tax expenditures that taxpayers may claim. The three approaches would have markedly different effects on households, and the impact of each would vary substantially across the income distribution.

The Recent History of Tax Expenditures

The Tax Reform Act of 1986 (TRA86) sharply reduced tax expenditures, in part by removing them from the tax code and in part by cutting tax rates and hence reducing their value.[2] In 1985, tax expenditures reported in the federal budget totaled nearly 9 percent of gross domestic product (GDP).[3] Three years later, after TRA86 had taken full effect, tax expenditures totaled just 6 percent of GDP (figure 6.1). They remained at roughly that level for a decade before climbing steadily to nearly 8 percent of GDP in 2003. Since then, they have fluctuated around 7 percent of GDP as the state of the economy has varied and Congress has enacted short-term stimulus provisions.[4] Tax expenditures are projected to rise modestly over the next few years as tax rates on higher-income taxpayers increase and the economy recovers more fully from recession.

Business versus Personal Tax Expenditures

Most of the variation in tax expenditures over the past twenty-five years has come from personal rather than business taxes (figure 6.2).[5] TRA86 cut business tax expenditures by nearly half from 1.8 percent of GDP in 1985 to just under 1 percent in 1988. They shrank further over the next three years and have remained roughly constant at about 0.8 percent of GDP since that time. Personal tax expenditures dropped by about a quarter after TRA86—from 6.7 percent of GDP in 1985 to 5

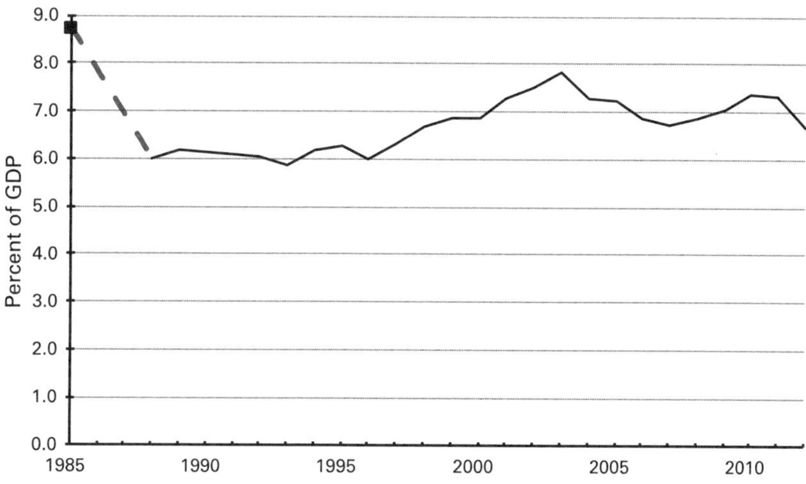

Figure 6.1
Sum of Tax Expenditure Costs, 1985–2012.
Source: Tax Policy Center calculations, based on tax expenditure estimates reported in the Budget of the Federal Government, Fiscal Years 1987 and 1990–2014.

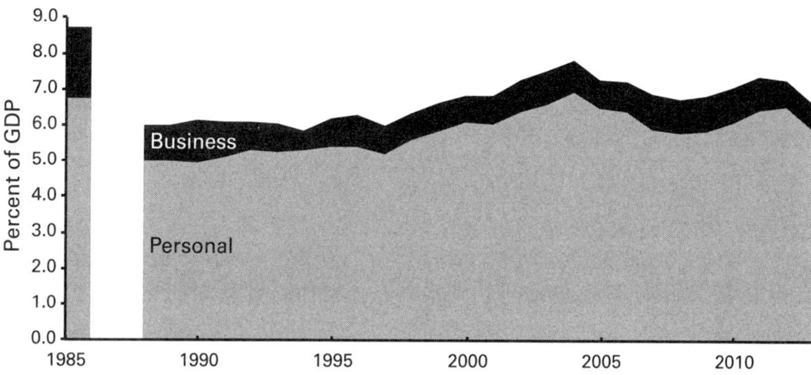

Figure 6.2
Cost of Tax Expenditures, Business versus Personal, 1985–2012.
Source: Tax Policy Center calculations, based on tax expenditure estimates reported in the Budget of the Federal Government, Fiscal Years 1987 and 1990–2014.

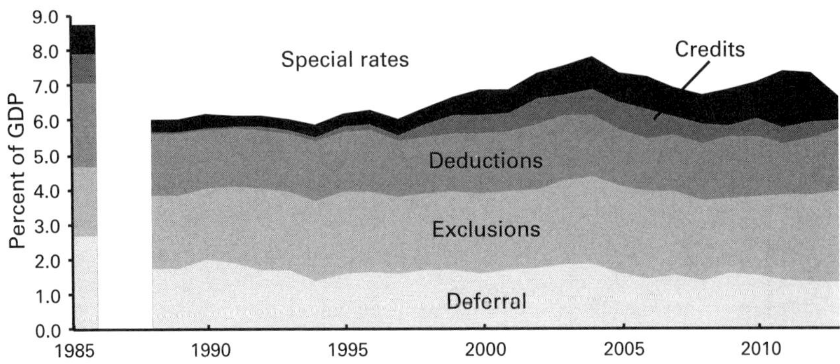

Figure 6.3
Cost of Tax Expenditures, by Form of Benefit, 1985–2012.
Source: Tax Policy Center calculations, based on tax expenditure estimates reported in the Budget of the Federal Government, Fiscal Years 1987 and 1990–2014.

percent in 1988—but rose fairly steadily over the next two decades to 6.9 percent of GDP in 2003. They have subsequently fallen to about 6 percent of GDP and fluctuated around that level ever since.

Types of Incentives

As indicated by their definition, tax expenditures arise from many sources: deferrals, exclusions, deductions, preferential tax rates, and credits reduce tax liabilities. The revenue costs of those different sources have changed in different ways over the past twenty-five years (figure 6.3).

- *Deferrals* allow taxpayers to delay recognition of current income to a future year. For example, small businesses may deduct the cost of qualifying investments immediately rather than over time based on economic depreciation. Individuals may choose to defer tax on retirement savings until they withdraw funds. TRA86 cut tax expenditures from deferral by one-third from 2.7 percent of GDP in 1985 to 1.8 percent in 1988. They stayed at roughly that level for more than a decade before falling below 1.5 percent of GDP in recent years.
- *Exclusions* leave income from specific sources out of the income tax base. For example, employer contributions to health insurance plans and interest paid on most state and municipal bonds are excluded from the taxable income of employees and bondholders. The cost of exclusions has risen gradually over the past few decades, from 2.0 percent of GDP in 1985 to 2.6 percent in 2012. That increase has

resulted in large part from increases in health care costs, which have driven up the share of employee compensation coming from tax-free employer-paid health insurance premiums.

- *Deductions* allow taxpayers to subtract specified outlays such as home mortgage interest and charitable contributions from taxable income. TRA86 reduced the cost of deductions as a share of GDP primarily by lowering marginal tax rates, thereby reducing the tax savings from deductible expenses. The revenue loss from deductions fell from 2.4 percent of GDP in 1985 to 1.7 percent in 1988 and has roughly maintained that level since that time.

Deferrals, exemptions, and deductions all reduce the present value of income subject to tax, and all provide larger tax reductions to taxpayers in high marginal rate brackets than to taxpayers in low marginal rate brackets or to those who would have no income tax liability even without these provisions. And itemized deductions (deductions for home mortgage interest, state and local taxes, charitable contributions, medical expenses, and miscellaneous expenses) have no value to the approximately two-thirds of taxpayers who use the standard deduction.

- *Special rates* reduce the tax rates on income from specific sources below those that generally apply. For example, the maximum 15 percent tax rate on both long-term capital gains and qualified dividends that was in effect from 2003 through 2012 was less than half the maximum 35 percent rate on most other forms of income. Legislated changes in tax rates on capital gains, dividends, and ordinary income, as well as large swings in stock prices, have caused the cost of special rates to fluctuate widely since 1985. TRA86 removed the preference for capital gains entirely and cut the cost of special rates from 0.8 percent of GDP in 1985 to less than 0.1 percent in 1988. Tax legislation in 1990 and 1993 imposed new, higher tax rates on ordinary income but left the rate on gains unchanged; the restoration of the differential between capital gains and ordinary income rates recreated the tax expenditure and raised the cost of special rates. Subsequent reductions in the maximum tax rate on long-term capital gains and on qualified dividends to 15 percent further increased the revenue loss to about 0.8 percent of GDP in 2005. The cost has fallen to about half that level more recently, largely because the sharp drop in equity prices after 2007 greatly reduced capital gains realizations.[6]
- *Tax credits* directly lower tax liability by the amount of the credit. The $1,000 child credit and the earned income tax credit are examples.

TRA86 eliminated the investment tax credit, causing credits to fall sharply from 0.9 percent of GDP in 1985 to 0.3 percent in 1988. Expansion of the earned income tax credit (EITC) in the 1990s and the 1997 introduction and 2001 expansion of the child credit combined to push the cost up to 1 percent of GDP in 2003. Temporary credits enacted to stimulate the economy increased the cost to 1.6 percent of GDP in 2010, but the cost has since returned to 1 percent of GDP as the largest of those temporary credits (the Making Work Pay credit) have expired.

Most of the cost of tax expenditures takes the form of reduced revenues, but the federal budget counts refundable credits—credits that may be claimed in excess of income taxes otherwise owed—differently. The portion of the credit that offsets tax liability counts as a revenue loss while the payment is an outlay. The EITC is fully refundable, while the child tax credit and the American Opportunity Tax Credit are partially refundable. The total budgetary cost of the outlay portion of refundable credits has grown over recent decades from less than one-tenth of a percent of GDP in 1985 to nearly 0.8 percent in 2010, representing 10 percent of the total budgetary cost of all tax expenditures. Outlays associated with tax expenditure provisions are scheduled to increase further in 2014 when the health insurance exchange subsidies associated with the Patient Protection and Affordable Care Act (PPACA) legislation take effect.

Despite significant variation over the years, tax expenditures impose substantial costs on the federal budget and will continue to do so. In 2011, they were projected to cut revenues and raise outlays by $1.1 trillion, more than we collected from individual income taxes and nearly half of total federal revenue collections for the year.

Who Benefits from Tax Expenditures?

We estimate that tax expenditures in 2011 saved households an average of about $6,500 in reduced taxes. Those savings went to households throughout the income distribution, but the largest share accrued to those at the top of the distribution. Households in the top income quintile (total income over about $103,000) received two-thirds of the benefits of tax expenditures in 2011 with average savings of more than $30,000 (figure 6.4). Those in the top 1 percent (income over about $533,000) got nearly a quarter of the tax savings, an average of nearly

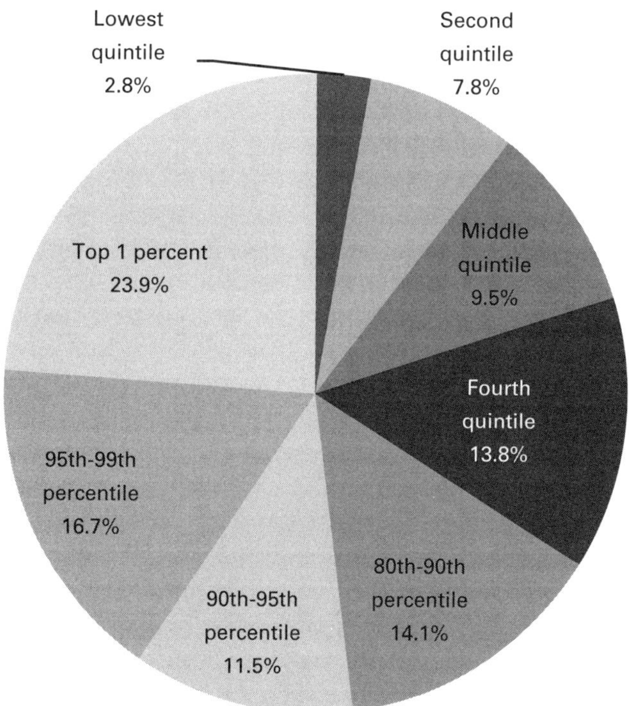

Figure 6.4
Distribution of All Tax Expenditures by Income Percentile, 2011.

$220,000. In contrast, households in the bottom three quintiles (income under about $60,000) saved an average of less than $2,000 each, totaling just one-fifth of the tax savings from all tax expenditures.

Tax expenditures have a striking effect on the taxes people pay, cutting the overall effective federal tax rate by more than a third to 18.1 percent, relative to a rate of 28.2 percent with no tax expenditures. The effect is greatest at the bottom of the income distribution—tax expenditures cut the effective tax rate (ETR) by 90 percent for the lowest quintile and by 61 percent for the second quintile (figure 6.5). For the rest of the income distribution, tax expenditures reduce ETRs by about a third.

Particular kinds of tax expenditures provide relatively higher benefits for taxpayers in different parts of the income distribution. For the purpose of displaying their distributional effects, we classify individual tax expenditures into six categories (figure 6.6), depending on where they appear on the income tax return: (1) special rates for capital gains

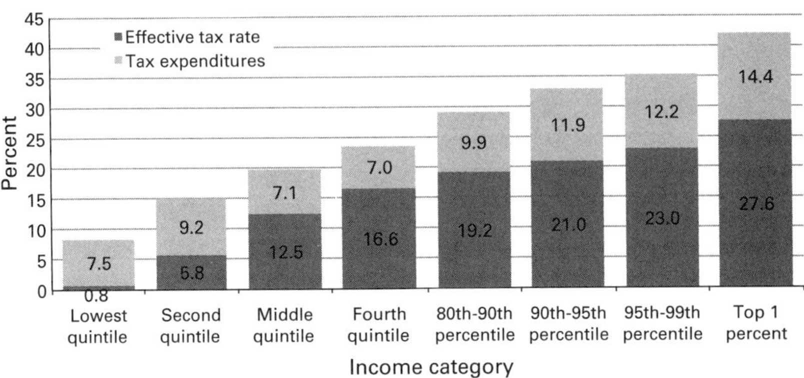

Figure 6.5
Effect of Tax Expenditures on Effective Federal Tax Rates by Income Percentile, 2011.
Source: Tax Policy Center Microsimulation Model (version 0411-2).

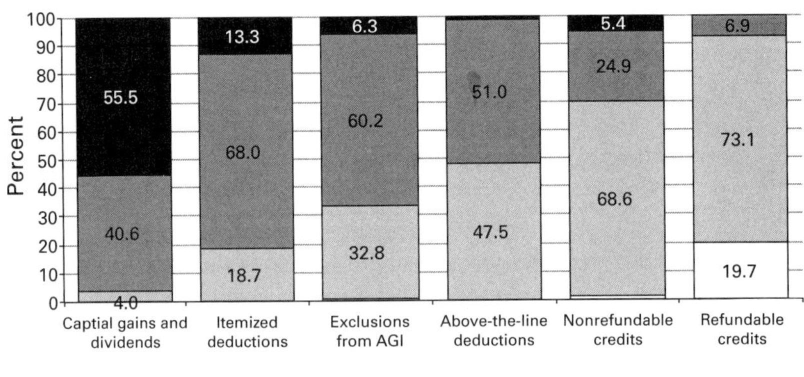

Figure 6.6
Distribution of Tax Change from Different Kinds of Tax Expenditures by Income Percentile, 2011
Source: Tax Policy Center Microsimulation Model (version 0411-2).

and dividends, (2) itemized deductions, (3) exclusions from AGI, (4) above-the-line deductions, (5) nonrefundable credits, and (6) refundable credits. Lower tax rates on capital gains and dividends, itemized deductions, and exclusions primarily benefit households in the top income quintile. Above-the-line deductions and nonrefundable credits provide the largest benefits to taxpayers in the middle three quintiles of the distribution. Refundable credits provide the largest benefits as a share of income to taxpayers in the bottom two quintiles, although the child credit also provides substantial benefits to households in the third and fourth quintiles.

- *Capital gains and dividends*. According to our estimates, fully 96 percent of the tax savings from preferential tax rates on long-term capital gains and qualified dividends went to people in the top income quintile in 2011: 75 percent to the top 1 percent and 55 percent to the top tenth of 1 percent (figure 6.6). That situation reflects the fact that gains and dividends go disproportionately to high-income households: in 2011, nearly half of households in the top quintile had income from those sources, compared to just 7 percent of those in the bottom four quintiles. The top quintile received 92 percent of total capital gains and dividend income, and those in the top 0.1 percent accounted for 47 percent of the total. Preferential rates substantially reduce the effective tax rates paid by people who get much of their income from gains and dividends. In 2011, the effective tax rate (ETR) under the individual income tax for taxpayers with cash income over $1 million was 18.7 percent. People in that income category who got at least two-thirds of their income from long-term capital gains and qualified dividends, however, faced an ETR of just 11.9 percent, compared with an ETR of 22.6 percent for those who got less than a tenth of their income from those sources.[7]
- *Itemized deductions*. More than 80 percent of the tax savings from itemized deductions accrued to taxpayers in the top income quintile in 2011, and 13 percent went to those in the top 0.1 percent. That situation resulted in part because high-income households are much more likely to itemize than are those with lower incomes. More than 80 percent of taxpayers in the top quintile itemized deductions in 2011, compared with just 16 percent of those in the bottom four quintiles. In addition, the value of a given amount of tax deductions is proportional to a person's marginal tax rate. A dollar of deductions reduces tax liability by 35 cents for a taxpayer in the 35 percent top tax bracket but by only 10 cents for someone in the 10 percent bracket.

- *Exclusions from AGI.*[8] Income from particular sources is excluded from AGI and therefore goes untaxed. Important exclusions include employer-paid health insurance benefits, a portion of Social Security benefits, all or part of foreign-sourced earnings, and the interest paid on bonds issued by state and local governments. About two-thirds of the tax savings from exclusions benefit tax units in the top income quintile, largely because they face higher tax rates.
- *Above-the-line deductions.* Taxpayers who claim the standard deduction rather than itemizing may still benefit from some deductions that they can use to reduce their AGI. Above-the-line deductions include a broad array of expenses, ranging from the first $250 of classroom expenses paid by educators and interest paid on student loans to tuition and fees for postsecondary education. In 2011, less than half of these deductions—but just over half of the tax savings they provide—went to people in the top income quintile. But savings as a share of income were highest for taxpayers in the middle 60 percent of the distribution.
- *Nonrefundable and refundable tax credits.* Tax credits differ from other tax expenditures in that the tax savings they provide are independent of tax rates. The $1,000 child credit, for example, is the same for all eligible families.[9] Credits do differ, however, in whether they are refundable—that is, whether tax filers can claim credits in excess of their basic tax liability. Most credits are not refundable; they can only reduce a person's income tax bill to zero. In contrast, refundable credits can result in payments to tax filers who would otherwise have no income tax liability. The child credit, the EITC, the American Opportunity tax credit, and a few other small credits are refundable.

Tax credits, particularly refundable ones, provide relatively more benefits to low- and middle-income tax units than do other tax expenditures. Over two-thirds of nonrefundable credits and more than 90 percent of refundable credits went to households in the bottom four quintiles in 2011. Taxpayers in the bottom quintile got less than 4 percent of pretax income but received about 20 percent of the benefit of refundable credits. In contrast, taxpayers in the second quintile received less than 9 percent of pretax income but almost 40 percent of the benefit from refundable credits. Taxpayers in the top 0.1 percent get virtually no benefit from refundable credits, primarily because those credits generally phase out at higher levels of AGI.[10]

Conceptual Issues in Defining and Measuring the Benefit from Tax Expenditures

The definition and measurement of tax expenditures is not without controversy. Originally defined in the 1974 Budget Act, tax expenditures must be measured relative to a "normal" income tax system. Both the Joint Committee on Taxation and the U.S. Treasury produce annual estimates of tax expenditures, although the method has differed over time and across agency. Altshuler and Dietz (2011) provide a summary of the history and difficulties that arise in performing tax expenditure analysis.

The benefits from tax expenditures reported in this section are measured using the Tax Policy Center's microsimulation tax model and are defined as the "static" change in tax liability associated with repealing the various tax provisions—that is, absent behavioral responses and under the assumption that the benefit of the tax expenditure accrues entirely to the taxpayer.[11] By design, tax expenditure estimates do not incorporate behavioral responses and therefore may differ substantially from conventional revenue estimates (see the discussion for more on the treatment of behavioral responses in distributional analysis), and in no case do such estimates incorporate an underlying model that could estimate the shifting of the calculated tax burdens among taxpayers.

Limiting Tax Expenditures

The complexity created by tax expenditures, the unequal benefits they provide to taxpayers, and the resulting revenue loss all provide strong arguments for curtailing or eliminating them. President George W. Bush's 2005 tax commission proposed sharply constraining tax expenditures. President Obama's fiscal commission considered complete elimination of all tax expenditures as a way to simplify the tax code, lower rates, and provide additional revenue. And most economists argue that cutting tax expenditures to broaden the tax base and lowering tax rates would yield a more efficient tax system.

But cutting back on tax expenditures is politically difficult. Taxpayers who benefit from specific tax preferences have a strong interest in maintaining them, and politicians hesitate to eliminate or even pare back popular tax provisions. For example, President Obama's repeated proposal to limit the value of itemized deductions to 28 percent brought quick condemnation from both the real estate industry and the philanthropic sector, which worried about the impact of reducing the tax savings from deducting mortgage interest and charitable contributions. Although interest groups would almost certainly levy similar objections to any similar broad reduction, reforming tax expenditures through across-the-board cuts, possibly accompanied by substantial marginal rate cuts, may stand a better chance of legislative success than attacking specific provisions one by one.

In this section, we simulate the effects of three broad approaches to limiting tax expenditures. The first would substitute nonrefundable credits for some deductions and exclusions, making the subsidy rate of tax expenditures the same in all marginal rate brackets. The second would place an overall limit on the tax savings any taxpayer can receive from a selected group of tax expenditure provisions. The third would scale back certain deductions, credits, and exemptions by a fixed proportional amount.

Methodology

Six tax expenditures are in our benchmark simulations:

- *Exclusion for employer-sponsored health insurance.* Premiums paid for employer-sponsored insurance (ESI) are not included in taxable compensation and therefore not taxed under the federal income tax.[12]
- *Deduction for medical expenses.* Taxpayers who itemize deductions may deduct the portion of medical and dental expenses (including health insurance premiums) that exceeds 10 percent of their adjusted gross income.[13]
- *Deduction for state and local taxes paid.* Taxpayers who itemize deductions and are not subject to the individual AMT may deduct either state and local income or general sales taxes paid, in addition to residential real estate, property, and certain other annual value-based personal property taxes.
- *Deduction for mortgage interest paid.* Taxpayers who itemize deductions may deduct interest paid on mortgages for owner-occupied housing and home equity loans. The deduction is limited to interest paid on up to $1 million in outstanding debt on new mortgages and $100,000 of debt on home equity loans.
- *Deduction for charitable contributions.* Taxpayers who itemize deductions may deduct gifts of cash and property donated to registered charitable organizations.

- *Preferential rates on capital gains and dividends.* For tax years 2003 through 2012, long-term capital gains and certain qualified dividends were taxed at a maximum rate of 15 percent. Beginning in 2013, taxpayers in the top income tax bracket will be subject to a maximum rate of 20 percent on long-term capital gains and qualified dividends. The PPACA will impose an additional surtax of 3.8 percent on dividends and capital gains of high-income taxpayers, beginning in 2013.

These six tax expenditures represent roughly 40 percent of the total sum of all tax expenditures as defined in the 2013 annual budget. The ESI exclusion is the largest single income tax expenditure, reducing revenues by nearly $184 billion in fiscal year 2012. The mortgage interest deduction is the next largest ($82 billion), and the deductions for charitable contributions and state and local taxes paid, along with preferential rates on capital gains and qualified dividends, all rank in the top ten according to OMB estimates.

Proposals to Limit Tax Expenditures

We examine three approaches for reducing the revenue cost of tax expenditures in the federal individual income tax by limiting the overall value of the selected provisions we listed rather than reducing or eliminating specific preferences. The first would replace the selected tax expenditures with a nonrefundable credit, the second would limit the value of the tax expenditures to a percentage of a taxpayer's income, and the third would impose an equal percentage reduction in the value of each of the tax expenditures. We set parameters in each of the options at levels that would result in roughly the same average tax increase in 2011. The three options for reforming the tax treatment of tax expenditures are:

- *Convert to a 15 percent credit.* This option would convert the selected tax expenditures into a single nonrefundable tax credit. It would include currently excluded ESI premiums in taxable income; repeal the preferential tax rates on capital gains and dividends; and eliminate the deductions for medical expenses, state and local taxes paid, mortgage interest, and charitable contributions. In their place, taxpayers would receive a credit equal to 15 percent of the sum of those deductions and exclusions. For capital gains and dividends, the credit would equal 15 percent of qualified gains and dividends, so it would effectively apply tax rates that are 15 percentage points lower than ordinary income rates.

- *Limit value to 3.9 percent of AGI*. This option would cap the total value of the selected tax expenditures at 3.9 percent of adjusted gross income.[14] Taxpayers would have to calculate their income tax liability under an alternative tax structure that disallows all the included tax expenditures. They would then subtract 3.9 percent of their AGI from their tax liability under the alternative structure and pay the larger of that amount or their regular tax liability.
- *Apply a 39 percent haircut*. This option would apply a uniform 39 percent reduction to each of the selected exclusions, deductions, and credits. Specifically, taxpayers would include 39 percent of currently untaxed ESI premiums in taxable income and would be allowed to subtract only 61 percent of the amounts currently deductible for medical expenses, state and local taxes paid, mortgage interest paid, and charitable contributions. Similarly, the value of the child tax credit would be reduced by 39 percent (the maximum credit amount of $1,000 would be reduced to $610). To achieve a similar percentage reduction in the benefit from preferential rates, the top tax rate on long-term capital gains and qualified dividends would increase to a level where the benefit to taxpayers in the top tax bracket would be reduced by 39 percent. In 2011, that corresponds to increasing the rate from 15 to 22.8 percent.[15]

Behavioral and Other Taxpayer Responses

Our analysis acknowledges that taxpayers may respond to changes in tax laws in a number of ways. Consistent with conventional distributional analysis, we distinguish between two broad categories of responses: (1) changes in "tax form" behavior and (2) changes in real economic behavior. The distinction is important because although both are included in our revenue estimates, only the former are included in our distributional results. The rationale for excluding behavioral responses from distributional tables is that changes in the so-called static burden provide a better approximation to the real economic burden of the tax change than the change in taxes paid.[16]

The following changes in tax form behavior are included in both our revenue and distributional results:

- We treat the standard deduction as part of the normal tax system and therefore not a tax expenditure. In all three options, our simulations allow taxpayers who would otherwise itemize their deductions to claim the standard deduction instead if it results in lower overall tax liability.

- Homeowners respond to a limitation on deductible mortgage interest by drawing down assets that generate taxable interest income (but not their stock portfolios) and using the proceeds to reduce mortgage debt.[17] Several studies have explored the mechanism and magnitude of this response, including Gale, Gruber, and Stephens-Davidowitz (2007) and Poterba and Sinai (2011). We follow the methodology of Gale et al. by allowing taxpayers to use up to 90 percent of reported taxable interest income to reduce their mortgage balance in response to a limit on the deductibility of mortgage interest.

Our revenue estimates also include the following behavioral responses:[18]

- Taxpayers reduce taxable income in response to an increase in marginal tax rates. A large literature exists on the responsiveness of taxable income to individual income tax rates, often summarized in the elasticity of taxable income (ETI). Empirical estimates of the ETI account for a broad range of possible behavioral responses, including changes in real labor supply, the composition of income and deductions, and tax evasion and avoidance behavior. Saez, Slemrod, and Giertz (2012) provide a thorough review of the theoretical and empirical literature on the ETI and conclude that a reasonable range for the long-run elasticity is 0.12 to 0.40. Our simulations use an ETI of 0.25, the midpoint of that range.[19]
- Taxpayers change the amount and timing of their capital gains realizations in response to changes in tax rates. Specifically, they realize more gains ahead of announced increases in the tax on gains and fewer gains once the higher tax rates take effect. They also realize less capital gains permanently in long-run equilibrium, although this permanent response is smaller than the transitory response. Our simulations use a permanent elasticity of capital gains realizations of -0.7 and a transitory elasticity of -1.2, both expressed at a tax rate of 20 percent. Those assumptions are broadly consistent with recent empirical evidence reported in Dowd, McClelland, and Muthitacharoen (2012).
- Donors reduce their charitable contributions in response to an increase in the net-of-tax price of giving. This is consistent

with a large body of empirical research that has documented responsiveness in the level of charitable giving to the income tax incentive, although estimates vary as to the magnitude. While Randolph (1995) found an overall (weighted) permanent elasticity of -0.5, more recent evidence in Bakija and Heim (2011) suggests a permanent elasticity in excess of -1.0. Our simulations use an elasticity of -1.0, although the revenue estimates would not be substantially affected if we used -0.5.

To provide a fair comparison among the three alternative tax increases, we calibrate each one to cause roughly similar increases in average tax burdens—about $1,050 in 2011. Because of differences in design and behavioral responses, however, the three options yield different increases in revenue over the ten-year budget period (table 6.1). The credit option would bring in nearly $2.8 trillion in added revenue over this period, compared with $2.4 trillion for the haircut and AGI limit. The main reason for this difference is the various tax provisions that are scheduled to expire under current law, in particular previously scheduled increases in marginal tax brackets that would have caused the 15 percent credit option to reduce the subsidy from deductions and exemptions by more after 2012 than in 2011 and 2012.[20] Some differences in the timing of behavioral responses, especially with respect to capital gains realizations, also lead to revenue differences.

Results

Distributional Effects

By design, all three proposals would have roughly similar effects on the average taxpayer in 2011. Each would increase the average federal tax rate that year by 1.6 percentage points from 18.1 to 19.7 percent of pretax income (table 6.2). As a result, each would reduce after-tax income by an average of just under 2 percent. The similarities end there, however. The AGI limit would affect the fewest households—just one in three—but would impose the largest tax increases on those with the highest incomes. In contrast, the 39 percent haircut would raise taxes for 54 percent of all tax units. The 15 percent credit would increase taxes for nearly 40 percent of households but would also cut taxes for 5 percent of them because the credit would generate larger tax savings than they currently get from the deductions affected by the proposal.

The effects of the three proposals would differ across the income distribution. Relatively few people in the lowest quintile would

Table 6.1
Impact on Individual Income Tax Revenue (billions of current dollars), 2011–2021

	Calendar Year											
Proposal	2011	2012	2013	2014	2015	2016	2017	2018	2019	2020	2021	2012–21
15 percent tax credit	10	118	215	230	249	270	290	312	334	358	384	2,769
3.9 percent AGI limit	31	53	159	193	212	233	254	278	303	330	361	2,407
39 percent haircut	16	111	179	207	223	239	255	272	289	308	327	2,426

Source: Urban-Brookings Tax Policy Center Microsimulation Model (version 0411–2).
Note: Proposals are effective January 1, 2012. Estimates include a microdynamic behavioral response and assume that taxpayers shift the timing of capital gains realizations in anticipation of a change in the capital gains tax rate. Estimates also assume that taxpayers adjust their investment portfolio and optimally pay down their mortgage balance if their tax benefit from mortgage interest is reduced. Finally, estimates assume that taxpayers adjust charitable contributions in proportion to the change in the tax price of giving compared with current law.

Table 6.2
Effects of Three Tax Proposals in 2011

	Tax Units with Tax Increase or Cut[a]						Average Federal Tax Rate[c]	
	With Tax Cut		With Tax Increase					
Proposal	Percent of Tax Units	Average Tax Cut ($)	Percent of Tax Units	Average Tax Increase ($)	Percent Change in After-Tax Income[b]	Average Federal Tax Change ($)	Change (% Points)	Under the Proposal
15 percent credit	5.4	-301	38.7	2,758	-2.0	1,051	1.6	19.7
3.9 percent AGI limit	0.0	0	33.7	3,112	-2.0	1,049	1.6	19.7
39 percent haircut	0.4	-179	54.0	1,940	-2.0	1,047	1.6	19.7

Source: Urban-Brookings Tax Policy Center Microsimulation Model (version 0411–2).
a. Includes both filing and nonfiling units but excludes those that are dependents of other tax units.
b. After-tax income is cash income less individual income tax net of refundable credits; corporate income tax; payroll taxes (Social Security and Medicare); and estate tax.
c. Average federal tax (includes individual and corporate income tax, payroll taxes for Social Security and Medicare, and the estate tax) as a percentage of average cash income.

experience a tax increase under any of the options, reflecting the fact that they benefit little from the tax expenditures the proposals would affect (table 6.3). In contrast, both the 15 percent credit and the 39 percent haircut would increase taxes for more than 90 percent of people in the top income quintile, while the AGI limit would raise taxes for just 75 percent of tax units in that quintile, largely because many high-income taxpayers have a large enough AGI to keep the limit from binding.

Although the three proposals would generate roughly equal average tax increases, the tax rise for affected tax units would be largest for the AGI limit and smallest for the haircut. The AGI limit would boost tax bills by an average of more than $3,100 in 2011 for the one-third of tax units whose taxes would go up. In contrast, the 15 percent credit would raise 2011 taxes by an average of nearly $2,800, and the haircut would increase them an average of less than $2,000 for tax units experiencing a tax increase. Those different effects are magnified at the top of the income distribution: affected tax units in the top quintile would see their 2011 tax bills go up by an average of more than $7,500 under the AGI limit, compared with about $6,000 for the 15 percent credit and just over $5,200 for the haircut.

About 5 percent of households would get a tax cut from the 15 percent credit.[21] That outcome results from the fact that they currently receive tax savings that are less than 15 percent of the value of the affected tax expenditures. For example, a taxpayer in the 10 percent tax bracket saves just 10 percent of any deductions or exclusions under current law but would save 15 percent of those items under the credit proposal. Taxpayers facing marginal income tax rates above 15 percent (but below 30 percent) can benefit from receiving a larger tax saving on capital gains and qualified dividends under the 15 percent credit than under current law. For example, a taxpayer in the 28 percent bracket would see her tax savings increase from 13 percent (28 percent ordinary tax rate minus the current 15 percent top rate on gains and dividends) of capital gains and qualified dividends with the current 15 percent top rate on gains to 15 percent of gains with the credit.

All three proposals would be moderately but unevenly progressive across the income distribution. Tax units in the bottom four quintiles would see their after-tax income in 2011 drop by less than average, while those in the top quintile would experience larger-than-average declines (table 6.4 and figure 6.7). For example, the 15 percent credit would reduce after-tax income by about 1 percent for those in the

Table 6.3
Tax Cuts and Tax Increases from Three Tax Proposals in 2011

Cash Income Percentile[1]	15 Percent Tax Credit				3.9 Percent AGI Limit				39 Percent Haircut			
	Tax Units with Tax Increase or Cut[a]				Tax Units with Tax Increase or Cut[4]				Tax Units with Tax Increase or Cut[4]			
	With Tax Cut		With Tax Increase		With Tax Cut		With Tax Increase		With Tax Cut		With Tax Increase	
	Percent of Tax Units	Average Tax Cut ($)	Percent of Tax Units	Average Tax Increase ($)	Percent of Tax Units	Average Tax Cut ($)	Percent of Tax Units	Average Tax Increase ($)	Percent of Tax Units	Average Tax Cut ($)	Percent of Tax Units	Average Tax Increase ($)
Lowest quintile	3.5	-116	4.3	464	0.0	0	5.5	168	0.1	-184	7.2	164
Second quintile	9.2	-128	19.5	1,317	0.0	0	19.9	404	0.5	-112	43.2	445
Middle quintile	5.9	-139	46.9	837	0.0	0	39.4	838	0.6	-82	71.5	698
Fourth quintile	3.7	-269	66.3	1,267	0.0	0	57.1	1,597	0.6	-212	88.9	1,273
Top quintile	4.2	-1,547	92.2	6,037	0.0	0	75.6	7,609	0.4	-447	96.8	5,230
All	5.4	-301	38.7	2,758	0.0	0	33.7	3,112	0.4	-179	54.0	1,940
Addendum												
80–90	3.9	-351	91.0	3,206	0.0	0	76.3	3,164	0.3	-128	95.8	2,682
90–95	3.9	-1,058	94.2	5,151	0.0	0	83.8	4,633	0.4	-77	98.0	4,005
95–99	5.1	-1,794	92.3	6,848	0.0	0	67.2	7,207	0.6	-801	97.3	5,342
Top 1 percent	4.4	-13,105	92.9	35,055	0.0	0	61.6	84,201	0.5	-2,278	97.4	35,890
Top 0.1 percent	2.8	-121,149	95.5	194,398	0.0	0	68.3	535,033	0.3	-16,232	97.9	218,137

Source: Urban-Brookings Tax Policy Center Microsimulation Model (version 0411–2).
a. Includes both filing and nonfiling units but excludes those that are dependents of other tax units. Tax units with negative cash income are excluded from the lowest income class but are included in the totals.

Table 6.4
Effects of Three Tax Proposals on After-Tax Income and Tax Rates by Income Percentile in 2011

	15 Percent Tax Credit			3.9 Percent AGI Limit			39 Percent Haircut		
Cash Income Percentile[a]	Percent Change in After-Tax Income	Average Federal Tax Change ($)	Change in Average Federal Tax Rate (% points)	Percent Change in After-Tax Income	Average Federal Tax Change ($)	Change in Average Federal Tax Rate (% points)	Percent Change in After-Tax Income	Average Federal Tax Change ($)	Change in Average Federal Tax Rate (% points)
Lowest quintile	-0.2	16	0.2	-0.1	9	0.1	-0.1	12	0.1
Second quintile	-1.1	245	1.0	-0.3	79	0.3	-0.8	192	0.8
Middle quintile	-1.0	384	0.9	-0.8	329	0.7	-1.3	498	1.1
Fourth quintile	-1.3	830	1.0	-1.4	911	1.2	-1.7	1,130	1.4
Top quintile	-2.8	5,499	2.2	-3.0	5,749	2.3	-2.6	5,058	2.0
All	-2.0	1,051	1.6	-2.0	1,049	1.6	-2.0	1,047	1.6
Addendum									
80–90	-2.8	2,904	2.2	-2.3	2,413	1.9	-2.4	2,570	2.0
90–95	-3.3	4,812	2.6	-2.7	3,881	2.1	-2.7	3,926	2.1
95–99	-2.5	6,228	2.0	-2.0	4,844	1.5	-2.1	5,193	1.6
Top 1 Percent	-2.9	31,988	2.1	-4.7	51,823	3.4	-3.2	34,961	2.3
Top 0.1 Percent	-3.8	182,282	2.7	-7.7	365,465	5.3	-4.5	213,543	3.1

Source: Urban-Brookings Tax Policy Center Microsimulation Model (version 0411–2).
a. Includes both filing and nonfiling units but excludes those that are dependents of other tax units. Tax units with negative cash income are excluded from the lowest income class but are included in the totals.

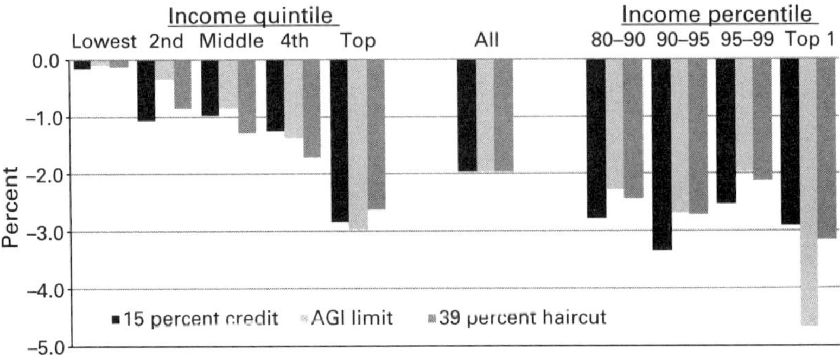

Figure 6.7
Average Change in After-Tax Income from Three Proposals by Income Percentile, 2011.
Source: Tax Policy Center Microsimulation Model (version 0411-2).

middle three quintiles (and just 0.2 percent for the lowest quintile), compared with a 2 percent overall average reduction and a 2.8 percent reduction in income for the top quintile. Similar patterns hold for the other two proposals.

Under any of the three proposals, taxes would rise much more, relative to income, for taxpayers in the top 0.1 percent. Their after-tax income would drop an average of about 4 percent under either the credit or haircut options and by nearly twice that much under the AGI limit. The size of their tax increases reflects the fact that the tax expenditures included in the options increase their after-tax income relatively more than they raise after-tax income for people further down the income distribution.

Alternative Specifications

Itemized deductions and the employer health insurance exclusion affect a relatively large number of taxpayers. In contrast, other tax expenditures, such as the preferential tax rates for long-term capital gains and qualified dividends and the child tax credit (CTC), provide significant benefits to specific groups of taxpayers—investors and families with children, respectively. For example, very high-income taxpayers receive most of the benefit from preferential rates for gains and dividends but almost none of the benefit from the child credit, which phases out at higher levels of AGI. To examine the distributional effects of protecting those tax expenditures from our three proposals, we analyzed two sets of alternatives: one that removes the preferential rates from the list of tax expenditures that are pared back and another that adds the CTC to the list. In each case, we used the 15 percent credit option as a benchmark against which to calibrate the AGI limit and haircut options so that all three result in roughly similar average tax increases in 2011.

Retaining Preferential Tax Rates for Long-Term Capital Gains and Qualified Dividends

If we retain the current tax expenditures for capital gains and dividends, the 15 percent credit would raise average tax liability by nearly $980, about 7 percent less than the $1,050 increase for our base proposal (table 6.5). Making the other two proposals roughly match that average tax increase while retaining the preference for capital gains and dividends required changing their parameters—reducing the AGI limit from 3.9 to 2.5 percent and increasing the haircut from 39 to 46 percent.

Both the credit and haircut options would increase tax burdens on about the same fractions of taxpayers as our base option—just under 40 percent for the credit and about 54 percent for the haircut. The lower AGI limit, however, would raise taxes burdens for nearly a third more taxpayers—44 percent compared with 34 percent for the base option. That increase, combined with the lower revenue gain for all three options under this variant, yields a much smaller average tax increase for affected taxpayers: just under $2,200 compared with more than $3,100 for the base case.

Exempting capital gains and dividends from cuts in tax expenditures mostly benefits higher-income taxpayers, who receive the largest share of income from those sources (table 6.6). That is particularly true for the AGI limit, which would increase taxes for only half of taxpayers in the top 0.1 percent compared with the two-thirds affected by our base option. The AGI limit would affect additional middle-income households; for example, more than half of those in the middle quintile would pay more tax under this version compared with 40 percent under the base option. Average tax increases differ much more, however, than the number of tax units affected. The AGI limit would raise taxes for affected taxpayers in the top 1 percent by an average of about $24,000 if gains and dividends retain their tax advantage, compared with over $84,000 when the capital gains and dividends preferences are subject to the limit.

Omitting gains and dividends from the proposals has a smaller effect on the number of tax units affected by the credit and haircut options than the number affected by the 15 percent credit, but

Table 6.5
Effects of Three Tax Proposals in 2011: Variants Retaining Current Law Treatment of Capital Gains and Dividends

	Tax Units with Tax Increase or Cut[a]						Average Federal Tax Rate[c]	
	With Tax Cut		With Tax Increase					
Proposal	Percent of Tax Units	Average Tax Cut ($)	Percent of Tax Units	Average Tax Increase ($)	Percent Change in After-Tax Income[b]	Average Federal Tax Change ($)	Change (% Points)	Under the Proposal
15 percent credit	4.4	-172	38.9	2,533	-1.8	977	1.5	19.6
2.5 percent AGI limit	0.0	0	44.4	2,209	-1.8	981	1.5	19.6
46 percent haircut	0.5	-304	53.8	1,821	-1.8	978	1.5	19.6

Source: Urban-Brookings Tax Policy Center Microsimulation Model (version 0411–2).

a. Includes both filing and nonfiling units but excludes those that are dependents of other tax units.

b. After-tax income is cash income less individual income tax net of refundable credits, corporate income tax, payroll taxes (Social Security and Medicare), and estate tax.

c. Average federal tax (includes individual and corporate income tax, payroll taxes for Social Security and Medicare, and the estate tax) as a percentage of average cash income.

Table 6.6
Tax Cuts and Tax Increases from Three Tax Proposals in 2011: Variants Retaining Current Law Treatment of Capital Gains and Dividends

	15 Percent Tax Credit				2.5 Percent AGI Limit				46 Percent Haircut			
	Tax Units with Tax Increase or Cut				Tax Units with Tax Increase or Cut				Tax Units with Tax Increase or Cut			
	With Tax Cut		With Tax Increase		With Tax Cut		With Tax Increase		With Tax Cut		With Tax Increase	
Cash Income Percentile[a]	Percent of Tax Units	Average Tax Cut ($)	Percent of Tax Units	Average Tax Increase ($)	Percent of Tax Units	Average Tax Cut ($)	Percent of Tax Units	Average Tax Increase ($)	Percent of Tax Units	Average Tax Cut ($)	Percent of Tax Units	Average Tax Increase ($)
Lowest quintile	3.5	-117	4.3	464	0.0	0	7.8	206	0.1	-204	7.6	195
Second quintile	8.7	-133	19.5	1,318	0.0	0	32.5	449	0.5	-109	43.7	529
Middle quintile	4.9	-155	46.8	839	0.0	0	56.3	906	0.6	-85	71.8	817
Fourth Quintile	2.4	-284	66.6	1,277	0.0	0	73.8	1,730	0.7	-203	87.9	1,482
Top quintile	1.1	-822	93.4	5,326	0.0	0	83.9	5,341	0.8	-855	94.6	4,438
All	4.4	-172	38.9	2,533	0.0	0	44.4	2,209	0.5	-304	53.8	1,821
Addendum												
80–90	1.1	-218	91.7	3,221	0.0	0	86.0	3,603	0.5	-137	93.6	3,104
90–95	0.9	-370	95.7	5,138	0.0	0	89.2	5,173	0.6	-192	96.3	4,385
95–99	1.2	-850	94.8	6,760	0.0	0	77.2	6,677	1.3	-823	95.2	4,903
Top 1 percent	2.0	-4,825	93.3	21,297	0.0	0	62.7	23,939	2.6	-3,003	94.1	16,161
Top 0.1 percent	3.5	-16,258	91.2	93,883	0.0	0	50.3	135,806	3.7	-9,871	93.8	73,670

Source: Urban-Brookings Tax Policy Center Microsimulation Model (version 0411–2).
a. Includes both filing and nonfiling units but excludes those that are dependents of other tax units. Tax units with negative cash income are excluded from the lowest income class but are included in the totals.

high-income taxpayers would see their taxes rise much less with gains and dividends excluded under these options as well. For example, people in the top 1 percent affected by the changes would see their taxes rise an average of just over $21,000 under the credit option with gains and dividends excluded, compared with about $35,000 when the limits apply to the gains and dividends preferences. Comparable estimates for the haircut option are $16,000 and $36,000, respectively. These differences reflect the fact that high-income households receive most capital gains and dividends and would thus benefit most from continuing the preferential tax treatment of income from those sources.

Exempting gains and dividends from the three proposals reduces or undoes the progressivity of the tax increases, particularly at the top of the income distribution (table 6.7). On average, for example, the AGI limit would then reduce after-tax income by 1.8 percent for all tax units but only by 1.4 percent for those in the top 1 percent. Similarly, it would boost tax rates by 1.5 percent on average but by only 1 percent for the top percentile. The haircut option would have similar effects, while the 15 percent credit would affect those with the highest incomes, about the same as the overall average. Of the three options, the 15 percent credit would have the largest adverse effect on tax units with the highest incomes and the smallest impact on households in the fortieth to eightieth percentile range. In contrast, the AGI limit and haircut options would affect these middle and upper-middle-income taxpayers more. All three options have relatively small effects on taxpayers in the bottom two quintiles, who get little income from gains and dividends.

Including the Child Tax Credit

Including the CTC in the base of tax expenditures subject to limitation would increase the impact of the AGI limit and haircut proposals on tax units in the lower quintiles while imposing smaller tax increases on those with the highest incomes.[22] This results primarily from the higher AGI limit (4.8 percent compared with 3.9 percent for the base option) and the smaller haircut (35 percent versus 39 percent for the base option) required to generate the same average effect on tax units. As was the case for the base option, those parameters would increase taxes by an average of around $1,050 in 2011 (table 6.8). The AGI limit and the haircut would affect slightly more tax units than in the base option, and the average tax increase for the affected tax units would be correspondingly smaller. For example, 38 percent of all tax units would

Table 6.7
Effects of Three Tax Proposals on After-Tax Income and Tax Rates by Income Percentile in 2011: Variants Retaining Current Law Treatment of Capital Gains and Dividends

Cash Income Percentile[a]	15 Percent Tax Credit			2.5 Percent AGI Limit			46 Percent Haircut		
	Percent Change in After-Tax Income	Average Federal Tax Change ($)	Change in Average Federal Tax Rate (% points)	Percent Change in After-Tax Income	Average Federal Tax Change ($)	Change in Average Federal Tax Rate (% points)	Percent Change in After-Tax Income	Average Federal Tax Change ($)	Change in Average Federal Tax Rate (% points)
Lowest quintile	-0.2	16	0.2	-0.2	16	0.2	-0.2	15	0.2
Second quintile	-1.1	245	1.0	-0.6	145	0.6	-1.0	231	0.9
Middle quintile	-1.0	385	0.9	-1.3	510	1.1	-1.5	586	1.3
Fourth Quintile	-1.3	843	1.1	-1.9	1,276	1.6	-2.0	1,302	1.6
Top Quintile	-2.6	4,964	2.0	-2.3	4,478	1.8	-2.2	4,191	1.7
All	-1.8	977	1.5	-1.8	981	1.5	-1.8	978	1.5
Addendum									
80–90	-2.8	2,952	2.3	-2.9	3,097	2.4	-2.8	2,904	2.2
90–95	-3.4	4,913	2.7	-3.2	4,616	2.5	-2.9	4,219	2.3
95–99	-2.6	6,397	2.0	-2.1	5,156	1.6	-1.9	4,655	1.5
top 1 percent	-1.8	19,763	1.3	-1.4	15,005	1.0	-1.4	15,137	1.0
top 0.1 percent	-1.8	85,079	1.2	-1.4	68,285	1.0	-1.5	68,714	1.0

Source: Urban-Brookings Tax Policy Center Microsimulation Model (version 0411–2).
a. Includes both filing and nonfiling units but excludes those that are dependents of other tax units. Tax units with negative cash income are excluded from the lowest-income class but are included in the totals.

Table 6.8
Effects of Three Tax Proposals in 2011: Variants Limiting Current Law Child Credit

	Tax Units with Tax Increase or Cut[a]						Average Federal Tax Rate[c]	
	With Tax Cut		With Tax Increase					
Proposal	Percent of Tax Units	Average Tax Cut ($)	Percent of Tax Units	Average Tax Increase ($)	Percent Change in After-Tax Income[b]	Average Federal Tax Change ($)	Change (% Points)	Under the Proposal
15 percent credit	5.4	-301	38.7	2,758	-2.0	1,051	1.6	19.7
4.8 percent AGI limit	0.0	0	38.4	2,698	-1.9	1,037	1.6	19.7
35 percent haircut	0.3	-196	59.2	1,757	-1.9	1,039	1.6	19.7

Source: Urban-Brookings Tax Policy Center Microsimulation Model (version 0411–2).
a. Includes both filing and nonfiling units but excludes those that are dependents of other tax units.
b. After-tax income is cash income less individual income tax net of refundable credits, corporate income tax, payroll taxes (Social Security and Medicare), and estate tax.
c. Average federal tax (includes individual and corporate income tax, payroll taxes for Social Security and Medicare, and the estate tax) as a percentage of average cash income.

pay an average of nearly $2,700 more tax under the AGI limit that affects the CTC, compared with 34 percent facing an average tax increase of just over $3,100 if the CTC is unchanged.

Compared with our base option, the AGI limit on preferences, including the CTC, would raise taxes by a larger amount and for more tax units in the bottom two quintiles and raise less from fewer taxpayers in the top two quintiles (table 6.9). For example, 31 percent of those in the second quintile would see their taxes rise by an average of nearly $830, compared with 20 percent facing an average tax increase of just $400 under the base case. This reflects the fact that the CTC makes up a larger share of tax expenditures for low-income families than for those in the higher quintiles (many of whom receive no benefit from the credit because it phases out at higher levels of AGI) and the fact that the base option set a lower AGI limit. The same pattern occurs for the 35 percent haircut, but for that option, the difference in tax changes in the bottom quintiles from including or excluding the child credit is smaller.

Including the child credit makes both the AGI limit and haircut options less progressive, increasing the tax increases on lower-income tax units and decreasing those on high-income households compared with the tax changes they would face for comparable limits that exclude the child credit (tables 6.4 and 6.10). This again results from the combination of the distributional benefits of the CTC and the less strict AGI limit and smaller haircut required to meet revenue targets for this option. For example, households in the second quintile would see their after-tax income drop by nearly $300 (1.2 percent) under this variant of the haircut, compared with about $200 (0.8 percent) under the base case. In contrast, tax units in the top 1 percent would see their taxes go up by about $31,000 on average, 10 percent less than under the base case.

Additional Policy Considerations

The simulation results we have presented are meant to be illustrative and demonstrate the significant role that across-the-board tax expenditure limits could play in future efforts to reform the tax system and reduce federal deficits. Toder, Rosenberg, and Eng (2013) discuss some of the general issues in designing across-the-board tax expenditure limits, including versions of the three options we have modeled. To be sure, such across-the-board limits are not a substitute for more thoughtful and comprehensive efforts to overhaul the tax system, a process that

Table 6.9
Tax Cuts and Tax Increases from Three Tax Proposals in 2011: Variants Limiting Current Law Child Credit

	15 Percent Tax Credit				4.8 Percent AGI Limit				35 Percent Haircut			
	Tax Units with Tax Increase or Cut				Tax Units with Tax Increase or Cut				Tax Units with Tax Increase or Cut			
	With Tax Cut		With Tax Increase		With Tax Cut		With Tax Increase		With Tax Cut		With Tax Increase	
Cash income percentile[a]	Percent of Tax Units	Average Tax Cut ($)	Percent of Tax Units	Average Tax Increase ($)	Percent of Tax Units	Average Tax Cut ($)	Percent of Tax Units	Average Tax Increase ($)	Percent of Tax Units	Average Tax Cut ($)	Percent of Tax Units	Average Tax Increase ($)
Lowest quintile	3.5	-116	4.3	464	0.0	0	14.3	380	0.1	-153	11.7	204
Second quintile	9.2	-128	19.5	1,317	0.0	0	30.9	827	0.3	-92	54.2	529
Middle quintile	5.9	-139	46.9	837	0.0	0	43.4	1,171	0.4	-95	77.1	778
Fourth quintile	3.7	-269	66.3	1,267	0.0	0	57.5	1,755	0.4	-226	90.9	1,326
Top Quintile	4.2	-1,547	92.2	6,037	0.0	0	68.0	7,241	0.4	-460	97.0	4,748
All	5.4	-301	38.7	2,758	0.0	0	38.4	2,698	0.3	-196	59.2	1,757
Addendum												
80–90	3.9	-351	91.0	3,206	0.0	0	71.3	3,145	0.3	-101	96.3	2,543
90–95	3.9	-1,058	94.2	5,151	0.0	0	75.5	4,221	0.4	-67	98.1	3,607
95–99	5.1	-1,794	92.3	6,848	0.0	0	55.8	6,542	0.6	-810	97.4	4,782
Top 1 percent	4.4	-13,105	92.9	35,055	0.0	0	47.1	96,084	0.5	-2,191	97.6	32,019
Top 0.1 percent	2.8	-121,149	95.5	194,398	0.0	0	59.3	557,579	0.3	-14,468	98.0	195,045

Source: Urban-Brookings Tax Policy Center Microsimulation Model (version 0411–2).
a. Includes both filing and nonfiling units but excludes those that are dependents of other tax units. Tax units with negative cash income are excluded from the lowest income class but are included in the totals.

Table 6.10
Effects of Three Tax Proposals on After-Tax Income and Tax Rates by Income Percentile in 2011: Variants Limiting Current Law Child Credit

	15 Percent Tax Credit			4.8 Percent AGI Limit			35 Percent Haircut		
Cash Income Percentile[a]	Percent Change in After-Tax Income	Average Federal Tax Change ($)	Change in Average Federal Tax Rate (% points)	Percent Change in After-Tax Income	Average Federal Tax Change ($)	Change in Average Federal Tax Rate (% points)	Percent Change in After-Tax Income	Average Federal Tax Change ($)	Change in Average Federal Tax Rate (% points)
Lowest quintile	-0.2	16	0.2	-0.6	54	0.6	-0.3	24	0.3
Second quintile	-1.1	245	1.0	-1.1	255	1.0	-1.2	286	1.2
Middle quintile	-1.0	384	0.9	-1.3	508	1.1	-1.5	599	1.3
Fourth quintile	-1.3	830	1.0	-1.5	1,009	1.3	-1.8	1,205	1.5
Top quintile	-2.8	5,499	2.2	-2.5	4,926	2.0	-2.4	4,606	1.8
All	-2.0	1,051	1.6	-1.9	1,037	1.6	-1.9	1,039	1.6
Addendum									
80–90	-2.8	2,904	2.2	-2.1	2,243	1.7	-2.3	2,449	1.9
90–95	-3.3	4,812	2.6	-2.2	3,187	1.7	-2.4	3,538	1.9
95–99	-2.5	6,228	2.0	-1.5	3,649	1.1	-1.9	4,653	1.5
Top 1 percent	-2.9	31,988	2.1	-4.1	45,298	3.0	-2.8	31,229	2.0
top 0.1 Percent	-3.8	182,282	2.7	-7.0	330,379	4.8	-4.0	191,126	2.8

Source: Urban-Brookings Tax Policy Center Microsimulation Model (version 0411–2).
a. Includes both filing and nonfiling units but excludes those that are dependents of other tax units. Tax units with negative cash income are excluded from the lowest income class but included in the totals.

would ideally assess tax expenditures on an individual basis and retain, reduce, or eliminate them based on their merits.

While our analysis has focused on the magnitude and distribution of changes in average tax burdens, policymakers should be aware of the impact such proposals might have on other important dimensions, such as the economic incentives to work and invest. While the disincentive effects of raising revenue from reducing tax expenditures are almost certainly less than from increasing tax rates, these proposals would all tend to raise effective marginal tax rates for a variety of reasons. By subjecting more income to tax, these proposals would shift taxpayers up the graduated rate schedule, directly increasing statutory marginal rates. In addition, to the extent that the magnitude of an individual's tax preferences depends on one's income—either directly, as in the case of the state and local tax deduction, or systematically, as in the case of charitable giving and the generosity of employer-provided health insurance plans—limiting the preferences will reduce incentives to work by reducing after-tax wages, net of deductions for additional charitable contributions or exemptions for additional use of health insurance. Limiting the preferential rates on long-term capital gains and dividends directly increases effective marginal rates on those forms of income. While estimating the magnitude of such effects is beyond the scope of this exercise, we would expect the disincentive effects to be smallest and most evenly spread in the 39 percent haircut option, larger and more concentrated among taxpayers in higher-income tax brackets for the 15 percent credit option, and largest and most concentrated among taxpayers subject to the 3.9 AGI limit.

In addition, policymakers should be aware of the broader economic effects that might accompany sharp reductions in existing subsidies. Some examples include the effect of limiting the mortgage interest deduction on home financing decisions (Poterba and Sinai 2011) and home prices (Harris 2013), the effect of limiting the state and local tax deduction on nonfederal government spending (Metcalf 2011), and the effect of limiting the charitable deduction on charitable contributions (Toder et al., 2013). Eliminating a large portion of the subsidy provided to employer-sponsored health insurance might erode the employer-based group insurance markets (Gillette et al. 2010) and put strain on the new state-run exchanges established as part of the PPACA, including the potential to increase the federal cost of providing exchange subsidies.

Conclusion

Compelling economic and political reasons make tax expenditures a logical focus of future efforts at deficit-reducing tax reform. While an ideal tax reform process would comprehensively evaluate each tax expenditure on its merits, eliminating some and restructuring or retaining others, broad-based limitations on tax expenditures may be easier to enact and would still produce net benefits. We have examined alternatives for implementing across-the-board limits applied to a selected group of the largest and most widely used tax preferences. The three options—a fixed percentage credit, a cap based on income, and a constant percentage reduction—can all be designed to raise significant revenue for deficit reduction. The effects of the options vary across the income distribution and depend on the types of tax expenditures subject to the limitations. But variants of all three options can be designed to be progressive in the sense that the limits would reduce after-tax income for higher-income taxpayers by more than they would reduce incomes of lower-income taxpayers.

References

Altshuler, Rosanne, and Robert Dietz. 2011. Reconsidering Tax Expenditure Estimation. *National Tax Journal* 64 (2): 459–90.

Auerbach, Alan J. 1995. Public Finance and Tax Policy. In Distributional Analysis of Tax Policy, edited by David F. Bradford, 135–47. Washington, DC: AEI Press.

Bakija, Jon, and Bradley T. Heim. 2011. How Does Charitable Giving Respond to Incentives and Income? New Estimates from Panel Data. *National Tax Journal* 64 (2): 615–50.

Carroll, Robert, and Warren Hrung. 2005. What Does the Taxable Income Elasticity Say about Dynamic Responses to Tax Changes? *American Economic Review* 95 (2): 426–31.

Dowd, Tim, Robert McClelland, and Athiphat Muthitacharoen. 2012. New Evidence on the Tax Elasticity of Capital Gains. CBO Working Paper 2012–09, Congressional Budget Office, Washington, DC.

Feldstein, Martin, Daniel Feenberg, and Maya MacGuineas. 2011. Capping Individual Tax Expenditure Benefits. NBER Working Paper 16921, National Bureau of Economic Research, Cambridge, MA.

Gale, William G., Jonathan Gruber, and Seth I. Stephens-Davidowitz. 2007. Encouraging Homeownership through the Tax Code. *Tax Notes* 115 (12): 1171–89.

Gillette, Robert, Gillian Hunter, Ithai Z. Lurie, Jonathan Siegel, and Gerald Silverstein. 2010. The Impact of Repealing the Exclusion for Employer-Sponsored Insurance. *National Tax Journal* 63 (4, Part 1): 695–708.

Harris, Benjamin H. 2013. *Tax Reform, Transaction Costs, and Metropolitan Housing in the United States*. Washington, DC: Urban-Brookings Tax Policy Center.

Joint Committee on Taxation. 1993. Methodology and Issues in Measuring Changes in the Distribution of Tax Burdens. JCS-7–93, Joint Committee on Taxation, Washington, DC.

Metcalf, Gilbert E. 2011. Assessing the Federal Deduction for State and Local Tax Payments. *National Tax Journal* 64 (2, Part 2): 565–90.

Neubig, Thomas S., and David Joulfaian. 1988. The Tax Expenditure Budget before and after the Tax Reform Act of 1986. OTA Paper 60, U.S. Department of the Treasury, Office of Tax Analysis, Washington, DC.

Poterba, James M., and Todd Sinai. 2011. Revenue Costs and Incentive Effects of the Mortgage Interest Deduction for Owner-Occupied Housing. *National Tax Journal* 64 (2, Part 2): 531–64.

Randolph, William C. 1995. Dynamic Income, Progressive Taxes, and the Timing of Charitable Contributions. *Journal of Public Economics* 103 (4): 709–38.

Rogers, Allison, and Eric Toder. 2011. *Trends in Tax Expenditures, 1985–2016*. Washington, DC: Urban-Brookings Tax Policy Center.

Saez, Emmanuel, Joel Slemrod, and Seth H. Giertz. 2012. The Elasticity of Taxable Income with Respect to Marginal Tax Rates: A Critical Review. *Journal of Economic Literature* 50 (1): 3–50.

Toder, Eric, and Daniel Baneman. 2012. *Distributional Effects of Individual Tax Expenditures: An Update*. Washington, DC: Urban-Brookings Tax Policy Center.

Toder, Eric, Joseph Rosenberg, and Amanda Eng. 2013. Evaluating Broad-Based Approaches for Limiting Tax Expenditures. *National Tax Journal 66* (4): 807–32.

U.S. Office of Management and Budget. Various years. *Analytical Perspectives, Budget of the United States Government. Fiscal Years 1987, 1990–2014*. Washington, DC: U.S. Office of Management and Budget.

Discussion

Edward D. Kleinbard

Daniel Baneman, Joseph Rosenberg, Eric Toder, and Roberton Williams have performed two important services. First, they skillfully remind readers in a few pages of the central role that tax expenditures play in explaining both the modest revenues collected by our current income tax and the distribution of the resulting tax burdens. Second, they demonstrate how different approaches to curbing tax expenditures can yield very different distributional consequences, even as they raise the same revenues.

The topic could not be more timely, in light of the juxtaposition of the body politic's widespread dissatisfaction with the current state of the income tax against the need for increased government revenues as a component of any rational deficit reduction plan. Within the confines of an income tax, scaling back tax expenditures is the smart way to raise inframarginal tax rates and revenues while leaving headline rates unchanged. In short, curbing tax expenditures is the key move required to bridging income tax reform and deficit reduction (Kleinbard 2011) among others.

The heart of the first essay in this chapter is a series of true revenue estimates, drawn from the Tax Policy Center's microsimulation model, that show the projected effects of three different strategies for paring back tax expenditures, as applied to six specific tax expenditures that the authors identify: the income tax exclusion for employer-sponsored health insurance,[23] the itemized deduction for medical expenses, the itemized deduction for state and local taxes paid, the itemized deduction for home mortgage interest paid, the itemized deduction for charitable contributions, and the preferential rates on capital gains and dividends.

These revenue estimates are by now already somewhat out of date, particularly as a result of the tax rate reductions made permanent in the American Taxpayer Relief Act of 2012 (the January 2013 fiscal cliff tax deal). Nonetheless, they still forcefully illustrate the authors' points that curbing tax expenditures can raise a great deal of revenue and that different instruments for doing have significantly different distributional consequences.

The three different strategies the authors identify for capping tax expenditures are converting the six identified tax expenditures into a 15 percent nonrefundable tax credit,[24] limiting the tax savings resulting from a taxpayer's use of the identified tax expenditures to 3.9 percent of the taxpayer's adjusted gross income, and a 39 percent "haircut" in the amount of each tax expenditure that could be claimed (or, in the case of the preferential tax rates on capital gains and dividends, a 39 percent increase in the tax rate, from 15 to 22.8 percent in 2011). The first of these strategies can be viewed as the base case, as it has been vigorously advanced in the literature (Batchelder, Goldberg, and Orszag (2006), although those authors advocated a refundable rather than nonrefundable credit).

Baneman and coauthors calibrated the other two strategies as having the same aggregate revenue-raising consequences as the first in respect of 2011—about a $1,050 tax increase for the average tax return. Over the standard ten-year budget window, however, the three strategies have divergent revenue estimates. The 15 percent tax credit approach would raise the most—some $2.8 trillion over the ten-year window.

This extraordinary revenue pickup alone shows the profound fiscal power of addressing tax expenditures. For example, the Congressional Budget Office (CBO) estimated in August 2011 that the aggregate federal deficit for the period 2011 to 2021, under the CBO's standard current law assumptions for tax matters (i.e., assuming what in retrospect proved to be the counterfactual expiration of all the 2001–2003 temporary tax cuts), and further assuming the application of the $1.2 trillion expenditure sequestration contemplated by the Budget Control Act of 2011, would total roughly $3.5 trillion (CBO, 2011). Adopting the 15 percent nonrefundable tax credit for the six tax expenditures that Baneman and coauthors modeled would reduce the aggregate deficit to about $700 billion—only about 0.36 percent of the country's projected $196 trillion in GDP over the same period. (Again, these estimates would change as a result of the 2013 resolution of the 2001–2003 temporary tax cuts, but their direction and approximate magnitude would not.)

Their projections also demonstrate that the three different strategies for limiting the benefits of tax expenditures lead to profoundly different distributional consequences in 2011 (the year for which distributional analysis was performed). The fifteen nonrefundable tax credit approach actually would reduce tax bills for 5.4 percent of tax units because the credit would be worth more than the health care exclusion and other benefits are worth to those tax units today. At the other end of the spectrum, the AGI limit that the authors specify would apply to far fewer taxpayers in the upper quintile than would the other two strategies. In sum, "all three proposals would be moderately but unevenly progressive across the income spectrum." On the other hand, if one drops the dividends and capital gains preference from the package of tax expenditures modeled (again calibrating the second two to yield the same 2011 revenues as the 15 percent nonrefundable credit), then the authors unsurprisingly find that for 2011, most or all of the progressivity pickup at the highest-income levels is eroded.

I referred earlier in passing to the fact that the authors' results constitute "true" revenue estimates. This observation is worth dwelling on, because it goes to the real strength of their essay. We all are the beneficiaries of the perspicacity of the authors and others over the years at the Tax Policy Center in developing their microsimulation individual tax model.[25] This model closely mimics the design—and, I understand, the results—of the models employed by the Treasury Department and the Joint Committee on Taxation (JCT) staff in preparing the individual income, payroll and estate tax revenue estimates on which tax policy decisions actually rely.

Because the Tax Policy Center's model is a microsimulation model, it is populated by thousands of representative agents whose characteristics and behaviors are drawn from some 140 million actual taxpayers, comprising both filers and nonfilers. For the model to yield meaningful predictions of how tax revenues will be affected by proposed changes in law, each representative agent must be fully specified with, first, a complete set of relevant economic characteristics, and, second, a set of behavioral responses to changes in its environment. The operation of the model can be analogized to a virtual reality computer game like *The Sims*: since each representative agent has a unique set of personal characteristics and behavioral responses to environmental inputs, the model's operators can introduce a change in the tax environment, comprising a proposed change in the tax law, and then observe how all the virtual taxpayers inside the model adjust their behaviors and resulting tax liabilities.

To develop these two sets of specifications (the characteristics of each virtual taxpayer, and his or her behavioral responses to changes in the tax environment) requires a huge investment of intellectual capital. The starting points for the first set are the 140 million or so tax returns filed in the relevant year. While the Treasury Department and the JCT Staff can look to actual tax returns to specify the representative agents in their models, the Tax Policy Center works with the IRS Public Use Files. These are "blurred" in some respects to protect the identity of actual taxpayers; the most important of these elisions is the removal of some of the nation's very highest-income taxpayers, because their identity might be deduced from other publicly available information. For the same reason, the Tax Policy Center and others have been stymied in developing a corporate tax microsimulation model; the relevant data are simply too company specific and therefore cannot be made available to researchers through Public Use Files without aggregating the information, thereby defeating their utility for use in a microsimulation model.

Tax return data are insufficient in several dimensions to specify fully the characteristics of each virtual taxpayer who resides inside a microsimulation model. By definition, for example, tax return data exclude nonfilers (whether individuals whose incomes fall below filing thresholds or tax evaders). Tax return data also fail to specify expenditures that would give rise to itemized deductions under current law but fall below the threshold where it would be advantageous for a taxpayer to switch from the standard deduction. And tax return data simply do not pick up a wide range of information (wealth, as opposed to income or educational status, for example) that is necessary to model the take-up rate for proposed new tax incentives or to refine how a virtual taxpayer will react to a new tax environment.

The solution is to impute the missing data, from sources like the Current Population Survey and the like. But this requires not simply finding and inputting the nontax data, but also statistical matching of the different data sets, so that each virtual taxpayer residing in the model ends up with the appropriate aggregation of personal economic characteristics. It is my understanding that the Tax Policy Center's microsimulation model is unparalleled in the depth and sophistication of its imputations when compared with other private sector tax models. In its current version, the model contains imputations for wealth, consumption, health, retirement, and educational status, as well as the tax-specific sorts of data described earlier that are not visible from the face of tax returns (and therefore the Public Use Files). This gives a richness to the model's results that other private sector models cannot match.

For many years, the Tax Policy Center's microsimulation individual tax model was a static one: the model knew a great deal about the personal characteristics of each virtual taxpayer, but nothing about how that taxpayer would react to changes in the tax environment. For example, if the charitable contribution itemized deduction were to be curbed, how would that new rule affect the quantum of contributions made in the future? In years past, the Tax Policy Center's model would assume that the amount of contributions would be unaffected.

Recently, Baneman and his coauthors and others at the Tax Policy Center have extended the microsimulation model to encompass behavioral responses to changes in the tax environment—in other words, to endow each virtual taxpayer with a true economic personality, not simply a comprehensive set of identifying characteristics.[26] To do this requires the specification of a wide range of behavioral reactions to new tax rules, captured for purposes of the model in a set of elasticities of representative agents' responses to different inputs. These elasticities in turn must be derived from empirical research, modulated by the revenue estimator's experience and intuitions.

This development, which has not yet attracted widespread attention, means that for the first time, the Tax Policy Center is able to produce genuine dynamic revenue estimates that are comparable in design, and in many cases in result, to those derived by the JCT staff and the Treasury Department. The virtual taxpayers inside the model now react in different ways to new tax inputs, depending on their economic identifying characteristics and the nature of the change in law being considered. The result is a much closer approximation of the consequences that one might expect in the real world were the proposed change to be adopted.

My description of the revenue estimates prepared by the JCT staff, the Treasury Department, and now the Tax Policy Center as "dynamic" is deliberate. It is unfortunate that contemporary political discourse on tax policy often demonizes these estimates as "static," because they all contain a "fixed GNP" constraint—that is, the models contemplate that a revenue measure will affect the allocation of goods and services within the economy, but will not change the overall level of gross national product) There are good reasons for relying on microsimulation models for revenue estimates. The most important are that efforts to model the macroeconomic consequences of tax policy necessarily require making assumptions about matters wholly exogenous to tax policy (in particular, future Federal Reserve policies and the economic cycle). These assumptions can swamp the measurable impact of most tax policy changes, and thereby lead to errors not simply of degree, but even of direction, in revenue estimates. Particularly given that the United States has incurred deficits in every year for the past few decades, other than at the end of the Clinton administration, and that most of the 2001–2003 tax cuts were recently made permanent, the argument that microsimulation revenue estimates are unfairly unkind to tax cuts seems not to capture the zeitgeist of the times.

Baneman and coauthors' "Curbing Tax Expenditures" is thus an exciting signal of future empirical work as much as it is an important contribution to current policy debates. The Tax Policy Center's extended microsimulation model should offer academic researchers the opportunity to model actual policy alternatives with more precision than has previously been the case. And at a minimum, the new model should yield results that, even if they do not perfectly predict the future, will at least reasonably accurately predict the official government revenue estimates on which the future of any actual policy proposal hinges.

Having lavished praise on the importance of the Tax Policy Center's extended microsimulation model, I might seem a bit churlish if I were to express any criticism of "Curbing Tax Expenditures." Nonetheless, it is appropriate to note a few qualifications to Baneman and coauthors' presentation.

First, their essay is a bit opaque as to some of the critical terms of its revenue estimates and distributional analyses. Those who work directly in the area know that JCT staff revenue estimates (the ones that count for budget scorekeeping purposes) assume current law, including the expiration of any temporary tax provisions. Baneman and coauthors follow this convention but do not explicitly identify it. Moreover, their specification of their base-case 15 percent tax credit is not as clear as it might be in respect of capital gains and dividends. Under current law, qualifying net capital gain will be taxed at a maximum rate of 20 percent after 2012; dividends will not receive any preference at all, and therefore will face a maximum rate of 39.6 percent.[27] The 15 percent tax credit scenario in fact contemplates a post-2012 rate of 24.6 percent on both capital gains and dividends, which in the case of dividends would constitute a tax *cut* relative to current law.

By the same token, Baneman and coauthors provide a distributional analysis only for 2011, which has its own issues, particularly when applied to the capital income components they analyze. In effect, the base case for distributional analysis purposes is a maximum 20 percent tax rate on capital gains and dividends (a 15 percent reduction of the maximum ordinary income tax rate, which in 2011 was 35 percent), in contrast to current law's maximum rate of 15 percent. As noted, however, the revenue estimates assume the expiration of all temporary tax provisions, so that capital income rates under the 15 percent credit scenario, for example, will jump in 2013 to 24.6 percent. Similarly, the value of existing law's other tax expenditures also will change after 2012 by virtue of both higher tax rates and the reintroduction of the unpatched alternative minimum tax. As a result, the distributional analysis of "Curbing Tax Expenditures" in respect of 2011 cannot be extended to post-2012 years. A note of caution would have been appropriate.

A second issue, inherent in all distributional analysis, is that the ideal measure of what should be distributed is the net effect of government inflows and outflows on individuals, not just their tax burdens. The proposals modeled in "Curbing Tax Expenditures" would raise as much as $2.8 trillion over the ten-year budget window. If those or similar proposals are not adopted, how will the resulting deficits be financed? One answer might be that certain government spending programs would be cut, but that would have its own distributional consequences; we see precisely this unhappy result in the uneven effects of sequestration on individuals' welfare in 2013. While we sometimes consider the distributional consequences that might fall on the programmatic side of government in respect of a new tax policy, we also need to keep in mind that in the current deficit environment existing policies have their own distributional consequences that have not yet fully been revealed (and therefore have not been reflected in projections). Distributional analysis could be considerably sharpened if the full fiscal consequences of different tax policies were modeled in relation to the spending consequences that they imply, at least through a few stylized alternatives.[28]

A third issue is that the basic package of six tax expenditures that Baneman and coauthors analyze mixes tax expenditures for capital income (which many might argue are just tax rate specifications) with tax expenditures for social programs (e.g., the exclusion for employer-sponsored health care). The particular mix reflects intuitions about political feasibility and perhaps some preferences on the part of the authors, but this combination of conceptually different tax expenditures reduces the clarity of the presentation and makes it difficult to tease out how much each contributes to the outcomes that the essay summarizes.

In fairness, Baneman and coauthors attempt to address this concern by considering the 2011 distributional consequences of the five non-capital income tax expenditures separately later in the presentation, and by separately modeling a cutback in an income support program (the child credit). They paper do not, however, provide a ten-year revenue estimate for either of these alternatives, and for the reasons described earlier, the 2011 distributional analysis might look quite different from that of a post-2012 year.

I believe that a more logical base case would have been to model the revenue consequences of curbing the five non-capital income tax expenditures against the tax law as it stood in 2011 (i.e., assuming the expiration of all the temporary tax cuts and the AMT "patch"). One could then model in a second step a reduction of dividend income rates to the same rate as qualifying net capital gain, on the theory that a large difference in those two rates is inefficient and unstable. Finally, the revenue estimates in each case could be paired with both 2011 and 2013 distributional analyses, for the reasons implied earlier.

More generally, it is a pity in this regard that one theme of the JCT staff's ephemeral restatement of tax expenditure analysis (JCT, 2008) has received so little attention. This was the idea that tax expenditure analysis could be enhanced by dividing tax expenditures into different conceptual groupings (income support expenditures, social expenditures, and business expenditures, for example), so that tax expenditure apples are compared with apples.

It would be interesting to extend Baneman and coauthors' analysis in future work by considering the standard deduction. Their essay follows standard JCT staff practice by treating the standard deduction as simply part of the "normal tax system." But in fact the standard deduction operates as a sort of floor on allowable itemized deductions, because it is available to all taxpayers and reduces a taxpayer's highest tax bracket income. It would be interesting and instructive to see what the revenue and distributional consequences would be if the standard deduction were recast as a nonrefundable tax credit, set at the lowest tax rate for the year in question. It would then serve to create a bottom layer of zero-taxed income rather than a layer of tax sheltered top-bracket income.[29] One of the authors of "Curbing Tax Expenditures" coauthored a paper exploring just this idea (Kleinbard and Rosenberg 2012).

Finally, it might be desirable to focus on the personal itemized deductions as a group, without considering any other tax expenditures. The exclusion for employer-sponsored health insurance is the largest single individual tax expenditure and can fairly be faulted on many policy grounds, but the country has just gone through a wrenching debate on health care, and if the subtext of "Curbing Tax Expenditures" is to point to ways in which tax reform can work in aid of deficit reduction, one wonders whether this is a politically useful expenditure to introduce into the mix. Similarly, the taxation of capital income has its own efficiency concerns, and many economists might argue that preferential rates for capital income are not tax expenditures at all. Moreover, as Baneman and coauthors suggest, the personal itemized deductions as a group are enormously costly, regressive, and distortionary—a trifecta of poor policy judgments. The base case for analysis should be the disallowance of all the personal itemized deductions (or, if you prefer, a nonrefundable tax credit rate of zero). Future work that harnesses the power of the Tax Policy Center's extended microsimulation tax model to show the revenue and distributional consequences of this simple proposal (ideally combined with a conversion of the standard deduction to a credit at the bottom bracket rate) might have a salutary impact on tax policy debates in the immediate future, notwithstanding the apparent failure of the first such paper along these lines (Kleinbard and Rosenberg 2012) to incite an immediate revolution in policy outcomes.

References

Batchelder, Lily L., Fred T. Goldberg Jr., and Peter R. Orszag. 2006. Efficiency and Tax Incentives: The Case for Refundable Tax Credits. Stanford Law Review 59:23–76.

Congressional Budget Office. 2001. *The Budget and Economic Outlook: An Update.* Washington, DC: Congressional Budget Office.

Joint Committee on Taxation. 2008. *A Reconsideration of Tax Expenditure Analysis, JCX–37–08. Joint Committee on Taxation, Washington, D.C., Joint Committee on Taxation, 2008b. Summary of Testimony for Senate Finance Committee Hearing: Health Benefits in the Tax Code: the Right Incentives, JCX–66a–08.* Washington, DC. Joint Committee on Taxation.

Kleinbard, Edward D. 2011. The Role of Tax Reform in Deficit Reduction. *Tax Notes* 133:1105–19.

Kleinbard, Edward D., and Joseph Rosenberg. 2012. The Better Base Case. *Tax Notes* 135:1237–47.

Rohaly, Jeffrey, Adam Carasso, and Mohammed Adeel Saleem. 2005. *The Urban-Brookings Tax Policy Center Microsimulation Model: Documentation and Methodology for Version 0304, Tax Policy Center Doc. No. 411136*. Washington, DC: Urban Institute.

Yang, Shu-Chun Susan. 2007. Do Capital Income Tax Cuts Trickle Down? National Tax Journal 60:551–67.

Discussion

Thomas S. Neubig

As U.S. federal policymakers become more serious about both deficit reduction and federal tax reform, there has been an increasing focus on tax expenditures. Tax expenditures are seen as a form of federal spending and as a potential source of base broadening to lower future deficits and pay for lower marginal income tax rates. Baneman and coauthors' work provides some important analysis of the distributional effects of three alternative approaches to limiting the value of tax expenditures and thus using the additional revenue for deficit reduction or tax reform.

I have three general comments on the analysis. First, in addition to the distributional analysis of the three approaches, more policy analysis of the three alternative approaches would be helpful. Besides differences in the distributional effects, there are other economic differences among the three approaches, which policymakers should consider. Second, the three approaches should be made more equivalent in their total deficit reduction and composition to make the distributional comparisons more direct. Third, as a subject for further research, the coauthors should consider extending their analysis to more tax expenditures.

More Policy Analysis Would Be Helpful

I wrote a paper on the role of the tax expenditure budget in U.S. policymaking twenty-three years ago for a Canadian conference on tax expenditures. Not much has changed in the tax expenditure area since 1988, except the number and size of tax expenditures have continued to steadily increase.

Policymakers clearly view tax expenditures as a close, or even perfect, substitute for direct government spending. For example, the

2009 economic stimulus legislative allowed cash grants in lieu of tax credits for certain energy tax credits.[30] This expands the number of refundable tax expenditures, even on the business tax side, beyond mortgage credit certificates and Build America Bonds. One of the disadvantages of tax expenditures was the need to have tax liability, but that barrier has been easily breached with the use of refundable credits and even alternative direct grant programs.

If serious deficit reduction or tax reform, or both, is going to be pursued, then tax expenditures will need to be part of the legislative changes. There are two general approaches to limiting the value of tax expenditures. The first is to propose changes to specific tax expenditures. The 1984 Treasury tax reform analysis singled out specific tax expenditures that would be repealed or limited. The Treasury staff evaluated individual tax expenditures, as well as many nontax expenditures, to see if they should be part of a tax base broadening to lower the marginal tax rates.

It was only in the political process of the Tax Reform Act of 1986 that tax expenditures were included as part of indirect limitations through the Pease haircut on itemized deductions and inclusion of certain tax expenditures in the individual alternative minimum tax (AMT).

This second, indirect, approach is what Baneman and coauthors analyze. They examine how six individual income tax expenditures could be converted into a 15 percent nonrefundable tax credit, how the value of seven tax expenditures could be capped at 4 percent of a taxpayer's adjusted gross income (AGI), and how the value of seven individual income tax expenditures could be reduced with a 35 percent haircut. Each of these proposals reduces the value of tax expenditures, but the approach would not address whether each activity still continues to merit government assistance and, if so, what level of assistance would be optimal.

Three times in 2010 as part of legislation to extend expiring tax provisions, the House of Representatives included a provision requiring the Congressional Joint Committee on Taxation to conduct an analysis of each of the expiring business and energy tax expenditures on its success in achieving its objective, its beneficiaries, and its cost effectiveness.[31] This provision was not adopted as part of the final legislation, thus suggesting, as in 1986, that an indirect approach may be more politically feasible.

One reason an indirect, broadbrush, approach might be used is if tax expenditures were ever subject to a sequestration process. To date, tax expenditures have been excluded from the earlier Gramm-Rudman-Hollings sequestration process and the current 2011 budget act sequestration. One of the unique things about the Canadian paper was an appendix that categorized tax expenditures into those that were common to both an income and consumption tax and those that could also be subject to a sequestration and those that would be difficult to do some form of value haircut.

An important policy addition to Baneman and coauthors' essay would be some discussion of how all tax expenditures might be limited. They pick seven individual income tax expenditures that are easy to limit indirectly. Many other tax expenditures, such as tax-exempt bond income or retirement pension tax treatment, would benefit from a discussion of options of how they might be included as part of a sequestration.

Finally, their essay would benefit from a policy comparison of the three alternatives analyzed beyond just their distributional consequences. Converting "upside-down" tax expenditures into an equivalent 15 percent credit could be part of a rationalization of government assistance. But why should such assistance be made nonuniform by being a nonrefundable credit? A 4 percent AGI limitation is somewhat akin to an alternative minimum tax, preventing excess deductions or exclusions from reducing tax liability beyond a certain point. Would the AGI limitation on tax expenditures be in addition to the current individual AMT? Besides revenue, I am not sure of the policy rationale for an AGI cap. A cap, unlike a floor, would eliminate the marginal incentive effects of the provisions (e.g., charitable contributions) for taxpayers subject to the cap.

More Equivalent Policy Alternatives

The conference version of the paper kept the average federal tax change in 2011 from the three proposals in a close range of $1,032 to $1,051. The ten-year aggregate revenue effects of the limitations, however, ranged from $1.9 trillion to $2.8 trillion over ten years. Since the distributional comparisons used 2011 law and data extrapolated to 2011, it makes sense to compare the alternatives that raise roughly the same amount in the year of the analysis.

Since the principal purpose of indirect limitations on tax expenditures is to raise revenue to lower the federal deficit or finance lower income tax rates, an alternative analysis could hold the ten-year revenue estimates fixed. This would require a lower AGI limitation and a higher percentage haircut, which would change the distributional effects.

The analysis also changes the composition of the tax expenditures being limited. Because Baneman and coauthors were not clear about how a fixed-dollar child tax credit could be reconstructed into a percentage credit, they left the child credit out of the analysis of the 15 percent credit option. This affects the direct comparability of the three alternative options, especially in terms of the distributional effects. How to handle various existing tax credits under a 15 percent credit option depends on the rationale of the approach. If the rationale is to make the tax subsidies more uniform, then there could be a rationale for keeping a 15 percent credit for exclusions and deductions and a uniform child tax credit. But if the 15 percent credit is nonrefundable, should the child credit continue to be refundable?

In the final version of the conference paper, which is the essay in this chapter, the authors limited the main analysis to a consistent set of six tax expenditures, while doing a separate analysis of the child tax credit as one of two variants. This made the ten-year estimates much closer.

Extending the Analysis to More Tax Expenditures

The issue of comparable analysis also raises the issue of which tax expenditures are included in the analysis and reraises the issue of how all tax expenditures might be subject to a limitation approach (e.g., sequestration). Baneman and coauthors limited their analysis to only seven individual income tax expenditures.

Based on the most recent JCT tax expenditure estimate, the seven tax expenditures account for slightly more than 40 percent of the estimated individual income tax expenditures, and include only six of the top fifteen largest individual tax expenditures. The analysis does not include any indirect limitations on any corporate tax expenditures.

In the context of tax reform, I have been troubled by the recent tax reform proposals (the 2005 Advisory Commission, the 2007 Treasury studies, and the 2010 Simpson-Bowles Advisory Commission) that limit their tax base broadening simply to a universal repeal of tax expenditures. Especially on the corporate side, that approach reminds me of the story about the drunk looking for his keys under the nearest lamppost. In the Tax Reform Act of 1986, over 40 percent of the corporate base broadening was not from tax expenditures, and 60 percent of the president's fiscal year 2012 budget business tax increases were not from tax expenditures. When federal tax reform gets really serious, tax policymakers will look beyond tax expenditures to reduce individual and corporate tax rates. On the individual side, significant payroll tax base broadening is also possible.

Conclusion

The Baneman et al. analysis is an important addition to the analysis of proposals to rationalize or limit tax expenditures. The analysis provides important information on the number of tax returns with tax cuts and with tax increases, and the distributional effects of the overall tax increases. Given the "upside-down" nature of most individual tax expenditures, the three alternative approaches show how the federal tax system could be made moderately more progressive.

The Tax Policy Center's revenue and distributional analyses of federal tax policy proposals is filling a void that was previously served by the Congressional Joint Committee on Taxation and the Treasury's Office of Tax Analysis. The authors should also supplement their strong empirical work with more policy analysis of the three analyzed options. The design and policy rationale for each of the options will also be important for future policy debates.

References

Carroll, Robert, Morgan Cox, and Tom Neubig. 2011. *Tax Reform Lessons: Composition of Tax Changes in the Tax Reform Act of 1986*. Washington, DC: Ernst and Young LLP Center for Tax Policy.

Neubig, Thomas. 1988. The Role of the Tax Expenditure Budget in US Policymaking. In *Tax Expenditures and Government Policy, John Deutsch Roundtable on Economic Policy*, edited by Neil Bruce. Kingston, Ontario: Queen's University.

Notes

1. This discussion of the history of tax expenditures draws heavily from Rogers and Toder (2011).

2. Neubig and Joulfaian (1988) find that 40 percent of the reduction in the value of tax expenditures from TRA86 was attributable to base broadening, while the remaining 60 percent was due to lower tax rates.

3. The Office of Tax Analysis in the U.S. Department of the Treasury estimates the value of tax expenditures in the federal income tax each year for the Office of Management and Budget. Historical tables in the annual Budget of the United States report those estimates for the two previous fiscal years and the next five years. The Joint Committee

on Taxation (JCT) prepares similar estimates for Congress. Unless otherwise noted, we use the Treasury estimates throughout this essay.

4. OMB and JCT estimate each tax expenditure as if all other tax expenditure provisions were in place, so tax expenditures are not strictly additive. Toder and Baneman (2012) estimate that the revenue loss of most individual tax expenditures estimated simultaneously is about 10 percent higher than the cost of adding up the separate estimates for each of those provisions.

5. Business tax expenditures include those in the corporate income tax as well as provisions in the individual income tax that affect business income reported on schedules C (business income), E (partnership income), and F (farm income).

6. The data reported here adjust the OMB figures for several years when OMB did not classify special rates on capital gains on corporate stock and dividends as a tax expenditure. Rogers and Toder (2011) used the relationship between JCT and OMB estimates to impute what the OMB values would have been using a consistent methodology for all years.

7. Urban-Brookings Tax Policy Center, Table T11–0317, http://www.taxpolicycenter.org/numbers/Content/PDF/T11-0317.pdf.

8. For the purpose of the distributional results shown in figure 6.6, and in contrast to the numbers presented in the previous section, tax preferences for retirement savings (including the above-the-line deduction for individual retirement accounts) are treated as exclusions instead of deferrals. A more complete classification would assign just the portion of the tax expenditure that comes from the exemption of income earned inside tax preferred retirement accounts as an exclusion and the portion that represents the net revenue change from deducting contributions and taxing withdrawals as a deferral. Since the latter portion is relatively small, classifying it as an exclusion instead of a deferral does not significantly affect the results.

9. The credit phases out for high-income tax filers and is refundable to low-income families only under specific circumstances.

10. The earned income tax credit phases out at relatively low incomes. The child and education credits phase out at higher income levels.

11. For a description of the Tax Policy Center model, see http://www.taxpolicycenter.org/numbers/related.cfm.

12. The estimates of the excluded amounts used in our analysis include the portion of health insurance premiums paid by employees under section 125 cafeteria plans, which are treated as employer contributions. Employer-sponsored health insurance premiums are also excluded from Social Security and Medicare payroll taxes. The simulations presented here do not alter any tax preferences for payroll tax purposes.

13. Prior to 2013, the deduction was limited to amounts above 7.5 percent of AGI (10 percent for taxpayers subject to the individual alternative minimum tax). The PPACA of 2010 raised the floor on the deduction to 10 percent of AGI for all taxpayers, beginning in 2013.

14. This option is similar to that proposed by Feldstein, Feenberg, and MacGuineas (2011), but includes a different group of tax expenditures and imposes a less stringent limit as a share of AGI—3.9 percent of AGI rather than 2 percent.

15. In 2011, the tax savings for people in the 35 percent top tax bracket is 20 percentage points, the difference between the 35 percent rate on ordinary income and the 15 percent rate on gains and dividends. Reducing that differential by the 39 percent haircut corresponds to a 7.8 percentage point increase in the preferential rate to 22.8 percent.

16. See Joint Committee on Taxation (1993) and Auerbach (1995) for more discussion on measuring changes in the distribution of tax burdens. An example of the problem associated with doing distributional analysis on a taxes paid basis is a reduction in the tax on realized capital gains, which would likely induce investors to realize more gains, resulting in their paying more tax than if they did not change their investment activity. A large enough increase in realized gains could result in their paying more total tax and thus appearing to be worse off, despite the fact that a lower tax rate would make them unambiguously better off.

17. We classify this response as "tax form" behavior since it leaves taxpayers' total housing wealth and net debt unchanged, but allows them to reduce their tax liability (with little or no transaction cost) by eliminating the use of nondeductible interest payments to finance holdings of assets that generate taxable income.

18. Other behavioral responses are not included in our analysis either because they are likely to be small or because data and model limitations prohibit doing so. One example is the impact of a significant change to the tax exclusion for employer health insurance on the overall marketplace for health insurance. Incorporating such responses requires more complete modeling of the structure of the national health insurance market and is beyond our scope here. Gillette et al. (2010) provide simulations that suggest that partial repeal of the income tax exclusion (with full retention of the payroll tax exclusion) would have a relatively modest overall effect.

19. An elasticity of 0.25 is also consistent with Carroll and Hrung (2005). They begin with an ETI of 0.4, but then derive a "microdynamic" elasticity that is consistent with the assumptions that underlie traditional revenue scoring (e.g., holding aggregate output, interest rates, and price level fixed), specifically by removing the effects of changes in aggregate labor supply and adjusting for shifts between the individual and corporate income tax bases.

20. The revenue numbers shown in table 6.1 were estimated prior to the passage of the American Taxpayer Relief Act of 2012 (ATRA). ATRA permanently extended many of the temporary tax provisions originally enacted in 2001 and 2003. Since lower marginal rates reduce the value of most tax expenditures, the actual revenue gain would be somewhat lower than what is reported here.

21. The 39 percent haircut would also provide tax cuts to a small number of taxpayers because it would reduce the tax on state and local income tax refunds. Because it would reduce taxpayers' income tax deduction for state and local income taxes, the proposal would also exclude from AGI 39 percent of their refunds of those taxes.

22. Because it is not clear how the fixed-dollar child tax credit would be converted to a percentage credit (or even what the rationale would be), it is excluded from all versions of the 15 percent credit option. As a result, the revenue and distributional effects of that option are identical in the base version and this version that includes the child credit.

23. Apparently the estimates do not include the payroll tax consequences of curbing this exclusion. In one study a few years ago, the staff of the Joint Committee on Taxation estimated that the payroll tax revenues forgone by the health care exclusion amounted

to about 69 percent of forgone income tax revenues—$100 billion a year, at a time when forgone income taxes were estimated at $145 billion a year. JCT (2008b), p. 3.

24. As applied to the preferential tax rates for dividends and capital gains, this proposal contemplates reducing the otherwise-applicable ordinary income tax rate by 15 percentage points. Thus, a taxpayer in 2013 in the 39.6 percent income tax bracket would face an effective tax rate on qualifying dividends and capital gains of 24.6 percent (without regard to new section 1411's 3.8 percent tax rate on the net investment income of certain high-income taxpayers). The 24.6 percent rate on dividends would actually be a tax cut when compared to the tax rates currently scheduled to take effect after 2012.

25. For a detailed description of the Tax Policy Center model, see Rohaly, Carasso and Saleem (2005). While this documentation is slightly out of date (and in particular does not reflect the introduction of behavioral responses of representative agents in the model), it is vastly more comprehensive than any description that the JCT staff has ever published of the components of its individual income tax model.

26. This development is not yet reflected in the Tax Policy Center's documentation (Rohaly et al., 2005) of its microsimulation model.

27. In each case, the tax rates presented in the text ignore new section 1411's 3.8 percent tax on the net investment income of high-income taxpayers.

28. Yang (2007) is an example of this sort of thinking; in that paper, the author models the welfare consequences across income distributions of different approaches to financing a cut in capital income taxation.

29. In this regard, Baneman and coauthors perhaps understate the complexity of their AGI cap alternative once the standard deduction is considered. In practice, a taxpayer would be required to calculate the tax value of the list of proscribed tax expenditures and compare that value to the AGI cap. If the AGI cap were binding, a taxpayer might abandon his or her itemized deductions and switch to the standard deduction. The taxpayer then would have to repeat the exercise all over again with the remaining tax expenditures—in particular, the exclusion for employer-sponsored health insurance—that are not itemized deductions.

30. IRC Section 1603: Grants in lieu of tax credits for renewable electricity generation facilities.

31. Additional analysis of tax expenditures, including cost–benefit and cost-effectiveness analyses, would be important for policymakers to have for both deficit reduction and tax reform. It is not clear how serious the effort was since the legislative language directed the JCT to report on the least costly expiring tax expenditures first, http://www.jct.gov/publications.html?func=startdown&id=3684.

7 Raising Revenue from Reforming the Corporate Tax Base

Jane G. Gravelle

Advocates of reform of the corporate income tax fall into three camps: those who support a rate cut, those who support revenue-neutral tax reform, and those who propose revenue increases, generally through base broadening. Not surprisingly, it is largely business representatives who favor cutting rates without broadening the base and also moving to a territorial tax (where income earned abroad is exempt). President Barack Obama and other political leaders have supported a rate cut if the revenue loss can be offset with corporate base broadening. Citizens for Tax Justice has urged a revenue-raising reform, while some business leaders have urged setting deficit concerns aside (Donmoyer and Cohn 2011). At the same time, President Obama has proposed in his three budgets a number of changes that largely raise revenue, including increases in taxes on foreign source corporate income. The National Commission on Fiscal Responsibility and Reform (2010) recommends using base broadening for both raising revenue and rate reduction, but some other major deficit reduction proposals favor revenue-neutral reform.

There is no question that the most common issue mentioned when discussing corporate taxes (whether raising them, lowering them, or implementing a revenue-neutral reform) is the effect of the tax in a global economy. The traditional concerns economists raised in the past about distortions in the allocation of capital and the sources of finance are less frequently mentioned. Nevertheless, while "international competitiveness" is frequently invoked as a reason to cut corporate taxes, or at least not raise them, and reducing rather than increasing the taxation of foreign source income of multinationals, the term is rarely defined and its effects are rarely quantified.

Similarly, many proposals that envision tax reform refer in a general way to eliminating corporate tax expenditures while rarely assessing the desirability of these revisions. Yet there may be some corporate tax expenditures that should be kept on their merits and some provisions outside the standard list of tax expenditures that might be considered for elimination.

This essay contains three major sections. The first outlines possible corporate revenue-raising reforms, drawing on proposals from a number of sources. Some proposals simply refer generically to eliminating corporate tax expenditures, while others specify provisions outside the traditional tax expenditure list. The second section addresses the fundamental question: What are the overall economic consequences of increasing corporate taxes (especially in a way that affects marginal effective tax rates), and why have observers from very different political views proposed revenue-neutral corporate tax reform in an era of deficits? This section essentially addresses the question of whether corporate taxes should be considered off-limits for reducing the deficit. The final section considers a number of specific tax provisions and the merits and drawbacks of eliminating or revising them.

An Inventory of Revenue-Raising Options

Corporate revenue could be raised by raising tax rates or broadening the base. Congressional Budget Office (CBO) (2011) projections show that an additional percentage point rate increase would raise revenues in fiscal year (FY) 2014 and on average for FY 2012–21 by $10.1 billion, about 2.3 percent of corporate tax revenue. Most of the discussion of corporate tax increases is aimed, however, at broadening the base. Base broadening could also be used in a revenue-neutral reform to lower the statutory rate. The remainder of this section inventories base-broadening provisions, first examining official corporate tax expenditures and then provisions contained in a variety of proposals and reviews.

The estimates vary in the degree to which they include behavioral responses, which I note in each case. However, while some estimates include allocational effects and other microeconomic changes, they do not generally include aggregate economy-wide changes that alter total output in the economy by altering labor or capital inputs or productivity, the types of effects that might be captured in dynamic models. There continues to be a lack of consensus on the effects of changing corporate tax burdens (or taxes in general) due to model differences, details of the changes, and other assumptions that have to be made.

For example, although a tax increase could (although would not necessarily, given income and substitution effects) induce reductions in savings, the addition to the deficit would eventually swamp these effects, so it makes a difference whether the gain is offset by reductions in taxes elsewhere. Some models require some offsetting change to be solved. Moreover, since these other changes can have economic effects, they would need to be specified. Similarly, tax increases could contract the economy in the short run, but that effect would depend on actions taken by the Federal Reserve. Several of these issues are discussed in Joint Committee on Taxation (2011b), CBO (2012b), and Gravelle (2007). As discussed below (and referring to Gravelle 2011a) corporate tax changes are unlikely to have large economy-wide effects or large revenue feedback effects even under the most generous assumptions.

Tax Expenditures

A natural place to start examining tax expenditures that might be eliminated or curtailed is with the tax expenditure estimates prepared each year by the JCT (2010b) and the Office of Management and Budget (2011). Table 7.1 reports, for FY 2014, projected corporate tax expenditures, how large the corporate revenue loss is as a percentage of projected corporate revenues, and where there are also benefits that cannot easily be retained for unincorporated businesses, the individual revenue loss.

Tax expenditure estimates do not include behavioral responses and estimate what revenues would be had the provision never been enacted. Thus, for permanent provisions, they reflect a steady-state effect but no behavioral effects.

There are many more tax expenditures with separate revenue estimates listed in the JCT (2010a) document, since some of the tax expenditures, which are allocated according to budget function, are combined in table 7.1. For example, all of the tax-exempt bond interest provisions, along with tax credit bonds, which are normally spread over many functions, are combined. Similarly charitable contributions are normally found in three places (health, education, and social welfare) depending on the recipients. In several cases, tax expenditures for specific industries were summed.

Tax expenditures are concentrated, in terms of potential revenue gain, in a small number of categories. The top five expenditures are accelerated depreciation (current depreciation compared to an

Table 7.1
Corporate and Business Tax Expenditures, FY 2014

Provision	Corporate Revenue (billions)	Loss as a Percent of Corporate	Individual Revenue (billions)
Accelerated depreciation			
Equipment and structures	$29.0[a]	6.6[a]	$6.5[a]
Rental housing	0.4	0.2	4.0
Deferral of tax on foreign source income	15.8	3.5	
Bonds, tax exempt: credits for corporations	15.5	3.5	
Research and experimentation credit	10.6[b]	2.4	
Production activity deduction (targeted domestic production subsidy)	9.8	2.2	5.1
Title passage rule (export subsidy)	7.8	1.7	
Insurance company subsidies	7.2	1.6	
Research expensing	6.9	1.5	
Low-income housing credit	6.1	1.4	0.3
Deferral of gain, nondealer installment sales	5.8	1.3	1.9
LIFO and lower of market or cost inventory	4.9	1.1	0.8
Reduced rates for small corporations	3.1	0.7	
Energy conservation, alternative fuels	2.8	0.6	0.1
Corporate charitable contributions	2.6	0.6	
Like kind exchanges	2.6	0.6	1.5
Fossil fuels	2.4	0.5	1.9
Energy conservation, alternative fuels	2.4	0.5	
Employee stock ownership plans	1.2	0.4	2.5
Special tax rate on nuclear decommissioning	1.1	0.3	
Other international (largely relating to foreign tax credit)	0.8	0.2	0.1
Completed contracts	0.8	0.2	
Exemption of credit unions	0.7	0.2	
Small business employer health insurance credit	0.7	0.2	4.5
Orphan drug credit	0.6	0.1	
Timber and mineral subsidies	0.5	0.1	
Rehabilitation credits	0.5	0.1	
New markets tax credit	0.3	0.1	0.4
Disaster relief	0.3	0.1	0.4
Work opportunity tax credit, new hires credit	0.3	0.1	
Deferral of tax on shipping companies	0.1	0.0	

a. Estimates for 2012 are from Gravelle (2010b), purged of bonus depreciation effects and updated.
b. This temporary provision has been extended since 1981, estimates are taken from U.S. Department of the Treasury (2011), which proposes making the credit permanent.
Source: Unless otherwise specified, tax expenditure estimates are from JCT (2010a). Corporate revenue projections are from CBO (2010).

alternative depreciation baseline), deferral of tax on foreign source income of subsidiaries of U.S. firms, tax-favored bonds (about two-thirds of which are general obligation bonds of state and local governments), the research and experimentation credit, and the production activities deduction (which allows a 9 percent deduction from taxable income for domestic production in certain industries). These five provisions account for 59 percent of the total. Elimination of accelerated depreciation and the production activities deduction would also likely involve significant revenue gains from unincorporated businesses because it would not be administratively efficient to maintain separate tax systems. Tax-exempt bond interest for individuals is significantly larger than for corporations, but it would not be difficult to eliminate only corporate provisions (although behavioral responses would likely offset most of the gain if individual provisions are retained).

The next five largest tax expenditures are the title passage rule (which allows half of income from exports to be allocated to foreign sources for the foreign tax credit limit), a set of tax benefits relating to the insurance industry, a provision allowing intangible research expenditures to be deducted immediately rather than capitalized, the credits for construction of low-income housing, and the deferral of gain on the sale of assets by those who do not regularly deal in them (largely benefiting sellers of farms, small businesses, and small real estate properties). These ten provisions account for 85 percent of total tax expenditures.

The only remaining tax expenditure that is at least 1 percent of corporate revenues is the allowance of LIFO (last-in, first out) and the lower of cost or market inventory accounting. About 90 percent of the cost of this provision is from LIFO, which effectively allows deductions for costs to be higher when prices are rising.

Although most estimates are taken directly from the tax expenditure estimates of the JCT (see the notes to table 7.1), some provisions are affected by legislation in place at the time the expenditure was estimated and have been corrected to purge them of these effects. They include accelerated depreciation whose revenue loss is projected to be much smaller due to the 50 percent bonus depreciation enacted in 2008–10 (and would be even smaller if the estimates captured the increase to 100 percent for 2011 and the continuation of 50 percent through 2012). The research and experimentation tax credit is one of the provisions that expires every year but is generally continued.

Base-Broadening Provisions in Other Proposals

The revenue effect going forward for provisions that involve timing, such as accelerated depreciation, can be very different in the near term from the tax expenditures that are calculated assuming alternative rules were permanently in place. In addition, some proposals or options might have modified versions of these provisions or introduce provisions that are not in the tax expenditure list.

Unlike the tax expenditure estimates, the JCT includes microeconomic behavioral responses in their revenue estimates. For example, they might modify their revenue estimates of the effects of the foreign source provisions to reflect tax planning or reallocation of investments that firms might make in response to the change.

Two proposals have been introduced as bills and can illustrate some of the modifications of cost, modification of provisions, or introduction of base-broadening provisions outside tax expenditures. The first is a series of proposals sponsored or cosponsored by Senator Ron Wyden (D-OR), with the most recent bill cosponsored with Senator Dan Coats (R-IN). Table 7.2 provides estimates of the revenue gains from the major corporate provisions of the virtually identical 111th Congress bill, H.R. 3018, (introduced in 2010 and cosponsored by Senator Judd Gregg (R-NH)) as estimated by the JCT. This bill also substantially reduces the corporate tax rate and is not designed as a revenue raiser, but the provisions and their revenue gains are instructive.

The estimates for the Wyden-Gregg bill illustrate all of the types of modifications and changes to tax expenditures and their costs that might influence base-broadening exercises for the purpose of raising revenues. Although this bill includes several provisions in table 7.1, it also shows the dramatically different revenue estimate going forward for the largest provision, accelerated depreciation. Rather than an average gain of about $35 billion (including unincorporated business), the average gain over the next ten years is $58 billion. As implied by the way in which revenue estimates are made, this difference suggests that short-term gains may not persist, an important consideration when addressing long-run budget shortfalls.

Second, this bill would add important new provisions not on the tax expenditure list. The bill would not only eliminate deferral of tax on foreign source income (which for subsidiaries' active income is not subject to tax until paid to the U.S. parent as a dividend) but also would increase the taxation of foreign source income by limiting the foreign tax credit to a per country basis. This change significantly increases the

Table 7.2
Corporate and Business Tax Provisions in the Wyden-Gregg Bill, S. 3018, Introduced in 2010

Provision*	Average Cost: FY 2011–20, (billions)
Eliminate deferral of foreign source income and impose a per country foreign tax credit limit	$58.3
Accelerated depreciation	56.9
Index interest for inflation	16.3
Eliminate production activities deduction	15.4
Eliminate title passage rule	7.7
Prohibition on advance refunding	1.2
Eliminate percentage depletion, capitalize intangible drilling costs, and mine development costs	1.6
Repeal LIFO for large oil and gas producers, eliminate lower of cost or market inventory	0.8
Apply inversion rules retroactively to 2002	0.2
Eliminate special tax rate on nuclear decommissioning	0.1

Source: JCT (2010a).

revenue gain from around $15 billion to $58 billion. Currently the U.S. has an overall limit, which allows foreign tax credits that cannot exceed the amount of U.S. tax on overall foreign source income, a rule that allows cross-crediting, that is, the use of credits in excess of U.S. tax in high-tax countries to offset tax due on income from low-tax countries. The per country limit eliminates the ability to cross-credit. In addition, S. 3018 also has a significant revenue gain from a provision disallowing the deduction of the inflation portion of interest. It also has some new smaller provisions and a partial revision in the treatment of inventories.

The second legislative proposal is House Ways and Means Committee chairman Charles Rangel's (D-NY) tax reform bill, H.R. 3970 introduced in 2007, reviewed in Gravelle (2007). This proposal actually includes only two tax expenditures, although it has modifications of the deferral provision. Rather than repealing deferral, it disallows the share of head office expenses such as interest and research and experimentation deductions by the share of total income that is deferred. It also addresses cross-crediting by limiting the share of foreign tax credits available for crediting to the share of income paid out as dividends. Its other provisions are not in the tax expenditure list. As in the case of

Table 7.3
Corporate Revenue Raisers in Chairman Rangel's Tax Reform Bill, H.R. 3970, 2007

Provision	Average Annual Revenue Gain, FY 2008–17 (billions)
Repeal production activities deduction	$11.5
Repeal of LIFO and lower of cost or market inventory	11.4
Allocation of expenses for repatriation of foreign income; pooling of foreign tax credits	10.6
Amortize intangibles over 20 years	2.6
Treaty shopping	0.6
Reduce dividend received deduction	0.5

Note: This bill also included repeal of worldwide income allocation with an average benefit of $2.6 billion; this provision has been delayed to 2020 by other legislation but could include revenue in the future. The bill also included the economic substance doctrine ($0.4 billion), which was enacted in health care legislation in 2010.
Source: Gravelle (2007), using estimates originally provided by the JCT.

any JCT revenue estimates, they are not steady-state estimates and incorporate some behavioral effects.

The CBO also provides JCT estimates of various deficit reduction options, generally concentrating on the larger provisions, as shown in table 7.4, which are estimated under the same conventions.

While several of the tax expenditures are also in table 7.4, the CBO considers a different revision of the depreciation provision. The depreciation provision in the tax expenditure list compares current provisions with a system with many more classes of assets, longer lives, and a straight-line depreciation method that spreads deductions proportionally over the useful life rather than concentrating them in the earlier years of the investment as is done with accelerated methods. The CBO option is much simpler (maintaining a few classes) and less restrictive since it does not alter depreciation methods. The revenue gain is less than half that of the depreciation revision in the Wyden-Gregg bill.

The CBO options study also considers an alternative to deferral, which is to move to a territorial tax under which foreign source income is exempt but deductions of overhead costs are disallowed based on the share of income excluded. This proposal was also included in the reform proposal of the President's Advisory Panel on Federal Tax Reform (2005). Because so little revenue is raised from the current tax

Table 7.4
Congressional Budget Office: Corporate Tax Options for Reducing the Deficit

Provision	Average annual revenue gain, FY 2012–21 (billions)
Extend depreciable lives of equipment from 3, 5, 7, 10, 15, and 20 years to 4, 8, 11, 20, 30, and 39 years,	$24.1
Eliminate production activities deduction	16.3
Eliminate deferral	11.5
Eliminate LIFO and lower of cost or market inventory	9.8
Territorial tax with allocation of deductions	7.6
Eliminate title passage rule	5.4
Eliminate graduated corporate rates	2.4
End expensing of exploration and development for the extractive industries	1.0

Source: Congressional Budget Office (2011).

system, this exclusion raises revenue, in part because of the disallowance of deductions and in part because no foreign taxes would be available for credits for exempt income. This provision prevents the current possibility of using excess credits on active income to shield royalties, which are generally not taxed abroad, from U.S. tax.

Although President Obama has proposed revenue-neutral tax reform, he also included some corporate revenue raisers in his budget proposals, as shown in table 7.5. While the administration has not clearly indicated estimating methodologies, they likely include behavioral changes.

This proposal raises $41 billion per year on average, with about a third from international provisions, a third from life insurance company provisions, and the remainder from inventory revisions and fossil fuel provisions. The two major international proposals are the same deduction allocation and foreign tax credit pooling proposals in the Rangel bill, but research expenditures are excluded from the allocation provision.

Finally, to make the inventory complete, several additional options are reviewed. Table 7.6 reports both general revisions and some international revisions for which revenue estimates can be calculated or found. Table 7.7 provides some specific international provisions, although with no revenue estimates.

Table 7.5
Corporate Revenue Raisers in President Obama's FY 2012 Budget Proposal

Provision	Average Annual Revenue Gain, FY 2012–21 (billions)
International provisions	$14.0
Disallow interest expense for unrepatriated income	3.8
Foreign tax credit pooling	5.1
Restrictions on intangibles profit shifting, including taxing excess returns to United States	2.3
Disallow credits for dual-capacity taxpayers (e.g., oil producers)	2.1
Limit earnings stripping by expatriates	0.4
Disallow deduction of insurance company premiums to foreign affiliates	0.3
Insurance company provisions	14.0
Expand pro-rata interest expense disallowance for life insurance company separate accounts	7.7
Reduce dividend-received deduction for life insurance companies	5.1
Modify rules that apply to sales of life insurance contracts	1.2
Eliminate LIFO and lower of market or cost inventory	6.1
Eliminate oil and gas preferences	4.4
Eliminate coal preferences	2.6

Source: U.S. Department of the Treasury (2011).

In general, the estimates in table 7.6 do not allow for behavioral responses (with the exception of those taken directly from the JCT or Treasury Department, which are the last two provisions). The two largest provisions in table 7.6 relate to international taxation and involve more far-reaching changes than even the international provisions of the Wyden-Gregg bill. Repealing deferral and allowing a foreign tax deduction was proposed in the 1970s by the Burke-Hartke proposal (see McClure and Bouma 1989 for a history) and conforms to the optimal rule for maximizing U.S. welfare with respect to foreign source income. Formula apportionment (in this case, allocating income based on the distribution of sales) should shift large amounts of income back to the United States that are probably shifted abroad due to tax-avoidance activities (although Altshuler and Grubert 2010 argue that behavioral responses would undermine these differences). These

Table 7.6
Major or General Additional Revenue-Raising Options

Provision	Estimated Revenue Gain, FY 2014 (billions)
Repeal deferral and allow deduction for foreign taxes	$123
Move to formula apportionment	105
Roll back 2003 dividend and capital gains tax cuts	58
Tax large pass-through firms as corporations	32
Eliminate deduction for state and local income taxes	25
Capitalize advertising expenses	8
Tax income of state and local business enterprises	4
Eliminate check-the-box	3
Restore foreign tax credit baskets eliminated in 2004	1

Source: Estimates for adopting current taxation with a foreign tax deduction, moving to formula apportionment, eliminating the deduction for state and local taxes, and capitalizing advertising expenses are described in the appendix. The estimate for rolling back the 2003 dividend and capital gains tax cuts and taxing large pass-through entities is adapted from Gravelle (2011a). The estimate for taxing the income of state and local business enterprises is from Gravelle and Gravelle (2007). The estimate for eliminating the check-the-box provision is from U.S. Department of the Treasury (2009). The estimate for restoring foreign tax credit baskets is from JCT (2005).

estimates in part reflect international profit shifting, with the latest estimates by Clausing (2011) ranging from $58 billion to $90 billion for 2008.

There are two other internationally related provisions. Check-the-box is a provision that allows the disregarding of foreign subsidiaries (treating their income as if it belonged to the corporate parent). This provision facilitates profit shifting by reducing the taxation of easily shifted income. An example might be a subsidiary in a low-tax country that lends to its own subsidiary in a high-tax country, reducing taxes by generating deductions at a high tax rate while taxing that income at a low rate. Under standard antiabuse rules (Subpart F) this income would be taxed, but check-the-box makes the transaction invisible to U.S. tax authorities. The small estimate may reflect the expectation that rather than continue these activities and pay taxes with repeal, many transactions will not occur in the first place and other high-tax countries will benefit. The second provision would increase foreign taxes by increasing the number of (generally passive activity) foreign tax credit limit baskets to those that existed before 2004, reducing to some extent the ability to cross-credit foreign taxes.

The non-foreign-related provisions in some cases could yield significant revenue. For example, although raising the corporate tax rate might be off the table because of issues of international competitiveness, increasing tax rates at the personal level, which would not raise that possibility, may be considered. This option involves restoring the ordinary tax treatment of dividends and the 20 percent rate on capital gains that existed before 2003 when those rates were cut to 15 percent. A second option involves taxing as corporations large pass-through entities, such as limited liability companies and Subchapter S corporations (small business corporations electing treatment as partnerships) when there are many shareholders. A similar proposal to treat all large businesses as corporations was also made by the President's Advisory Panel on Federal Tax Reform (2005).

Another significant provision is disallowing the deduction of state and local corporate income taxes. Although the deduction of these taxes is treated as a tax expenditure under the individual income tax, including taxes on profits of unincorporated businesses, the corporate provision is not included in the tax expenditure list.

Although the ability to expense research expenses is considered a tax expenditure, the ability to expense advertising costs, which can also create benefits into the future through brand establishment, is not included. The estimates in table 7.6 suggest that the value of expensing advertising is larger than the estimated tax expenditure for expensing research costs.

The final provision in table 7.6 is the estimated revenue gain from treating state and local business enterprises as taxable corporations, an issue along with the state and local corporate tax deductions, discussed in Gravelle and Gravelle (2007).

Table 7.7 lists some additional tax expenditures relating to international taxation for which there are no revenue estimates but which are discussed in Gravelle (2009b). There are two options for limiting cross-crediting. One would prevent the use of excess foreign tax credits to offset U.S. tax due on royalties, and the other would eliminate cross-crediting between high- and low-tax countries. The latter provision might also be considered along with elimination of deferral for low-tax countries. This deferral provision might raise most of the revenue that would come with a complete end to deferral and, combined with a separate foreign tax credit basket, could raise a large amount of revenue as in the Wyden-Gregg bill. Current taxation of income of low-tax

Table 7.7
Additional International Options, without Revenue Estimates

Provision
Foreign tax credit revisions
Separate basket or foreign sourcing for royalties
Separate basket for low-tax countries
Deferral
Eliminate for low-tax countries
Eliminate for products produced abroad and exported
Eliminate for products produced abroad and exported to United States
Require minimum payout of foreign source income
Tighten this capitalization rules for U.S. multinationals and U.S. subsidiaries of foreign parents

countries acting as tax havens was recently adopted by Japan when it moved from a deferral system with a foreign tax credit to a territorial tax (Kleinbard 2011; JCT 2011a).

There are three other deferral options: one eliminating deferral where firms move to a second country to produce and export, one eliminating deferral where firms move to second country and produce for export back to the United States, and one that requires a minimum payout ratio.

The final provision would restrict the amount of interest deducted relative to income (or debt versus assets). These rules (called thin capitalization rules) exist in the United States but are weak. In the case of U.S. multinationals, Kleinbard (2011) suggests a system such as that used in Germany, which has a very restrictive cap that can be relaxed only if it is shown that foreign subsidiaries as a whole also have similar debt-to-asset ratios.

Recently there have been a number of comprehensive budget proposals. However, by and large they have been vague about corporate tax changes. The National Commission on Fiscal Responsibility and Reform (2010) is modeled on the Wyden-Gregg proposal but includes a territorial tax rather than the broader tax provision included in S. 3018. The commission is vague about how much goes for revenues and how much for rate reduction and also proposes a broader set of eliminated tax expenditures. Most other major plans make only a general reference to what is often a revenue-neutral corporate tax reform, although the Gang of Six Plan (2011) plan specifies a territorial tax.

Should Revenue Raised from Corporate Taxes Be Off-Limits?

Perhaps the first question that might be raised about the corporate tax is whether this tax, because of its flaws, should even be considered as a source of increased revenue or whether base broadening should be considered only as part of a revenue-neutral reform. As the issues surrounding the corporate tax have increasingly been focused on those relating to global trade and investment and away from more traditional concerns of the distortionary effects of the tax in a closed economy, some have argued that it is not only crucial not to raise corporate taxes, but to lower the rate and, at a minimum, use base broadening for a revenue-neutral reform.

Traditional Issues

Before the focus on international capital flows began to dominate the debate about the corporate tax, the major criticism leveled at the corporate tax was primarily the distortions it produced in investment behavior, although many supported the tax as a reliable source of revenue, a contributor to a progressive system, and a necessary element to protect individual income tax revenues. Harberger (1962) and subsequent studies identified significant distortions that favored investment in the noncorporate sector (see Gravelle (2009a) for a review of developments). Economists also addressed the effects of the favorable treatment of debt finance in the corporate sector.

The distortions caused by the corporate tax have been reduced over time due to lower effective tax rates, the decline in inflation (which particularly affects the debt equity distortion), the revisions of the corporate tax in 1986 that lowered the rate and broadened the base (virtually eliminating most interasset distortions across types of physical capital), the lowering of the tax rates on capital gains and dividends, and the increasing share of corporate equities in tax-preferred accounts such as pension plans and individual retirement accounts (where noncorporate investment is generally not an option).

Gravelle and Hungerford (2008) adjust existing estimates for changes in the tax wedge and find that the largest tax differential is between equity and debt finance. They estimate the cost of this distortion to be about 5 percent of revenues, given estimates of small substitution elasticities, confirmed in a review article by de Mooji (2011). The overall distortion between corporate and noncorporate investment suggests a cost of 4 to 7 percent of revenues. Combined with some small effects on payouts and capital gains realizations, they estimate the overall distortion as between 10 and 15 percent of revenue. These measures may be overstated because the tax rates they are based on do not include investments in intangibles, which probably lower the effective marginal tax corporate rate from around 27 to 22 percent (Gravelle 2011a).

This cost, while smaller than it has been in the past, is nevertheless significant as a percentage of revenues, although not as a percentage of output. With corporate tax revenues currently equal to about 2 percent of output, these distortions are about 2/10 of 1 percent of output. At the same time, some base-broadening provisions, such as reducing the amount of interest that can be deducted or treating large pass-through firms as corporations, might reduce, or at least not further expand, these distortions.

The corporate tax was also criticized, along with other taxes on capital income, for potentially discouraging savings, although it is not clear that higher taxes on capital income do so because of opposing income and substitution effects, and patterns of savings rates over time seem, if anything, to show lower savings rates with lower taxes. As noted earlier with respect to incorporating macroeconomic effects in revenue estimating, many studies have raised questions about the magnitude and even the direction of the overall economic effect (JCT 2011b; CBO 2012b; Gravelle 2007). Even in the dynamic models that tend to be most favorable to large savings responses, the effects depend on how the change in revenues is accommodated (Auerbach and Kotlikoff 1987; Engen, Gravelle, and Smetters 1997). In general, these dynamic models make powerful assumptions about the abilities of individuals to make extremely complex decisions over a long time horizon and have not been empirically tested. In many cases, the responses are quite inconsistent with empirical evidence (Gravelle 2007). Finally, this issue regarding savings arises with all taxes on capital income and not just corporate taxes.

Even with a small or even nonexistent savings response, taxes on the return to savings could still cause a distortion between present and future consumption (broadly defined to include leisure). But as in the case of savings responses, the effects depend on what policy is being contemplated. Most dynamic models have not reported excess burdens; however, Gravelle (1991) uses a method of compensating each generation to estimate excess burden in the case of the Summers (1981) and Auerbach and Kotlikoff (1987) life cycle models and finds considerable variation depending on the model, elasticity assumptions, and method of replacing the lost revenue, including, in some cases, welfare losses from eliminating capital income taxes (because of increased distortions from other taxes).

The two major arguments in support of the corporate tax, aside from its value as a reliable revenue source, are that it provides a backstop for the individual income tax and that it falls on capital owners and thus contributes to a progressive income tax. If the corporate tax did not exist or if its rate is too low, high-income taxpayers could use corporations to shelter retained earnings. The ideal tax treatment of the corporate sector is to treat shareholders like partners and pass through the income to shareholders. In practice, with millions of shares changing hands constantly, such treatment is not feasible.

Analysis of the corporate income tax in a closed economy, as shown by Harberger (1962) and confirmed in later studies, indicated that the tax was borne by capital. Since capital income is more concentrated among higher-income individuals, the tax contributes to the progressivity of the system. Of course, this distributional reason is not nearly as compelling as the protection of the individual tax base since greater progressivity could be achieved through the individual income tax.

International Tax Issues

Even as attention has focused on the U.S. corporate tax rate in an open economy, with critics citing the high rates relative to the rest of the world and the negative consequences for "competition" (whatever that is), the most notable thing about the corporate tax is its shrinking size. In 1953, the corporate tax was 5.6 percent of output and 30 percent of federal revenues; currently, it is 2 percent of output and about 10 percent of federal revenues. Effective tax rates fell as well, from 63 percent to about 30 percent (Gravelle 2004).

Considering corporate taxes in an open economy introduced two important issues into the debate. First, it increased the possibility that the burden could fall in part on labor income due to capital mobility. Second, it introduced international competitiveness as an argument in the debate in a way that did not fit with traditional allocational efficiency arguments.

Capital mobility meant that the capital stock in the United States was not fixed even if savings was fixed. Higher corporate taxes in the United States could discourage inbound capital and encourage outbound capital, which not only potentially affected output but raised questions about the incidence of the corporate tax. It is fairly easy to prove that in a small, open economy where capital is perfectly mobile and there is a single homogeneous good, labor bears 100 percent of the burden of a source-based corporate tax (a tax that applies only to earnings of firms located in that country). Critics of the corporate tax also made claims that U.S. corporate rates were considerably higher than those in the rest of the world and that the discouragement of capital investment provided significant restraints on growth. These same critics, however, also argued, in something of a tail-biting exercise, that we should reduce, or at least not increase, U.S. taxes on the foreign source income of U.S. firms (see, for example, National Commission on Fiscal Responsibility 2010). Since low taxes on these investments encourage capital to leave the country, proponents have to engage in some specialized arguments to make the case that we should simultaneously reduce domestic and foreign taxes in the interests of international competiveness. (These issues are reviewed in the section on raising revenue from increasing taxes on foreign source income.)

With an increasingly global economy, economists began to study the open-economy incidence of a corporate tax in a more complicated economy with multiple goods, and imperfect mobility and product substitution, using the same type of general equilibrium model as in the original Harberger (1962) model. The introduction of a number of reasonable moderating factors suggests that the corporate tax is still largely borne by capital. These moderating factors include the facts that the United States is large (which by itself would limit the labor share of the burden to about 70 percent for a single good economy), that capital is imperfectly mobile, that domestic products and imports are imperfect substitutes, that debt finance (which is more mobile) is subsidized by higher tax rates, that some profit is excess profit borne by shareholders, and that other countries impose corporate taxes that are not much different, when effective tax rates are considered, from the corporate tax in the United States. Many of these effects are discussed in detail by Jennifer Gravelle (2013), and tax rate comparisons are provided in Gravelle (2011a).

Some researchers have recently taken a different approach: estimating corporate tax effects on wages using reduced-form regressions with wages as the dependent variable and some measure of the corporate tax as an independent variable. Some of these studies, using cross-country panel data, found large reductions in wages from the corporate tax. Reviews of these studies by Gravelle and Hungerford

(2008), Jennifer Gravelle (2011), and Clausing (2013) suggest a number of problems. Some of the studies that found an effect reported one that was implausible (e.g., a burden on labor that was twenty-five times the size of the tax, which is theoretically impossible). A number of methodological and specification issues have also been raised (as discussed in these reviews). In addition, some of these studies are attempting to capture the effects of corporate taxes on reduced rents and the sharing of that tax with labor through bargaining rather than general equilibrium effects. Most of these studies used European data, where (unlike in the United States) the power of unions is significant. A serious problem with all of these studies is that the corporate tax tends to be dwarfed by the size of labor income, and it is difficult to detect the effect of a small variable on a much larger one when so many more significant factors affect wages.

Recently three groups that regularly prepare distributional analysis of U.S. taxes—the CBO (2012a), the Treasury Department (Cronin et al. 2013) and the Tax Policy Center (Nunns 2012)—modified their incidence assumption from the tax being borne 100 percent by capital, but they all still assume that between 75 and 82 percent of the burden is borne by capital.

While the debate over the incidence of the corporate tax fits into a standard economic paradigm, the other claim—that corporate rates need to be lowered and, in some cases, simultaneous arguments that income abroad should be fully exempt from tax (rather than deferred until repatriated and eligible for foreign tax credits)—was long on rhetoric, short on theory, and generally asserted rather than quantified.

The allocational effects discussed in a closed economy gave rise to welfare costs that stemmed from an inefficient allocation of capital; efficiency, in turn, absent market distortions, leads to welfare maximization. That is, treating capital income uniformly is optimal and the welfare cost of the corporate tax arises from the failure to do so. There were debates about how precisely to model the corporate tax and about the magnitude of distortions, reviewed in Gravelle (2009b), but these issues were precisely defined.

By contrast, the discussion of competitiveness is based on a concept not generally clearly defined and whose use as a metric is unclear. When competitiveness was invoked regarding trade and industrial policy in the early years of the Clinton administration, Krugman (1994) wrote that not only was competitiveness a meaningless concept for a country, but relying on it to guide to policy is likely to lead to poor policy. While Krugman was addressing trade, the same issues arose with respect to cross-border capital flows. Countries do not compete, and do not fail to exist if they cannot, in the way a firm would: they trade with other countries, normally each gaining something in the process.

Free markets in trade mean welfare maximization for the world (absent market failures), while optimization for a single country could involve interventions (such as optimal tariffs). Standard economic theories also exist for the tax rules that would produce an efficient allocation of capital around the world—namely, that each country's firms face the same tax rate regardless of where they invest, a system that is termed *capital export neutrality* and is consistent with a residence-based system of taxation. Under capital export neutrality, firms are not required to face the same tax rate in a given country as other firms because their after-tax returns differ (depending on the tax rate of their home country). This system can be duplicated with a worldwide system that taxes foreign source income currently with a foreign tax credit that allows the first right of taxation to the source country. In practice, this system generally requires a limit on the foreign tax credit to protect revenues, which approximates, albeit imperfectly, capital export neutrality.

Such a system also, again absent market failure, maximizes world welfare. For an individual country acting alone, there are different rules for optimization: for inbound capital (foreign-owned capital invested in the United States), the desirable tax rate depends on the elasticity of capital flows, and for outbound capital, current taxation of foreign source income with a deduction for foreign taxes is indicated. This approach is called *national neutrality*, as it equates the returns to domestic and foreign investment received by the home country, whether in the form of home country taxes or company profits. (In theory, if a country is large, there is a case for even heavier taxes on foreign source income.)

An alternative concept, unfortunately termed *capital import neutrality*, is defined as firms facing the same tax rate wherever they operate; this approach would, given nonuniform rates around the world, require a territorial tax (where income was taxed only in the host country). But such a system is not neutral, efficient, or optimal, and it results in too much capital being allocated to low-tax countries.

Two issues arise with respect to concerns about the allocation of capital in a global economy. The first is the effect of increasing the

Table 7.8
Effects of a 10 Percentage Point Cut in the Corporate Rate

Effect	Percentage Change
Percentage change in output from increased capital	0.15
Percentage change in national income from increased capital	0.01
Percentage offset in revenue loss from feedback	6.00
Increase in revenue due to reduced profit shifting	3.00
Percentage decrease in output due to crowding out (in ten years)	0.40
Percentage increase in revenue loss from crowding out (in ten years)	19.00

Source: Gravelle (2011a), showing midpoints of ranges of estimates.

domestic tax (through either increased rates or reductions in benefits that affect marginal investments), which can discourage inbound capital and encourage outbound capital. The second is about the tax burden on foreign source income and the provisions that reduce that burden relative to the tax burden on domestic investment.

The claims by advocates of lower taxes (other than those associated with the incidence of the corporate tax) are largely about the importance of lower rates and the tax regime that would be most conducive to growth in the United States. However, estimates in Gravelle (2011a) suggest that the effects of cutting the corporate tax rate by 10 percentage points (without other changes) on output and welfare are small. As shown in table 7.8, the estimated effect of cutting the corporate tax rate by 10 percentage points (about 0.7 percent of output) is minimal, increasing output by 15/100 of a percentage point. Moreover, virtually all of that gain in the aggregate is paid to foreigners as returns on their investments; the gains to the United States are only 1/100 of a percentage point. The gains from profit shifting, while small, are probably also optimistic, since they are proportional to the rate change even though there is a case to be made that profit shifting is constrained only by the relatively lax rules restricting it and not necessarily sensitive to this type of tax rate change (unless tax rates are cut to a very low level). Finally, note that if the rate reduction were enacted alone, any gains in output would be more than offset by the crowding out of investment due to an increased deficit.

The results arising from international capital flows in table 7.8 are based on the preferred estimates of Gravelle and Smetters (2006). However, even in the most optimistic scenario (with perfect capital mobility and perfect product substitution), the effects on output are an increase of 0.5 percent accompanied by an increase in national income of only 5/100 of 1 percent. The gain in U.S. income is small because it arises from collecting more taxes (excess burdens are quite small). Taxes collected from profits on additional capital inflows are offset by the loss of revenues on foreign-owned capital already in the United States. Similar effects can be estimated from data in a study by the Organization for Economic Cooperation and Development (OECD) (Johansson et al., 2008). Details are discussed in the appendix to this essay.

These modest effects suggest that raising revenue from the corporate tax, even if it increases the domestic tax burden, would not be very harmful to economic growth and would have a negligible effect on U.S. income, a finding that is not surprising given the small amount of current revenue collected from the corporate tax and the ownership claims of foreign investors. Given the current pressing need for reducing a growing debt, the corporate tax appears to be a reasonable potential source of revenue.

Revenue could also be used to finance rate reductions. As a rough rule of thumb, a revenue increase of x percent of tax revenue should allow a rate reduction of approximately 0.35 divided by $(1 + x)$, or perhaps slightly less depending on the effect on tax credits (Gravelle 2011a).

Note that according to the theory discussed in this section, raising revenue by raising taxes on foreign source income would also have small effects, but these effects would be reinforcing. The increased capital in the United States would increase output, and revenue effects would result in crowding in of investment. According to standard economic theory, raising revenue in this way would be beneficial to the economy as well as to the federal budget.

Evaluating Alternative Base-Broadening Approaches

This section examines specific types of base-broadening provisions, addressing them largely in order of their size. Topics include increasing the taxation of foreign source income, accelerated depreciation, tax benefits for intangibles, tax expenditures that are conduits for other beneficiaries, the production activities deduction, the title passage rule, LIFO inventory accounting, industry-specific tax preferences, limits on interest deductions, and provisions related to the taxation of capital income under both the corporate and individual income tax bases.

Increasing the Taxation of Foreign Source Income

Many critics, even those who believe that the United States should move toward a territorial system, consider the current system less desirable than some alternatives because it collects very little revenue from foreign source income while encouraging the retention of profits abroad and requiring complicated tax planning. As shown in table 7.4, a territorial tax with allocation of deductions and maintenance of antiabuse provisions (Subpart F) would actually raise revenue, although the amounts would be small (slightly under 2 percent of corporate revenues).

A major argument advanced for moving to a territorial tax is that under the current system, deferring taxes until dividends are paid by foreign subsidiaries to U.S. parents has caused firms to retain earnings abroad. Recent evidence from the shift to a territorial tax in Japan and the United Kingdom, however, has suggested a smaller and largely transitory effect (Gravelle 2012). Of course, eliminating deferral would also eliminate any incentive to retain profits abroad while gaining more revenue.

As I have already demonstrated, the potential for revenue gain from base broadening is large for foreign source income. The proposal listed in table 7.6 for current taxation of foreign source income with a deduction, a reform consistent with maximizing national income according to optimal taxation theory, is $123 billion, which is 28 percent of corporate revenue. (Behavioral responses would likely reduce this amount, since the initial effects would cause firms to earn lower profits abroad; they would therefore shift investments back to the United States and recoup some of those profits while driving down U.S. returns.) The system that, practically, comes closest to one consistent with maximizing worldwide efficiency—the provision eliminating deferral and instituting a per country foreign tax credit limit—raises $58 billion, or 13 percent of revenues. Formula apportionment, which largely addresses profit shifting, is estimated to raise $105 billion, or 23 percent of revenues.

The worldwide system that theory suggests is optimal for the United States (current taxation with a deduction for foreign taxes) might nevertheless be criticized on two grounds. The first is that other countries might retaliate in some way against such a regime. The second is that the United States might wish, given its wealth and power, to be a better global citizen and set its policies to maximize world welfare. These objections do not apply to the worldwide system with a credit, and in this case it could be argued that it is appropriate for a wealthy country that is a world leader to model good behavior.

A number of provisions associated with moving toward a worldwide system, but with a more limited reach, include eliminating deferral (3.5 percent of revenues), the specialized provisions in the FY 2012 budget proposals (3 percent of revenues), or a variety of other revisions, such as those focused on tax havens. That potential for revenue, although it may be smaller as a result of behavioral responses, as well as the general focus on international issues, makes this category of revenue raisers an important area to consider.

Are there reasons, despite the fundamental theory indicating that a territorial tax is neither efficient nor optimal, to nevertheless support such a system? Analysts have indeed presented a series of specific arguments that support a territorial tax.

Perhaps the most straightforward argument is that, politically, a worldwide tax is not likely to be adopted and the current system could be improved by moving to a properly designed territorial system. This view is generally expressed in the report of the President's Advisory Panel on Federal Tax Reform (2005), which gives lip-service to competitiveness but is largely focused on two issues: eliminating the incentive under a deferral regime to retain earnings abroad and reducing the opportunities to shift profits abroad by disallowing a share of parent company deductions, such as interest, to the extent of exempt income. Both of these factors would also reduce the costs associated with tax planning. These benefits could potentially offset the revenue losses due to the additional incentives for foreign investment that might arise from an exclusion since firms would no longer have any concerns about trapping future earnings abroad.

Note that this territorial tax is far from the simple exclusion of all foreign source income, which is estimated to result in a revenue loss of about $34 billion for FY 2014, or a loss of about 7.7 percent of revenue (see the appendix for details). Many critics have raised concerns about a territorial tax because it might result in more artificial profit shifting, especially with respect to profits from intangibles that—unlike the other principal method, leveraging—may not be fully addressed by a provision requiring an allocation of deductions. For example, although such an approach would allocate research deductions as well as interest deductions, successful companies with big hits may have much larger profits relative to these costs to shift abroad. In general, concerns about the consequences for profit shifting led Japan, for example, when it moved to a territorial system, to tax currently the income of operations in countries with tax rates below 20 percent (as described in Kleinbard 2011 and JCT 2011a). This treatment would be the equivalent of ending deferral and providing a separate foreign tax credit basket for tax havens in the context of the current U.S. system.

When profit shifting with intangibles is added to the other objections to a territorial tax, its improvement relative to the current system become less clear. It seems possible that the system proposed by the President's Advisory Panel on Federal Tax Reform (2005) might end up not only inducing additional investment abroad but losing rather than gaining revenue. What other reasons have been advanced for proposing a territorial tax?

Other Countries Use a Territorial Tax and the United States Is No Longer Dominant

Clearly one country alone cannot achieve efficiency in a world economy, and critics of the traditional standard of capital export neutrality argue that while such an objective may have made sense when the United States dominated the world after World War II and was the principal exporter of capital, it is no longer applicable in today's economy. Since most other countries have chosen a territorial tax, in this second-best world, U.S. firms are at a competitive disadvantage in low-tax countries and would be more so under a true worldwide system (such as current taxation with a per country foreign tax credit limit). However, even if this is the case (and as Kleinbard 2011 shows), Japan is not the only country that uses stricter controlled foreign corporation rules to limit the tax benefits of a territorial system), the reduction of investment abroad induced by a worldwide system would benefit the United States by drawing investment from operations with low pretax returns in tax haven countries to investments with higher returns in the United States. In this situation, it does not pay to adopt the same inefficient policies as other countries do.

Foreign Investment Results in More Domestic Investment

The standard theory about the efficient allocation of capital is that there is a fixed amount of capital available in a country, and lower taxes abroad cause the capital to flow abroad from the United States, causing productive inefficiency in the allocation of capital and reducing wages at home. Thus, a territorial tax reduces world welfare, U.S. welfare, and the welfare of U.S. labor (although U.S. capital owners benefit).

Proponents of territorial taxes argue that investment abroad increases investment at home. They do not address the obvious question of where this investment comes from. Rather, the argument rests wholly on empirical estimates, which are not appropriate to answer the question.

Consider the analysis of Desai, Foley, and Hines (2009), which is frequently cited to support this view. (Note that as reviewed in the Desai et al. study, other studies have in some cases found similar results and in some cases results in the other direction.) Desai et al. examined individual company data and found a correlation between growth in assets abroad and growth of assets in the United States. The authors estimated foreign investments based on foreign countries' growth rates and then used this variable to estimate predicted domestic growth in investment. They found that 10 percent growth in foreign investment led to 2.6 percent growth in domestic investment. The driving factor is foreign demand growth rather than changes in the relative costs of producing through an affiliate versus exporting. It is not unreasonable to imagine that firms both export to foreign affiliates and invest abroad and that demand growth could have driven both activities.

In any case, even if foreign and domestic investment are complements, this analysis does not capture all of the general equilibrium effects of investment abroad. Investments abroad may simultaneously increase both capital abroad and the domestic capital of multinationals to export to foreign operations by diverting capital from other activities in the domestic economy.

In sum, this argument is inconsistent with theory and rests on unpersuasive evidence.

The Capital Ownership Neutrality Argument

A third argument appears to be due to a new concept of neutrality, capital ownership neutrality, due to Desai and Hines (2003). Essentially capital ownership neutrality is the same as capital import neutrality in that, under certain very restrictive assumptions, it is achieved by source-based taxation; indeed, some discussions view it as a resurrection of capital import neutrality.

Capital ownership neutrality is based on the notion that the ownership of assets affects productivity. For example, a U.S. firm may make a higher profit because it has some type of intangible asset. If the United States imposes high taxes on operations in low-tax countries, then another firm not subject to home country corporate taxes might acquire the asset even if its pretax return is not as high because it is less productive. In that case productivity will be reduced because the U.S. firm is more productive. If the United States had a territorial tax, this effect would not occur.

As Gravelle (2009b, 2010c) argued, capital ownership neutrality can be efficient only if physical capital is not mobile. Otherwise the gains from capital ownership neutrality must be offset against any losses in either world welfare or national welfare due to the misallocation of capital as the United States adopts a territorial tax.

Perhaps more important, the analysis assumes that there are no mechanisms available to obtain the benefits of productive efficiency short of owning the capital asset. If the greater productivity of the U.S. firm is due to the employment of managers with greater skills, then that productivity arises at a cost, and these management skills could be employed elsewhere. If the asset is uniquely tied to the firm, such as value due to a trademark, intangible R&D, or even a management structure, the model does not allow for the fact that ownership of the productive assets and ownership of the intangible asset can be separated in most cases. Trademarks and patents can be franchised or sold, or firms can operate by leasing capital assets or engaging in contract manufacturing. As long as they are making an excess profit, they should continue to exploit the intangible. In light of the many ways in which the efficiency costs of capital ownership nonneutrality are unlikely to be significant compared to location distortions, it seems questionable to use this concept to support a territorial tax.

Portfolio Investment Allows the Benefit of Territorial Taxes

Another argument is that U.S. citizens can avoid restrictions on U.S. taxation of the foreign source income of its companies by investing directly in the stock of firms based in countries with low taxes or in countries with territorial systems. Some of this argument has arisen because of the growth of portfolio investment in foreign firms. As Gravelle (2009b, 2010c) has noted, in 1960 U.S. residents held less than 1 percent of their portfolios in foreign stock; by 2007 they held 23 percent of their portfolios in foreign stock.

However, several important facts should be noted about this change. There is little evidence that this growth was motivated by tax considerations rather than the increasing ease of international portfolio diversification. If portfolios were perfectly substitutable, U.S. residents should own the same share of foreign stocks in their portfolios as foreign stock shares are as a percentage of the total, and this amount is three times as large as actual stock shares. Moreover, foreign shares are largely in countries with high tax rates. These observations suggest a large home bias in stock holdings and that portfolio substitution responses to taxes are not very large.

There is, however, a more fundamental flaw in this argument. Investors purchase stocks to earn a rate of return. That rate of return will be influenced by numerous factors, of which the tax treatment of foreign source income is likely to be only a small factor, especially in the United States, where domestic investment is so large. Presumably the overall tax burden regardless of the source of that burden drives portfolio investors to purchase shares.

Firms Can Change Nationality

Another argument supporting a territorial tax and rejecting a move toward worldwide taxation is that firms are not tied to any one nationality so that if U.S. taxes are too high or too burdensome on foreign operations, the firm can reconstitute itself as a firm with another nationality so as to better compete in foreign jurisdictions. There are three ways in which this might be accomplished directly: inversion, merger, or original incorporation outside the United States.

Inversion, where an existing U.S. firm reorganizes itself to recreate a firm with a foreign parent, was the subject of much discussion when this activity was taking place at the beginning of this century. Legislation enacted in 2004, which treats inverted firms as U.S. firms either indefinitely or for a period of time (depending on continuity of ownership), appears to have ended this practice. And, as Kleinbard (2011) pointed out, were the United States to move closer to a worldwide system, there are additional methods of addressing this problem, including toll taxes on assets and facts and circumstances determination of the location of management.

A second method of changing the nationality of ownership is through mergers with foreign companies where the foreign firm becomes the parent. Mergers impose many other costs and are not likely to be motivated by purely tax motives. But as with inversions, Kleinbard (2011) notes that current tax rules limit transfers of U.S. assets to foreign firms and notes that there are additional measures that could be taken if these rules prove insufficient.

The third method is the possibility that new start-up firms will incorporate as non-U.S. firms. It seems fairly unlikely that many firms facing the challenges of succeeding with an initial public offering would abandon the familiarity and safety of U.S. incorporation for a distant and uncertain tax benefit. In fact, recent evidence by Allen and Morse (2013) suggests that such incorporations are quite rare. In addition, the United States still has technical remedies to address such effects by determining residence. One possibility, for example, is defining residence based on where effective management occurs, an approach recommended by the President's Advisory Panel on Federal Tax Reform (2005).

Summing Up

Although many arguments have been advanced to suggest that territorial taxation is a better approach to taxing U.S. corporations, this analysis finds each weak, especially relative to the problems associated with a territorial tax: losses in efficiency and national welfare and, perhaps even more important, the facilitation of profit shifting. On fundamental economic grounds, a movement toward an effective worldwide system with current taxation and a deduction for foreign taxes seems a change that can both raise revenue and increase economic efficiency, especially by reducing tax incentives to retain earnings abroad.

If, for political reasons, such a move is not feasible, a territorial tax that not only allocates deductions and adopts a management and control standard, as proposed by the President's Advisory Panel on Federal Tax Reform (2005), but also provides current taxation of profits from low tax or tax haven operations might be a desirable alternative.

Accelerated Depreciation

Of the items listed among traditional corporate tax expenditures, the single largest provision is accelerated depreciation for equipment, which, abstracting from the effect of temporary bonus depreciation, costs a little more than 6 percent of revenue (table 7.1). This measure is based on an alternative depreciation system as described above. As indicated in table 7.2, a much larger amount of revenue would be raised in the first ten years, so it is important not to rely on the initial gain for the longer term. The modified system analyzed in the CBO budget options would raise a little over 40 percent of the revenue raised by moving to the alternative depreciation system.

As shown in table 7.9, equipment in particular is estimated to be taxed at rates well below the statutory rate, at least at current inflation rates, while structures are taxed at rates closer to the statutory rate. The revisions would bring the assets' tax rates into close alignment. This

Table 7.9
Aggregate Effective Tax Rates, No Change in Statutory Rate

Asset Type	Current Law (percent)	Alternative Depreciation (percent)	CBO Budget Options (percent)
Equipment	26	36	34
Structures	32	34	34
Total	30	35	34

Source: Gravelle (2011b). Calculations assume a 5 percent real discount rate and a 2 percent inflation rate.

table presents broad aggregates, but the variation in tax rates for individual assets is larger, as Gravelle (2011b) showed. For example, under current law, effective tax rates for equipment range from 17 percent for ships and boats and 18 percent to 35 percent for autos; under the alternative system, ships and boats still have the lowest tax rate, 27 percent, but the highest rate, 44 percent, is on aircraft. For the CBO options, the lowest rates are on ships and boats and railroad equipment (25 percent and 24 percent, respectively), with the highest tax rates on autos.

The change in the tax treatment of structures is largely due to public utility structures whose estimated tax rates rise from 27 to 31 percent under the alternative system and to 33 percent under the CBO option. Tax rates on industrial and commercial buildings remain the same, 36 percent and 37 percent, respectively. Although not reflected in the table and relatively unimportant for the corporate sector, tax rates on rental structures rise from 30 percent under current law to 33 percent under the alternative system.

Tax rates on structures and equipment were much closer when depreciation was revised in 1986, as Gravelle (1994) showed, when tax rates on equipment were estimated at 30 percent and structures 32 percent, a revision that was a significant improvement over preexisting tax rates of 8 and 30 percent, respectively. This differential has grown in part due to the fall in inflation rates (which benefits short-lived assets more than longer-lived ones) and in part due to the increased life for nonresidential buildings (from 31.5 years to 39 years) adopted in 1993. Of course, were inflation to increase substantially, equipment could be significantly overtaxed.

Either of the revisions in table 7.9 would bring tax rates of equipment and structures closer together, largely by increasing the tax rates on equipment as well as bringing the overall tax burden more in line with the statutory tax rates.

Nevertheless, the desirability of restricting depreciation as a revenue raiser is not straightforward. Reducing investment incentives raises the effective tax rate more for a given revenue gain than lowering statutory tax rates because the rate reduction applies to the return to existing capital. Moreover, while tax rates between equipment and structures would be brought closer together, tax rates between physical capital and intangibles (which are taxed at zero or negative rates and arise from research, advertising, and human capital investment) would be exacerbated. This problem may not be of great concern for intangibles created by research but might be of concern with respect to advertising (although such issues might be addressed separately). In addition, if no changes are made in the taxation of foreign source income, raising revenues through reductions in accelerated depreciation would exacerbate the differences between taxes on U.S. and foreign income. It could also discourage inbound capital, although the evidence presented previously suggests that this effect would be small.

One other advantage of raising revenues by reducing depreciation allowances rather than increasing corporate rates is that the change in depreciation deductions would not exacerbate existing distortions in the way that a rate increase would. Reducing depreciation allowances would also raise taxes on both debt and equity-financed capital and on both corporate and noncorporate income.

One observation about raising revenue by restrictions in depreciation allowances is that for administrative reasons, it might not be desirable to return to the numerous classes under the alternative system. The CBO option retains the simplicity of the current system, and if more revenue were needed, the recovery method could be shifted to straight-line methods, as in the alternative system.

A more far-reaching approach would be to adopt a system proposed in the past for open-ended accounts, where the undepreciated basis would be added to new investment each year with a percentage taken as a deduction. Such an approach was included in the recommendations of the President's Advisory Panel on Federal Tax Reform, although the number of categories was limited. Such a system could be easily indexed for inflation.

Tax Benefits for Intangibles

A significant portion of capital investment and of the value of assets is in intangible property, which accounts for an estimated 27 percent of reproducible assets, with about half arising from research and development, according to Gravelle (2011a). The remaining intangibles arise from human capital investment and advertising. (Asset shares are 24.2 percent for equipment, 39.6 percent for structures, 9.7 percent for inventories, and 26.5 percent for intangibles.) Since all intangibles are expensed, the effective tax rate is zero, although the research and experimentation credit implies that the effective tax rate is negative. This effective tax rate is estimated to be -10.1 percent, based on data from Canada's Department of Finance (2009).

The incentives for research and development, taken together, are 3.9 percent of corporate revenues and are larger than the cost of any other single tax expenditure other than accelerated depreciation for equipment. In addition to the basic research credit, there is a therapeutic research credit included in the credit total and an orphan drug credit with a small cost. Estimated benefits for expensing of advertising are another 1.7 percent, for a total of 5.6 percent, almost as large as depreciation. The subsidies would be even larger if there were a way to estimate the subsidy for expensing human capital investment.

There is a justification for a subsidy for R&D, since it can have significant spillover effects. R&D actually has two offsetting external effects. First, because firms may not be able to capture the full returns from innovation, they underinvest in research. At the same time, overinvestment may occur in the race for discovery. Evidence reviewed in Hall, Mairesse, and Mohnen (2010) suggests the former effect dominates, as there are high, and in some cases extremely high, estimated rates of return. Overall, the investment encouraged by the R&D tax benefits is desirable. In addition, in the case of expensing of R&D, it is difficult to determine the useful life of essentially heterogeneous investments.

There are, however, critics of these provisions, especially the research credit, which does not face the administrative problem of determining a write-off period, because it subsidizes activities that do not have spillover effects. The latest of these criticisms has been levied at the programming of video games (Kocieniewski 2011). It might be possible to scale back some of the research expenditures that are eligible for the credit. In the past, for example, legislation was adopted to eliminate social science research. Restrictions on the subsidy for proprietary software might also be considered.

Advertising has no powerful justification for a subsidy. Although it is recognized to have value in providing information, there is no general consensus that the overall uncaptured social benefits are positive, and they may be negative. As is the case with research, measuring the useful life of advertising could be difficult; at the same time, it might be better to get the average tax burden right rather than undertax the returns to much investment.

The final source of intangibles, investment in human capital, would be difficult to isolate for either measurement or tax administration purposes. There is a case for favoring investment in human capital because some of that capital formation is generally applicable rather than firm specific, and firms may be reluctant to invest in it due to the possibility the worker will leave and another firm will capture the fruits of training.

Note that the Rangel bill also included a provision to lengthen the life of acquired intangibles. Having a fixed (currently fifteen-year) life for assets acquired by purchase was a compromise to simplify taxpayer disputes over useful lives, and a longer life may be justified because many of these intangibles, such as trademarks and customer lists, do not deteriorate or are replenished by deductible expenses.

Tax Expenditures That Are Conduits for Other Beneficiaries

Another large tax expenditure is the exclusion of income for state and local bonds (or, in a minority of cases, a special credit). About two-thirds of tax-exempt bonds are general obligation state and local bonds; the remainder are private activity bonds. The intended beneficiaries of these subsidies are not corporations or their investments. Also falling into this category are the low-income housing credit (designed to benefit low-income tenants), charitable contributions, and possibly rehabilitation credits, subsidies directed at areas with poverty such as the new markets credit, disaster relief, and the work opportunity credit (the new hires credit is temporary).

These types of subsidies might be better provided by direct spending, and whether they should be retained in the absence of spending programs is an issue that has less to do with corporate taxation and more with the other objectives. Allowing a conduit frequently means a program is less target efficient if intermediaries get a cut of the benefit, as is usually thought to be the case for taxpayers with the highest marginal rates in the case of tax-exempt bonds. In addition, eliminating the corporate exclusion without eliminating the individual exclusion would probably largely shift the source of the revenue loss from corporations to individuals. Charitable contributions, if the elasticity of giving is low, induce less in contributions than they cost in revenue. Charitable contributions also reflect the preferences of the donor rather than the public at large, which may be either a desirable or an undesirable attribute. The corporate charitable deduction is especially beneficial because it eliminates two levels of tax. In addition, questions can be raised about whether large public corporations should be making contributions on behalf of their shareholders.

Deductions for state and local taxes have a less clear interpretation, although to some extent, they benefit state and local governments by making taxes less burdensome on firms. The federal deduction also dampens the distorting effects of differential corporate taxes, although many of those taxes are allocated according to sales rather than investment. The exemption for tax on state and local government enterprises may, if anything, burden private corporations as it encourages public production.

Production Activities Deduction

Another large tax expenditure is the production activities deduction, which allows a deduction of 9 percent of taxable income for domestic production for certain industries, primarily manufacturing, electricity and natural gas production, and construction. Because the deduction applies to taxable income, it is equivalent to a rate reduction from 35 to 31.5 percent where applicable. One of the original rationales was to benefit manufacturing. This provision has been criticized as distorting the tax treatment of different industries by granting differential tax rates. In addition, it creates administrative and compliance problems in both distinguishing domestic content and identifying eligible activities.

About a quarter of the subsidy benefits unincorporated businesses, although that share is growing and is projected to reach 35 percent by FY 2014, according to Sherlock (2011). Of the corporate component, the manufacturing share is 66 percent, while its taxable income was 40 percent of corporate profits. Assuming little of the benefit in the noncorporate sector is for manufacturing, manufacturing receives only about half the benefit. About 12 percent of the corporate benefit is from firms in the information sector, which is responsible for 6 percent of profits. The mining sector claims 6 percent.

A reason to question eliminating this deduction relates to international capital flows. This deduction is more likely to apply to multinationals because of the industry restrictions. A revenue-neutral rate substitution could lower the effective statutory rate (estimated by

Gravelle 2011a) by about 1.2 percentage points, comparing the benefit with tax liability before tax credits. Therefore, to the extent that lower domestic tax rates are attractive because they induce capital inflows or reduce profit shifting, the production activities deduction may be more targeted than a general rate reduction. It is doubtful, however, that this issue outweighs the drawbacks of the provision, making this change a good candidate for revenue raising. A middle course might be to limit the benefit to corporate manufacturing, which would recoup about half the revenue loss.

Title Passage Rule

The next largest tax expenditure is the title passage rule, also referred to as the sales source rule exception. This provision is essentially an export subsidy, but because of its design, it is available only to multinational firms that have foreign operations and excess foreign tax credits. The provision allows half of income from sales of inventory produced by the firm to be allocated to the country in which the title passes for purposes of the foreign tax credit, which increases the limit on the foreign tax credit and the tax credits available for firms with excess credits. The provision also allows income from the purchase from another party and resale to be sourced in the country where title passes.

It is difficult to justify this provision, whose origins date to the early days of the tax code. Since title passage can easily be arranged abroad, firms that produce exports for sale abroad can readily take advantage of this provision if they otherwise qualify. In general, an export subsidy benefits foreign consumers rather than U.S. citizens. Moreover, there is little justification for allowing a benefit to a limited number of firms that have no related characteristic other than foreign income in high-tax countries.

LIFO Inventory Accounting

Another option is the repeal of LIFO accounting, which allows firms to treat goods sold as the latest acquired. This provision can be contrasted with FIFO (first in, first out) accounting, where goods sold are assumed to be the oldest purchased. A much smaller provision available to FIFO taxpayers would eliminate the opportunity to choose the lower of cost or market value (LCM). By choosing market value, a firm can recognize losses of goods in inventory. Only 10 percent of the cost of the inventory tax expenditure is for LCM. There is also a negligible (a revenue cost of less than $50 million) for another method that allows specific identification of homogeneous goods (so that subnormal or damaged goods can be chosen, allowing a loss).

Most firms do not use LIFO because they must conform their financial and tax accounting methods. There is, however, a justification for LIFO: on average, it eliminates tax on inflationary gains; however, it can eliminate real gains. It is also used primarily by certain industries, and a change in treatment is unlikely to lead to large consequences because inventory holdings, on average, are very short-lived and therefore, as Gravelle (2001) showed, less sensitive to tax treatment. There is no apparent justification for LCM or specific identification.

Special Provisions for Specific Industries

Special provisions for insurance companies are almost the size of the title passage rule and are a revenue-raising option, as are the relatively smaller provisions for fossil fuels. Although I will not discuss each of these provisions (Congressional Research Service 2010 provides a broader discussion), many of them could be considered for reduction. The president's budget proposals would restrict insurance company provisions and benefits for fossil fuels. There is little reason that these industries, credit unions, timber, mining, or investment in shipping should be tax favored. A number of energy subsidies are directed at conservation or alternative energy production, where issues such as global warming and pollution may justify government intervention. These benefits might be better accomplished through direct spending but are currently linked with the more general issues.

Many provisions whose revenue cost was too small to appear in the list, or that have expired, are also industry specific, including numerous energy conservation and alternative energy subsidies, as well as subsidies for film production and railroad tracks.

Other Minor Provisions

Although it is small, the provision allowing graduated corporation rates is not justified by normal distributional concerns, since there is no reason to expect that owners of small corporations are less wealthy than owners of large ones. Most small corporations have the option of pass-through treatment, and the main effect of this provision may be to permit individuals to shift income to lesser-taxed forms.

The provisions that defer the recognition of income—deferral of tax on nondealer installment sales, like-kind exchanges (where similar properties can be exchanged without realizing capital gain), and completed contracts—also do not appear to have a rationale, and the like-kind exchange provision has spawned an industry to determine what qualifies and has added to administrative and compliance costs.

Special provisions that benefit employee stock ownership plans are frequently justified because employees with a stake in the business are argued to be more productive. Once a firm reaches any reasonable size, this effect becomes unimportant, and the concentration of retirement assets in the employee's firm increases the potential negative consequences to employees if the firm becomes bankrupt, as was seen in the Enron scandal.

Limits on Interest Deductions

Restricting the deduction of interest would address one of the more significant distortions in the corporate income tax. Gravelle and Hungerford (2008) report effective tax rates indicating that corporate equity is taxed at rates at or close to 40 percent while debt is taxed at very low, or possibly slightly negative, rates even when allowing for higher taxes on interest income at the individual level (which is taxed as ordinary income). These differentials occur because nominal interest is deductible. One option is to disallow the deductibility of the inflation portion of interest by excluding a share of interest as a deduction or imputing income equal to the inflation rate times the stock of net debt. Given the dramatic differences in tax rates on corporations and their recipients, this restriction could be disallowed at the corporate level without a corresponding benefit at the individual level and achieve reasonable parity with equity tax burdens. Alternatively, to avoid involving individual investors in these adjustments, only a portion of the inflation premium could be disallowed.

Such a limit might cause less debt capital to flow into the United States, but optimal tax theory does not indicate that a negative tax is beneficial for inbound capital, so U.S. national income would likely increase. Such a change might also reduce the use of debt as a method of profit shifting (through borrowing in high-tax countries from lenders in low-tax countries, including tax havens).

Shifts between Individual and Corporate Taxes: Restrictions on Using the Noncorporate Form and Shifting Tax Burdens to the Shareholder Level

According to a U.S. Department of the Treasury (2007) study, the share of business income that is in corporate form has declined from 80 percent to 50 percent since the early 1980s, primarily through an increase in the number of shareholders for small corporations that are allowed to elect partnership treatment (Subchapter S corporations) and the growth in new organizational forms such as limited liability corporations that are taxed as partnerships. These are firms that have the general characteristics of corporations. The estimate in table 7.6 is based on calculations in Gravelle (2011a) and assumes average estimated marginal rates and a return to the early 1980s ratio of business organized in the corporate form.

In a global economy, it is better to raise revenue within the corporate sector at the individual rather than the corporate level, since the individual-level tax is residence based. One option is rolling back the 2003 cuts in dividends and capital gains that set the rates at 15 percent and returning to ordinary rates for dividends and a 20 percent rate for capital gains. Note that the estimates in table 7.6, taken from Gravelle (2011a), assume the much smaller realizations response indicated by recent research than that used by the JCT. Raising these taxes, however, is similar to raising the corporate tax rate in that it magnifies the basic domestic economy distortions (between corporate and noncorporate investment and between debt and equity) and might be more usefully considered as a source for financing a corporate rate cut. Even in that case, the marginal tax rate on corporate equity could rise because about half of corporate income is received in tax-exempt form; the overall effect depends on what investments are marginal.

The last two options interact, however. The more taxes are collected at the individual level by raising taxes on dividends and capital gains, the larger the gain from shifting income into the corporate sector. If dividends were taxed at full rates and capital gains at 20 percent, then at a 30 percent individual tax rate and a 35 percent corporate rate, the reduction in the differential is 6.5 percentage points. These effects depend as well, of course, on how the individual tax rate on ordinary income develops.

Conclusion

This analysis has identified a number of possibilities for raising revenue from corporate base-broadening provisions without exacerbating (or at least having only a minimal effect on) existing tax distortions. Some of these reforms might improve efficiency. The most important area, measured by potential revenue, would include increases in taxes on foreign source income, such as that proposed in the Wyden-Gregg bill. A territorial tax with teeth (e.g., taxing not only passive income and allocating deductions but also income from low-tax countries or tax havens) might also be desirable if political constraints prohibit a worldwide system. Eliminating the title passage rule is another option, although it might disappear with some reforms of foreign source income. There are also numerous smaller items that have little justification, including graduated corporate tax rates, many industry-specific subsidies, and provisions that defer income recognition.

A number of options that are not in the traditional tax expenditure list also might be candidates for raising revenues; these include disallowing a portion of interest deductions, capitalizing advertising, and taxing large pass-through entities as corporations. If the resulting revenues were used to reduce the corporate rate, increasing individual taxes on dividends and capital gains is an option that might not exacerbate, and could reduce, current distortions.

Two of the largest tax expenditures, accelerated depreciation and the production activities deduction, are difficult to assess. Restricting accelerated depreciation for equipment would more closely equate the treatment of equipment with structures and inventories but would also widen differentials with intangibles. Preferential tax treatment of intangible investments is, however, probably justified. The taxation of advertising could also be increased by capitalizing such expenses. Because reductions in depreciation allowances apply only to new investment, they raise tax burdens more for a given steady-state gain in revenue than is the case with a rate increase. The production activities deduction, while causing industry distortions and administrative burdens, targets multinationals where international capital mobility may be an issue. If the deduction is retained, however, it could be narrowed to corporate manufacturing.

Appendix

This appendix describes the methods used in the text to estimate the revenue effects of adopting a deduction for foreign taxes, moving to formula apportionment, eliminating the deduction for state and local taxes, capitalizing advertising expenses, and adopting a territorial tax that eliminates the residual U.S. tax. It also explains the estimates of economic effects of changing corporate taxes derived from Johansson et al. (2008).

Estimating the effect of adopting a foreign tax deduction must account for foreign taxes not credited due to the overall limit and foreign tax credits not claimed because the income is not repatriated. For 2006, the last year that data are available on these details, the data on U.S. corporations and their controlled foreign corporations indicate that $97 billion of income tax was paid, while the data on foreign tax credits claimed indicate that deemed-paid dividends were $40 billion. These comparisons indicate that $57 billion was not claimed as foreign taxes because the income was not repatriated. For foreign tax credits claimed, current foreign tax credits of $86 billion, disallowed taxes of $9 billion, and carryovers of $31 billion result in a total of $108 billion.[1]

The foreign tax credit limit in that year was also $108 billion. The actual credits taken were $78 billion, presumably because some firms had credits over the limit or insufficient tax liability to use the credits. Under the assumption that with a deduction there would no longer be carryovers, comparing the deduction of $86 billion, which is worth $30 billion (86 × 0.35), to the $78 billion credit, implies a loss of $48 billion. In addition, assume that under elimination of deferral, another $57 billion in credits would be taken, which can be compared to a deduction of $58 billion, which is worth $37 billion (58 × 0.65). The resulting total of $85 billion is 24 percent of total corporate tax revenues in 2006 of $354 billion. Applying that ratio to FY 2014 estimates results in a revenue gain of $107 billion, which, added to the $16 billion for deferral alone, yields a total revenue gain of $123 billion.

The estimates for moving to formula apportionment are based on the $50 billion estimate for 2002 in Clausing and Avi-Yonah (2007), scaled up to current revenues. Since the 2002 revenue was only 1.4 percent of gross domestic product (GDP) because of bonus depreciation and slow growth, the FY 2002 revenue of $148 billion was first scaled up to 2 percent of GDP and then adjusted to FY 2014 levels. The $50 billion was multiplied by the ratio of FY 2014 revenue and then scaled up FY 2002 revenue.

Revenue estimates for eliminating the deduction for state and local taxes are based on OECD data reported in Gravelle (2011a), indicating combined statutory rates are 39.6 percent, which with a statutory rate of 35 percent implies state and local tax rates of 7 percent. Thus, the ratio of the tax benefit to tax liability before credits should be 7 percent, suggesting an estimate of $31 billion. Alternatively, the estimates for 2006 (which was a more normal year) reported in Gravelle and Gravelle (2007) were scaled up by the increase in corporate taxes between those two years, yielding $25 billion. (The years 2007 to 2010 were significantly distorted by the recession.) The smaller estimate was used.

Revenue estimates for capitalizing advertising were based on Internal Revenue Service (2006), which indicates advertising expenditures of $227 billion for firms with net income. The estimate assumes a depreciation rate of 60 percent, based on Corrado, Hulten, and Sichel (2006). Assuming a 5 percent nominal growth rate, the steady-state deductions will be 92 percent of their size with expensing (0.6/(0.6 + 0.05)), leading to an estimate of revenue gain of $6.4 billion (0.08 × $227 billion × 0.35). This amount is 2 percent of revenues in 2006 and is scaled up to FY 2014 by the projected growth in revenues from $354 billion to $447 billion, yielding a total revenue gain of $8 billion.

Estimation of the revenue raised from a territorial tax that simply eliminates the residual U.S. tax is based on data presented in Gravelle (2010a), which indicates that capital abroad was 16 percent of the U.S. capital stock and that corporate capital is 50 percent of the total, and equity capital is two-thirds of total corporate capital. As a result, corporate equity capital is one-third of the total, while the effective residual tax rate on foreign source income is 4 percent and the U.S. effective domestic rate is 25 percent. These numbers imply a revenue loss of 34.7 billion (0.04 × 0.16)/(0.25 × 0.33) times total revenue of $447 billion.

Translating the OECD (Johansson et al., 2008) investment demand responses into output effects leads to an effect of essentially the same range of economic effects as those estimated using the Gravelle-Smetters model. In 2006, before the recession (and thus a more normal year), gross investment plus inventories was $2.387 trillion and GDP was $13.377 trillion. The ratio of investment to value added (output minus investment) is 21.7 percent. Using the OECD investment responses, this amount would increase to 21.9 percent at their lower bound and 22.2 percent at their upper bound with a 5 percentage point rate reduction. Since investment appears in both the numerator and denominator, the ratio of investment to GDP is 0.217/1.217. Holding output constant, investment and ultimately the capital stock would increase from between 0.76 percent and 1.88 percent. Since the corporate rate reduction of 10 percentage points would be twice as large as the reduction in the OECD study, but corporate capital is about half of capital, these estimates would only need to be multiplied by factor shares of approximately one-third to produce output effects between 0.25 percent and 0.6 percent of GDP. The increase in output net of depreciation, more comparable to the results in the text, would be about the same: 2/10 of 1 percent to one-half of 1 percent. Data on investment and GDP are at http://www.gpo.gov/fdsys/pkg/ERP-2012/pdf/ERP-2012-table1.pdf.

Notes

The views in this study do not reflect the views of the Congressional Research Service.

1. Internal Revenue Service statistics on controlled foreign corporations and foreign tax credits are located at http://www.irs.gov/uac/SOI-Tax-Stats-International-Business-Tax-Statistics.

References

Allen, Eric J., and Susan C. Morse. 2013. Tax Haven Incorporation for U.S.-Headquartered Firms: No Exodus Yet. *National Tax Journal* 66 (2): 395–420.

Altshuler, Rosanne, and Harry Grubert. 2010. Formula Apportionment: Is it Better Than the Current System and Are There Better Alternatives? *National Tax Journal* 62 (4): 1145–84.

Auerbach, Alan J., and Laurence J. Kotlikoff. 1987. *Dynamic Fiscal Policy*. Cambridge: Cambridge University Press.

Clausing, Kimberly A. 2011. The Revenue Effects of Multinational Firm Income Shifting. *Tax Notes* 28: 1580–86.

Clausing, Kimberly A. 2013. Who Pays the Corporate Tax in a Global Economy? *National Tax Journal* 66 (1): 151–84.

Clausing, Kimberly A., and Reuven S. Avi-Yonah. 2007. Reforming Corporate Taxation in a Global Economy: A Proposal to Adopt Formulary Apportionment." Hamilton Project Discussion Paper, Brookings Institution, Washington, DC.

Congressional Budget Office. 2010. *The Budget and Economic Outlook: An Update*. Washington, DC: Congressional Budget Office.

Congressional Budget Office. 2011. *Reducing the Deficit: Spending and Revenue Options*. Washington, DC: Congressional Budget Office.

Congressional Budget Office. 2012a. *The Distribution of Household Income and Federal Taxes, 2008 and 2009*. Washington, DC: Congressional Budget Office.

Congressional Budget Office. 2012b. *The Economic Impact of the President's 2013 Budget*. Washington, DC: Congressional Budget Office.

Congressional Research Service. 2010. Tax Expenditures: Compendium of Background Material on Individual Provisions. In Senate Committee on the Budget, 111–2, Committee Print S. Prt. No. 111–58.

Corrado, Carol A., Charles R. Hulten, and Daniel E. Sichel. 2006. Intangible Capital and Economic Growth. Finance and Economics Discussion Series, Working Paper 2006–24, Federal Reserve Board, Washington, DC.

Cronin, Julie Ann, Emily Y. Lin, Laura Power, and Michael Cooper. 2013. Distributing the Corporate Income Tax: Revised U.S. Treasury Methodology. *National Tax Journal* 66 (1): 239–62.

de Mooij, Ruud A. 2011. The Tax Elasticity of Corporate Debt: A Synthesis of Size and Variations. Working Paper 11/95, International Monetary Fund, Washington, DC.

Canada. Department of Finance. 2009. Tax Expenditures and Evaluations, 2009. Canada: Department of Finance.

Desai, Mehir A., and James R. Hines, Jr. 2003. Evaluating International Tax Reform. *National Tax Journal* 56 (3): 487–502.

Desai, Mehir A., C. Fritz Foley, and James R. Hines, Jr. 2009. Domestic Effects of the Foreign Activities of U.S. Multinationals. *American Economic Journal: Economic Policy* 1 (1): 181–203.

Donmoyer, Ryan J., and Peter Cohn. 2011. Obama Backs Corporate Rate Cut along with Tax Simplification. *Bloomberg*, January 26. http://www.bloomberg.com/news/2011-01-26/obama-backs-cut-in-u-s-corporate-tax-rate-only-if-it-won-t-affect-deficit.html.

Engen, Eric M., Jane G. Gravelle, and Kent A. Smetters. 1997. Dynamic Tax Models: Why They Do the Things They Do. *National Tax Journal* 50 (3): 657–82.

Gang of Six Plan. 2011.Senators Saxby Chambliss, Tom Coburn, Kent Conrad, Mike Crapo, Dick Durbin, and Mark Warner, *A Bipartisan Plan to Reduce Our Nation's Deficit: Executive Summary*. http://thehill.com/images/stories/gangofsix_plan.pdf.

Gravelle, Jane G. 1991. Income Consumption and Wage Taxation in a Life Cycle Model: Separating Efficiency from Redistribution. *American Economic Review* 81 (4): 985–95.

Gravelle, Jane G. 1994. *The Economic Effects of Taxing Capital Income*. Cambridge, MA: MIT Press.

Gravelle, Jane G. 2001. Whither Tax Depreciation? *National Tax Journal* 54 (3): 513–26.

Gravelle, Jane G. 2004. The Corporate Tax: Where Has It Been and Where Is It Going? *National Tax Journal* 57 (4): 903–23.

Gravelle, Jane G. 2007. *Issues in Dynamic Revenue Estimating*. CRS Report RL31949, Congressional Research Service, Washington, DC.

Gravelle Jane, G. 2008. *The Tax Reduction and Reform Act of 2007: An Overview.* CRS Report RL34249, Congressional Research Service, Washington, DC.

Gravelle, Jane G. 2009a. Corporate Income Tax: Incidence, Economic Effects, and Structural Issues. In *Tax Reform in the 21st Century*, edited by John G. Head and Richard Krever, 355–84. Amsterdam: Kluwer Law International.

Gravelle, Jane G. 2009b. International Corporate Tax Reform: Issues and Proposals. *Florida Tax Review* 9 (5): 469–96.

Gravelle, Jane G. 2009c. Tax Havens: International Tax Avoidance and Evasion. *National Tax Journal* 62:727–54.

Gravelle, Jane G. 2010a. International Tax Policy: Are We Heading in the Right Direction? In *Proceedings of the One-Hundredth-and-Third Annual Conference on Taxation*, 103–6. Washington, DC: National Tax Association.

Gravelle, Jane G. 2010b. Practical Tax Reform for a More Efficient Income Tax. *Virginia Tax Review* 30 (2): 389–406.

Gravelle, Jane G. 2010c. Reform of U.S. International Taxation: Alternatives. CRS Report RL34115, Congressional Research Service, Washington, DC.

Gravelle, Jane G. 2011a. International Corporate Tax Rate Comparisons and Policy Implications. CRS Report R41743, Congressional Research Service, Washington, DC.

Gravelle, Jane G. 2011b. Reducing Depreciation Allowances to Finance a Lower Corporate Tax Rate. *National Tax Journal* 64 (4): 1039–54.

Gravelle, Jane G. 2012. Moving to a Territorial Income Tax: Issues and Design. In *Proceedings of the One-Hundredth-Fifth Annual Conference on Taxation*. Washington, DC: National Tax Association,.

Gravelle, Jane G., and Jennifer C. Gravelle. 2007. How Federal Policy Makers Account for the Concerns of State and Local Governments in the Formulation of Federal Tax Policy. *National Tax Journal* 60 (3): 631–48.

Gravelle, Jane G., and Thomas L. Hungerford. 2008. Corporate Tax Reform: Should We Really Believe the Research? *Tax Notes* 121 (4): 419–38.

Gravelle, Jane G., and Kent A. Smetters, 2006. Does the Open Economy Assumption Really Mean That Labor Bears the Burden of a Capital Income Tax? *Advances in Economic Analysis and Policy* 6 (1), article 3.

Gravelle, Jennifer. 2011. Corporate Tax Incidence: A Review of Empirical Estimates and Analysis. Working Paper 2011–01, Congressional Budget Office, Washington, DC.

Gravelle, Jennifer C. 2013. Corporate Tax Incidence: Review of General Equilibrium Estimates and Analysis. *National Tax Journal* 66 (1): 185–214.

Hall, Bronwyn H., Jacques Mairesse, and Pierre Mohnen. 2010. Measuring the Returns to R&D. Working Paper 2010s-02, Cirano, Montreal, Canada.

Harberger, Arnold C. 1962. The Incidence of the Corporation Income Tax. *Journal of Political Economy* 70 (3): 215–40.

Internal Revenue Service. 2006. *Statistics of Income, Corporation Income Tax Returns*. Washington, DC: Internal Revenue Service.

Johansson, Åsa, Christopher Heady, Jens Arnold, Bert Brys, and Laura Vartia. 2008. Tax and Economic Growth. Working Paper 620, Organization for Economic Development and Cooperation, Paris, France.

Joint Committee on Taxation. 2010a. *Estimates of Federal Tax Expenditures for Fiscal Years 2010–2014*. Washington, DC: Joint Committee on Taxation.

Joint Committee on Taxation. 2010b. Estimates of the Revenue Effect of S.3018, The Bipartisan Simplification Act of 2010. Washington, DC: Joint Committee on Taxation, http://wyden.senate.gov/imo/media/doc/Score.pdf.

Joint Committee on Taxation. 2011a. *Background and Selected Issues Related to the U.S. International Tax System and Systems that Exempt Foreign Business Income. JCX-33–11*. Washington, DC: Joint Committee on Taxation.

Joint Committee on Taxation. 2011b. *Testimony of the Staff of the Joint Committee on Taxation Before the House Committee on Ways and Means Regarding Economic Modeling. JCX-48–11*. Washington, DC: Joint Committee on Taxation.

Kleinbard, Edward D. 2011. The Lessons of Stateless Income. *Tax Law Review* 65:99–171.

Kocieniewski, David. 2011. Rich Tax Breaks Bolster Makers of Video Games. *New York Times*, September 10, http://www.nytimes.com/2011/09/11/technology/rich-tax-breaks-bolster-video-game-makers.html

Krugman, Paul. 1994. Competitiveness: A Dangerous Obsession. *Foreign Affairs* 73 (2): 28–44.

McLure, William P., and Herman B. Bouma. 1989. The Taxation of Foreign Income from 1909 to 1989: How a Tilted Playing Field Developed. *Tax Notes* 43:1379–1410.

National Commission on Fiscal Responsibility and Reform. 2010. *The Moment of Truth: Report of the National Commission on Fiscal Responsibility and Reform*. Washington, DC: U.S. Government Printing Office.

Nunns, Jim. 2012. *How TPC Distributes the Corporate Income Tax*. Washington, DC: Urban-Brookings Tax Policy Center.

President's Advisory Panel on Federal Tax Reform. 2005. *Simple, Fair and Pro-Growth: Proposals to Fix America's Tax System*. Washington, DC: President's Advisory Panel on Federal Tax Reform.

Sherlock, Molly. 2001. The Section 199 Production Activities Deduction: Background and Analysis. CRS Report R41988, Congressional Research Service, Washington, DC.

Summers, Lawrence H. 1981. Taxation and Capital Accumulation in a Life Cycle Growth Model. *American Economic Review* 71 (4): 533–54.

U.S. Department of the Treasury. 2007. Treasury Tax Conference on Business Taxation and Global Competitiveness: Background Paper. U.S. Government Printing Office, Washington, DC.

U.S. Department of the Treasury. 2009. *General Explanations of the Administration's Fiscal Year 2010 Revenue Proposals*. Washington, DC: U.S. Government Printing Office.

U.S. Department of the Treasury. 2011. *General Explanations of the Administration's Fiscal Year 2012 Revenue Proposals*. Washington, DC: U.S. Government Printing Office.

U.S. Office of Management and Budget. 2011. *Analytical Perspectives: Budget of the United States Government, Fiscal Year 2012*. Washington, DC: U.S. Office of Management and Budget.

Discussion

Rosanne Altshuler

The essay that opens this chapter examines a broad range of ideas for reform of the corporate tax system. The policies have one important feature in common: all would increase the revenues we currently derive from the taxation of business income. The author, a noted expert on corporate tax policy, divides her analysis into three sections. The first section presents a large inventory of revenue-raising options. The next takes a step back and considers whether raising additional revenues from the corporate tax system should be off-limits for efficiency and competitiveness concerns. The final section evaluates some approaches to corporate base broadening that have been or are actively being discussed by policymakers.

Gravelle's conclusions should be of interest to economists and policymakers alike. Gravelle argues that policies that increase corporate tax payments should be squarely on the table. Her analysis suggests that there are numerous options available to policymakers that would raise additional tax revenues from corporations without worsening (and, in some cases, lessening) the distortions of the existing corporate tax system.

Gravelle presents readers with an exhaustive set of revenue raisers. The list includes corporate tax expenditures as well as options from various policy proposals floated in recent years. I have one quibble with this presentation. Almost all of the options include revenue estimates. But readers cannot readily compare the cost of many of the options because different methodologies, time periods, and baselines have been used to produce the revenue estimates. While difficult to do, conforming the estimates so that comparisons could be made across options would be helpful. This would also allow readers to roughly estimate how much the statutory corporate tax rate, or other rates, could be lowered in a revenue-neutral reform. Even without conforming the revenue estimates, however, one important theme emerges. There are a few large expenditures in terms of forgone revenue and a slew of smaller ones. Not surprisingly, the most costly expenditures in terms of forgone tax revenues—the deferral of taxation of foreign source income and accelerated depreciation for equipment—have been targets of reform proposals.

One goal of the conference associated with this book was to consider fiscal reforms that would lower the deficit. Gravelle offers up the corporate tax as a potential source of revenue in the second section of her essay. She reviews existing research on the efficiency costs of the corporate tax system and ends with a provocative conclusion: that raising the corporate tax rate would have few ramifications for the U.S. economy. While Gravelle does not quantify how much the rate could be raised without inducing significant economic costs, a 10 percentage point increase is implicit. She argues that given the small efficiency cost, raising revenue from the corporate tax should be on the table. This conclusion is based on her previous research using an open economy general equilibrium simulation model.

The model requires some strong assumptions and, of course, parameter estimates that are difficult to pin down. The general equilibrium model does not allow for the presence of debt financing, assumes a fixed worldwide capital stock, and assumes away the presence of excess economic profits, which is particularly important in the context of international taxation since multinationals are likely to generate returns in excess of normal returns to capital. Furthermore, the model assumes that the United States does not tax any of the foreign earnings of U.S. corporations. However, under the current tax system, both the domestic and foreign earnings of U.S. corporations are subject to U.S. taxation.

Table 7.8 presents estimates from Gravelle's work simulating the economic impact of a 10 percentage point cut in the corporate tax rate. This result forms the basis of the conclusion that the corporate tax could be increased at a small welfare cost. It is not clear, however, that the effects of a decrease in the statutory rate on output, revenue, and profit shifting would be symmetric to an increase in the rate. Corporate decisions may respond to increases and decreases in the corporate tax in ways that are not smooth. For example, consider the incentive to operate in the noncorporate form. As the statutory corporate rate goes up, it will eventually reach top individual rate, and corporations have an incentive to switch to the noncorporate form to the extent they are able. The foreign tax credit creates a cliff that affects a range of economic incentives.

It is quite possible, however, that as Gravelle writes, raising revenue from the corporate tax "would not be very harmful to economic growth and would have a negligible effect on U.S. income." One wonders, however, whether this result in itself is sufficient to guide policy. Many important questions are left unanswered. Do the results differ depending on how the revenue is raised? Will hiking the corporate rate to raise a certain amount of revenue have the same impact as the same revenue increase from base broadening? How does raising revenue from the corporate tax compare to raising revenue from the individual tax? How do the economic effects of raising revenue from corporate income compare to increasing the taxation of capital income at the individual level (through higher rates on dividends and capital gains, for example)?

Gravelle then evaluates a range of base-broadening proposals, including increasing the taxation of foreign source income and changes to depreciation allowances, the two largest tax expenditures in terms of lost revenues. This section is extremely useful. Gravelle provides the rationale for existing corporate tax benefits as well as the potential costs and benefits of their elimination. This is important as policy decisions certainly cannot be made based on revenue considerations alone.

Gravelle's essay presents an informed and comprehensive view of how corporate tax reform may be used to reduce the deficit from one of the foremost scholars of corporate tax policy. Although controversial in parts, the essay is a terrific starting point for anyone trying to get up to speed on how the United States taxes corporations, how much revenue is lost from exclusions from the corporate tax base, policies designed to encourage certain types of investments, and the merits of different reforms.

Discussion

Robert J. Carroll

Jane Gravelle provides a catalogue of potential ways to raise revenue from the corporate income tax base. She also evaluates various international reforms, analyzes the broad economic effects of raising additional revenue from the corporate income tax, and considers whether the corporate income tax can be viewed as falling primarily on labor or capital owners.

Broadening the Corporate Income Tax Base

Gravelle relies on a number of potential sources for estimates of possible revenue raisers impacts, including the Joint Committee on Taxation's annual tax expenditure pamphlet, the Congressional Budget Office's Options for Reducing the Deficit, House Ways and Means chairman Rangel's 2007 tax reform proposal (H.R. 3970), the Wyden-Gregg tax reform plan (S. 3018), and the administration's corporate revenue raisers included in its FY 2012 budget submission. Gravelle also includes some additional possible revenue raisers not included elsewhere.

The cataloguing of potential sources of revenue from the corporate income tax base is useful to the tax reform debate by indicating how much and from which provisions revenue could potentially be raised through base broadening. This information provides a sense for how much the corporate income tax rate could be lowered through a revenue-neutral base-broadening reform and where some of the trade-offs are with respect to base broadening and corporate rate reduction. Gravelle also suggests where some revenue beyond traditional tax expenditures might come to achieve additional reduction in the corporate income tax rate. She reports that most of the $136.7 billion in annual revenue from corporate tax expenditures can be attributed to a relatively small number of provisions with 59 percent of the revenue from the top five provisions and 85 percent of the revenue from the top ten provisions. Accelerated depreciation is the most important provision, accounting for nearly 22 percent of the revenue. Gravelle notes that a number of provisions would raise significant revenue from both C corporations, as well as pass-through businesses (e.g., S corporations, partnerships, limited liability corporations, and sole proprietorships), including accelerated depreciation, the production activity deduction, employee stock ownership plans, and the small business employer health credit. She notes, however, that eliminating some provisions for C corporations but maintaining them for pass-through businesses could pose significant administrative difficulties associated with the maintenance of separate systems.

The cataloguing of provisions also indicates that more than half of the revenue from corporate tax expenditures is concentrated in provisions with the three broad purposes of promoting investment (e.g., accelerated depreciation—22 percent), research (e.g., research and development credit and research expensing—13 percent), and socially orientated objectives (e.g., charitable contributions, tax-exempt bond financing, the low-income housing tax credit and new markets tax credit—18 percent). If, as Gravelle suggests, the corporate income tax rate could be reduced only to the 27 to 28 percent range with repeal of all tax expenditures, retaining the provisions with these objectives would imply that only half of this amount of corporate rate reduction could be achieved with base broadening that focuses on traditional tax expenditures.

In the current debate, much of the discussion on tax reform has focused on base broadening to repeal or reduce tax expenditures. In contrast, the Tax Reform Act of 1986 may be instructive on where an eventual tax reform plan may raise revenue: more than 40 percent of the 1986 act's $528 billion in tax increases was derived from nontax expenditures (Carroll, Cox, and Neubig 2011). The administration's fiscal year 2012 budget, for example, shows that additional base broadening is possible, since 59 percent of its proposed tax increases are not tax expenditures. As in 1986, the current tax reform effort is likely to include more base broadening than simply reducing or repealing tax expenditures.

Gravelle indicates where some of this additional revenue may come from. The tax plan put forward by Senators Ron Wyden (D-OR) and Dan Coats (R-IN) includes provisions that would raise additional revenue through an across-the-board limitation on the deduction for interest expenses ($16.3 billion annually) and two international tax changes that would eliminate the deferral of tax on active foreign source income and impose a per country foreign tax credit limit ($58.3 billion annually). Other possible revenue raisers that Gravelle identified include taxing large pass-through businesses as C corporations ($32 billion annually), repealing the corporate deduction for state and local income taxes ($25 billion annually), and capitalizing advertising expenses ($8 billion annually).

Reform of the U.S. System for Taxing International Income

Gravelle focuses on a number of potential changes to the U.S. system for taxing international income. One observation is that the current system creates a significant incentive for U.S. multinational corporations to keep foreign earnings outside the United States—the so-called lockout effect—a significant distortion. The United States is now unique as being the only country with both a high corporate income tax rate (39.0 percent, including both federal and state tax rates in 2014), and a worldwide system for taxing foreign source income. An important aspect of reform to the U.S. system for taxing international income, however, is that depending on important design elements, moving to either a worldwide or territorial system could raise additional revenue.

Also important to international tax reform is the rapidly changing global economy, where more of the world's economic growth is forecast to occur outside the United States over the next several decades, primarily in the developing world. Tax policy can be expected to play an important role in today's competitive world economy.

An analysis of headquarter location of Fortune Global 500 (FG500) companies between 2000 and 2012 found a significant rise in FG500 company headquarters in emerging market countries at the expense of developed countries (Kinrade and Neubig 2013). In 2012, the United States had forty-seven fewer headquarters in the FG500 than in 2000. All of the top ten countries with corporate income tax rates above 30 percent in 2012 had fewer FG500 company headquarters than in 2000. These shifts are not due to the relocation of headquarters, but instead the displacement from the FG500 by non-US companies in terms of revenue and the rise of state-owned enterprise. A prominent issue is the importance of U.S. multinationals to the U.S. economy and the extent to which they provide significant economic benefits directly and indirectly through their supply chains and distribution networks.

Globalization may make it easier for business and investors to reallocate capital in response to differences in countries' tax policies. In addition, globalization may amplify the effects of the United States being out of line with respect to the rest of the world.

Economic Benefits of a Lower Corporate Income Tax Rate

Gravelle concludes that the benefits to the U.S. economy from lowering the corporate income tax rate might well be small. In a simulation of a 10 percent percentage point cut in the corporate income tax rate, she reports small increases in output of 0.15 percent, with most of this gain being paid to foreigners in returns to their investment. This result is generally consistent with some earlier research evaluating the potential gains from a revenue-neutral reduction in the corporate income tax rate (U.S. Department of the Treasury 2007). The result from these earlier analyses, however, did not necessarily fully account for the extent to which some capital might respond to differentials in tax rates, the importance of firm-specific capital, or the sensitivity of the U.S. corporate income tax base to the differential in countries' tax rates. In the revenue-neutral reforms analyzed, a lower corporate tax rate, which reduces the tax on both new and existing investment at the time of the reform, is refinanced with base broadening consisting of the repeal of investment-related provisions whose tax advantages are focused on new investment.

There is considerable evidence that foreign direct investment is highly sensitive to differentials in countries tax rates (U.S. Department of the Treasury 2007). As well, research suggests that the corporate income tax base is sensitive to differentials in corporate income tax rates between countries, particularly as it relates to debt financing and income from intangibles (Clausing 2009). Some estimates suggest that the U.S. tax base may be smaller by as much as $300 billion annually due to such considerations. A lower corporate income tax rate would attract additional FDI and help expand the U.S. corporate income tax base. The former would result in greater economic output, while the latter would result in additional revenues that could be used in ways consistent with increased economic growth (e.g., further reductions in the corporate tax rate, reduction in federal debt).

Summary

Gravelle provides a broad view of base broadening that goes well beyond traditional tax expenditures. This may reflect the likely path of tax reform if the 1986 act is taken as a guide. An overly pessimistic view is taken on the potential economic benefits of a lower corporate income tax rate, with the implication that the corporate income tax could potentially be a source of additional revenue. This is at odds with the rate-reducing trends in other developed countries over the past several decades and does not fully embrace some of the economic research suggesting potential benefits from a lower corporate income tax rate, especially when viewed from the perspective of an increasingly integrated world economy.

References

Bull, Nicholas, Tim Down, and Pamela Moomau. 2011. Corporate Tax Reform: A Macroeconomic Perspective. *National Tax Journal* 64 (4): 923–41.

Carroll, Robert, Morgan Cox, and Tom Neubig. 2011. Tax Reform Lessons Composition of Tax Changes in the Tax Reform Act of 1986. In *EY Tax Insight*. Washington, DC: EY Center for Tax Policy.

Clausing, Kimberly A. 2009. Multinational Firm Tax Avoidance and Tax Policy. *National Tax Journal* 57 (4): 703–25.

de Mooij, Ruud, and Sjef Ederveen. 2008. Corporate Tax Elasticities: A Reader's Guide to Empirical Findings. *Oxford Review of Economic Policy* 24 (4): 680–97.

Gordon, Roger, and James R. Hines. 2002. International Taxation. In *Handbook of Public Economics*, edited by Alan J. Auerbach and Martin Feldstein, 1347–1421. Atlanta, GA: Elsevier.

Kinrade, Thomas, and Tom Neubig, 2013. Changing Headquarters Landscape, 2000–2012: Corporate Taxation and the Impact of Emerging Market Economies. *Daily Tax Report*, 142 DTR J-1, July 24, 2013.

Klassen, Kenneth J., and Stacie K. LaPlante. 2012. Are US Multinational Corporations Becoming More Aggressive Income Shifters? *Journal of Accounting Research* 50 (5): 1245–85.

U.S. Department of the Treasury. 2007. *Approaches to Improve the Competitiveness of the U.S. Business Tax System for the 21st Century*. Washington, DC: U.S. Department of Treasury.

8 The Dynamic Economic Effects of a U.S. Corporate Income Tax Rate Reduction

John W. Diamond, George R. Zodrow, Thomas S. Neubig, and Robert J. Carroll

The U.S. corporate income tax system has not been changed significantly since the much-celebrated Tax Reform Act of 1986 (TRA86). In the interim, most countries have dramatically reduced their statutory corporate income tax rates below the U.S. rate, prompted in large part by the inexorable forces of globalization and increasing international tax competition (Zodrow 2008). The U.S. statutory corporate income tax rate is now the highest in the world among industrialized countries, sparking concerns about the extent to which the tax system makes it difficult for the United States to compete successfully in the world economy today. These issues were the focus of a comprehensive report, *Approaches to Improve the Competitiveness of the U.S. Business Tax System for the 21st Century*, prepared by the U.S. Department of the Treasury (2007).

Such concerns have prompted calls for reform, ranging from dramatic changes in the corporate income tax system to replacing the income tax system with some form of consumption-based taxation. We focus on one such reform—a reduction in the statutory corporate income tax rate. Of course, a reduction in the corporate tax rate would have to be financed by expansion of the corporate tax base, an increase in other taxes, a reduction in spending, an increase in the deficit, or some combination of these. This analysis considers three potential financing alternatives: elimination of a wide range of business tax expenditures, an increase in individual income taxes on labor income, and a decrease in government expenditures in the form of income transfers. Each package is designed to be revenue neutral in a dynamic sense, that is, taking into account the effects of the reform over time on saving, investment, labor supply, and other macroeconomic variables. The dynamic analysis in this essay reflects simulations of the macroeconomic effects of reform using a modified version of a dynamic, overlapping-generations, computable general equilibrium model developed by Diamond and Zodrow.

We discuss the case for a significant reduction in the statutory corporate income tax rate in the United States in the following section, focusing on several key issues that must be addressed in any analysis of corporate income tax reform in the global economy. An outline of the model, including various extensions made to more accurately analyze the effects of such a reform, follows; details of the model are provided in Zodrow and Diamond (2013). We then present the simulation results.

The Case for a Corporate Income Tax Rate Cut

In this section, we describe the case for corporate income tax reform in the United States. We then discuss the case for a specific reform—a revenue-neutral corporate tax rate reduction, with business tax base broadening as the principal financing mechanism, similar to the approach used in TRA86 (Diamond and Zodrow 2011); this discussion includes a brief description of some relevant empirical work. We also compare the advantages and disadvantages of this particular reform to the alternative approach of keeping the statutory tax rate at its current relatively high level while adding investment incentives.

The Need for Reform

Policymakers and economists have long advocated income tax reforms that lower tax rates while broadening the base of the tax structure by eliminating tax expenditures, generally defined as deviations from a broad-based income tax. TRA86 is a prime example in the United States of this classic approach to tax reform.[1] Such reforms are generally desirable because they reduce costly distortions of economic decisions and thus promote economic growth and economic efficiency in resource allocation, simplify tax administration and compliance, reduce incentives for tax evasion and tax avoidance, and create both the perception and the reality of a fairer tax system.

These arguments are especially compelling in the case of the corporate income tax, which has often been characterized as a singularly complex and inefficient tax instrument that significantly distorts a wide variety of decisions, including those regarding asset mix and thus the allocation of investment across different industries, the method of finance (debt versus equity in the form of retained earnings or new share issues), organizational form (corporate versus noncorporate), and the mix of retentions, dividends paid, and share repurchases (Gravelle 1994; Cnossen 1996; U.S. Department of the Treasury 2007; Nicodème 2008). Moreover, in the case of equity finance, the magnitude of these distortions is increased to the extent that the effective tax rate on corporate income is increased by the double taxation of such income at both the business level under the corporate tax and then again at the individual level as dividends or capital gains (and under the estate tax), although to an increasingly limited extent).[2] The taxation of capital income inherent in the corporate income tax also reduces saving and investment, which in turn reduces the size of the capital stock, labor productivity, and wage growth.

In addition, many recent proposals for tax reform have focused on international issues, especially increasing international capital mobility, more aggressive international tax competition from both advanced and emerging economies, and legitimate tax planning that arises in response to significant differences in tax rates across countries, often referred to as income shifting.[3] Proponents of such reforms argue that both statutory tax rates and the overall tax burden on capital income in the United States are quite high by international standards and that the corporate income tax should be reformed in the interest of attracting and retaining mobile capital, promoting economic growth, improving economic efficiency, reducing opportunities for tax arbitrage, and reducing administrative and compliance costs.[4] The ongoing process of globalization also implies that the tax system increasingly has important effects on the competitiveness of U.S. multinationals and the investment decisions of multinationals based in both the United States and other countries. All of these factors suggest that the corporate income tax is ripe for reform.

The need for corporate income tax reform has also been recognized in the political arena. Indeed, both parties have supported reform plans that included reductions in the corporate income tax rate, including House Ways and Means Committee chair Dave Camp's tax reform discussion draft and President Obama's framework for reforming business taxation.[5] The case for such an approach is buttressed by the U.S. Department of the Treasury (2007, i) report noted above, which stresses that "the United States, which had a low corporate tax rate in the late 1980s as compared to other countries in the Organisation for Economic Co-operation and Development (OECD), now has the second-highest statutory corporate tax rate among OECD countries. Moreover other

OECD countries continue to reduce their corporate income tax rates leaving the United States further behind."

Clear evidence of this trend in corporate tax rates is provided by a comprehensive data set on international statutory and effective marginal tax rates (EMTRs) in nineteen OECD countries maintained by the Institute for Fiscal Studies (IFS).[6] Prior to the passage of TRA86, the U.S. statutory corporate income tax rate, including both federal and state corporate income taxes, was 49.6 percent, roughly equal to the average tax rate of the G7 countries and 3.3 percentage points higher than the (unweighted) average rate for the nineteen-country sample of 46.3 percent. In 1987, the U.S. combined statutory rate fell to 38.4 percent, 8.0 percentage points below the G7 average rate of 46.4 percent and 6.0 percentage points lower than the nineteen-country average rate of 44.4 percent. However, by 2005 (the last year of the IFS data available at the time of publication), the U.S. statutory tax rate of 39.3 percent was 3.0 percentage points above the G7 average rate of 36.3 percent and 7.9 percentage points higher than the nineteen-country average rate of 31.4 percent, in the latter case reflecting a swing of nearly 14 percentage points in relative statutory rates since the passage of TRA86. Recent rate reductions among the OECD countries have only exacerbated these trends; indeed, with recent reforms in Japan (formerly the highest tax country), the United States in 2013 had the highest combined national and subnational corporate income tax rate among the thirty-nine member nations of the OECD (table 8.1).

A roughly similar, though less pronounced, pattern is observed for EMTRs, defined by the IFS as the business-level tax rate applied to a marginal (breakeven) equity-financed investment in plant and machinery. Because TRA86 was in general a base-broadening, rate-reducing reform, it left the EMTR in the United States largely unchanged; indeed, it increased slightly from 21.8 to 22.9 percent between 1986 and 1987. In 1987, the EMTR in the United States was 5.2 percentage points below the G7 average rate of 28.1 percent and 4.8 percentage points below the nineteen-country sample average of 27.7 percent. However, by 2005, the EMTR in the United States had increased slightly, while EMTRs in the other OECD countries had declined considerably; as a result, the EMTR in the United States, 23.6 percent, was equal to the G7 average and 3.3 percentage points higher than the nineteen-country sample average of 20.3 percent.

As discussed above, relatively high corporate income taxes cause a variety of problems, distorting a wide variety of economic decisions,

Table 8.1
Statutory Corporate Income Tax Rates, 2013 (Combined National and Subnational)

Country	Statutory Tax Rate %
Australia	30.0
Austria	25.0
Belgium	34.0
Canada	26.1
Chile	20.0
Czech Republic	19.0
Denmark	25.0
Estonia	21.0
Finland	24.5
France	34.4
Germany	30.2
Greece	26.0
Hungary	19.0
Iceland	20.0
Ireland	12.5
Israel	25.0
Italy	27.5
Japan	37.0
Korea	24.2
Luxembourg	29.2
Mexico	30.0
Netherlands	25.0
New Zealand	28.0
Norway	28.0
Poland	19.0
Portugal	31.5
Slovak Republic	23.0
Slovenia	17.0
Spain	30.0
Sweden	22.0
Switzerland	21.1
Turkey	20.0
United Kingdom	23.0
United States	39.1

Source: OECD Tax Database, Corporate and Capital Income Taxes, Table II.1, http://www.oecd.org/ctp/tax-policy/tax-database.htm#C_CorporateCapital.

magnifying problems of administration and compliance, and increasing incentives for tax arbitrage. Beyond these problems, a central question is the degree to which the relatively high tax rates on capital income in the United States reduce investment and thus the size of the capital stock, thereby resulting in lower levels of output, reduced growth rates, and diminished labor productivity and thus lower wages and living standards. Although the early empirical evidence on the tax sensitivity of investment was mixed, the more recent evidence, which accounts for the costs of adjusting the capital stock in response to changes in taxes and uses improved econometric techniques, is consistent with significant effects of taxes on investment as captured by tax-induced changes in the cost of capital (Cummins, Hassett, and Hubbard 1994; Hassett and Newmar 2008; de Mooij and Ederveen 2008). For example, de Mooij and Ederveen (2008) conduct a meta-analysis of the literature on tax effects on various corporate decisions and conclude that a consensus estimate of the elasticity of domestic investment with respect to the cost of capital is between -0.5 and -1.0. They also provide consensus estimates of the corporate tax rate semielasticities of the corporate share of business activity (-0.7) and the corporate debt-asset ratio (0.3).

In addition, of particular interest in the modern global economy is whether high corporate tax rates reduce foreign direct investment (FDI). Again, empirical evidence demonstrates clearly that FDI is sensitive to tax factors and suggests that this sensitivity is increasing over time. For example, recent surveys by Gordon and Hines (2002) and de Mooij and Ederveen (2003, 2005, 2008) conclude that FDI is quite responsive to corporate tax rates, with the most recent and careful studies tending to obtain the largest estimates (Altshuler and Grubert 2006). For example, de Mooij and Ederveen (2008) conclude that a consensus estimate of the semielasticity of foreign direct investment with respect to the effective marginal tax rate is -4.0, and with respect to the effective average tax rate which, as will be discussed below, better captures tax effects on the location of highly mobile firm-specific capital that earns economic rents, of -3.2.

If the relatively high rate of corporate income taxation in the United States is a problem that should be addressed with reform, the next logical question is the direction that such a reform should take. In this essay, we focus on reform of the existing corporate income tax system rather than fundamental tax reform in the form of replacing the existing income tax with some form of consumption-based tax system.[7] In particular, we analyze the dynamic economic effects of a reduction in the statutory corporate income tax rate, financed in three alternative ways under the constraint of dynamic revenue neutrality. Before proceeding to a description of the model and a simulation analysis of the effects of corporate income tax rate reduction, we examine in more detail the case for such a reform, especially in comparison to the alternative—discussed at length in the U.S. Department of the Treasury (2007) report—of reducing effective marginal tax rates by increasing tax incentives for new investment while maintaining statutory tax rates at relatively high levels.

Rate Reduction versus Tax Incentives

A question that inevitably arises in discussions of lowering the corporate tax rate is whether maintaining a high statutory rate, coupled with investment incentives such as an investment tax credit or more accelerated depreciation allowances (including partial expensing) for new investment, is not a preferable approach. The investment incentive approach is often touted as having more "bang for the buck" in that the revenue cost per dollar of induced investment is lower than with a rate reduction;[8] that is, revenue losses are comparatively small because the new tax incentives apply only to new investment, while the relatively high statutory rate continues to apply to the income earned by old investments.[9] In addition, the use of investment incentives implies that the effective marginal tax rate applied to normal returns is reduced, while above-normal returns are still taxed at the statutory rate. By comparison, revenue losses are argued to be significantly higher under a reduction in the statutory tax rate because the rate reduction applies to both the income earned by old investments and by investments that generate above-normal returns. Finally, to the extent that a lower statutory corporate tax rate increases a positive rate differential between the personal and corporate income tax rates, it creates incentives for shifting income from the personal tax base to the corporate tax base (Gordon and Slemrod 2000).

Each of these three arguments clearly has some validity; nevertheless, each must also be qualified. First, there is no question that a corporate tax rate reduction benefits existing investments, an issue that does not arise with investment incentives. However, the bang for the buck from rate reduction may not be as small as sometimes envisioned, because the rate cut may result in larger investment responses than those associated with investment incentives in the form of increased deductions from income. As Neubig (2007) stressed, the key distinction is that investment incentives lower the taxation only of "normal" returns to investment, while a rate reduction applies to both normal and "above-normal" returns. As a result, to the extent that above-normal returns reflect firm-specific rents attributable to highly mobile investments in invention and innovation or firm-created intangible assets, a lower corporate tax rate will stimulate such investments by lowering the average effective tax on such returns—a result that does not obtain under investment incentives.

Second—and closely related—is the fact that although a lower statutory tax rate reduces the taxation of above-normal returns, the implications of such reduced taxation of above-normal returns must be examined carefully (Zodrow 2010). To the extent that above-normal returns are location specific (e.g., rents associated with access to lucrative markets), a statutory tax rate reduction lowers the level of taxation of relatively immobile factors of production. However, to the extent that above-normal returns are firm specific (e.g., returns that arise from unique entrepreneurial or managerial skills, or intangibles such as unique technological knowledge, proprietary production techniques, patents, goodwill, and reputations), a lower statutory tax rate is desirable because it increases the returns to those investments, including especially investments by multinationals—both those based in the United States and in other countries—that represent capital that is highly mobile internationally. By comparison, investment incentives are of relatively little value to firms with assets that generate firm-specific above-normal returns, as their level of profit will be affected primarily by the statutory tax rate applied to such returns. Indeed, Devereux and Griffith (2003) argue that under these circumstances, the key tax factor affecting investment decisions is the average effective tax rate (AETR), which they define as a weighted average of the EMTR and an adjusted statutory tax rate, with the weights equal to the normal and above-normal rates of return available on a representative firm's investments.[10]

Recent empirical evidence confirms the importance of AETRs and thus statutory tax rates in determining the investment decisions of U.S. multinationals that are relatively likely to make investments that generate above-normal returns. For example, Devereux and Griffith (2003) construct a model in which the level of investment is determined primarily by the effective marginal tax rate, while the choice of investment location among several alternative options is determined primarily by the average effective tax rate. Their empirical results indicate that a 1 percentage point increase in the effective average tax rate in a country reduces the probabilities that a U.S. firm will choose to produce there by between 0.5 and 1.3 percentage points. Many other studies have linked FDI and average tax rates and found rather high elasticities. Finally, recent empirical evidence indicates that the dispersion of relative profitability in the United States has increased significantly in recent years, suggesting an increase in the relative importance of investments that generate above-normal returns (Auerbach 2006).

Third, a corporate tax rate that is low relative to the top personal income tax rate does encourage shifting labor income to a corporation, and recent empirical work suggests that the magnitude of this effect is important. For example, Gordon and Slemrod (2000) estimate that a 1 percentage point increase in the tax rate differential between corporate and personal income raises reported personal income by 3.2 percent. Of course, the importance of this effect depends on the extent to which tax administration and enforcement are effective in limiting opportunities for tax rate arbitrage and on the extent to which a decrease in the relative corporate income tax rate results only in deferral, rather than complete exemption, of individual-level taxation on the income—for example, because the income is eventually distributed as taxable dividends, capital gains, or wages.

Lower statutory tax rates have the important advantage of reducing the importance of tax planning in all types of business decision making. A high statutory corporate tax rate exacerbates the tax bias favoring debt financing over issuing new shares or retained earnings. It also encourages new firms to structure if possible as S corporations or partnerships, where income is taxed currently at the individual owners' personal tax rates. A high statutory corporate tax rate encourages firms to use legal tax planning strategies, including supply chain management, location of debt, and location of patents and other intangible assets, to reduce the share of taxable income realized in relatively high-tax-rate countries like the United States, while increasing the share of taxable income realized in relatively low-tax countries. Such "financial reallocation," which is much easier to put into effect than physical reallocation of capital assets, can reduce taxable corporate income reported and taxes paid in high statutory tax rate countries. In addition, a high corporate tax rate increases the returns to illegal tax evasion.

A number of empirical studies show that tax rate arbitrage takes place despite various governmental mechanisms, such as thin capitalization rules, advance pricing agreements, interest allocation rules, and special treatment of passive investment income. Taken together, these empirical results, discussed in detail in appendix B, strongly suggest that a lower U.S. corporate tax rate would have a positive effect on the U.S. corporate tax base due to reduced tax arbitrage, thereby offsetting a significant part of any static revenue loss.

Another potentially important rationale for a low statutory corporate income tax rate is the "headline tax rate" argument. Specifically, multinationals may, at least in the initial stages of choosing among competing locations, focus on a comparison of statutory tax rates across competing locations, independent of special provisions that might lower the effective marginal tax rate, such as accelerated depreciation allowances, which are considered only in a subsequent evaluation of countries that make the short list of potential investment locations.

For all these reasons, a move to a corporate income tax with a lower statutory rate could be desirable in the United States, depending on the overall design of the tax reform. This is especially true since the statutory tax rate in the United States is the second highest among the OECD countries and differentials in statutory tax rates between the United States and its competitors have been increasing recently. Moreover, recent experience around the world suggests that many countries have arrived at this same conclusion. The tax reform experience in the mid-1980s, including TRA86 in the United States, was largely one of base-broadening, rate-reducing reforms (Boskin and McLure 1990). Moreover, more recent tax changes, prompted in large part by increasing international tax competition in the face of increasing globalization, have followed a similar pattern. In particular, Devereux (2007) stresses that statutory tax rates in the OECD have fallen significantly in recent years, but that these rate reductions have been accompanied by base-broadening efforts, so that overall corporate tax revenues as well as average and especially effective marginal tax rates have declined considerably less; indeed, he notes that despite significant statutory rate reductions, corporate tax revenues as a fraction of GDP have been roughly constant over the past forty years, and indeed they have increased in recent years. More generally, a revenue-neutral lowering of the corporate tax rate has both positive and negative effects, and its desirability can be determined only with an explicit analysis of its economic effects. We turn next to the details of our analysis of this issue.

Modeling the Effects of a Corporate Income Tax Rate Reduction

In this and the following section, we present our analysis of the economic effects of lowering the corporate income tax rate. This section first provides a short description of the dynamic, overlapping-generations, computable general equilibrium model used for our simulation analysis and then turns to a number of extensions to the basic model that were made for purposes of this analysis. The simulation results are presented in the following section.

Our basic model is a dynamic general equilibrium model of the U.S. economy that is well suited for analyzing major business tax reforms. It builds on several other well-known general equilibrium models but includes important extensions that facilitate the analysis of the short- and long-run economic effects of tax policy changes. Versions of the model have been used in analyses of tax reforms by the U.S. Department of the Treasury (President's Advisory Panel on Federal Tax Reform 2005), the Congressional Joint Committee on Taxation (Joint Committee on Taxation 2005), and in a number of other recent tax policy studies (Diamond and Zodrow 2007, 2008a; Diamond and Viard 2008; Carroll et al. 2010; Zodrow and Diamond 2013).

Overview of the Basic Model

The distinguishing feature of the analytical approach used in the basic model is the treatment of both composite consumption goods and owner-occupied and rental housing markets in the context of a dynamic, overlapping-generations, life cycle, computable general equilibrium model that explicitly calculates reform-induced changes in all asset values during the transition to a new equilibrium.

The model has owner-occupied housing and rental housing production sectors, and corporate and noncorporate composite good production sectors that include all nonhousing goods and services. The time path of investment demands in all production sectors is modeled explicitly, taking into account capital stock adjustment costs. On the consumption side, consumer demands for all housing and nonhousing goods and for a bequest are modeled using an overlapping-generations structure in which a representative individual in each generation maximizes lifetime utility.

Thus, the model allows a fairly detailed description of both the transitional and the long-run effects of implementing a base-broadening, rate-reducing corporate income tax reform. The basic structure of the model combines various features from similar and well-known models constructed by Auerbach and Kotlikoff (1987), Goulder and Summers (1989), Goulder (1989), Keuschnigg (1990), Fullerton and Rogers (1993), and Hayashi (1982). A short description of the structure of the model and details on the calibration of the initial equilibrium are provided in appendix C. More detailed descriptions of the basic model are provided in Diamond and Zodrow (2007, 2008a) and Zodrow and Diamond (2013).

Extensions to the Basic Model

The basic model is extended in this analysis in several ways in order to better capture the economic effects of eliminating business tax expenditures and reducing the corporate income tax rate. The key feature of the reform proposal being analyzed is a significant reduction in the corporate income tax rate in the United States, coupled with the elimination of a wide variety of business tax expenditures. In the benchmark case analyzed, the reform analyzed is revenue neutral, with the corporate rate reduction fully financed by the elimination of business tax expenditures. Note that revenue neutrality in this context is defined in the aggregate, that is, for both the corporate and noncorporate business sectors. This implies that effective tax rates on the noncorporate sector would increase, since the elimination of noncorporate tax expenditures is not offset by a reduction in the personal income tax rates at which such income is taxed. As a result, the effective tax rate differential between the corporate and noncorporate sectors is narrowed, which improves the efficiency of capital allocation across the two sectors,[11] but at the same time raises effective tax rates on, and thus reduces investment in, the noncorporate sector.[12]

In order to analyze these reforms, the model is extended to take into account explicitly a wide variety of such business tax expenditures, modeling in detail how their elimination would affect the cost of capital in the corporate and noncorporate sectors. Business tax expenditures are classified into four types with different economic effects: rate-reducing preferences, production incentives, investment incentives, and lump-sum deductions.[13] The classification of tax expenditures and descriptions of their different economic effects are provided in appendix A.

In addition to this differentiated modeling business tax expenditures, we modify the structure of the basic model in three ways to better capture the effects of the base-broadening, rate-reducing reform analyzed in this essay. Specifically, we add an imperfectly competitive sector earning above-normal returns, allow for reform-induced capital inflows from abroad, and consider in a relatively ad hoc way the effect of a rate reduction on corporate tax rate arbitrage. The latter two extensions are especially important in modeling the effects of tax reform in the modern globalized economy and have been the focus of much recent attention, including—among many others—reports issued by the President's Advisory Panel of Federal Tax Reform (2005) and the U.S. Department of the Treasury (2007); both of these reports considered sweeping reforms to the taxation of foreign income, including the possible movement from the current worldwide tax system with a foreign tax credit to a "territorial" tax system that would exempt active foreign source income from tax and is currently being debated in Congress and the broader policymaking community. Appendix B describes these three additional model extensions in detail.

Simulation Results

In this section, we report the results of several simulations of rate-reducing corporate income tax reforms with alternative deficit-neutral financing approaches. We focus on short-run and long-run effects on GDP, but include some discussion of reform-induced changes in other macroeconomic variables as well.

Overview of Modeling

We begin with a dynamic revenue-neutral corporate tax rate reduction, assuming the elimination of all business tax expenditures, simulated in the basic Diamond-Zodrow model. We then consider the implications of adding the three extensions to the basic model described above: an imperfectly competitive sector, an elastic supply of foreign capital, and a reduction in tax rate arbitrage.

We also consider an alternative treatment of business tax expenditures that follows the approach used in the U.S. Department of the Treasury (2007). The Treasury report assumed that all business tax expenditures other than accelerated depreciation have no effects on marginal investment decisions, that is, they do not affect the cost of capital and thus the level of investment. Although this is true for tax expenditures that can accurately be characterized as lump sum in nature, the vast majority of the tax expenditures detailed in table 8.2 reflect investment incentives, production incentives, or rate reductions

Table 8.2
Business Tax Expenditures, Average Annual FY 2008

Tax Expenditure Item	Corporate (billions)	Noncorporate (billions)	Category
Business synthetic tax expenditures			
Inventory property sales source rule exception	$6.8	$0.0	II
Deduction for income attributable to domestic production activities	5.5	1.8	PI
General science, space, and technology credit for increasing research activities	4.9	0.1	II
Housing: credit for low-income housing	4.8	0.0	PI
Inventory methods and valuation: last in, first out	3.5	0.5	II
Reduced rates on first $10 million of corporate taxable income	3.3	0.0	RR
Expensing of research and experimental expenditures	3.1	0.1	II
Deferral of gain on like-kind exchanges	3.0	0.0	II
Exclusion of investment income on life insurance and annuity contracts (estimate of $26.8 billion ignored on noncorporate side)	2.6	0.0	DL
Lower of cost or market	2.2	0.6	II
Expensing of exploration and development costs: oil and gas	2.1	0.0	II
Special treatment of life insurance company reserves	2.0	0.0	PI
Financial institutions: exemption of credit union income	1.4	0.0	RR
Excess of percentage over cost depletion: oil and gas	1.3	0.0	II
Deferral of gain on nondealer installment sales	1.1	0.5	PI
Separate grouping of affiliated financial companies	1.0	0.0	DL
Special deduction for Blue Cross and Blue Shield companies	1.0	0.0	PI
Expensing under section 179 of depreciable business property	1.0	4.4	II
60–40 rule for gain or loss from section 1256 contracts	0.1	2.2	II
Accelerated depreciation tax expenditure	19.6	4.9	II
JCT social spending business tax expenditures			

Table 8.2
(continued)

Tax Expenditure Item	Corporate (billions)	Noncorporate (billions)	Category
Social services: deduction for charitable contributions other than for education and health	2.4	0.0	DL
Gulf opportunity zone	0.3	1.3	PI
Other tax expenditures	8.7	4.7	
Total tax expenditures	**81.7**	**21.1**	

Note: RR = rate reducing; PI = production incentive; II = investment incentive; DL = deduction lump sum.
Source: JCT (2008).

that would affect the cost of capital. As noted previously, recent empirical evidence is consistent with the view that reductions in the cost of capital have a positive effect on investment, as predicted by the theory of firm behavior (Hassett and Newmark 2008). Accordingly, in most of our simulations, we distinguish between the different tax expenditures and model explicitly the effects of investment incentives, production incentives, or rate reductions in lowering the cost of capital; we refer to this as "differentiated treatment of business tax expenditures."

In two of our simulations (one with the basic model and one with the extended model), we examine the effects of adopting the Treasury approach of treating all business tax expenditures other than accelerated depreciation as lump-sum deductions. Note that one possible rationale for this approach is that our analysis understates the efficiency gains from a base-broadening, rate-reducing corporate income tax reform because it ignores the benefits of improved intrasectoral allocation of capital and reduced reliance on debt finance. These effects might be significant, as the Congressional Budget Office (2005) estimates that effective corporate taxes on different types of assets vary widely. Such variation in effective tax rates suggests that intrasectoral distortions are sizable, and moving to a more neutral system could generate some modest additional efficiency gains.[14]

Finally, we consider three modified versions of rate-reducing corporate income tax reforms. In each of these simulations, the federal corporate income tax is reduced, but the extent of corporate income base broadening is either limited to dampen its negative effects on investment incentives or there is no base broadening and the lost revenues are made up with a proportional increase in wage taxes or reductions in government spending in the form of transfer payments.

Corporate Rate Reduction with Business Tax Base Broadening

The first simulation considers a business base-broadening, corporate rate-reducing reform. All of the business income tax expenditures listed in table 8.2, including special provisions for corporate, noncorporate, and rental housing, are eliminated, with all of the resulting increase in revenues devoted solely to corporate income tax rate reduction.[15] With the elimination of $81.7 billion in annual corporate tax expenditures and an additional $21.1 billion in annual noncorporate tax expenditures (with no offsetting rate decrease for noncorporate income), a dramatic reduction in the federal corporate income tax rate is possible.[16] Initially the corporate rate declines from 35 to 25.6 percent, and in the long run the corporate rate declines to 19.7 percent.[17] As shown in table 8.3, the effects of such a reform on GDP, however, are moderately negative in the long run, as GDP increases by 0.08 percent two years after the enactment of reform, but then declines by 0.01 percent after five years, 0.14 percent after 10 years, 0.30 percent after 20 years, 0.51 percent after 50 years, and 0.56 percent in the long run (150 years). The 50-year figure translates into a loss of GDP per household of $1,081 (in 2011 dollars).

These results reflect the classic problem with a base-broadening, rate-reducing reform of the corporate income tax—the combination of reducing the rate and eliminating tax expenditures (the vast majority of which are assumed to reduce the cost of capital at the margin in our analysis) has offsetting effects on the incentives for new investment,

Table 8.3
Dynamic Macroeconomic Effects of Revenue-Neutral Corporate Rate Reduction Financed by Repealing All Business Tax Expenditures with Basic Model (percentage changes from initial steady states)

Years after Reform	2	5	10	20	50	150
GDP	0.08%	-0.01%	-0.14%	-0.30%	-0.51%	-0.56%
Capital stock	-0.19	-0.64	-1.15	-1.72	-2.22	-2.35
Labor supply	-0.09	-0.10	-0.08	-0.07	-0.07	-0.06
Consumption	0.26	0.03	-0.19	-0.33	-0.17	-0.14
Investment	-2.57	-2.65	-2.76	-2.81	-2.95	-2.99

Note: Basic Diamond-Zodrow model with differentiated treatment of business tax expenditures.

and the rate reduction reduces revenues on income earned by existing capital.[18] The reduction in revenues implies that the tax rate is higher than it would be in the absence of this effect, which in turn reduces incentives for new investment. Indeed, investment decreases by 2.57 percent two years after the enactment of reform, 2.65 percent after five years, 2.76 percent after 10 years, and 2.99 percent in the long run. The smaller capital stock (a decline of 2.35 percent in the long run) implies that labor is less productive, wages decline, and labor supply declines as well, by 0.06 percent in the long run.

These negative macroeconomic effects are exacerbated when an imperfectly competitive sector is added to the model, as the corporate rate reduction applies to the above-normal returns earned in this sector, further driving down revenues and thus further limiting the rate reductions that can be achieved with a revenue-neutral reform. Allowing for an elastic supply of foreign capital in principle could increase the amount of reform-induced investment, especially in the imperfectly competitive sector where above-normal returns are taxed at lower rates. However, the net effect of the reform on after-tax interest rates is very small, as the beneficial effects of the rate cut are roughly offset by the negative effects of eliminating tax expenditures that benefit capital investment. This in turn implies that changes in capital inflows and outflows, which are assumed to be determined by differences in relative after-tax interest rates, are similarly very small.[19] More positive results occur, however, when reform-induced reductions in tax rate arbitrage are added to the model, which results in higher revenues at each tax rate. Thus, reduced tax arbitrage results in a reduction in the corporate tax rate that does not require offsetting base-broadening measures that increase the cost of capital and reduce investment. Indeed, the effects of incorporating reduced tax rate arbitrage are sufficiently large that implementation of the base-broadening, rate-reducing reform results in small gains in GDP in the model.

The effects of incorporating the three additions to the basic Diamond-Zodrow model are shown in table 8.4. In this simulation, the changes in GDP are small but positive, always on the order of 0.1 to 0.2 percent and equal to 0.12 percent in the long run. The effects of corporate base broadening and reduced tax arbitrage allow the corporate tax rate to be reduced to 16.8 percent in the long run.

These results may appear to be surprising given the negligible or slightly positive effects on GDP from a base-broadening, rate-reducing reform reported by the U.S. Department of the Treasury (2007) that did

Table 8.4
Dynamic Macroeconomic Effects of Revenue-Neutral Corporate Rate Reduction Financed by Repealing All Business Tax Expenditures with Expanded Model (percentage changes from initial steady states)

Years After Reform	2	5	10	20	50	150
GDP	0.11%	0.17%	0.19%	0.22%	0.18%	0.12%
Capital stock	0.31	-0.25	-0.21	-0.20	-0.23	-0.36
Labor supply	-0.13	-0.17	-0.17	-0.16	-0.17	-0.16
Consumption	0.47	0.25	0.21	0.28	0.70	0.73
Investment	-1.16	-1.06	-0.91	-0.77	-0.78	-0.94

Note: Diamond-Zodrow model with differentiated treatment of business tax expenditures, imperfectly competitive sector, foreign capital flows, and tax rate arbitrage.

not consider reductions in tax arbitrage. The Treasury study examined the effects of eliminating an average $93.2 billion in corporate tax expenditures[20] and an additional $39.4 billion in noncorporate tax expenditures (although the effect of eliminating these noncorporate tax expenditures on the corporate tax rate was largely eliminated by assuming that noncorporate income was taxed at a lower rate). The Treasury analysis assumed that all tax expenditures other than accelerated depreciation had no effects on marginal investment decisions, that is, they did not affect the cost of capital and thus the level of investment. At the same time, however, our analysis ignores the efficiency gains that would arise from eliminating intrasectoral distortions in the allocation of capital and reducing tax incentives for debt finance, so that the Treasury treatment might be rationalized as a rather ad hoc means of adjusting the results to reflect the potential for such efficiency gains.

Primarily for purposes of comparison to the Treasury results, we provide two sets of simulation results for the case in which all tax expenditures other than accelerated depreciation are treated as lump-sum deductions. In the first case, we follow Treasury in assuming that all markets are perfectly competitive, the economy is closed, and there is no income shifting. However, we maintain our assumption that noncorporate tax expenditures are also eliminated, with no offsetting decrease in the tax rate on income that is passed through to the owners of noncorporate businesses. In this case, as shown in table 8.5, the effects of eliminating all business tax expenditures and lowering the corporate tax rate are, unsurprisingly, significantly more positive than

Table 8.5
Dynamic Macroeconomic Effects of Revenue-Neutral Corporate Rate Reduction Financed by Repealing All Business Tax Expenditures with All Expenditures Treated as Lump Sum except Accelerated Depreciation with Basic Model (percentage changes from initial steady states)

Years after Reform	2	5	10	20	50	150
GDP	0.12%	0.27%	0.41%	-0.51%	0.53%	0.52%
Capital stock	-0.08	-0.22	-0.25	-0.11	0.07	0.06
Labor supply	–0.01	0.00	0.01	0.02	0.01	0.01
Consumption	0.02	-0.12	-0.15	0.00	0.51	0.60
Investment	-0.97	-0.58	-0.24	0.00	0.00	-0.01

Note: Basic Diamond-Zodrow model.

Table 8.6
Dynamic Macroeconomic Effects of Revenue-Neutral Corporate Rate Reduction Financed by Repealing All Business Tax Expenditures, with All Expenditures Treated as Lump Sum except Accelerated Depreciation with Expanded Model (percentage changes from initial steady states)

Years After Reform	2	5	10	20	50	150
GDP	0.17%	0.46%	0.77%	1.09%	1.25%	1.25%
Capital Stock	0.29	0.35	0.75	1.46	1.84	1.85
Labor Supply	-0.06	-0.07	-0.07	-0.08	-0.10	-0.10
Consumption	0.26	0.20	0.30	0.66	1.40	1.58
Investment	0.41	1.10	1.70	2.30	2.26	2.24

Diamond-Zodrow model with imperfectly competitive sector, foreign capital flows, and tax rate arbitrage.

when virtually all tax expenditures are assumed to affect the cost of capital (compare to table 8.3). Indeed, rather than declining, GDP increases by 0.12 percent two years after the enactment of reform, 0.27 percent after five years, 0.41 percent after ten years, and 0.52 percent in the long run. The long-run effect translates into an increase in GDP per household of $1,104. The corporate tax rate declines significantly in this case—to 20.3 percent initially and 17.0 percent in the long run.

For the reasons discussed above, the magnitudes of these positive effects are increased when the model is expanded to include an imperfectly competitive sector, foreign capital flows, and especially the income-shifting response. For example, as shown in table 8.6, GDP increases by 0.17 percent two years after the enactment of reform, 0.46

percent after five years, 0.77 percent after ten years, and 1.25 percent in the long run. The corporate tax rate declines to 20.0 percent initially and 12.9 percent in the long run. The treatment of tax expenditures other than accelerated depreciation is thus critical in determining the simulated effects of a base-broadening, rate-reducing corporate income tax reform.

We now return to our standard approach under which we assume that virtually all business tax expenditures reduce the cost of capital (rather than treating all such expenditures other than accelerated depreciation as lump-sum deductions). As discussed previously, the GDP effects under this assumption are either negative or relatively small (tables 8.3 and 8.4), reflecting the negative effects of reducing the taxation of the income earned by existing capital. A natural question is whether it is possible to design alternative reforms that lower the corporate income tax rate and have more positive macroeconomic effects. We consider three such reforms.

Three Reforms with a 25 Percent Corporate Tax Rate and Alternative Financing

We conclude our study by analyzing three reforms under which the long-run corporate income tax rate is cut to 25 percent and financed by (1) selective business base broadening, (2) a proportionate increase in wage taxation, and (3) a reduction in government spending in the form of income transfers. In each case, we use the fully expanded version of the model, including an imperfectly competitive sector, international capital flows, and tax rate arbitrage.

Under the first reform, we take into account the fact that of the various categories of business tax expenditures, investment incentives, including accelerated depreciation, have the largest effect on the cost of capital since they are focused solely on investment decisions. By comparison, other tax expenditures, such as production incentives and rate-reducing expenditures, have smaller effects on investment since they are general incentives that apply to all production and lump-sum tax expenditures and have no effects on marginal investment decisions.

Specifically, in the simulation presented in table 8.7, we reduce the corporate income tax rate to 25 percent in the long run and finance the rate reduction with partial base broadening in which we order the elimination of tax expenditures so that investment incentives, including accelerated depreciation, are "stacked" last. (By comparison, recall

Table 8.7
Dynamic Macroeconomic Effects of Long-Run Revenue-Neutral 25 Percent Corporate Rate Reduction Financed with Partial Base-Broadening, Retaining Accelerated Depreciation and Other Investment Incentives with Expanded Model (percentage changes from initial steady states)

Years after Reform	2	5	10	20	50	150
GDP	0.06%	0.13%	0.19%	0.30%	0.40%	0.41%
Capital stock	0.27	0.08	-0.04	0.35	0.54	0.56
Labor supply	-0.04	-0.07	-0.07	-0.06	-0.07	-0.07
Consumption	0.21	0.16	0.13	0.24	0.54	0.65
Investment	-0.04	0.07	-0.03	0.43	0.52	0.52

Note: Diamond-Zodrow model with differentiated treatment of business tax expenditures, imperfectly competitive sector, foreign capital flows, and tax rate arbitrage. Reform assumes accelerated depreciation and 65 percent of investment incentives are retained.

that the elimination of all business tax expenditures allowed a reduction in the corporate tax rate to 19.7 percent in the long run.) This implies that all tax expenditures in categories other than investment incentives are eliminated, but accelerated depreciation is maintained and only 35 percent of the remaining investment incentives are repealed. The macroeconomic effects of this reform are somewhat more favorable than the full base-broadening option analyzed above (compare to table 8.4). For example, GDP increases by 0.06 percent two years after the enactment of reform, 0.13 percent after five years, 0.19 percent after 10 years, and 0.41 percent in the long run.

In the second simulation, the corporate rate is reduced to 25 percent, but there is no corporate tax base broadening whatsoever, as the rate reduction is assumed to be financed with a proportionate increase in wage taxation. The results of this simulation, presented in table 8.8, show that this reduction in capital income taxation stimulates investment, which increases by 0.43 percent two years after the enactment of reform, 1.37 percent after five years, 2.27 percent after ten years, and 2.73 percent in the long run. Labor supply declines slightly—by 0.44 percent two years after reform and 0.14 percent in the long run. Although GDP also declines initially, it increases by the fifth year after reform (by 0.13 percent), by 0.47 percent ten years after enactment, and by 1.02 percent in the long run.

In the third simulation, the corporate rate is reduced to 25 percent and is financed with a reduction in federal government spending in the form of transfer payments. The simulation results in this case,

Table 8.8
Dynamic Macroeconomic Effects of Long-Run Revenue-Neutral 25 Percent Corporate Rate Reduction Financed by a Proportionate Wage Tax Increase with Expanded Model (percentage changes from initial steady states)

Years after Reform	2	5	10	20	50	150
GDP	-0.22%	0.13%	0.47%	0.82%	1.01%	1.02%
Capital stock	0.38	0.90	1.75	2.01	2.32	2.35
Labor supply	-0.44	-0.31	-0.21	-0.14	-0.14	-0.14
Consumption	-0.15	–0.02	0.21	0.44	0.82	0.95
Investment	0.43	1.37	2.27	2.68	2.76	2.73

Note: Diamond-Zodrow model with differentiated treatment of business tax expenditures, imperfectly competitive sector, foreign capital flows, and tax rate arbitrage.

Table 8.9
Dynamic Macroeconomic Effects of Long-Run Revenue-Neutral 25 Percent Corporate Rate Reduction Financed by Reduction in Government Spending with Expanded Model (percentage changes from initial steady states)

Years after Reform	2	5	10	20	50	150
GDP	0.17%	0.49%	0.81%	1.10%	1.22%	1.23%
Capital stock	0.40	1.10	1.95	2.27	2.52	2.54
Labor supply	0.09	0.10	0.10	0.07	0.04	0.04
Consumption	0.07	0.22	0.46	0.69	1.04	1.15
Investment	1.63	2.38	3.00	3.10	3.08	3.05

Note: Diamond-Zodrow model with differentiated treatment of business tax expenditures, imperfectly competitive sector, foreign capital flows, and tax rate arbitrage.

shown in table 8.9, indicate that this reform, which finances rate reduction with a nondistortionary reduction in transfer payments rather than a distortionary increase in wage taxes, has somewhat more positive effects than the previous reform analyzed. Investment increases by 1.63 percent two years after the enactment of reform, 2.38 percent after five years, 3.00 percent after ten years, and 3.05 percent in the long run. Labor supply increases by 0.09 percent two years after reform and 0.04 percent in the long run. GDP increases by 0.17 percent two years after enactment of reform, 0.49 percent after five years, 0.81 percent ten years after enactment, and 1.23 percent in the long run.

To summarize the results, table 8.10 compares the results of the different versions of the model, different treatments of tax expenditures, and alternative methods of financing a corporate rate reduction. The table shows the dynamic revenue-neutral corporate tax rate that can be

Table 8.10
Summary of Simulated Dynamic Economic Effects of Corporate Rate Reductions. Change in GDP: Description of Modeling Change in GDP (%) per household ($)

	Revenue-Neutral Base-Broadening Reform?	Imperfectly Competitive Sector?	Foreign Capital Inflows?	Tax Rate Arbitrage Response?	Tax Expenditures Treated as Lump-Sum Changes?	Long-Run Revenue-Neutral Corporate Rate (%)	10 Years	50 Years	10 Years	50 Years
Table 8.3	Yes	No	No	No	Generally no	19.7	-0.14	-0.51	-202	-1,081
Table 8.4	Yes	Yes	Yes	Yes	Generally no	16.8	0.19	0.18	272	379
Table 8.5	Yes	No	No	No	Yes, except depreciation	17.0	0.41	0.53	572	1,104
Table 8.6	Yes	Yes	Yes	Yes	Yes, except depreciation	12.9	0.77	1.25	1,184	2,623
Table 8.7	Yes; retain accelerated depreciation and 65% of investment incentives	Yes	Yes	Yes	Generally no	25.1	0.19	0.40	269	849
Table 8.8	No; wage tax offset	Yes	Yes	Yes	NA	25.0	0.47	1.01	657	2,120
Table 8.9	No; spending offset	Yes	Yes	Yes	NA	25.0	0.81	1.22	1,143	2,564

achieved in the long run and presents the economic effects in terms of the changes in GDP over ten and fifty years, as well as the effects on GDP per household. For example, the proposal that finances a reduction in the corporate tax rate to 25 percent with a proportional wage tax increase would increase annual GDP per household by over $650 within ten years (in 2011 dollars).

Conclusion

The U.S. corporate income tax system has not changed significantly since 1986, while most other countries have dramatically reduced their statutory corporate income tax rates below the U.S. rate. We have analyzed the dynamic macroeconomic effects of a reduction in the U.S. corporate tax rate financed in a revenue-neutral manner through different types of business tax base broadening, a wage tax increase, and a reduction in government spending.

Focusing on the results, which assume that virtually all business tax expenditures affect the cost of capital, the model simulations of standard corporate rate-reducing, business base-broadening tax reforms show fairly modest effects on overall U.S. GDP, capital stock, labor supply, and consumption. These results obtain primarily because the revenue-neutral rate-reduction reform plans analyzed include offsetting base-broadening measures that have adverse effects on capital investment, and because the lower corporate tax rates apply not only to new investments but also to the income earned from existing capital (and also because the model does not capture all of the economic efficiency improvements that would occur with implementation of the reforms). The more positive results occur when corporate rate reductions reduce the extent of tax arbitrage and most investment incentives are retained. These results suggest that the effects of corporate income tax reform depend both on how the reform is designed and the context in which it is imposed.

Additional model simulations show that rate-reducing reforms coupled with increases in wage taxes or cuts in government spending in the form of income transfers can have more positive macroeconomic effects, with increases in GDP ranging from roughly 0.5 to 0.8 percent ten years after the enactment of reform and long-run increases of 1.0 to 1.2 percent.

These results illustrate the importance of differentiating among current business tax expenditures, examining alternative financing mechanisms, and considering the positive benefits of a lower corporate tax rate in reducing tax rate arbitrage when analyzing the economic effects of a base-broadening, rate-reducing corporate income tax reform. In particular, including imperfect competition, foreign capital inflows, and reductions in tax arbitrage in the simulation model resulted in increases in long-run GDP on the order of 0.7 percent (from -0.56 percent in table 8.3 to 0.12 percent in table 8.4). Moreover, these results are likely to understate the potential positive economic effects of a lower corporate tax rate due to the incomplete modeling of the global economy, including the movements of highly mobile firm-specific capital that earns above-normal economic rents and the effects on domestic demand of reform-induced reductions in income shifting, as well as the potential benefits of a more level playing field across different types of assets and industries—all topics we plan to investigate in future research.

Acknowledgments

We thank the Ernst and Young LLP Thought Leadership Program for financial support, Ruud de Mooij, Alan Viard, and the participants at a Baker Institute conference on "Defusing the Debt Bomb: Economic and Fiscal Reform," held October 5–6, 2011 at Rice University for helpful comments, and James Dargan for research assistance.

Appendix A: Extension of the Basic Diamond-Zodrow Model to Differentiate among Business Tax Expenditures

In order to analyze these reforms, the model is extended to take into account explicitly a wide variety of such business tax expenditures, modeling in detail how their elimination would affect the cost of capital in the corporate and noncorporate sectors. Specifically, the simulated reform assumes that a wide variety of business tax expenditures, as delineated in the annual report on tax expenditures issued by the Joint Committee on Taxation (2008), are eliminated, with the resulting revenues used to finance a reduction in the corporate tax rate. Such a reform is modeled as follows.

The business tax expenditures under current law are classified into the four categories listed below. Examples are provided in each category, with an estimate of the cost of each tax expenditure at the corporate level provided in parentheses; all estimates come from Joint

Committee on Taxation (2008) unless otherwise noted. The examples listed include all tax expenditures in excess of $1 billion, which account for virtually the entire corporate tax expenditure budget ($81.7 billion in FY 2008), which in turn is roughly four times the size of the tax expenditure budget for the noncorporate sector ($21.1 billion).[21]

1. **RR** refers to *rate-reducing* preferences that effectively lower the tax rate applied to corporate income, such as the graduated corporation income tax rate structure ($3.3 billion) and various income exemptions (for which the tax rate is zero), including exemption of income earned by credit unions ($1.4 billion).

2. **PI** refers to provisions that provide *production incentives* for specific business activities, such as the deduction for domestic production activities ($5.5 billion), the credit for low-income housing ($4.8 billion), the special treatment of life insurance reserves ($2.0 billion), deferral of gain on nondealer installment sales ($1.1 billion), and the special deduction for Blue Cross and Blue Shield insurance companies ($1.0 billion).

3. **II** refers to provisions that provide *investment incentives* for certain types of investment activities, such as accelerated depreciation of buildings, machinery, and equipment in excess of that required to offset the effects of inflation ($20 billion);[22] the inventory property sales source rule exception ($6.8 billion);[23] research tax credits for incremental investment in science, space, and technology ($4.9 billion); the LIFO (last in, first out) and LCM (lower of cost or market) methods of inventory accounting ($6.7 billion);[24] deferral on like-kind exchanges ($3.0 billion); expensing of research and experimentation expenditures ($3.1 billion); and various provisions that provide for expensing of costs related to energy exploration and development ($2.1 billion), percentage depletion for the oil and gas industry ($1.3 billion), and expensing of depreciable property for small businesses ($1.0 billion).

4. **LD** refers to deductions in the calculation of taxable income that we treat as *lump-sum deductions*, on the grounds that the deductions are unrelated to either production levels or investment levels, such as the exclusion of investment income on life insurance and annuity contracts ($2.6 billion), and separate grouping of affiliated financial companies ($1.0 billion). In addition, the revenues gained from recapturing the LIFO reserve associated with eliminating LIFO inventory accounting are treated as reflecting the elimination of a lump-sum deduction.

These preferences are then included in the expressions for total taxes paid in the revenue equations for the representative corporate and noncorporate firms in the model. Corporate tax rates are adjusted to reflect the rate-reducing preferences, while production and investment incentives are assumed to reduce the sizes of the corporate and noncorporate tax bases by amounts sufficient to generate revenue losses equal to the estimated tax expenditures.[25] The resulting modified expressions for corporate and noncorporate firm profits are then used in determining the cost of capital and the profit-maximizing investment and output decisions of the firm.

The classification of the business tax expenditures listed in the JCT report into these four categories is noted in table 8.2. Several items listed as business tax expenditures in the JCT report are not included as business base broadeners in our analysis. These include incentives for state and local governments (e.g., tax exemption of interest on state and local bonds) or tax expenditures that reduce labor income taxes (e.g., employee stock ownership plan rules for tax-preferred compensation on company stock). Our analysis focuses solely on provisions that affect capital income; thus, it is conservative in the sense that it ignores these tax expenditures that could be used to finance further corporate rate reduction.

Several issues merit further discussion. In particular, the treatment of LIFO inventory accounting, which is the fifth largest item on the JCT list of corporate tax expenditures, is controversial. Proponents of eliminating LIFO, such as Kleinbard, Plesko, and Goodman (2006), argue that LIFO is a highly imperfect method of inflation adjustment and is undesirable because it often results in quasi-permanent deferral of taxes on increases in inventories. In contrast, Viard (2006) argues that the current ad hoc inflation adjustments due to the combination of LIFO inventory accounting and accelerated depreciation for depreciable assets achieves rough neutrality across investment in inventories and depreciable assets. Moreover, as long as one adopts the LIFO rule for ordering which items are sold from inventory, the increases in wealth attributable to the use of LIFO accounting for the stock of inventory are unrealized capital gains, which are typically exempt under the current U.S. income tax code.[26]

In any case, LIFO accounting is currently treated as a tax expenditure by the JCT, and eliminating LIFO accounting was included in the tax reform proposal of House Ways and Means Committee chairman Charles Rangel (D-NY). Thus, we include it among our base-broadening provisions in this analysis. The JCT (2007), in its analysis of the Rangel proposal, estimates the effects of eliminating LIFO accounting under the assumption that bringing the existing "LIFO reserve"—the difference between the valuation of inventory under FIFO accounting and the considerably smaller value under LIFO accounting rules, which reflects prices in effect at the time the assets were initially added to inventory—is spread out over eight years. In addition, the Rangel proposal would eliminate on a phased-in basis the LCM inventory method, which allows taxpayers who do not use LIFO inventory accounting to choose between valuing inventories at cost or the lower of cost or market value. Together these provisions would raise $6.7 billion in 2008 and $113.7 billion over 2008 to 2017.[27]

A separate but closely related issue is the treatment of generally accelerated deductions for depreciation—that is, accelerated deductions that apply to all depreciable assets. JCT (2008) no longer treats accelerated depreciation as a tax expenditure but instead classifies it as a "tax-induced structural distortion." Such a distortion is defined as an element of the tax code that is similar to most tax expenditures in that it causes substantial economic efficiency costs, but different in that the resulting inefficiencies cannot be eliminated by reverting to "the general rule of present law" and instead requires "a more fundamental reexamination and redesign of present law."[28]

Accelerated deductions for depreciation can be thought of as consisting of two components: a substantial element that adjusts deductions based on historical costs for inflation and thus improves the measurement of real economic income, and a second component that serves as an incentive for investing in depreciable assets, much like the sector-specific investment incentives classified as tax expenditures above. It is difficult to separate accelerated depreciation deductions into these two components, especially since the inflation rate varies over time. The JCT (2008) estimates of accelerated depreciation deductions vary widely over 2008 to 2012, ranging from $6 billion to $32 billion. For our simulations, we simply take the average value over that five-year period, which is $20 billion, and treat that as the size of the tax expenditure associated with accelerated depreciation deductions. Even if one believes that only the portion of accelerated depreciation in excess of that required for inflation adjustment should be treated as a tax expenditure, the JCT estimate is sufficiently low (e.g., relative to the U.S. Department of the Treasury 2007 average estimate of 35.6 billion) that it could be interpreted as roughly reflecting such treatment.[29]

Before proceeding further, several limitations of the analysis in capturing the efficiency gains of a reform that involves eliminating business tax expenditures and reducing corporate income tax rates should be noted. First, because we consider only four production sectors in our model, we understate the intersectoral efficiency gains obtained from eliminating tax expenditures and thus tax distortions across the many different industries within these four aggregated production sectors. Second, because it does not include uncertainty or the costs of bankruptcy, the model does not capture the efficiency gains from reduced reliance on debt rather than equity finance in response to reductions in the corporate tax rate and thus the value of interest deductions, including any external costs associated with excessive leverage. Third, our model overstates the efficiency gains from a base-broadening, rate-lowering reform to the extent that there are economic benefits associated with the eliminated tax expenditures—for example, any beneficial effects on productivity and economic growth of the research and experimentation tax credit or the benefits of less pollution due to various environmental provisions. Finally, the model does not capture the revenue costs arising from the shifting of labor income by the individual owners of closely held corporations from the personal tax base to the business tax base in response to relatively low corporate tax rates; similarly, it does not consider any equity benefits that might arise from certain corporate tax expenditures, such as lower-priced housing for the poor due to the credit for low-income housing.

Appendix B: Diamond-Zodrow Model Extensions for Corporate Tax Reform Analysis

This appendix describes three extensions made to the basic Diamond-Zodrow model in order to capture additional dimensions of the U.S. economy and better measure tax effects important for modeling corporate tax reform. It also provides some empirical support for the parameters chosen.

An Imperfectly Competitive Corporate Sector Earning Above-Normal Returns

An important difference between lowering the statutory corporate tax rate and the alternative reform option of using tax investment incentives such as accelerated depreciation is that only the former approach reduces the tax rate applied to above-normal returns (both reforms reduce the tax rate applied to normal returns). In order to capture the effects of a reduction in the statutory corporate tax rate on above-normal returns, we extend the model to include an imperfectly competitive sector in which investments permanently earn such above-normal returns. This is accomplished by splitting the corporate sector into two production sectors—a perfectly competitive sector characterized by normal returns and an imperfectly competitive corporate sector that is characterized by above-normal returns, even in the long-run steady-state equilibrium.

In the imperfectly competitive corporate sector, the equilibrium price of output is assumed to reflect a markup at a fixed rate m_{IPC}, that is, the gross price of output in this sector received by firms is $p(1+m_{IPC})$. The remainder of the profit function for firms in this sector is the same as the profit function in the perfectly competitive sector. The above-normal returns that arise due to the price markup are assumed to be attributable to firm-specific factors such as unique entrepreneurial or managerial skills, or intangibles such as unique technological knowledge, proprietary production techniques, patents, and goodwill and reputations. Note that these above-normal returns are assumed to persist in the long run, so that in the steady state, the after-tax return to capital invested in the imperfectly competitive corporate sector always exceeds the analogous return to capital in the perfectly competitive sector by the same factor, which equals the after-tax revenues attributable to the price markup, expressed as a percentage of firm value in the imperfectly competitive corporate sector. The ownership shares of capital in the two corporate sectors are determined in the initial equilibrium and are assumed to remain constant. In particular, these ownership shares are passed on to an individual's heirs as part of the bequest.

Thus, capital is allocated to (1) the imperfectly competitive corporate sector in the model until in equilibrium it earns a rate of return that reflects the after-tax value of the price markup and is thus permanently higher than the normal return, and (2) the perfectly competitive sector until it earns the normal rate of return. This implies that the model captures the greater inflow of capital into the imperfectly competitive sector (relative to the perfectly competitive sector), including capital inflows from abroad, that occurs in response to the reduction in the statutory corporate income tax rate; that is, since average tax rates fall relatively more in the imperfectly competitive sector, a relatively larger capital inflow is required to return the system back to the differential rate-of-return equilibrium described. At the same time, the model also captures the reduction in revenues associated with reduced taxation of above-normal returns associated with the corporate rate reduction—that is, the reduction in the relatively high average tax rate in that sector due to the taxation of all above-normal returns at the statutory tax rate often stressed by proponents of increasing investment incentives rather than lowering corporate tax rates.

Choosing the size of the markup in the imperfectly competitive sector is difficult given the problems associated with measuring this parameter accurately and the resulting wide range of estimates. For example, Bayoumi et al. (2004) estimate a price markup of 23 percent, and Judd (1997) argues that a range of 10 to 40 percent is plausible, given the existing empirical literature. We assume a price markup of 20 percent.

Similarly, the size of the imperfectly competitive sector is far from clear. The firms in this sector are characterized by investments that generate firm-specific above-normal returns, and we assume that such returns characterize investments by large U.S. multinational corporations. The analysis thus assumes that the imperfectly competitive sector comprises large U.S. multinational corporations, with all remaining corporations in the perfectly competitive sector. The division of the corporate sector into perfectly competitive and perfectly competitive components is based on Compustat data for 2007. These data provide information on over 4,300 U.S.-based multinationals with assets of $24.7 trillion and pretax income of $906 billion, almost evenly split between domestic and foreign source income. Accordingly, for the simulation analysis, we assume that the imperfectly competitive sector accounts for $451.4 billion, or 21.3 percent of total U.S. corporate gross income in 2007 of $2.1 trillion; the remainder of U.S. corporate gross income is attributed to the perfectly competitive corporate sector. Capital and labor are allocated between the two components of the corporate sector in such a way as to be consistent with this split of corporate income. For purposes of the international income-shifting calculation, we assume that half of total income earned by U.S. multinationals comes from foreign sources.

Effects of Increased Imports of Capital

Even if the U.S. economy were closed, a reduction in the statutory corporate tax rate that increased after-tax returns to saving would stimulate increased saving and thus increased investment. However, in an open economy context, this effect would be augmented by additional imports of capital from abroad in response to an increase in the after-tax rate of return to investment in the United States. In this essay, we extend the basic model to include the potential for such capital imports as follows.

Following Goulder, Shoven, and Whalley (1983), capital imports (or exports) in period s are governed by the constant elasticity expression,

$$\frac{K^W - K_s^F}{K^W} = \left(\frac{r_s^{US}}{r^W}\right)^{\varepsilon\kappa},$$

where K^W is the fixed rest-of-the-world capital stock,[30] r^W is the fixed rest-of-the-world return to capital after corporate-level taxes, r_s^{US} is the return after corporate taxes to capital in the United States (given the fixed debt-to-asset ratio of b), K_s^F is foreign exports of capital to the United States in period s, and $\varepsilon\kappa$ is a constant (positive) elasticity that determines the extent of international capital flows in the model. Thus, foreign exports of capital to the United States are

$$K_s^F = K^W\left[1-\left(\frac{r^W}{r_s^{US}}\right)^{\varepsilon\kappa}\right].$$

For example, if $r_s^{US} > r^W$ as a result of the reform, then the United States has positive capital imports in period s ($K_s^F > 0$). The appropriate value of $\varepsilon\kappa$ is difficult to determine.[31] Gravelle and Smetters (2006) stress that the U.S. economy cannot be modeled as a small, open economy that faces a perfectly elastic supply of capital. They argue that the empirical literature suggests values of the foreign and domestic capital portfolio elasticity roughly between 1.0 and 3.0, and we use a capital supply elasticity consistent with the bottom of that range. Note that a relatively low value is appropriate to the extent that a dramatic reduction in the U.S. corporate income tax rate may prompt further reductions in the corporate income tax rates of our competitors, which would mute reform-induced capital inflows from above.[32] Note also, however, that we do not consider the possibility that certain types of capital—for example, firm-specific capital that earns above-normal rents such as patents or other proprietary technology, brand names, goodwill, unique managerial skills, or knowledge of production processes—are much more mobile than other forms of capital. Such capital would be likely to be more responsive to taxes, including changes in the statutory tax rates that are more relevant to the taxation of above-normal profits than the taxation of normal profits we analyze in this essay. We leave this extension to future research.

Capital imports are treated as perfect substitutes for domestic capital in all production functions. Given the level of capital imports in each period, the model is closed simply by assuming that the returns, after U.S. corporate taxes, to foreign capital are included in aggregate demand for the corporate good and noncorporate goods, in fixed proportions equal to the ratio of these two goods in the initial equilibrium. This approach effectively implies that the United States is renting capital services from abroad in each period, with foreign capital owners spending an amount equal to their after-tax returns on purchases of exports of the two U.S. composite goods, so that aggregate demands equal aggregate supplies for those goods. These goods do not enter the utility functions of U.S. residents.

Effects of Reducing Tax Arbitrage

An important advantage of a lower U.S. statutory tax rate is that it reduces the tax rate differentials between the U.S. rate and other countries' tax rates; these differentials encourage legal tax rate arbitrage, which can lower the amount of taxable profit reported in the United States. Corporations have some discretion with respect to where they earn and report taxable income, as companies make incremental investment decisions about the location of new factories, research facilities, and supply chain, as well as financial decisions that can affect the location of debt and intangibles.

The key factor in determining the extent of tax rate arbitrage is the magnitude of the statutory tax rate in the United States, relative to statutory rates in competing countries, since shifted taxable income is taxed at the statutory rate. In particular, a reduction in the statutory tax rate in the United States relative to statutory tax rates in other countries increases the U.S. corporate tax base compared to what it would be in the future if there is less tax rate arbitrage against the United States. Since some tax rate arbitrage can occur without significant reallocation of the physical assets, it is likely to be significantly more sensitive to tax factors than reallocations of physical assets and personnel.

To capture tax rate arbitrage, the basic model is extended in an admittedly ad hoc way to include a reform-induced increase in government tax revenues from a lower relative U.S. tax rate. Tax rate arbitrage is assumed to occur only in the imperfectly competitive sector, which consists solely of large multinationals. Specifically, suppose that in the initial equilibrium, the representative firm in the imperfectly competitive industry has a pool of domestic and foreign profits and that there is no residual U.S. tax on the firm's foreign income. When the United States lowers its statutory corporate tax rate from an initial value of τ_c^o by an amount $\Delta\tau_c$, some fraction ϕ_{IS} of the static domestic revenue loss in the imperfectly competitive sector that would occur in the absence of any tax rate arbitrage (the product of $\Delta\tau_c$ and initial profits in the imperfectly competitive corporate sector) is offset by an increase in taxable income in the United States.

In addition, the model assumes that the associated increase in after-tax profits is reinvested abroad; this simplifying assumption is necessary, given the incomplete open-economy treatment in the current model, so that U.S. private income is not increased and thus does not affect domestic demand. Note, however, that this assumption implies the model may understate the potential beneficial effects of the reduced income shifting due to a lower U.S. corporate tax rate. For example, if a reduction in the U.S. corporate rate reversed income shifting by U.S. parent firms to subsidiaries in foreign countries with lower tax rates, foreign source income used to purchase imports to the United States would decline and domestic income and consumption would increase. A closely related point is that if a foreign subsidiary in the United States reduced the income it shifted abroad, more foreign source income would be available abroad to purchase U.S. exports. Both of the effects would tend to increase demand for U.S.-produced goods and services but are not captured in the model, and they reflect extensions left to future research.

The magnitude of the tax rate arbitrage parameter, ϕ_{IS}, is difficult to determine. A number of empirical studies have estimated the effects of different types of tax rate arbitrage. For example, studies have found that after-tax profitability tends to be high in low-tax countries (Hines 1999). Grubert (2003) estimates that tax-minimizing choices regarding the location of intangible income and the allocation of debt explain all of the observed differences in profitability across countries with high and low statutory tax rates. Other studies find that deductible interest payments tend to be made by subsidiaries in high-tax countries, while nondeductible dividend payments tend to be made in low-tax countries (Altshuler and Grubert 2002; Grubert 1998; Huizinga, Laeven, and Nicodème 2006) and that deductible royalties are substituted for nondeductible dividends in host countries with high tax rates (Grubert, Randolph, and Rousslang 1996; Grubert 1998).

Also important is the fact that research and development expenses and other intangible inputs are increasingly mobile. Hines (1996) finds that the allocation of research and development expenditures is highly sensitive to international tax differentials, Altshuler and Grubert (2004) show that low-tax countries are becoming much more important destinations for intangibles initially produced in the United States, and Mutti and Grubert (2006) estimate that less than half of the contribution of parent research and development expenditures to subsidiary income is reflected as royalties. Moreover, increasing economic integration, including especially the greater intrafirm trade that now accounts for nearly 40 percent of all U.S. international trade (Clausing 2003), suggests that such tax arbitrage is likely to become more prevalent over time. This conjecture is supported by empirical evidence presented in Grubert (2001) and Altshuler and Grubert (2006), who find large increases in tax arbitrage over time.

The most striking results are obtained in four recent studies that directly estimate the effect of tax arbitrage. Bartlesman and Beetsma (2003) find that a 1 percent increase (decrease) in a country's tax rate leads to a decline (an increase) in reported before-tax income of 2.7 percent, based on a sample of fifteen industrial sectors in a group of sixteen OECD countries. Their estimates suggest that the revenue increase (decrease) from a unilateral increase (decrease) in the statutory tax rate is on average reduced by roughly more than 65 percent. Broadly similar results are obtained by Huizinga and Laeven (2008), who estimate that the elasticity of the taxable corporate income tax base to the statutory corporate tax rate in Europe is 0.45. Clausing (2003) finds that prices for intrafirm imports and exports are strongly affected by international tax differentials. Her estimates indicate that relative to goods that are not traded within the firm, a reduction in a country's statutory tax rate of 1 percentage point results in changes in the prices of intrafirm traded goods of roughly 2 percent, in the directions predicted by a tax minimization strategy. Clausing (2009) estimates that in 2004, "income shifting" reduced U.S. corporate income tax revenues by about 35 percent.

The most relevant paper is by Bartelsman and Beetsma (2003), who estimate that the revenue increase from a unilateral tax increase (decrease) by one country in their sample of sixteen OECD countries is reduced (increased) by more than 65 percent due to tax rate arbitrage in intercompany pricing (which does not include other forms of tax rate arbitrage). However, their tax rate arbitrage coefficient for the United States is statistically insignificant and of the wrong sign. In our analysis, we assume a value somewhat smaller than the OECD average that Bartlesman and Beetsma found; specifically, we assume $\phi_{IS} = 0.5$.

We conclude by noting that as in the case of the supply elasticity of capital, the appropriate value of ϕ_{IS} depends on the response of other governments. For example, a significant rate reduction in the U.S. corporate tax rate might be met with competing rate reductions in other countries, as was certainly the experience following the dramatic reduction in the statutory corporate income tax rate that occurred with the Tax Reform Act of 1986 in the United States, as foreign tax rates declined over time to the point that the United States is once again a relatively high-tax country. Yet to the extent that a statutory rate reduction in the United States is perceived as merely catching up to recent trends, it might not result in significant rate reductions in other countries, implying that a relatively high value of ϕ_{IS} would be appropriate. Finally, note that a lower corporate income tax rate in the United States would also encourage tax rate arbitrage by foreign multinationals, resulting in increased taxable profits in the United States not considered in our analysis—a consideration that argues for using a somewhat higher value for ϕ_{IS} than otherwise would be the case.

Appendix C: Model Description and Parameter Values Used in the Analysis

The Composite Good Production Sectors

Firms in the two composite-good production sectors produce output using a Cobb-Douglas production function with capital and labor as inputs. One sector is subject to the corporate income tax, while the other reflects noncorporate production and is subject to pass-through tax treatment, with all income taxation occurring at the individual level. Firms are assumed to choose the time path of investment to maximize the present value of firm profits or, equivalently, maximize firm value, net of all taxes and subject to quadratic costs of adjusting the capital stock. Total taxes assessed on the composite-good production sectors include the corporate income tax, state and local property taxes, and individual-level taxes on capital income. Each firm is assumed to maintain a fixed debt-to-asset ratio and pay out a constant fraction of earnings after taxes and depreciation in each period.

The model assumes individual-level arbitrage in the absence of uncertainty about rates of return, which implies that the after-tax return to bonds must equal the after-tax return received by the shareholders of the firm. The values of the firms in the composite-good sectors equal the present value of all future net distributions to the owners of the firm.

The Owner-Occupied and Rental Housing Production Sectors

Housing services are produced in the owner-occupied and rental housing production sectors where, following Goulder and Summers (1989) and Goulder (1989), rental housing services are produced by noncorporate landlords and owner-occupied housing services are produced by homeowners. The technology used in the production of rental housing and owner-occupied housing services is assumed to be identical—capital and labor combined in the same Cobb-Douglas production function. Landlords and owner-occupiers are also are assumed to choose time paths of investment to maximize the equivalent of "firm" value, net of total taxes.

In the case of the rental housing sector, the firm is modeled as a noncorporate entity, which implies that landlords are simply taxed at the individual level. In the owner-occupied housing sector, the tax burden takes into account the facts that imputed rents are untaxed and depreciation and maintenance expenditures are not deductible under the individual income tax, while mortgage interest and property taxes are deductible. The optimal investment path is calculated as above.

Individual Behavior

On the individual side, the model has a dynamic overlapping generations framework with fifty-five generations alive at each point in time. There is a representative individual for each generation, who has an economic life span (which begins with entry into the workforce) of fifty-five years, with the first forty-five of those years spent working, and the last ten years spent in retirement. Individual tastes are identical so that differences in behavior across generations are due solely to differences in lifetime budget constraints. An individual accumulates assets from the time of "economic birth" that are used to finance both consumption over the life cycle, especially during the retirement period, and the making of a bequest. The model follows Fullerton and Rogers (1993) in assuming a "target bequest" motive under which individuals give a fixed bequest.

Table 8.11
Parameter Values Used in the Model Simulations

Symbol	Description	Value
	Consumer Parameters	
ρ	Rate of time preference	0.001
σ	Intertemporal elasticity of substitution	0.35
ε	Intratemporal elasticity of substitution	0.8
σ_{CN}	Elasticity of substitution for composite good and housing	0.8
σ_{CM}	Elasticity of substitution for corporate and noncorporate	5.0
σ_{CM}	Elasticity of substitution for competitive and noncompetitive corporate good	0.75
σ_{CM}	Elasticity of substitution for rental and owner housing	2.0
α_E	Utility weight on leisure	0.28
α_C	Utility weight on composite consumption	0.71
α_G	Utility weight on composite good consumption	0.8
α_H	Utility weight on composite housing consumption	0.2
α_{C1}	Utility weight on corporate good	0.68
α_{C12}	Utility weight on corporate competitive good	0.71
α_R	Utility weight on owner housing	0.74
α_{LE}	Leisure share of the initial endowment	0.38
n	Population growth rate	0.01
	Producer Parameters	
g	Technological growth rate	0.01
α_1	Capital share in composite good production	0.25
α_2	Capital share in housing production	0.99
β_X	Composite good adjustment cost parameter	2
β_{rh}	Rental housing adjustment cost parameter	2
β_{oh}	Owner housing adjustment cost parameter	2
μ_X	Composite good adjustment cost function constant	0.1031
μ_h	Housing adjustment cost function constant	0.0451
ζ	Dividend payout ratio in the composite good sector	0.6
b	Debt-to-capital ratio (in all three sectors)	0.35
δ	Economic depreciation in the composite good sector	0.083
δ_h	Economic depreciation in the housing sector	0.025

The consumer is assumed to choose the time paths of consumption and leisure to maximize rest-of-life utility, a discounted sum of annual utilities, subject to a lifetime budget constraint that requires the present value of lifetime wealth, including inheritances to equal the present value of lifetime consumption including bequests. Annual utility is assumed to be a CES function of consumption of an aggregate consumption good, leisure, and the bequest. The aggregate consumption good is modeled as a CES function of the composite good and aggregate housing services, with aggregate housing services in turn modeled as a CES function of owner-occupied and rental housing services. In addition, the model includes a simple social security system, government purchases of the composite good, transfer payments, a hump-backed wage profile over the life cycle, a progressive tax on wage income, and constant average marginal tax rates applied to interest income, dividends, and capital gains. Table 8.11 provides a list of important parameter values used in the simulations.

References

Altshuler, Rosanne, and Harry Grubert. 2002. Repatriation Taxes, Repatriation Strategies, and Multinational Financial Policy. *Journal of Public Economics* 87 (1): 73–107.

Altshuler, Rosanne, and Harry Grubert. 2004. Taxpayer Responses to Competitive Tax Policies and Tax Policy Responses to Competitive Taxpayers: Recent Evidence. *Tax Notes International* 34 (13): 1349–62.

Altshuler, Rosanne, and Harry Grubert. 2006. Governments and Multinational Corporations in the Race to the Bottom. *Tax Notes* 110 (8): 459–74.

Altshuler, Rosanne, Harry Grubert, and T. Scott Newlon. 2001. Has U.S. Investment Abroad Become More Sensitive to Tax Rates? In International Taxation and Multinational Activity, edited by James R. Hines Jr., 9–32. Chicago: University of Chicago Press.

Altig, David, Alan J. Auerbach, Laurence J. Kotlikoff, Kent A. Smetters, and Jan Walliser. 2001. Simulating Fundamental Tax Reform in the United States. *American Economic Review* 91 (3): 574–95.

Auerbach, Alan J. 2006. Why Have Corporate Tax Revenues Declined? Another Look. NBER Working Paper 12463, National Bureau of Economic Research, Cambridge, MA.

Auerbach, Alan J., and Kevin A. Hassett. 2005. *Toward Fundamental Tax Reform*. Washington, DC: AEI Press.

Auerbach, Alan J., and Laurence J. Kotlikoff. 1987. *Dynamic Fiscal Policy*. Cambridge, MA: Harvard University Press.

Bartelsman, Eric J., and Roel M.W.J. Beetsma. 2003. Why Pay More? Corporate Tax Avoidance through Transfer Pricing in OECD Countries. *Journal of Public Economics* 87 (9–10): 2225–52.

Bayoumi, Tamim, Douglas Laxton, and Paolo Pesenti. 2004. Benefits and Spillovers of Greater Competition in Europe: A Macroeconomic Assessment. NBER Working Paper 10416, National Bureau of Economic Research, Cambridge, MA.

Becker, Johannes, and Clemens Fuest. 2005. Optimal Tax Policy when Firms Are Internationally Mobile. CESifo Working Paper 1592. CESifo, Munich.

Boskin, Michael J., and Charles E. McLure, Jr., eds. 1990. *World Tax Reform: Case Studies of Developed and Developing Countries*. San Francisco: ICS Press.

Carroll, Robert J., Robert J. Cline, John W. Diamond, Thomas S. Neubig, and George R. Zodrow. 2010. *The Macroeconomic Effects of an Add-On Value-Added Tax*. Washington, DC: Ernst and Young.

Carroll, Robert, Morgan Cox, and Tom Neubig. 2011. Tax Reform Lessons: Composition of Tax Changes in the Tax Reform Act of 1986." In *Tax Insights*. Washington, DC: February. Ernst and Young.

Clausing, Kimberly A. 2003. Tax-Motivated Transfer Pricing and U.S. Intrafirm Trade Prices. *Journal of Public Economics* 87 (9): 2207–23.

Clausing, Kimberly A. 2009. Multinational Firm Tax Avoidance and Tax Policy. Paper presented at the Spring Symposium of the National Tax Association, May 21–22, Washington, DC.

Congressional Budget Office. 2005. *Taxing Capital Income: Effective Tax Rates and Approaches to Reform*. Washington, DC: Congressional Budget Office.

Cnossen, Sijbren. 1996. Company Taxes in the European Union: Criteria and Options for Reform. *Fiscal Studies* 17 (4): 67–97.

Cummins, Jason G., Kevin A. Hassett, and R. Glenn Hubbard. 1994. A Reconsideration of Investment Behavior Using Tax Reforms as Natural Experiments. *Brookings Papers on Economic Activity* 2: 1–74.

de Mooij, Ruud A., and Sjef Ederveen. 2003. Taxation and Foreign Direct Investment: A Synthesis of Empirical Research. *International Tax and Public Finance* 11: 673–93.

de Mooij, Ruud A., and Sjef Ederveen. 2005. Explaining the Variation in Empirical Estimates of Tax Elasticities of Foreign Investment. Tinbergen Institute Discussion Paper TI 2005–108/3, Tinbergen Institute, Rotterdam, Netherlands.

de Mooij, Ruud A., and Sjef Ederveen. 2008. Corporate Tax Elasticities: A Reader's Guide to Empirical Findings. *Oxford Review of Economic Policy* 24 (4): 680–97.

Devereux, Michael P. 2007. Developments in the Taxation of Corporate Profit in the OECD since 1965: Rates, Bases and Revenues. Oxford University Centre for Business Taxation Working Paper 07/04, Oxford University Centre for Business Taxation, Oxford.

Devereux, Michael P., and Rachel Griffith. 1998. Taxes and the Location of Production: Evidence from a Panel of U.S. Multinationals. *Journal of Public Economics* 68 (3): 335–67.

Devereux, Michael P. and Rachel Griffith. 2003. Evaluating Tax Policy for Location Decisions. *International Tax and Public Finance* 10 (2): 107–126.

Diamond, John W., and Alan D. Viard. 2008. Welfare and Macroeconomic Effects of Deficit-Financed Tax Cuts: Lessons from CGE Models. In Tax Policy Lessons from the 2000s, edited by Alan D. Viard, 145–93. Washington, DC: AEI Press.

Diamond, John W., and George R. Zodrow. 2007. Economic Effects of a Personal Capital Income Tax Add-On to a Consumption Tax. *Finanz-Archiv* 63 (2): 374–95.

Diamond, John W., and George R. Zodrow. 2008a. Consumption Tax Reform: Changes in Business Equity and Housing Prices. In Fundamental Tax Reform: Issues, Choices and Implications, edited by John W. Diamond and George R. Zodrow, 227–60. Cambridge, MA: MIT Press.

Diamond, John W., and George R. Zodrow, eds. 2008b. *Fundamental Tax Reform: Issues, Choices and Implications*. Cambridge, MA: MIT Press.

Diamond, John W., and George R. Zodrow. 2011. *Fundamental Tax Reform: Then and Now.* Baker Institute for Public Policy Report, Rice University, Houston, TX.

Fuest, Clemens, and Thomas Hemmelgarn. 2005. Corporate Tax Policy, Foreign Firm Ownership and Thin Capitalization. *Regional Science and Urban Economics* 35 (5): 508–26.

Fullerton, Don, Yolanda K. Henderson, and James Mackie. 1987. Investment Allocation and Growth under the Tax Reform Act of 1986. In Compendium of Tax Research 1987. Washington, DC: U.S. Department of the Treasury Office of Tax Analysis.

Fullerton, Don, and Diane L. Rogers. 1993. *Who Bears the Lifetime Tax Burden?* Washington, DC: Brookings Institution Press.

Gordon, Roger H., and James R. Hines, Jr. 2002. International Taxation. In *Handbook of Public Economics*, vol. 4, *1935–1989*, edited by Alan J. Auerbach and Martin Feldstein. Amsterdam: North-Holland/Elsevier.

Gordon, Roger H., and Joel Slemrod. 2000. Are "Real" Responses to Taxes Simply Income Shifting between Corporate and Personal Income Tax Bases? In *Does Atlas Shrug? The Economic Consequences of Taxing the Rich*, edited by Joel Slemrod, 242–79. New York and Cambridge, MA: Sage Foundation and Harvard University Press.

Goulder, Lawrence H. 1989. Tax Policy, Housing Prices, and Housing Investment. NBER Working Paper 2814, National Bureau of Economic Research, Cambridge, MA.

Goulder, Lawrence H., John B. Shoven, and John Whalley. 1983. "Domestic Tax Policy and the Foreign Sector: The Importance of Alternative Foreign Sector Formulations to Results from a General Equilibrium Tax Analysis Model." In *Behavioral Simulation Methods in Tax Policy Analysis*, edited by Martin Feldstein, 333–368, Chicago: University of Chicago Press.

Goulder, Lawrence H., and Lawrence H. Summers. 1989. Tax Policy, Asset Prices, and Growth. *Journal of Public Economics* 38 (3): 265–96.

Gravelle, Jane G. 1994. *The Economic Effects of Taxing Capital Income*. Cambridge, MA: MIT Press.

Gravelle, Jane G. 2008. Discussion. In *Fundamental Tax Reform: Issues, Choices and Implications*, edited by John W. Diamond and George R. Zodrow. Cambridge, MA: MIT Press.

Gravelle, Jane G., and Kent Smetters. 2006. Does the Open Economy Assumption Really Mean That Labor Bears the Burden of a Capital Income Tax? *Advances in Economic Analysis and Policy* 6 (1): 1–42.

Grubert, Harry. 1998. Taxes and the Division of Foreign Operating Income among Royalties, Interest, Dividends and Retained Earnings. *Journal of Public Economics* 68 (2): 269–90.

Grubert, Harry. 2001. Tax Planning by Companies and Tax Competition by Governments: Is There Evidence of Changes in Behavior? In International Taxation and Multinational Activity, edited by James R. Hines Jr., 113–39. Chicago: University of Chicago Press.

Grubert, Harry. 2003. Intangible Income, Intercompany Transactions, Income Shifting, and the Choice of Location. *National Tax Journal* 56 (1, part 2): 211–42.

Grubert, Harry, William Randolph, and Donald Rousslang. 1996. Country and Multinational Company Responses to the Tax Reform Act of 1986. *National Tax Journal* 49 (3): 341–58.

Harberger, Arnold C. 2008. Corporation Tax Incidence: Reflections on What Is Known, Unknown and Unknowable. In *Fundamental Tax Reform: Issues, Choices and Implications*, edited by John W. Diamond and George R. Zodrow, 283–308. Cambridge, MA: MIT Press.

Hassett, Kevin A., and Kathryn Newmark. 2008. Taxation and Business Behavior: A Review of the Recent Literature. In *Fundamental Tax Reform: Issues, Choices and Implications*, edited by John W. Diamond and George R. Zodrow, 191 –214.. Cambridge, MA: MIT Press.

Haufler, Andreas, and Guttorm Schjelderup. 2000. Corporate Tax Systems and Cross Country G7. *Oxford Economic Papers* 52 (2): 306–25.

Hayashi, Fumio. 1982. Tobin's Marginal q and Average q: A Neoclassical Interpretation. *Econometrica* 50 (1): 213–24.

Hines, James R., Jr. 1996. Taxes, Technology Transfer and R&D by Multinational Firms. In *Taxing Multinational Corporations*, edited by Martin Feldstein, James R. Hines Jr., and R. Glenn Hubbard, 51–62. Chicago: University of Chicago Press.

Hines, James R., Jr. 1999. Lessons from Behavioral Responses to International Taxation. *National Tax Journal* 52 (2): 305–22.

Huizinga, Harry, and Luc Laeven. 2008. International Profit Shifting within Multinationals: A Multicountry Perspective. *Journal of Public Economics* 92 (5–6):1164–1182.

Huizinga, Harry, Luc Laeven, and Gaetan Nicodème. 2006. Capital Structure and International Debt Shifting. European Economy Economic Paper 263, European Commission, Brussels.

Joint Committee on Taxation. 2005. Macroeconomic Analysis of Various Proposals to Provide $500 Billion in Tax Relief. JCT Report JCX-4–05, Joint Committee on Taxation, Washington, DC.

Joint Committee on Taxation. 2007. Estimated Revenue Effects of Proposals Contained in "The Tax Reduction and Reform Act of 2007." JCT Report JCS-4–09, Joint Committee on Taxation, Washington, DC.

Joint Committee on Taxation. 2008. Estimates of Federal Tax Expenditures for Fiscal Years 2008–2012. JCT Report JCS-2–08, Joint Committee on Taxation, Washington, DC.

Judd, Kenneth L. 1997. The Optimal Tax Rate for Capital Income Is Negative. NBER Working Paper 6004, National Bureau of Economic Research, Cambridge, MA.

Keuschnigg, Christian. 1990. Corporate Taxation and Growth, Dynamic General Equilibrium Simulation Study. In Simulation Models in Tax and Transfer Policy, edited by J. Brunner and H. Petersen, 245–78. New York: Campus Verlag.

Kleinbard, Edward D., George A. Plesko, and Corey M. Goodman. 2006. Is It Time to Liquidate LIFO? *Tax Notes* 113 (3): 237–53.

Mutti, John, and Harry Grubert. 2006. New Developments in the Effect of Taxes on Royalties and the Migration of Intangible Assets Abroad. Paper presented at CRIW Conference on International Services Flow, April 28–29. Bethesda, MD.

[REMOVED IF= FIELD] Neubig, Thomas S. 2006. Where's the Applause? Why Most Corporations Prefer a Lower Rate. *Tax Notes* 111 (4): 483–86.

Neubig, Thomas S. 2007. Expensed Intangibles Have a Zero Effective Tax Rate . . . NOT! *Tax Notes* 116 (11): 959–68.

Neubig, Thomas S., and Estelle Dauchy, 2007. Rangel's Business Tax Reforms: Industry Effects by Sector. *Tax Notes* 117 (9).

Neubig, Thomas S., and Estelle Dauchy. 2008. Additional Dimensions to the Industry Effects of Rangel's Business Tax Reforms. *Tax Insights*. Washington, DC: April. Ernst and Young.

Nicodème, Gaëtan. 2008. Corporate Income Tax and Economic Distortions. CESifo Working Paper 2477, CESifo, Munich.

President's Advisory Panel on Federal Tax Reform. 2005. *Simple, Fair, and Pro-Growth: Proposals to Fix America's Tax System*. Washington, DC: U.S. Government Printing Office.

Slemrod, Joel. 1997. The Taxation of Foreign Direct Investment: Operational Policy Perspectives. In *Borderline Case: International Tax Policy, Corporate Research and Development, and Investment*, edited by James M. Poterba. Washington, DC: National Academy Press.

U.S. Department of the Treasury. 2007. *Approaches to Improve the Competitiveness of the U.S. Business Tax System for the 21st Century*. Washington, DC: U.S. Department of the Treasury Office of Tax Policy.

U.S. Office of Management and Budget. 2008. *Analytical Perspectives, Budget of the United States Government, Fiscal Year 2009*. Washington, DC: U.S. Office of Management and Budget.

Viard, Alan D. 2006. Why LIFO Repeal Is Not the Way to Go. *Tax Notes* 113 (6): 574–76.

Zodrow, George R. 2006. Capital Mobility and Source-Based Taxation of Capital Income in Small Open Economies. *International Tax and Public Finance* 13 (2–3): 269–94.

Zodrow, George R. 2007. Should Capital Income Be Subject to Consumption-Based Taxation? In *Taxing Capital Income*, edited by Henry Aaron, Leonard Burman, and C. Eugene Steuerle. Washington, DC: Urban Institute.

Zodrow, George R. 2008. Capital Mobility and Tax Competition. *National Tax Journal* 63 (4, Part 2): 865–902.

Zodrow, George R. 2010. International Taxation and Company Tax Policy in Small Open Economies. In Tax Reform in Open Economies: International and Country Perspectives, edited by Iris Claus, Norman Gemmell, Michelle Harding, and David White, 109–34. Northampton, MA: Elgar.

Zodrow, George R., and John W. Diamond. 2013. Dynamic Overlapping Generations Computable General Equilibrium Models and the Analysis of Tax Policy. In *Handbook of Computable General Equilibrium Modeling*, edited by Peter B. Dixon and Dale W. Jorgenson, 743–813. Oxford: Elsevier.

Zodrow, George R., and Peter Mieszkowski. 2002. *U.S. Tax Reform in the 21st Century*. Cambridge: Cambridge University Press.

Discussion

Ruud A. de Mooij[33]

Is a lower corporate income tax rate what the United States needs? Do we expect it to create jobs and boost growth? And is corporate tax rate relief the most pressing concern in U.S. tax policy?

Diamond, Zodrow, Neubig and Carroll (DZNC) address these issues in two ways. First, they provide a comprehensive review of arguments for corporate income tax rate reduction, based on findings in the literature. Second, they use a computable general equilibrium model developed by Diamond and Zodrow (DZ) to quantify the impact of corporate tax reform on the U.S. economy. In my comments, I focus primarily on the second issue: the modeling approach. I will frequently refer to my own earlier work, which is closely related to their work but applied to the European debate. At the end, I address the question as to whether the United States should reduce its corporate income tax rate.

Modeling Approach

The combination of, on the one hand, an outstanding review of arguments and, on the other hand, the use of simulations from a comprehensive overlapping generations (OLG) model makes the DZNC essay extremely valuable for the discussion about U.S. corporate tax reform. Often this debate is plagued by misleading claims and fuzziness between political and economic arguments. The modeling framework is probably the best possible starting point to discuss the impact of U.S. corporate tax reform in a more structured way, especially when placed in a broader context of arguments. The model is particularly welcome as it brings the three vital pillars of theory, empirics, and institutions together into one consistent framework.

First, theoretical underpinning structures thinking. The outcomes of the model are the logical mathematical consequence of the assumptions made by the modelers and hence verifiable, offering common ground and common terminology for a fruitful debate. Of course, many assumptions in the DZ model can be—and should be—criticized. A key question, for instance, is how the conclusions about policy reforms change if certain disputable theoretical assumptions are changed. But the possibility of doing so is precisely what makes the model so useful: without a model, such a debate would be much more difficult.

Second, empirics add numbers. This is important for policymakers who are generally interested in the quantitative impact of reforms. Assumptions in the DZ model are based on the best available knowledge from empirical studies. But to be honest, I think the numbers rolling out of the simulations should be taken with a grain of salt. In fact, numbers can be highly misleading when politicians and policymakers use them without referring to the uncertainties underlying them. Probably more important than the numbers is the story that the model tells us. Why does one reform have a positive impact on GDP and consumption and another reform does not? Why do certain parameters or elasticities matter a lot and others only marginally? Empirics help us to get a sense of the relative order of magnitude of various distortions and whether the balance of various effects is most likely positive or negative.

Third, the more detailed modeling of institutions reflecting actual policy parameters makes the analysis more interesting from a policy perspective. Models usually differ a lot in their level of detail on actual institutional parameters. The most aggregated models contain only a simple t-variable, reflecting a tax. The most elaborate models contain a whole range of rules and regulations reflecting details of the tax system. The DZ model is somewhere in between those extremes: being a general equilibrium model, it inevitably has less detail than some microsimulation models (which lack the general equilibrium framework), but the model is much richer in describing the corporate tax base than many other general equilibrium models. This allows the authors to explore policy-relevant reforms, such as base broadening with rate reduction in the corporate income tax.

Qualifications

The basic DZ model is essentially a neoclassical framework of investment. It thus ignores issues that many recent empirical studies emphasize, such as inframarginal investment decisions and international tax arbitrage. Indeed, studies have found that corporate income taxes probably have more sizable effects through these channels than through the traditional neoclassical ones (see De Mooij and Ederveen 2008 for an overview). I therefore have more faith in the extended DZ model than in the basic model. The extended model includes, for instance, imperfect product markets that lead to the presence of economic rents; it allows for (imperfect) international capital mobility; and it includes tax arbitrage through profit shifting by multinationals. The way in which these extensions are modeled, however, leaves room for further improvement. Moreover, a number of other relevant decision margins are still ignored in the DZ model. I elaborate on these points.

Investment

As an instrument for exploring the economic impact of corporate income tax changes, probably the most important omission of the DZ model is the absence of discrete location decisions (see Devereux and Griffith 2002 for an overview of this work). Many empirical studies have found that average effective tax rates exert a larger and more robust impact on foreign direct investment than marginal effective tax rates do. This can be explained by the behavior of multinationals. Their location choice will depend on the amount of after-tax profit that can be earned, that is, income related to location-specific and firm-specific rents. If a lower corporate tax rate would attract discrete investment projects to a country because the rents are firm specific, the DZ model will underestimate the effects of corporate tax rate relief.

The question is then how to model multinational behavior. This is not easy because the theory of multinationals is not particularly well developed. One option is to apply insights from the new economic geography literature, which has been used for corporate tax issues by, for example, Baldwin and Krugman (2004). These models explain the location of multinational firms across regions by trading off the benefits from agglomeration due to increasing returns to scale and the cost of transportation of goods to the final consumers. In an agglomeration-equilibrium, firms earn location-specific rents. High corporate tax rates can then be sustained without the immediate risk that multinationals relocate their firms. However, corporate tax rates that are too high may destroy the agglomeration equilibrium and multinationals will have many small subsidiaries in different locations, producing close to their home markets. Developing a structural model for multinationals along these or other theoretical lines is a challenge, but also an innovation that would increase the reliability of the DZ model for the purpose of corporate tax analysis.

Investment effects of corporate tax relief may also be underestimated for another reason. In the DZ model, there are no firms that are credit constrained. If this were important, a lower corporate tax rate would stimulate investment through its positive impact on the cash flow of firms. Indeed, some empirical studies have found that firm cash flows have significant effects on investment (Hubbard 1997). Today some firms may be credit constrained, especially small and innovative ones, although this is probably less important in the United States than elsewhere in the world.

Profit Shifting

Tax arbitrage through multinational profit shifting is important. Cross-country evidence suggests that base erosion due to high statutory corporate tax rates is significant and substantial (see Heckemeyer and Overesch 2013 for a recent overview). In the extended DZ model, this effect is captured by an ad hoc expression, that is, it is not integrated in the firm decision-making process. Hence, decisions regarding investment and profit shifting are taken independently. Some recent empirical studies, however, suggest that these interactions are important. For instance, Smart and Hong (2010) find that the possibility of tax arbitrage effectively makes high corporate tax rates less important for investment, as investing firms realize that they can shift profits to low-tax locations. Real distortions are thus mitigated by the opportunities for tax arbitrage. In that sense, the DZ model might overestimate the distortionary impact of corporate taxes on investment.

Capitalization

The DZ model keeps the ratio between debt and equity within corporations as exogenous. Endogenizing this choice would be both straightforward and important. Modeling the simultaneous choice of investment and finance has been done before by others (see various references in the DZNC essay in this chapter). Modeling the debt bias is also important because it adds a significant distortion of the corporate income tax. I have recently concluded that these welfare costs might be much larger than economists have previously thought (De Mooij 2012). One reason is that companies today appear to be responding more aggressively to tax than in the past in their capital structure choices. Another reason is that the harmful economic effects of excessive levels of debt might be much bigger, especially in the banking sector, due to externalities (De Mooij, Keen, and Orihara 2013). While debt bias can be reduced by a lower corporate tax rate, other reforms are more effective in doing so. An example is the allowance for corporate equity, which I discuss below.

Parameterization

Apart from the theoretical structure of the model, choices with respect to parameter values are critical. For some parameters, the literature might have converged to some consensus, such as the elasticity of labor supply, although even here the range of estimates is large. For other parameters, the evidence is very diverse, and consensus is lacking. This holds, for instance, for responses in (foreign) investment, the choice of legal form, and the importance of profit shifting. Also, other parameters in the DZ model, such as the size of economic rents, are very difficult to estimate and thus highly uncertain.

The best way to deal with this tremendous uncertainty in parameter values is by performing sensitivity analysis. This is currently missing from DZNC's essay. How sensitive are the quantitative outcomes for changes in the size of economic rents, the investment elasticity, and the elasticity of labor supply? Sensitivity analysis is important for a number of reasons. First, it gives the right message to policymakers—that there is not one number that represents the impact of corporate tax reform but a range of plausible outcomes, reflecting uncertainty. Second, sensitivity analysis gives an idea about which parameters are critical and which are less important for the quantitative outcomes. This gives guidance to researchers as to what parameters they should pay more attention to. Finally, sensitivity analysis is useful to get a better understanding of how the model works. A comprehensive model always hides secrets, which makes it difficult to grasp all the outcomes. By varying parameters, one gets to know the model a lot better.

Welfare

Models like the DZ model are well designed for performing welfare analysis. This is important because consumption and GDP are imperfect indicators for welfare and therefore not sufficiently comprehensive to assess the desirability of reforms. For instance, both indicators ignore the value of leisure. Moreover, while GDP may rise significantly if policies attract foreign direct investment, welfare may rise much less as capital returns will flow to the foreign owners. A comprehensive welfare measure is therefore superior in judging the attractiveness of policy reforms. This would be a straightforward calculation in a general equilibrium model, although some assumptions would need to be made regarding the distribution of welfare across generations.

Does the United States Need a Lower CIT Rate?

DZNC are not entirely consistent in answering this question. Although they forcefully advocate a reduction in corporate income tax rate in the United States, to be financed by base broadening, their basic model simulations do not support this conclusion. In fact, a policy of base broadening and rate reduction is not efficiency enhancing in these simulations. However, the extended model with profit shifting shows more consistent messages and supports the positive economic impact of a corporate tax rate cut. I think that both their text and models teach us important lessons.

Base Broadening and Rate Reduction

Many politicians and policymakers have a strong belief that base broadening with rate reduction is good for the economy. However, this is not always true, and particularly not in the corporate income tax area. The DZ model explains why this is so. In particular, tax expenditures generally reduce the cost of capital at the margin of new investment. In contrast, rate reduction also raises the after-tax economic profits. Tax expenditures are therefore more important for investment and GDP than low tax rates.

This result is generally poorly understood and therefore important to explain to policymakers. In fact, the risk of lower investment is a serious drawback of eliminating tax expenditures. Acknowledging this is better than changing the way in which tax expenditures are modeled—as DZNC do by following an assumption that all tax expenditures other than depreciation are lump-sum transfers. Of course, some tax expenditures might be more useful than others and some forms of base broadening may indeed be desirable. Yet base broadening is not in general an efficient way to finance rate reduction. In fact, proposals for base narrowing, such as the allowance for corporate equity, might have more appeal.

Allowance for Corporate Equity

The allowance for corporate equity involves a deduction for the normal return on equity. Its base is the book value of equity in corporations, minus equity participations in other firms (to avoid duplication of tax relief). The rate would be the risk-free return on capital—assuming that firms have full assurance that they will receive the full value of the deduction. This system has gained popularity in academic circles due to its neutrality properties (Institute for Fiscal Studies 2011). First, it eliminates the debt bias that currently characterizes corporate tax systems. Second, by allowing a deduction for the normal rate of return for equity, it charges no tax on projects with a return that matches the cost of capital. Thus, it transforms the corporate income tax into a tax on economic rents. Such a tax in principle would not distort the scale of investment. Finally, it offsets investment distortions induced by differences between economic depreciation and depreciation for tax purposes. For example, an increase in accelerated depreciation for tax purposes will reduce the book value of assets in the tax accounts, thereby also reducing the allowance for corporate equity in later years. This exactly offsets the benefits from earlier depreciation in present value terms. Hence, the present value of the sum of the depreciation allowance and the allowance for corporate equity are independent of the rate at which firms write down their assets in the tax accounts.

For the European Union, I have compared the economic impact of an allowance for corporate equity with corporate tax rate reduction, using a model similar to the one developed by DZ. It is the so-called CORTAX model (Bettendorf et al. 2010), which is heavily inspired by an earlier model that Sorensen (2000) developed. As the DZ model, CORTAX is an overlapping-generation framework describing saving, investment, and labor supply behavior. In addition, it models the behavior of multinationals. They choose the amount of foreign direct investment in different subsidiaries and the transfer prices charged for intracompany trade. The transfer price might be manipulated in order to shift profits across affiliates.

In De Mooij and Devereux (2011), we use CORTAX to explore an allowance for corporate equity in the EU, financed by an increase in the corporate income tax rate (thus effectively comparing an allowance for corporate equity with corporate tax rate reduction). What this simulation teaches us is the following. If an individual European country does this reform (i.e., with other European countries keeping their corporate tax policy unchanged), it is welfare improving in countries with a small multinational sector. For countries with a large multinational sector, however, the reform is welfare reducing. Indeed, while the cost of capital declines due to the allowance and the debt bias

Table 8.12
Effects of an Allowance for Corporate Equity in the European Union Financed by a Higher Statutory Corporate Tax Rate, according to the CORTAX Model

	Unilateral Reform	EU-Wide Reform
Investment	3.9	4.8
Employment	0.2	0.5
GDP	0.8	1.8
Welfare	-0.2	0.4

Source: De Mooji and Devereux (2011).

distortion disappears, multinational investment declines and the tax base erodes through outward profit shifting. Hence, an allowance for corporate equity is not necessarily better than corporate tax rate reduction in an individual European country. In fact, on average across countries, the model reports a small negative effect on welfare (table 8.12).

This result changes, however, if all European countries pursue the same reform. Table 8.12 shows that an allowance for corporate equity in the entire EU boosts investment, employment, and GDP and raises welfare even though it is financed by a higher corporate tax rate. The reason is that the higher corporate tax rate is much less distortionary for location choices and profit shifting if other countries increase their rate by a similar amount. A European-wide allowance for corporate equity is therefore more attractive than corporate tax rate reduction.

What does this teach us for the United States? The United States is probably better in comparison to the EU than to a single European country. Hence, the results from the right column in table 8.12 might be more relevant for the United States than those in the left column. Of course, this should be verified in a model that is calibrated for the United States, such as the DZ model, especially the extended model that includes profit shifting. I therefore encourage DZNC to simulate such a reform with their model. My guess would be that the results from the right column carry over.

Should the United States Follow International Trends?

Despite its appeal, the allowance for corporate equity receives little attention in the U.S. debate.[34] Corporate tax rate reduction is much more popular, probably because it is simpler to understand. Some people advocate a corporate tax rate cut in the United States also by pointing to international trends. Indeed, headline corporate tax rates have been declining rapidly. Especially in Europe, sharp rate reductions reflect a process of intense regional tax competition. Such rates might have become inefficiently low, leading to revenue loss and underprovision of public goods, as predicted by Zodrow and Mieszkowski (1986). Today the United States is an outlier (together with Japan and some large European economies, although rates are declining there as well) in having kept a relatively high corporate tax rate. The question is whether the United States should follow the worldwide trend and reduce its rate, or follow its own course and consider an alternative path toward reducing distortions of the corporate tax.

Broader Tax Issues

While an allowance for corporate equity might be attractive, its main obstacle will be its cost to the budget. In De Mooij (2012), I estimate the budgetary cost of an allowance for corporate equity in the United States at 0.43 percent of GDP. This, of course, is significant, especially in light of the large consolidation needs.[35] The same would apply to rate reduction when suitable options for base broadening are limited. This opens a broader discussion about U.S. tax reform. Of course, lower corporate taxes or an allowance for corporate equity could be financed by other tax increases. For instance, there is large untapped revenue potential in the United States in the form of consumption. Here, the United States can probably learn more from other countries, where the value-added tax (VAT) acts as a relatively efficient source of revenue raising multiple percentages of GDP. Introducing a VAT would allow the United States both to meet its fiscal challenges and enable it to have significant reforms in the corporate income tax. Perhaps the next paper with the DZ model could be devoted to this broader tax debate.

References

Baldwin, Richard E., and Paul Krugman. 2004. Agglomeration, Integration and Tax Harmonization. *European Economic Review* 48 (1): 1–23.

Bettendorf, Leon, Michael Devereux, Albert van der Horst, Simon Loretz, and Ruud A. de Mooij. 2010. Corporate Tax Harmonization in the EU. *Economic Policy* 25 (63): 537–90.

De Mooij, Ruud A. 2012. Tax Biases to Debt Finance: Assessing the Problem, Finding Solutions. *Fiscal Studies* 33 (4): 489–512.

De Mooij, Ruud A., and Michael Devereux. 2011. An Applied Analysis of ACE and CBIT Reforms in the EU. *International Tax and Public Finance* 18 (1): 93–120.

De Mooij, Ruud A., and Sjef Ederveen. 2008. Corporate Tax Elasticities: A Reader's Guide to Empirical Findings. *Oxford Review of Economic Policy* 24 (4): 680–97.

De Mooij, Ruud A., Michael Keen, and Masanori Orihara. 2013. Taxation, Bank Leverage, and Financial Crises. IMF Working Paper 13/48, International Monetary Fund, Washington, DC.

Devereux, Michael P., and Rachel Griffith. 2002. The Impact of Corporate Taxation on the Location of Capital: A Review. *Swedish Economic Policy Review* 9:79–102.

Heckemeyer, Josh H., and Michael Overesch. 2013. Multinational's Profit Responses to Tax Differentials: Effect Size and Shifting Channels. ZEW Discussion Paper 13–045, Center for European Economic Research, Mannheim, Germany.

Hubbard, R. Glenn, 1997. Capital-Market Imperfections and Investment. NBER Working Paper 5996, National Bureau of Economic Research, Cambridge, MA.

Institute for Fiscal Studies. 2011. Tax by Design: Mirrlees Review. In *Part 2: Reforming the Tax System for the 21st Century*. London: Institute for Fiscal Studies.

Kleinbard, Edward. 2007. Designing an Income Tax on Capital. In *Taxing Capital Income*, ed. Henry J. Aaron, Leonard E. Burman, and Eugene C. Steuerle. Washington, DC: Urban Institute Press.

Smart, Michael, and Qing Hong. 2010. In Praise of Tax Havens: International Tax Planning and Foreign Direct Investment. *European Economic Review* 54 (1): 82–95.

Sorensen, Peter B. 2000. The Case for International Tax Coordination Reconsidered. *Economic Policy* 15 (31): 429–72.

Zodrow, George, and Peter Mieszkowski. 1986. Pigou, Tiebout, Property Taxation, and the Underprovision of Local Public Goods. *Journal of Urban Economics* 19 (3): 356–70.

Discussion

Alan D. Viard

Diamond, Zodrow, Neubig and Carroll (DZNC) tackle a timely and important topic, analyzing the impact on long-run output of reducing the statutory corporate income tax rate. Their results support two broad conclusions, both of which are economically plausible. First, when corporate tax rate reduction is financed by the curtailment of traditional business tax expenditures, its impact on long-run output is limited and uncertain, depending on the selection of the tax expenditures to be curtailed and the relative magnitudes of various economic effects that are difficult to estimate precisely. Second, corporate tax rate reduction is more likely to increase long-run output if it is financed through other means.

The authors shed valuable light on these questions by skillfully exploiting the Diamond-Zodrow computable general equilibrium model. As I have noted elsewhere (Viard 2008), the basic Diamond-Zodrow model has several features that make it well suited for the analysis of tax policy, including a general equilibrium methodology, rational expectations, a careful representation of the tax code's key features, and separate sector detail for corporate business, noncorporate business, and owner-occupied and rental housing. The version of the model DZNC used also includes important extensions that address, at least in a rudimentary fashion, above-normal returns, international capital flows, and tax avoidance. To be sure, the model still has some limitations, notably its failure to model the debt-equity decision.

Why might corporate tax rate reduction be expected to boost long-run output? The simplest reason is that rate reduction, in isolation, reduces the effective marginal tax rate on new investment. As previous authors have found and as the authors confirm, however, that potential benefit can be fully, or more than fully, offset if the rate reduction is financed by curtailment of depreciation allowances and other business tax expenditures, such as those listed in table 8.2. I will refer to rate reduction financed in that manner as "the conventional rate-reduction strategy." DZNC's results confirm that the conventional rate-reduction strategy can offer only limited gains. The strategy's primary limitation is its treatment of old and new capital.

Old and New Capital

An extensive literature, beginning with Auerbach and Kotlikoff (1987), notes the fundamental economic importance of the relative treatment of old and new capital. All else equal, taxing old capital rather than new capital makes future generations better off and increases long-run output. That result is attributable to both efficiency gains, reflecting the fact that an unanticipated tax on old capital is theoretically a lump-sum tax, and intergenerational redistribution, reflecting the fact that the incidence of a tax on old capital falls on current rather than future generations.

Using the basic Diamond-Zodrow model, DZNC generally find that rate reduction has little impact on long-run output when it is financed by the curtailment of incentives that apply only to new investment. In principle, there are ways to limit the gain received by old capital. One of the authors, Zodrow (1988), has previously discussed the Treasury Department's 1985 windfall recapture proposal, which would have imposed a tax on old capital to offset part of its gain from rate reduction. And, the capital-cost recovery reform proposed by Senator Max Baucus (D-MT) in November 2013 would break with historical practice by slowing depreciation schedules for old capital, as well as new investment. In practice, though, the scope for such measures may be limited, a conclusion reinforced by the unceremonious rejection of the 1985 proposal and the uncertain prospects of the Baucus proposal.

Accordingly, the conventional rate-reduction strategy has limited potential to boost long-run output unless rate reduction offers other benefits that outweigh the strategy's shift of the tax burden from old to new capital. As it turns out, rate reduction potentially offers several such benefits, some of which are included in the basic Diamond-Zodrow model, some of which are included in DZNC's extension of that model, and some of which are omitted from DZNC's model. It is unclear, however, whether those benefits are large enough for rate reduction to yield a significant net gain in long-run output.

Other Potential Benefits of Rate Reduction

As DZNC observe, the conventional rate-reduction strategy affects the economy in ways other than altering the relative treatment of old and new capital. It also alters the allocation of resources across assets and industries and between the corporate and noncorporate business sectors, the choice between debt and equity finance, the treatment of above-normal returns, and the incentive to engage in tax avoidance.

The basic Diamond-Zodrow model captures one potential long-run output gain from rate reduction: the narrowing of the distortion between corporate and noncorporate businesses. A revenue-neutral reform that curtails tax expenditures in both sectors while lowering tax rates only in the corporate sector necessarily raises taxes on the noncorporate sector and lowers taxes on the corporate sector, thereby narrowing the current tax system's bias against the corporate sector. Although DZNC reasonably find that the proposals they examine offer long-run output gains through this channel, those gains are unlikely to be achieved by any tax reform plan that will ultimately be adopted in the United States. The required net tax increase on the noncorporate business sector is likely to be politically unviable because noncorporate businesses are viewed (somewhat inaccurately) as small businesses and therefore sacrosanct. Any politically viable reform plan is likely to reduce individual tax rates on noncorporate business income in order to avert a net noncorporate tax increase, thereby eliminating these gains.

DZNC usefully extend the basic Diamond-Zodrow model to include above-normal returns, which are important for understanding the effects of corporate tax rate reduction. Because above-normal returns receive smaller benefits from investment incentives than from rate reduction, the conventional rate-reduction strategy lowers the tax on above-normal returns. As DZNC observe, that fact makes the conventional strategy less attractive in a closed economy, in which a tax on above-normal returns raises revenue in an efficient lump-sum manner. The same conclusion would hold in an open economy under destination-based taxes or origin-based taxes with proper sourcing of royalties and perfect transfer pricing. Under imperfect origin-based taxes (such as actual corporate income tax systems), however, the taxation of above-normal returns inefficiently prompts investments generating such returns to relocate abroad, making the conventional strategy more attractive. DZNC's modeling of these phenomena is tentative and requires further refinement, but it represents a significant step forward. DZNC also extend the basic Diamond-Zodrow model to allow tax rate increases to generate accounting transactions that shift profits abroad, which they call tax rate arbitrage. Although the profit shifting does not directly affect output, it diminishes the revenue gain from a tax rate increase and thereby makes rate increases less attractive.

DZNC observe that their model omits the output gains that rate reduction can achieve by narrowing the debt-equity distortion. Although early studies concluded that the debt-equity decision was unresponsive to incentives, recent evidence points in a different direction. De Mooij (2011)'s meta-analysis of nineteen empirical studies of the effect of taxes on the debt-equity choice finds that a 10 percentage point reduction in the corporate tax rate induces a decline of 2.8 percentage points in the debt-asset ratio. Rate reduction can therefore generate significant gains by reducing the tax bias against equity.

DZNC state that their model omits another gain from the conventional rate-reduction strategy. In practice, though, this gain may be zero or even negative. They argue that the conventional strategy boosts output by narrowing differences in tax treatment between different assets and industries, an effect that their model cannot capture due to its lack of industry detail. As I have discussed (Viard 2009), however, making a tax base broader need not make it more neutral. The curtailment of some tax expenditures, such as LIFO inventory accounting, actually impedes neutrality by increasing taxes on assets that are already more heavily taxed than alternative assets. Whether the conventional strategy reduces or increases disparities between assets and industries cannot be resolved in the abstract, as it depends on which tax expenditures are curtailed.

In their most comprehensive simulation, as reported in table 8.4, the authors find a small net gain in long-run output from the conventional rate-reduction strategy. In a more general framework, the conventional rate-reduction strategy may either increase or reduce long-run output. Although the authors' model omits some gains (the narrowing of the tax bias against equity) offered by the conventional strategy, it includes other gains (the narrowing of the tax bias against the corporate sector) that the strategy is unlikely to achieve in the current political environment. Moreover, changes in the magnitudes of the various effects, all of which are highly uncertain, could easily change the sign of the net impact on long-run output. Given the current state of knowledge, it is difficult to do more than sketch the relevant factors and describe the range of uncertainty, as DZNC have ably done.

In summary, the conventional rate-reduction strategy may boost long-run output, but such an outcome is far from certain and any gain is unlikely to be large. Bigger and more certain gains can be achieved if rate reduction is financed in other ways. DZNC confirm this finding, but they consider a relatively limited set of financing mechanisms.

Other Ways to Pay for Rate Reduction

DZNC consider reforms in which corporate tax rate reduction is financed by wage tax increases or transfer payment reductions and find that these reforms boost long-run output. Surprisingly, they do not consider the use of consumption taxation, an approach that is likely to dominate the use of wage taxation. Whatever their economic merits, though, any of these options would be politically problematic because they would lower a tax that is (at least perceived to be) borne by the wealthy while raising taxes or cutting benefits for the broader population. They do not consider other options that offer clearer economic gains than the conventional strategy, but share its political advantage of not reducing the amount of tax collected from corporations and their investors.

One such option is to restrict the deduction for corporate interest payments, either through a percentage haircut or restrictions on highly leveraged firms. Although the interest deduction is not classified as a tax expenditure, curtailing it would reduce the current tax system's tax bias against equity. Brill (2012), Pozen and Goodman (2012), and others have offered proposals to curtail the corporate interest deduction in the United States, and de Mooij (2011) describes similar measures adopted abroad.

An even more promising option is to reduce corporate income tax rates while increasing individual income tax rates on dividends and capital gains, effectively swapping firm-level taxes for shareholder-level taxes. Taxation at the individual level allows the tax rate on corporate income to be tailored to the shareholder's ability to pay, permitting greater progressivity. A shift to taxation at the individual level offers additional benefits in a global economy. Unlike corporate income taxes, shareholder-level taxes tied to the shareholder's country of residence do not encourage corporations to invest or shift profits abroad and do not disadvantage domestic-chartered corporations relative to foreign-chartered corporations. Grubert and Altshuler (2008), Altshuler, Harris, and Toder (2010), Graetz (2011), Sullivan (2011), Viard (2013), and Gravelle (2014) discuss the economic advantages of shifting the taxation of corporate income toward the shareholder level. This option has also drawn attention in the current policy debate, winning support from Yglesias (2013), Pethokoukis (2013), Barro (2013), and Salam (2013).

Shareholder-level taxation poses some challenges. To ensure that retained corporate earnings do not escape tax, it may be necessary to tax shareholders on an accrual basis, a strategy that income taxation may have to embrace in any event in response to taxpayers' manipulation of realization and basis rules. DZNC's model could be used to analyze some of the effects of a move toward shareholder-level taxation.

Conclusion

DZNC's results confirm that corporate tax rate reduction financed by the curtailment of traditional business tax expenditures offers uncertain and modest economic gains. Both policymakers and economic modelers should focus greater attention on proposals to finance corporate tax rate reduction by restricting the corporate interest deduction or by increasing shareholder taxes on corporate income.

References

Altshuler, Rosanne, Benjamin H. Harris, and Eric Toder. 2010. Capital Income Taxation and Progressivity in a Global Economy. *Virginia Tax Review* 30 (2): 355–88.

Auerbach, Alan J., and Laurence J. Kotlikoff. 1987. *Dynamic Fiscal Policy*. Cambridge: Cambridge University Press.

Barro, Josh. 2013. Don't Tax Apple, Tax Its Shareholders. *Bloomberg*, May 24. http://www.bloomberg.com/news/2013-05-24/don-t-tax-apple-tax-its-shareholders.html.

Brill, Alex. 2012. A pro-Growth, Progressive, and Practical Proposal to Cut Business Tax Rates. AEI Tax Policy Outlook, no. 1 (January). http://www.aei.org/files/2012/02/10/-a-progrowth-progressive-and-practical-plan-to-cut-business-tax-rates_13472858147.pdf.

De Mooij, Ruud. 2011. The Tax Elasticity of corporate debt: A Synthesis of Size and Variations. International Monetary Fund Working Paper 11/95. http://www.imf.org/external/pubs/ft/wp/2011/wp1195.pdf.

Graetz, Michael M. 2011. Testimony before the Senate Finance Committee, March 8. http://www.finance.senate.gov/imo/media/doc/030811%20mg%20test.pdf.

Gravelle, Jane. 2014. *Corporate Tax Reform: Issues for Congress*. Congressional Research Service Report RL34229. http://www.ctj.org/pdf/crscorporatetaxreformissuesforcongress.pdf.

Grubert, Harry, and Rosanne Altshuler. 2008. Corporate Taxes in the World Economy: Reforming the Taxation of Cross-Border Income. In Fundamental Tax Reform: Issues, Choices and Implications, edited by John W. Diamond and George R. Zodrow, 319–54. Cambridge, MA: MIT Press.

Pethokoukis, James. 2013. What Tim Cook Should Say: Tax Me More, Apple Not at All. *AEIdeas*, May 21. http://www.aei-ideas.org/2013/05/what-tim-cook-should-say-tax-me-more-apple-not-at-all/.

Pozen, Robert C., and Lucas W. Goodman. 2012. Capping the Deductibility of Corporate Interest Expense. *Tax Notes* 137 (11): 1207–24.

Salam, Reihan. 2013. A Schumpterian Reason to Replace Corporate Income Taxes with Higher Capital Income Taxes on Individuals. *National Review Online, the Agenda,* May 22. http://www.nationalreview.com/agenda/349052/schumpeterian-reason-replace-corporate-income-taxes-higher-capital-income-taxes.

Sullivan, Martin. 2011. Corporate Tax Reform: Time to Think outside the Box. *Tax Notes* 130 (13): 1513–17.

Viard, Alan D. 2008. Discussion. In Fundamental Tax Reform: Issues, Choices and Implications, edited by John W. Diamond and George R. Zodrow, 319–54. Cambridge, MA: MIT Press.

Viard, Alan D. 2009. Two Cheers for Corporate Tax Base Broadening. *National Tax Journal* 62 (3): 399–412.

Viard, Alan D. 2013. *PPL*: Exposing the flaws of the foreign tax credit. *Tax Notes* 138 (5): 553–66.

Yglesias, Matthew. 2013. Scrap the Corporate Income tax. *Slate, Moneybox*, April 9. http://www.slate.com/articles/business/moneybox/2013/04/corporate_income_tax_reform_it_s_not_possible_we_should_just_get_rid_of.html.

Zodrow, George R. 1988. The Windfall Recapture Tax: Issues of Theory and Design. *Public Finance Quarterly* 16 (4): 387–424.

Notes

1. Numerous other countries also enacted base-broadening, rate-reducing reforms during this time period; see Boskin and McLure (1990). More recently, Devereux (2007) documents that recent corporate income tax reforms in numerous OECD countries have also moved in the direction of lower rates and broadened tax bases.

2. Note, however, that under the still controversial "new view" of dividend taxation, the taxation of dividends at the individual level has no effect on marginal incentives for investment financed with retained earnings. Our analysis follows most of the existing literature, including the U.S. Department of the Treasury (1992) report on the integration of business and individual level taxes, in assuming the validity of the traditional "double taxation" view of dividend taxes.

3. We shall refer to such activities as tax arbitrage, defined narrowly to include only such arbitrage that takes advantage of differences in corporate income tax rates across countries.

4. Indeed, some recent proposals would completely replace the current income tax system with a tax based on consumption, which would eliminate the taxation of "normal" returns to capital while subjecting "above-normal" returns to capital to taxation at the statutory rate. For a recent review of these arguments, see Zodrow (2007).

5. See http://waysandmeans.house.gov/taxreform/ and http://www.treasury.gov/resource-center/tax-policy/Documents/The-Presidents-Framework-for-Business-Tax-Reform-02-22-2012.pdf.

6. See the data set compiled by the Institute for Fiscal Studies, "Corporate Tax Rate Data," which is available at the IFS website: http://www.ifs.org.uk/publications.php?publication_id=3210.

7. For recent discussions of potential reforms in the United States, including various forms of consumption-based taxation, see Zodrow and Mieszkowski (2002), Auerbach and Hassett (2005), Aaron, Burman, and Steuerle (2007), and Diamond and Zodrow (2008b).

8. For example, see U.S. Department of the Treasury (2007).

9. Note, however, that even in this case, many of the incentives for new investments will nevertheless be inframarginal and will reduce taxes for investments that would have been made even in the absence of the incentive.

10. In their empirical application, Devereux and Griffith (2003) calculate average effective tax rates for prospective investments that earn various arbitrary pretax rates of return (30 percent, 70 percent, and 100 percent).

11. For example, the Congressional Budget Office (2005) estimates that combined business and individual-level effective marginal tax rates are 26.3 percent for corporate income and 20.6 percent for the noncorporate sector.

12. This reform thus differs from the proposal analyzed in Department of the Treasury (2007), which assumed that the elimination of tax expenditures in the noncorporate sector was accompanied by the introduction of a new, relatively low individual-level tax rate applied to noncorporate income and thus did not finance any reduction in the corporate tax rate.

13. We do not, however, address the issue of deferral of foreign source income. The Joint Committee on Taxation (2008) tax expenditure estimates do not include deferral as a "business synthetic tax expenditure," but rather as a "major provision not classified as a tax subsidy." Subsequently, the committee has reverted back to its traditional approach and includes deferral of active income and active financing income of controlled foreign corporations (CFCs) as tax expenditures. Our analyses do not include a change in the tax treatment of active income of CFCs other than the lower U.S. corporate tax rate that would apply to such income.

14. For example, although these results are quite dated, Fullerton, Henderson, and Mackie (1987) estimate that the Tax Reform Act of 1986, which broadened the corporate base while significantly reducing both corporate and individual tax rates (while slightly increasing marginal effective tax rates in the corporate sector), reduced the overall capital stock by 0.6 percent, but increased output by 0.2 percent due to the improved allocation

of capital attributable to more neutral taxation of business investment. Although effective tax rate differentials are smaller under current law than prior to the enactment of TRA86 Fullerton et al. 1987 estimate effective tax rates across different types of assets that vary from zero to 51 percent), these results suggest that improved allocation of capital under the base-broadening, rate-reducing reform analyzed in this essay might result in an increase in GDP on the order of 0.2 to 0.3 percent. This effect would be augmented by the gains attributable to reduced reliance on debt finance but diminished by the costs of income shifting from labor to capital and any losses in efficiency due to the elimination of well-targeted provisions that encourage activities that generate positive economic externalities.

15. The particular reform analyzed results in an increase in taxation of the noncorporate sector, since its tax expenditures are eliminated while personal income tax rates remain constant. This reduces the distortion between corporate and noncorporate investment but has an adverse effect on investment in the noncorporate business sector.

16. Note, however, that the amount of rate reduction is overstated to the extent that the cumulative effects of eliminating the tax expenditures are less than their simple sum due to interaction effects that we do not consider. On the other hand, Carroll, Neubig, and Cox (2011) report that over 40 percent of the corporate base broadening in the 1986 Tax Act was not from eliminating tax expenditures and suggest that additional business base broadening could be possible to lower rates further.

17. State corporate income taxes add approximately 4 percentage points to the corporate income tax rate.

18. Recall, however, that our analysis does not capture any reform-induced efficiency gains from eliminating the distortions across industries within the corporate and noncorporate production sectors.

19. One potentially interesting extension to the analysis, left to future research, would be to model international capital flows as also responsive to differences in after-tax returns in the imperfectly competitive sector.

20. The Treasury estimates of corporate tax expenditures differ from those of the Joint Committee on Taxation in many dimensions, and in the aggregate is about $12 billion greater. One important difference is that the committee estimate of accelerated depreciation is on average roughly $16 billion lower than that of the Treasury.

21. An additional $7.3 billion of tax expenditures apply to the rental housing sector and is included in the $21 billion of noncorporate tax expenditures.

22. The treatment of accelerated deductions for depreciation is discussed further below.

23. This provision allows revenue from selling U.S. inventory to be counted as foreign source income, which increases the foreign tax credits available for firms in excess foreign tax credit positions.

24. This estimate comes from Joint Committee on Taxation (2007) and includes the first year of the recovery of LIFO reserves, which is assumed to be phased in over eight years, a point discussed further below.

25. The base reduction equals the tax expenditure divided by the corporate tax rate.

26. See Kleinbard, Plesko, and Goodman (2006) and Viard (2006) for further details.

27. Since the JCT study provides estimates only for corporations, we do not consider the much smaller effects of eliminating these provisions in the noncorporate sector.

28. See Joint Committee on Taxation (2008, 25).

29. Calculations by the authors suggest that at a 2 percent inflation rate roughly 60 to 70 percent of the acceleration of depreciation deductions (relative to unadjusted economic depreciation) under current law reflects inflation adjustment.

30. Note that the world capital stock is fixed within a period, but must increase in each period at a rate equal to the growth rate of the U.S. economy so that a long-run equilibrium can be attained.

31. See Harberger (2008) and Gravelle (2008) for differing perspectives on this issue.

32. Note that such a response may be limited to the extent that the United States is perceived to be merely catching up to the rate reductions in other countries described above.

33. Fiscal Affairs Department, International Monetary Fund. The views expressed here are my own and should not be attributed to the IMF, its executive board, or its management.

34. An exception is Kleinbard (2007), who advocates a variant to the allowance for corporate equity: the business enterprise income tax.

35. In the short run, this cost could be reduced to almost zero if the allowance would be granted only to new investment, as Latvia did in 2010 and Italy in 2012. In the long term, the budgetary cost can also be significantly smaller due to the favorable dynamic scoring effects.

Subject Index